THE DIARIES OF EDNA ST. VINCENT MILLAY

Rapture and Melancholy

The Diaries of Edna St. Vincent Millay

Edited by

DANIEL MARK EPSTEIN

Foreword by

HOLLY PEPPE

Yale UNIVERSITY PRESS/NEW HAVEN & LONDON

Yale University Press books may be purchased in quantity for educational, business, or promotional use. For information, please e-mail sales.press@yale.edu (U.S. office) or sales@yaleup.co.uk (U.K. office).

Designed by Mary Valencia.
Set in Adobe Garamond type by Integrated Publishing Solutions.
Printed in the United States of America.

ISBN 978-0-300-24568-4 (hardcover : alk. paper)
Library of Congress Control Number: 2021941258
A catalogue record for this book is available from the British Library.

This paper meets the requirements of ANSI/NISO Z39.48-1992 (Permanence of Paper).

10 9 8 7 6 5 4 3 2 1

For India Kotis

CONTENTS

FOREWORD

Are personal diaries fair game for curious readers? Do we have the right to eavesdrop on a writer's intimate thoughts recorded in a worn leather journal or little red book bound by lock and key? Fifteen-year-old Edna St. Vincent Millay had no qualms answering those questions in her first diary, written in 1907, threatening, "whosoever, by stealth or any other underhand means, opens these pages to read, shall be subject to the rack, the guillotine, the axe, the scaffold, or any other form of torture I may see fit to administer." More than a century later, her razor-sharp wit and remarkable self-awareness, punctuated by vanity, insecurity, and cynicism, not to mention humor, generosity, compassion, and profound moments of joy, make her forbidden diaries irresistible reading.

Other than the poet's sister Norma, who died in 1986, very few people have had access to this astonishing collection of personal writing. Since 1998, when the diaries were transferred to the Library of Congress from Steepletop, Millay's home in Austerlitz, New York, they have remained safely out of view, available only to credentialed scholars.

With this book, Daniel Mark Epstein has changed all that. An award-winning poet and acclaimed biographer, he knows the diaries well, having used them as primary source material for his biography of Millay, *What Lips My Lips Have Kissed,* published in 2001. Passionate about their value as rare literary and historical documents, he provides insightful chapter introductions and detailed endnotes that help the reader navigate the many people and events that shaped Millay's spellbinding life. The ideal editor for this long-awaited volume, Epstein keeps the reader in mind, never sacrificing our fascination with human behavior to protect the integrity of his subject, one of America's most accomplished and, in her day, most popular and financially successful poets.

I first read selections from the diaries in 1984, sitting on a faded cream-colored sofa embroidered with exotic birds and flowers in Millay's living room at Steepletop, sipping Cointreau with Norma, who was then ninety, as we translated the poet's leggy scrawl one line at a time. I'd landed at Steepletop a few years earlier when I accepted Norma's invitation to stay with her while researching Millay's sonnets for a dissertation I was writing. It was an extraordinary experience to see the poet and her work through her sister's eyes, and a privilege to help care for Norma in the last months of her life.

Norma herself had moved there in 1951, the year after Millay's death, and spent the rest of her life organizing and preserving thousands of pages of writing, photos, and personal artifacts left in the house. As her sister's literary executor, she published a few new editions of poems and one collection of unpublished work, but tackling the diaries was too daunting and time intensive a task.

The value of Epstein's efforts to bring the diaries to light cannot be overestimated. They provide us with delicious new details about Millay's life, from her sweet revenge against high school boys envious of her talent, to vivid accounts of her sexual fantasies at age nineteen, to her sudden dissatisfaction with her husband after six years of marriage. During her writing career Millay continued to ward off jealous boys—this time, sexist male poets and critics—by publishing one best-selling poetry collection after another and attracting thousands of adoring fans during cross-country reading tours. But in later years, as her health began to fail and her popularity as a poet waned, her fighting spirit weakened and she chronicled her dependence on her elixirs of choice—gin, wine, champagne, and finally morphine—to numb her physical and emotional pain.

Reading these diaries is a wild and dangerous ride, but Epstein holds steady at the wheel, guiding us forward as we begin to understand that Millay's rich intellect, uncanny facility with language, and clever humor were countered by an obsessiveness that led to addiction. Yet long before that tragic turn, we're captivated by the mind of an unconventional woman who was already defining herself at age sixteen, setting the stage for what's to come: "Went to the ball at Lincolnville tonight . . . Wore my pink silk muslin. I was the only red-headed girl in pink, at which I was not surprised. Red-heads are supposed to wear blue."

Holly Peppe,
Literary Executor for
Edna St. Vincent Millay

NOTE ON THE EDITORIAL METHOD

In preparing the manuscript of this book I transcribed every diary and journal entry in Millay's hand that I could find among her papers. More than ninety percent of the diary entries were made in the years 1907–1914 and 1927–1935. The young woman's diaries from her adolescence through her first college year are so dramatic and integrated that it is impossible to abridge them without ruining the fabric of the story, so her entries for these years are complete except for a few verses she wrote in her journal that are extraneous to the narrative. There are some entries of interest between 1914 and 1927, including a brief and prosaic Japan travelogue. In the interest of focus, I have included Millay's impressions of Paris and Albania in the 1920s, which show her progress as a prose stylist and journalist, while omitting the Japan diary. In the later diaries recorded at Millay's farm in upstate New York there is a good deal of repetition of details about gardening and agriculture, so I have omitted a small portion of these sections, with no disturbance to the logic of her story. During her later years when she was in a lot of pain, she used her diary to keep obsessive records of her use of painkilling drugs; there is much repetition in these, so I have selected a dozen entries to represent a hundred similar ones.

The diaries as presented here are therefore very nearly complete. Pretty much everything of substance that has survived is here, preserving the force and coherence of the narrative and the historical integrity of the document. Before 1914, Millay wrote in more than one diary at a time. I have merged these diaries chronologically, and where I believe it will be helpful I have noted that she is shifting from one book to another.

All words in brackets are mine and not Millay's. These are mostly quick glosses and clarification for the sake of convenience; longer explanations and background details are found in the endnotes at the back of the book. For the most part I have preserved Millay's spellings and misspellings, silently correcting only those words and phrases that would otherwise be confusing. For the most part Millay did not indent paragraphs. Instead she marked paragraphs by lines or spacing that is difficult to reproduce on the printed page, so I have inserted paragraph indents in place of her markings.

Introduction

Edna St. Vincent Millay was born in Rockland, Maine, on George Washington's birthday, February 22, 1892. America was preparing for the World's Fair in Chicago to celebrate the four hundredth anniversary of Columbus's arrival in the New World.

Her elaborate name, a perfect double-dactyl (Higgledy Piggledy) with an extra syllable added for gravity, may be seen as an advance payment on the child's literary account: in its prime, the name would be printed and pronounced as frequently as that of Columbus, or even perhaps the Father of Our Country—if ceremonial usage be excepted. Her mother, Cora Buzzell Millay, a hair weaver, practical nurse, and published poet, may have had a premonition. No one knows where the homely "Edna" came from, but St. Vincent is the name of a Manhattan hospital where Cora's brother had been rescued from death by starvation a week before his niece was born.

Edna's father, Henry Tolman Millay, a ne'er-do-well salesman and school administrator, would remain in the picture not much longer than it took to conceive Edna's sisters, Norma, who was born a year later, and Kathleen, born in 1896. Henry gambled and failed to provide. After several years of conjugal agony, in 1900 Cora Millay—like her mother before her—divorced her husband. For a while she worked on nursing cases in Rockland, Camden, and Rockport until the summer of 1901, when all three of her girls were stricken with typhoid. Then it was all nurse Cora could do to keep her own children alive. Kind relations in her hometown, Newburyport, and Ring Island, Massachusetts, supported the young mother and her three daughters until they could afford to rent a bungalow in Newburyport in 1903.

The efforts of these women to lead their lives free of husbands and well-intentioned relatives, rich and poor, will become a major theme in the story of their lives and the pages of this book. They needed help but they didn't want it. Pride can hardly explain the choices they made to live as they did. In the cold winter of 1903–1904, Cora nearly died of influenza, and eleven-year-old Edna took charge of the household. When Kathleen, the youngest, contracted infantile paralysis, the little family left Newburyport for Maine, where they briefly accepted the hospitality of her husband's brother Fred on a farm outside of Camden. Then the vagabonds were taken in by the kindly Aunt Clara Millay who kept a boarding house on Washington Street at the edge of town. One of her boarders owned an abandoned house in a field downhill between the boarding house and the river that powered the Camden sawmills.

The weather-beaten two-story clapboard cottage had stood vacant in the field for so long that the landlord offered the Millays a month's free rent if they would paint it. There were two rooms upstairs, one of them heated by the only coal stove in the dwelling. The indoor plumbing consisted of a single cold water tap in the kitchen, where a small wood stove provided fire for cooking and some heat by day. In winter the house was unbearably cold, as the wind blew through gaps in the siding. Cora observed that "you could poke a broom-stick right out of doors through the wall."

In the autumn of 1904 the Millays, with a trunkload of classic books and another of clothing, moved into the little house. Cora and Kathleen slept in the room upstairs with the coal fire, and Edna and Norma shared the other bedroom. It was here that the twelve-year-old girl wrote her first publishable poems. And it was here in the spring of 1907 that Edna St. Vincent Millay began writing the journal that she would continue, intermittently, for the rest of her writing life.

People have been writing diaries and journals for about a thousand years. The earliest examples apart from travelogues are daily records of religious or mystical experience. Among them are the writings of Agnes Blannbekin and Elizabeth of Schonau, charting their spiritual journeys. It is likely that the diary as we know it marks a medieval awakening in human consciousness, a crucial stage in the evolution of personality. In any case, by the time of the Renaissance the pocket diary was ready for the reflections and effusions of Buonaccorso Pitti and Gregorio Dati; and by the seventeenth century for the omnivorous chronicles of Samuel Pepys, the Englishman who witnessed the Plague and the Great Fire of London, the earliest diarist to be widely known. Others have captured our attention, including the nineteenth-century figures Dorothy Wordsworth and Fanny Burney, the Civil War journals of George Templeton Strong and Marie Chesnutt; the colorful diaries of Virginia Woolf and Anaïs Nin; and most famously, *The Diary of Anne Frank.*

Strictly speaking the diary (or journal—both words derive from words for "day") is not a literary genre, although a diary entry or sequence of entries may rise to the level of great literature. Diaries get published, and are of value to us, because of the importance of the writer, the information the diary provides us about a historical period or a significant event; and only occasionally because the prose rises to the level of literature. Ronald Reagan's diaries fall into the first category, Marie Chesnutt's into the second, and the journals of Virginia Woolf into the third category, as this English novelist seemed incapable of writing a sentence that was not in itself memorable.

To what does Edna St. Vincent Millay owe the honor of having her diaries published and read in 2022, more than seventy years after her death? Her status as a poet and playwright of the first magnitude, secure until the 1940s, is now a subject of debate. Her poems remain in print and her play *Aria da Capo* is occasionally revived; but as of this writing her work is rarely included in textbooks or college syllabi. The reasons for this are largely political, or in any case extra-literary. The poet had the fortune and misfortune to become a legend in her own time, what we now quaintly call "a cultural icon." Her binge drinking and promiscuity were notorious even in the 1920s when such behavior was commonplace. She became the bad girl of American letters who published her modern escapades in verses that demonstrated mastery of the classic forms and meters. No one had seen anything like it. Ezra Pound and T. S. Eliot, who had enough Latin between them to recognize her achievement, ostentatiously ignored the upstart whose ballads and sonnets made her rich. She needed no one's help, and what she was writing did not fit the modernist's profile of "free verse."

Her success was a reproach to modernism. Meanwhile she behaved as badly as Byron and Baudelaire, Sappho in a cloche hat, chain-smoking, sipping gin, bed-hopping—a person who would not serve as a moral role model in those times. The poetry was transgressive and subversive. Compared with the unimpeachable verse of Elizabeth Bishop, Millay's poetry is still shocking.

There's really no need to repeat here the whole of an argument I made on behalf of Millay's poetry in the biography of her that I wrote twenty years ago. She is our greatest love poet with the possible exception of Walt Whitman. She has written many sonnets that compare favorably with the best of Shakespeare, Sir Philip Sidney, and John Donne. Without an axe to grind there is no knowledgeable reader who would dispute the evidence which print has made imperishable. The great poems won't go away no matter how many professors bar the classroom door against them. As long as there are lovers, they will be reading Millay.

And so, like George Washington, Edna St. Vincent Millay is of interest to us because she was important—a groundbreaking writer. No less an authority than the English author Thomas Hardy proclaimed that America had two great attractions: the skyscraper, and the poetry of Edna St. Vincent Millay. Her diary provides a window not only upon a unique personality and intelligence, but also the creative process that produced sublime works of art. Last but not least, it is of considerable value as "journalism," the impressions of a woman of a certain class growing up in a New England fishing village, traveling to New York for education and a literary career, and later to Europe, before settling down on a blueberry farm in the Taconic Mountains in 1925. Virtually overnight the small-town girl became dangerously famous; and the diarist's record of that adventure is one of the most dramatic chapters of her story.

The first diary entry is dated March 24, 1907, when Millay was a schoolgirl of fifteen. The last entry is May 10, 1949, about a year and a half before the writer's death on October 18, 1950. Like most writers, Millay struggled to make her diary a daily practice. The business of life, and travel, and other kinds of literary activity often interfere with the hour of leisure one requires to devote to a diary; and from the beginning Millay took herself to task for neglecting the routine. There are many days, months, and then decades when there is no diary that we know of, and for good reasons I shall try to explain as the document unfolds.

The diary is richest and most complete in the years 1907–1914, and again in 1927–1935. The entries for those fourteen years constitute ninety percent of Millay's diary, but from this book a full-length profile of a woman emerges: a young genius, a devoted daughter and sister; a rebellious but dedicated student; a celebrated poet and dramatist; a loyal friend and passionate wife; a public heroine, and finally a solitary, tragic figure. It is a portrait that cannot be found elsewhere, in Millay's poetry or in her marvelous letters. The letters, like the poems, are a kind of performance in which the writer discloses only the part of her that she wishes to reveal in that moment. The diaries—which the mature writer *never* intended for publication—are unfiltered. From beginning to end she writes without restraint or inhibition, recording thoughts, dreams, emotions, and impressions meant only for her own clarification and reflection.

In these pages we hear Millay's intimate voice, the woman speaking to herself about her most private and urgent concerns.

Finding Her Voice
(1907–1910)

An older friend named Ethel Knight, from the Congregational Church that Millay attended, who also belonged to the St. Nicholas League, a literary club for youngsters, encouraged Edna to start a diary. The idea of keeping a diary, especially when one beholds the voluminous crop of a friend's effort, is often more appealing than the daily commitment.

Millay struggled for several years before finding a rhythm. Also the girl had little privacy in the bedroom she shared with her sister Norma. Her six entries over a two-month period in 1907 suggest that earlier efforts have been lost. She trails off on May 21, then resumes, with apologies to the "dear old brown book" more than a year later.

Her eight entries in the summer of 1908 are substantial musings on religious and moral themes. And in the last of these she introduces a character, a confidant she will call, with sincere affection, "Ole Mammy Hush-Chile."

Before we consider the nature of this surrogate imaginary mother, we must acknowledge the terrible need that called her into being. Cora Millay's profession as an itinerant nurse was the family's only source of income, as Henry failed to pay the five dollars per month of child support ordered by the court. She was often away from Camden for days, and even weeks, leaving the girls in that house in a field. In Cora's absence, sixteen-year-old Edna was in charge of the household, shopping, cooking, cleaning, and minding her younger sisters. She loved her mother dearly and would do anything to please her. As a result, two themes dominate the diaries from 1909 until 1911: how painfully she misses her mother, and how exhausted she has become from the housework, the endless laundry, the dishes (and how the work chafes her delicate hands!), not to mention the challenges of supervising Norma and Kathleen, who naturally resisted taking orders from their sister.

Under these circumstances Millay's summoning of the black Mammy archetype to bring her comfort is of some significance—beyond what she might have understood. Slavery had been outlawed in this part of New England for more than a century. But the stereotype of the grandmotherly, stout, round-faced slave woman with the low sonorous and soothing voice was popular all over America. She appeared as Aunt Chloe in *Uncle Tom's Cabin,* in minstrel shows, and as grinning Aunt Jemima in the bandana (no longer in use) on a box of pancake mix. What the girl could not have known is that the real slave women who nursed and comforted white children on the plantations were not grandmothers but young women her own age. They also cooked, mopped the floors, and scrubbed laundry. Doing the work of a real antebellum servant, desperate for relief, she invoked the imaginary "Mammy Hush-Chile," whose very name recalls an old slave lullaby.

> Hush-a-bye, don't you cry
> Go to sleep you little baby.

And it seemed to work for her in the difficult year 1908, in that freezing house in the snowy field.

To Mammy she confides: "the first big disappointment of my life: I graduate in June—without the class poem." Millay had in fact written the prize-winning poem, but by a curious and cruel turn of events another student claimed to have written it. And he got the glory. "Something has broken the sweet childishness within me." A bitter truth, and the fact that she was able to capture such a moment in a lifetime, is what makes the diary great.

In October the family moved to a ground-floor tenement apartment on Chestnut Street, near the center of town and the harbor. And while the diary jottings, including a poem in 1909, are meager, they provide a glimpse of the ambition that would result in her first disciplined diary in the year 1910, as well as her first honors as a poet.

This year, 1910, is the first in which we get a full picture of the teen-ager's life and routine—which is not all work and no play by any means. She loves her piano lessons, and sailing on the waters of the harbor. She has good friends, including the minister's daughter Abbie Evans, Martha and Ethel Knight, and Stella Derry. These girls went to school together, taught Sunday school classes, sewed and embroidered dresses, attended parties and balls and picnics, and shared a passion for books and theater. In April she fell in love, and her account of her infatuation with the youth ("Am I in love with him? Or am I simply in love with love? Whatever it is I wish it would get either worse or better right off . . .") is a tantalizing preview of the rich autobiographical reflections soon to come.

Mar. 24 [1907]

I haven't written for two days and I suppose I must write a good lot now to make up for it. Our Glee Club Concert went off slick. We cleared over fifty dollars. The boys' double quartet in "Call John" got two encores. We shall probably have another Concert next term. Norma and I have been picking up our room today. Oh! Such a mess! It was half-past eight tonight before we got the letters and boxes and ribbons and collars and everything else off the bed. We are about flabbergasted we are so tired. Moral: Never clean up your room. We are going to take oath never to do it again. Our old alarm clock that has been froze up all winter, thawed out today and began to tick. I was so scairt I fainted dead away into a pile of clothes and Norma had to hit me over the head with a broom twice before I could condescend to come to. Moral: Never have a clock that will go. Mama is hollering from the sitting-room and saying that now that we have our bed made we might as well get into it, and I was planning on an hour to read. Moral: Never make your bed.

Mar. 25

Too tired to write much tonight and besides Norma is jiggling the bed and I am writing on a pillow. I am going to play Susie in "Triss," and we had a rehearsal tonight.[1] My lines only come in the IV Act, but I helped prompt the others. I can make a fine part out of mine although it is a short one. I have the stage all to myself for a while and I have a love scene with the villain. The villain is great. Probably the first rehearsal of my part will come the last of this week but I shall go all I can before then just to get acquainted with the others.

Mar. 31

Today is the last day of March and tomorrow will be April Fool's day. I must make a fool of someone—not a difficult matter around here.

My first rehearsal was last Thursday. I hated to go on at first, for I didn't know any of them very well. My part is going to be great,—at least they all told me how well I did. I am awfully glad for this will be my first appearance. I want to make it a dazzling one. I get rather sick of having Ed Wells forever hugging me while he is showing Mr. Keep how to do it. Mr. Wells seems to understand the performance all right. He has evidently had experience in that line. There has been talk of playing "Triss" in Rockland, one week from next Friday, but I'm not sure whether they will or not. I hope they will.

Apr. 8

"Triss" went off even better than I had expected, and we are going to Rockland as I had hoped. Everyone says it is the best home talent performance ever given here, and a great many consider it better than the productions of the traveling companies. I have received many congratulations on my acting of Susie Smith. My part isn't very large, but it is important and rather hard. I hope we will get as good a house in Rockland as we did here. The Opera House was crowded full and everything went off finely except when Allie Eldredge lost his wig. Of course something had to happen. But what of it?

June 27 [1911]

I had just read through to this point and I wish to remark that I consider myself at this period of my life an insufferable mutt and a conceited slush head.

March 20 [1907]

The first day of spring! And the snow so deep that I had to wade in a drift over my knees to get from the side-walk to the house. We had a Glee Club rehearsal tonight, and just as I turned the corner to Washington Street to go home, I heard some one calling, "Hi! Hi there! Young lady!," and when I turned around there was a man behind me pointing to a pretty sleigh drawn up by the curbing. I could not think what the man meant when he said, "Run and jump in. That team's going up to your house." And I did run and jump in, and was only too glad to get a ride home. The team was coming to take Mama to Rockport on a consumption case.[2] How I hate to have her go! Have to keep house all through vacation! Got a letter from George today, thanking me for the photograph. Got another from Ted, who didn't thank me for anything at all but just wondered why I hadn't answered a letter for a month. When I do write I will tell him that I have something more important to do than scribble notes to foolish boys. It is getting so dark that I can't see the lines and anyway I guess this is enough for one entry.

May 21

I have just finished reading Booth Tarkington's "Gentleman from Indiana."[3] It is a beautiful story. I don't know when I have enjoyed a book so much. I was two books short on my Home Reading List, so I got them out after school tonight and must pass the lists in before tomorrow noon. I have read this one but I don't know about the other. It is Irving's "Tales of a Traveler"—a lot of short stories and I don't know how to begin in on them. Besides it is half-past eleven now and I am so sleepy I can hardly see.[4] I don't believe I shall get done, I certainly sha'n't if I run on this way forever.

June 28 [1908]

Over a year since I have written in you, you dear old brown book! I hope you will forgive me, but I must ask more forgiveness for my neglect of myself. For in this year that has passed I had laid down for myself two commandments. These are the two.

1. Respect thyself.

2. Be worthy of thine own respect.

If I live up to those two I shall need no Ten Commandments. For I shall not respect myself unless I am worthy of it, and if I respect myself I shall have no gods before the real God; I shall make unto him no graven images; I shall honor my father and my mother; I shall not kill, nor steal, nor covet, nor commit adultery; —and as for remembering the Sabbath day and doing no work upon it, I work on Sunday if I see fit, and mean no irreverence to God in the doing, for honest work is no desecration, and dishonest work I have no use for,—though if I had it would be as bad one day as another. I remember the Sabbath Day and keep it holy as I keep any day, for I do not believe in saving up all one's praise, prayer, and song for Sunday, and then, to make up for the unnatural goodness of one day, going to the extremes of wickedness every other day in the week. This kind of religion does not appeal to me. I offer my praise at no stated time and in no stereotyped form. My God is all gods in one. When I see a beautiful sunset, I worship the God of Nature; when I see a hidden action brought to light, I worship the god of Truth; when I see a bad man punished and a good man go free, I worship the god of Justice; when I see a penitent forgiven, I worship the god of Mercy. And never a day passes that I do not, for something beautiful, for something truthful, for something just, or for something merciful,—give praise to my all-powerful Creator. My worship is spontaneous,—never forced. I give no praise because of things for which I ought to be grateful, but for things for which I am grateful. And I like my way of worship much better than all others. If I did not, I would not worship in that way; for I know that only one's best is good enough for God. Father, God of my praise, I offer this prayer.

Help me to be worthy of my own respect; help me to keep my own respect. For each bad act in my life, help me to do a good act; and for each good act in my life, let me do another good act, so that in my soul good may be stronger than bad. When I see aught that calls forth praise, let me not forget to whom that praise is due. Deal kindly with me, justly with my wrong deeds, and mercifully with my mistakes.

Amen.

To thee, God of my prayer, I offer praise.

For all things beautiful, for all things great and glorious, for every good action, for every noble sacrifice, for every wrong righted, for every penitent pardoned, praises be Thine. Thou hast made beauty, greatness, glory, goodness, nobility, right, and forgiveness. For these I thank Thee. Thou hast given me a life to live, a world to live in, and an object to live for. For these I thank Thee. God of life, help all creatures which thou hast made, to see thy might and to worship Thee as I do.

Amen.

June 29

I guess I am going to explode. I know just how a volcano feels before an eruption. Mama is so cross she can't look straight; Norma's got the only decent rocking-chair in the house (which happens to be mine); and Kathleen is so unnaturally good that you keep thinking she must be sick. I suppose this is an awful tirade to deliver after the sermon I wrote yesterday, for it was a sermon, although I had forgotten about it's [*sic*] being Sunday. But it is very hard to be sixteen and the oldest of three. It is such a relief to have a diary to run to, where you can spit out all your spite on something which can't spit back, and which is not hurt by your spitting. How much I have missed this year in not writing out my joys and sorrows for the edification of posterity. But "Never Mind!" as Miss Michels used to say. I will try and make up for it now that I am writing once more. I owe that much to Ethel, who started me in the first place and has spurred me on a second time. She has kept a diary ever since she was twelve and she is now nineteen. Seven years! And I can't keep it up for one! That shows how much back-bone I've got.

Dear Ethel! Yesterday she took her diary and some cushions and I took some magazines and some cushions, and we went over in the woods. She showed me the page in her diary which she had written on the night when we took our long walk back and forth between her house and mine, and talked so much about hope and dreams and ambitions. We both love Shakespeare and Tennyson and music and pictures. Ethel pointed out to me a line at the bottom of the page where she had written, "Vincent is a sweet girl." I'm glad she likes me, for I like her so well. She is a sweet girl herself, bless her! Mama is going to give a kind of picnic-party for us girls tomorrow. We have invited Jean Anderson for Norma; her little sister Eleanor, and little Ruth Knight for Kathleen; Ethel and Martha Knight for me.[5] We're going to have a strawberry lunch out under the trees,—Mama is going to make a short cake. Then we're going to have sardine and salmon sandwiches, bananas, fancy cookies and chocolate. At sunset we're going to play the "Rainbow Game" out in the tall grass. I do hope it won't rain but it looks like it might. I wish it would have a thunder storm right off now and get it over with. But if it rains tomorrow we'll have it on Wednesday. —I've just read over the first part of today's entry, and I don't feel so explosive as I did. Scribbling must be wholesome exercise.

June 30

I'm stealing just a few minutes this morning before I have to go down and get breakfast. It is the loveliest day for our out-door party, and I am so pleased I can hardly keep still. We can't help having a lovely time. Perhaps if I am not too tired tonight I'll write some more and tell about how it went off. —I've just noticed the June 30 at the top. The last day of June! Almost Fourth of July! Oh, dear! I'll have to go back to school before I know it. But then, it isn't going to be hard at all next year, my Senior year at C.H.S.[6] Our class is going to have to have a play every term and a supper every month, to see if we can raise money enough to get to Washington. And that reminds me, we did the play "Triss" in Rockland and did well with it. This year our class put on "Gypsy, the Mountain Maid," and the local talents presented "The Gypsy's Secret."[7] I played in both. Well, I must go get breakfast or Mama and the girls will starve, and I don't know but that I will too.

10 o'clock

Well, it's over with. Such a lovely day as we had and such a lovely time. The supper under the trees was such fun with the little cool breeze and the tiny new moon coming out for us to play by. After supper we played "Rainbow" and "Old Man's Soup" and made cocoa fudge. Ethel and I tried to slip off upstairs so that I could read her part of my diary, and just as we were getting interested, Martha and Norma and all the rest burst into the room and dragged us out. Martha even so far presumed as to lay defiling fingers upon the sacred pages of this, my diary. There was a little wrinkle left when she got through with it, but that only adds a more venerable aspect. We stole a little time later and managed to get through some of it before those lawless house breakers found it out. I am going down to Mrs. Knight's store tomorrow, to see Ethel. We've been talking over some lovely plans about note-books which we are to keep together, but I am too sleepy to tell about them now. O, we've had such a perfect day, they all said so and I know they must have for not a minute dragged. They're all coming over again some night and play "Pit." I had a few left of the pictures which I had taken last year, and Martha teased for one so bad that mama said she might have it. Ethel is to have one of my daisy pictures when Mr. Harris has them finished. Next year at commencement we're each to have some taken, and exchange.

Oh, I just must go to bed.

July 1

I can't take any time to write tonight. It's only nine o'clock, but Ethel and I are going to walk tomorrow at half past four. I walked over to her house tonight and she made me promise to go right to bed when I got home.

July 2

We took our walk this morning. I got up at 3:15 but I stayed so long out on the bridge watching the sun rise that it was 4:15 when I got over to Ethel's. She was sitting on the front steps waiting. We decided to go up to the lake and started off up Mountain St. O, it was lovely to be up so early. I don't think I can ever lie abed again. The sun was just glinting through the trees and throwing the first long, wet shadows upon the fields. There are no shadows like sunrise shadows! We passed one field where grass had just been mown and lay in long stretches upon the ground. The smell of the new-mown hay floated out to us, and we heard the song of two little robins who were hopping about in the dewy field. It would have made a beautiful picture—the smooth cut field with the first sunlight upon it and the two robins making the only spot of color.

As we went along we wished more and more that we had taken at least a camera. We had taken a few cookies and buns with us for lunch but we had no water, and by the time we had gone half the distance, our thirst grew very strong. So when we came to a farm house which looked as if the people were up, we went up to the steps to ask for a drink. A wood fire was crackling in the stove and from the barn beyond came the smell of milking. A young and pretty woman, standing in front of a table was washing milk pails and humming to herself. I knocked at the door and asked for a drink which she brought me at once. She was very kind. Sometimes I think that in the country one finds the truest hospitality.

When we had become refreshed by the water, we started off again, walking briskly so as to have a little time when we got there. The road wound in and out, green and cool, bordered with ox-eyed daisies and wild roses. On our way back we got our hands full of these. We were so entranced with the whole country that we must have been careless and have taken the wrong road, for instead of coming out on the side of the lake where the cottages were we emerged on the turnpike, just across the lake from the cottages. But this didn't spoil our good time. We took off our shoes and stockings and cooled our dusty feet in the water, and by the time we had laced our shoes again we thought it must be time to start back.

On the way home we went up into a field to look for strawberries and found, at the top of a hill, great clusters of ox-eyed daisies. I stumped Ethel to roll down the hill, and as she wouldn't be stumped, we both rolled, through wet grass, and daisies and thistles. By this time the sun was getting hot so we started again toward home. It was terribly dusty and we were thirsty, and when we went by Hortense Hopkins' house, she peeked out of her chamber window to speak to us and we found it was quarter to seven. We were still a mile from home but our thirst spurred us on in spite of dust and heat, so that we reached Camden in good time and in fairly good condition. It was a lovely walk and we are going again some morning, only this time we will be sure and take the right road and not come out with Megunticook Lake between us and our destination.[8]

July 18
First Entry

Backsliding again! More than two weeks since I last wrote! Well, I've got to pay for it. I called Ethel up today and 'fessed up all about it, whereupon Ethel said I must write six pages tonight to make up for it. Well, I suppose I must. But I may say things which I would rather have no one see. Therefore I make this resolution.

Resolved.

Firstly. That, henceforth, no one reads my diary.

Secondly. That whosoever, by stealth or any other underhand means, opens these pages to read, shall be subject to the rack, the guillotine, the axe, the scaffold, or any other form of torture I may see fit to administer.

There! It's done. And now I think I'd better put a big placard on the outside of this, bearing the inscription, "Who enters here leaves hope behind!" For I've written enough public entries. Ethel has read all the perfectly lovely things I've written about her and Martha all the perfectly horrid things I've said about her, and I think it has gone far enough. I am going to have some place where I can write my joys and sorrows, my benedictions and anathemas, without fear of scorn or censure. I'm going to write exactly what I think—(Mr. and Mrs. Olson have been calling, and have just gone. Now I'll resume.) I'm going to say exactly what I think, and if people come eavesdropping they may ferret out certain phrases slightly ungratifying to their vanity. I don't care if they do. They needn't be nosing around. Well, I guess I'll stop scolding and begin my second entry. Ethel told me to write three entries of two pages each, and she's my judge, so I'll have to. These two pages and a half are good measure.

Second Entry

Ethel and I took another walk last Thursday. This time we watched for signposts and really arrived at Lake City. But it wasn't so early as it had been on our last walk, so we had no time at all to stay. We got a drink of cold water from a spring and started home again. We must go again some day when we can to stop and rest, and perhaps go in wading.

Martha and I are reading Dickens' "Dombey and Son" together.[9] We take turns reading aloud, one chapter at a time. One morning last week, Friday I think, we took an early walk and started off into regions unexplored in company with Dombey and little Dombey. We saw a field which was newly mown and displayed a stubbly hill, very alluring to the unwary who "wist not" of the swamp which it concealed. We both got our feet wet and "Dombey and Son" nearly had a bath, but nothing very exciting happened and at last we gained the hill and sat down upon a big, gray rock which was just made for Martha and me and the Dombeys. In addition to our little party there was a large sign, turned slightly from us as if it did not like the company it was in.

We were very grateful for the cold shoulder, however, because since it did not face us we were under no obligations to read what it said and even now we don't know whether it said "All Trespassing Forbidden," or "Welcome!"

Third Entry

Kathleen came home from Knight's this evening and said that they had all gone to bed. Ruth retires at eight o'clock precisely, and the older girls are not far behind. Kathleen was very scornful. She says she doesn't see any sense in going to bed at eight and getting up at eight. We retire when we are tired,—which is sometimes half-past nine and sometime half-past eleven—and we usually arise about six. As a general thing we get about eight hours of sleep which is really all we need, but children ought to have more, so I am thinking of having Kathleen's bedtime set at nine o'clock— to be changed to half-past eight on the first night after she fails to be in on time. She doesn't like this a bit, but it is better than half-past eight all the time, which I threatened at first. Kathleen never surrenders uncondition- ally. If I had suggested nine she would have insisted on half-past nine, and so on until it would be time for breakfast before she got asleep. I suppose if I had really wanted her to retire at half-past eight I should have spoken of eight and let her think she was having her own way in setting half an hour later. And speaking of bed-time reminds me that I am tired, which to me means,—go to bed, and besides Norma wants me to hurry and is having no scruples about telling me so. I will write tomorrow.

July 19

I don't suppose I ought to write this morning because it is about time to be getting breakfast. There is a pretty, dainty tinted card above my desk which Abbie Evans, my Sunday School teacher, gave me last Christmas, (bless her!) This card bears the following legend; "Let us give thanks. Nature is beautiful, friends are dear, and duty lies close at hand."[10] In this case, duty lies very close at hand and is slumbering peacefully in the kitchen, where she may lie and snooze until I get this entry written. My diary is a duty which lies right under my nose and I must try and make up for the two weeks I've missed. My diary is and is to be my confidante, (that e on the end makes it feminine. It would be out of my power to tell all these things to a mere confidant.) My diary has become my confidante, not through chance, but through merit. She is the only one of my friends who can keep quiet long enough for me to talk, and talk I must or my boiler will burst, in which case there would be more an explosion than if the same thing should happen to the Camden Mills boiler.

Now I'll unburden. It's Sunday and therefore it's Sunday School, and I don't want to go one bit. It looks like rain, and I hope it will rain cats and dogs and hammers and pitchforks and silver sugar spoons and hay-ricks and paper covered novels and picture frames and rag carpets and tooth-picks and skating rinks and birds of Paradise and roof gardens and bur-docks and French grammars, before Sunday school time. There! If it does, I sha'n't have to go, anyway. Besides I don't see how I could if I wanted to, because I haven't anything to wear. And perhaps that is why I don't want to go—which is perhaps enigmatical to anything but "mens feminae" [a woman's mind]. My white muslin dress is all dirty around the bottom. It always is after I've worn it one afternoon. I think Burns must have had me in mind when he wrote: "She draigl't a' her petticoatie, comin' through the Rye."[11] I've certainly "draigl't" my "petticoatie" in good shape. The top of my dress is all nice and clean and the bottom of it looks like a dish towel which has been handed down from father to son even unto the third and fourth generation. If it's misty I couldn't wear it anyway, and if it is misty I couldn't wear anything else, because I haven't anything else to wear.

I've tried to take up a new hem in my blue skirt, and after I got it nicely sti[t]ched I found out that it was a sight. My green skirt has a darn in the back where a rusty nail became too familiar and intruded,—the entrance of which, or rather, the result of the entrance, I've darned with silkatees. I hate to mend anyway—And I can't very well go in mama's pink kimona and my own, which would be about as bad, is in the wash. I don't see but I've got to stay at home. Guess I'll weep a while. Guess I won't, I mean. Guess I'll dance a Highland fling on top of the ink bottle. There isn't enough in it to upset. That reminds me—I don't know why, I'm sure but it does—that I didn't bake beans yesterday, thinking it was Friday, so I must do it today. Beans are cheap, and we must have them at least once a week or we will be bankrupt. It will be real original to have beans baked on Sunday, and originality is my long suit. So baked beans it is.

Bonnie's lost his license tag and torn his collar. We don't dare let him out of the house. We rung up Mama to tell her about it and she only said, "Find his tag and mend his collar." Sounds easy, doesn't it. Just try it and see. It's harder than one of Plummie's examinations on French irregular verbs. Bonnie's a pretty dog, but he can just go and find his tag and mend his collar himself. He did the losing and tearing. Now he can do the repairing or go collarless and tagless. It would be terrible if anything should happen to him, though. He is a thoroughbred Scotch Collie, but that won't protect him, I'm afraid. Well, I must get breakfast.

Sunday evening

I didn't go to Sunday school but Kathleen did. If she goes every Sunday for a whole quarter, she will get a little Bible. She is trying hard for it and I am glad she takes an interest in going. I suppose I don't set a very good example but I don't see how I could have gone today. Martha is coming over tomorrow and we are going to read some more. She has been gone ever since last week so "Dombey and Son" have languished, since I promised not to read a word until she got back.

I have been thinking of a name for my diary and I think I'll call her Ole Mammy Hush-Chile, she so nice and cuddly and story-telly when you're all full of troubles and worries and little vexations.[12] It's such a comfort to confide in her and let cares roll off your mind. After this I'm going to talk right to her and not be content with a proxy. We need no interpreter, we understand each other too well.

Ole Mammy Hush-Chile, let's have a nice little chat, just you and I. You'll have to take the place of mama when she's gone, which is most all the time. It seems strange, doesn't it, that you, an old nigger mammy, who are not my real mama at all, but only a cuddle mammy, should take the place of my real mama even when she is away. You are so nice and strong, my mammy, that I can tell you little foolish things that I couldn't tell Mama, for fear of worrying her. She isn't very strong, you know, Mammy Hush-Chile. But it's so comfy when she's home to sit down in the kitchen—I keep the kitchen clean and shiny all the time, Mammy—to sit down near the stove when the wood is crackling and sending out little sparks and little stray flakes which light up so you don't need a lamp, when you hear the wind out doors and know that it can't get in where you are or where the little girls are sleeping in the other room. I make two cups of tea in the little blue china teapot, and we sit opposite each other and drink it nice and hot while we watch each other's faces in the first-light of the crackling stove.

19

It makes up for all the time she's gone, Mammy Hush-Chile; I forget all about the things that went wrong and she forgets all about the doctors and the patients and the surgery and the sleepless nights. It's nice to have a mama who is a trained nurse, for there are so many things she knows which you don't know anything about. It must be terrible to have a mama who doesn't know as much as you do. It must be terrible to be ashamed of your mother. I love my mama, Mammy Hush-Chile, more than I can ever think of loving you, and you mustn't be jealous a bit. You are very like her, Mammy, so I love you in something of the way in which I love her, though not one millionth part as much.

I must say good night to you, Mammy, before long for I must write some of my poems into my big book. I don't know as I've told you about it, Mammy Hush-chile, but I'll tell you now to make sure. I've written so many verses and keep on writing so many more, that I became afraid that if I didn't write them into one big book, I might forget some of them. I've had five of them published in the St. Nicholas, one of which, "The Land of Romance," took the first prize in March 1907, and for which I received a beautifully enameled badge made of a five dollar gold piece.[13] I'm so proud of my badge and I love my verses so that it would be like taking my heart out if I should wake up some morning and find that all I could re-member of one of my most loved—was the name. O, Mammy, I mustn't let it happen, you mustn't let me, you dear old white-souled, black-faced, cuddle-mammy. But I must get up early tomorrow and it's bed-time. I don't think I'll write anything in it tonight; I'll wait until tomorrow. This isn't just a vague promise for I mean tomorrow. I haven't neglected it; there are fifteen poems in it already. I'll just finish this page so as to make it an even six pages—I don't want to start on the seventh one tonight. I'll come and see you again tomorrow and we'll talk some more. Kiss me good-night, Mammy Hush-Chile, for I'm going to bed, I'm so sleepy. Good night, Mammy.

July 20

I've come to you again, mammy Hush-Chile, for a cuddle and comfort. I'm crying, mammy, just as hard as I can cry and I don't know as I ever shall stop. I've tried so hard ever since mama went to have things nice and pleas-ant and she's coming home tomorrow, mammy. This is the first time I've cried since she went. Just because I took more brass-headed picture tacks than I left to the girls they're just as hateful as they can be. They plan it all out to see how much they can torment me. There's no key to my room and I can't keep them out; they're likely to come in any minute now, and interrupt us. Just now Norma came out of her room with an old torn black ribbon she's had in there for months, and threw it at me, saying that she didn't want my old rags. Kathleen took an old white hat I wore out two years ago and hung it in my room over my white dress and Norma the hat which used to be hers and which she had given to me if I could do anything with it,—she tore it down from the hook and ripped all the ribbon from it.

Just a minute ago I heard a crash and came in here in time to see Kathleen going out laughing. She'd just tipped over all the boxes and bottles and things on my dressing-table. O, dear, Mammy, what makes them so mean! Just when mama's coming home, too. They're sweet and good-natured enough when they want anything done. Kathleen expects me to comb her hair, button her dress, and file her nails, every morning. Norma always has a bow she wants me to tie; and yesterday I took so much pains to darn a pair of her stockings just as nicely as I know how. She forgets it all quick enough and so does Kathleen.

It's lots easier in this world for people to forget than it is for them to remember; isn't it Mammy Hush-Chile? I suppose I forget things, too. Last night Kathleen brought me up a nice, cool drink of water when I was up here with you, and Norma let me wear her best night-dress that she has never worn just because mine was out on the line wet. I suppose they think I am cross and hateful and I am,—just as mean as they are, and meaner, too, because I ought to be patient with them and not so irritable, since I am the oldest. I know what you want me to do, Mammy Hush-Chile. You want me to go down and get them a nice, hot dinner, don't you? With tapioca cream and sliced oranges for dessert? Just what they like best? Of course you do, you dear old sermon, and that's just what I'm going to do. I might have known you would give me comfort and advice. You are such a comfy old thing anyway, I couldn't be cross very long with you around, could I? And, I've stopped crying, too, my eyes are just as dry. You did it all, bless your old heart. I'm going to be so sweet the girls won't know who I am. Good-bye, Mammy.

April 17 [1909]

I've come back to you, Mammy Hush-Chile. It is almost a year since I last came to see you but I knew I should come back some day. We were too good friends to forget it all so soon. Big things have happened since I saw you last, but I can't tell you all about them, it would take too long,— besides, some of them aren't pleasant to talk about. Still, there are some things you will have to know. One of them was a big pleasure. Norma and I have been to Newburyport where we used to live and had a beautiful time. How small seem the places you used to know when you go back to them after a lapse of years. Perhaps it is because bigger interests have come into your life. Another of the things I must tell you is this,—the first big disappointment of my life:—I graduate in June—without the class poem. You wouldn't have believed it, would you, Mammy? But it's true, all too cruelly true. I'll tell you to whom they gave it. There is a boy in my class who, when we were Juniors, used to amuse himself by writing to me queer rhymeless, meter-less things which I suppose he meant for poems. This year I was Editor-in-chief of our school periodical, the "Megunticook." I was at a loss for material for one of the issues and someone suggested that he write a poem. I thought that perhaps with care he might produce some funny verses. But when it was almost time for the material to come in he came to me and said that he had it partly done and could not possibly finish it. So I, about crazy for my paper, took the thing, finished it, changed it all over, rhymed lines that didn't rhyme, balanced the shaky meter of other lines, named the thing, and had him sign his name to it. When it was published the school had a fit over it. How many people,—oh the irony of it, told me how much they admired the ending.

Of course I couldn't tell them I had written it. When it came time for the writer of the class poem to be elected, the boys had an idea that Henry Hall was a poet and he—oh, he'll make a manly man some day, didn't have stiffening enough in his great fat sluggish, stolidity to get on his feet and tell them that the only poem he ever had printed in his life had been half written, wholly made over, and published by me.

Oh it makes me white when I think that it was my own fault. And I did it just for the paper. Oh, Mammy, Mammy, Mammy, how can he sit there in front of me in school and smile at me with his round, red face!

How can he speak to me with his great fat voice? How could he, yesterday, ask me to translate his French for him, ask me to help him! Didn't he think when he asked me about the last time I helped him? Oh, Mammy, I thought about it, I think about it all the time, but I smiled and said I didn't think I'd have time. And so I shall always smile and speak for I'll die before he shall know how the sight of him shrivels my heart up. But I will not help him again! I've helped him take away from me the only thing I cared about, and now—I can't help him any more. I despise him as I despise a snake. I shiver when his coat sleeve brushes against me. I hate the sight of his fat, white hand,—his pretty, lady-like white hand, that copied and copied in the symmetrical, self-satisfied writing that stole my poem, my class poem that belonged to me, away from me. Our class had a play this winter. He was my father. I put my arms around his neck and kissed him every night for weeks. Oh, I could strike my mouth! I can feel the touch of him now. I laid my head on his knee and clasped his hand. Oh, I loved him dearly in the play, but if I had known what I know now, my mouth would have burned him when it touched him. Oh, Mammy, I can tell it all to you, for it won't hurt you, it won't sadden you, except as you know it hurts and saddens me. I can't tell it all to Mama. She knows all that happened, but she doesn't know the way it feels to me. Only it worried her that I didn't cry about it. It would seem more like a little girl's trouble if I had cried, I suppose. But I couldn't cry even to please her. I cry when I'm angry, not when I'm hurt. Something has broken the sweet childishness within me. I feel too old to cry. Good night, Mammy.

September 30

Dear Mammy, I've come back again to see you. I've been away all summer in Newburyport and Lowell. Of course I had a splendid time but I was glad to get home. Aunt Clem almost drove me crazy. I had a foolish idea that because I was her guest I should be polite to her but she had no such opinions about the duties of a hostess, and so after she'd kept at me till I thought I should fly, I turned around and fought. Along toward the last of it we fought all the time. After this I think I shall stay at home where I can do as I please. Being told when I shall or shall not change my dress and when I shall not take my parasol and when I shall not mail a letter is not without its novel side at first but gets monotonous after a while. Honest, mammy, she did all those things and lots more like them. She said she thought I was too independent.

Out of respect to her age I didn't say what I thought, which is just as well perhaps.

One thing I like about you, Mammy, is that you never talk back. You are a big melting-pot into which at night I pour my joys and sorrows, and which in the morning gives back to me a well-mixed pill to be chewed until I feel better. My metaphor, incidentally, is also well-mixed. Now, Mammy. All ready for me to pour in a gladness. Graduation night gave me one big enough to cover all the disappointments which piled up in the weeks before it. You know it was one of the rules that each pupil should write an essay to deliver at commencement, out of which the best would be chosen to be delivered. Also, there was to be a prize of ten dollars each to the boy and the girl who should write the best essays. The composition might be in any form. I sent in a poem which I had written the summer before—when I was sixteen, which was not against the rules. This was one of the essays chosen to be delivered graduation night, and oh, mammy, they gave me the prize. Lots of my friends have asked for copies of the poem and so I'll give you one for I know you will love to have it. Perhaps, too, if you have a better knack at keeping things than I have, after I have lost my copies I may come sometimes and read yours. Here it is.

LA JOIE DE VIVRE
(The Joy of Living)

'Tis good to be alive a day like this!
'Tis good to be alive! I will not miss
One joy from out the living; I will go
Through valleys low, where deep-set mountains throw
A shadow and shelter from the heat,
In cool retreat where shall no city street
Intrude its noise and scare the stillness sweet.

Deep draw I in my breath,
    Deep drink of water cold;

There is no growing old,
There is no death.

The world and I are young!
　　Never on lips of man,—
　　Never since time began,
　　Has gladder song been sung.

　　Youth in our hearts doth live
　　And every day will he
　　His own society
　　For our lodging give.

Green are the fields and hills, and blue the sky;
Soft green and blue are pleasing to the eye,
　　　　And that is why
　　　　God made them so. . . .

[Millay's poem continues for another 59 lines that do not contribute to the content of the diary, but might be included in a collection of the poet's juvenilia.]

[What follows is from a small leather pocket diary from 1910.]

Sat. Jan. 1 [1910]　　*Weather Fair*

Mama came home today from a scarlet fever case in Rockland. She called on Aunt Fanny who was sick. Norma and I went to the New Year's ball at [Silas] Heale's last night and watched the Old Year out.[14]

Sun. Jan. 2　　*Weather Fair*

Went to Sunday School today—my first S[unday] as teacher while Abbie H[uston].E[vans]. is away at Radcliffe. Martha, Mildred and I were the only ones present. Ethel, Jess, and Clara are in Boston. Florence is in the Tel. Office.

Mon. Jan 3

Mendelssohn's birthday.[15] A year ago today, on his 100th anniversary, I played the Op. 30 "In a Gondola" at the High School exhibition—my first piano solo in public. Corinne called [in person].

Tues. Jan. 4   *Weather Cold*

N[orma,] K[athleen] and I went to the installation of the I.O.O.F. and to the ball.[16] Found out afterward that this night a man named Pendleton was knocked down and robbed near the shirt factory. The coldest night I ever knew. Alton Heale called [stopped by].

Wed. Jan. 5   *Weather Cold & Snowy*

Returned Corrine's [Corinne's] call. Had a lovely time and came home in a snowstorm with Percival as escort. Alton called and we discussed the robbery.

Thurs. Jan. 6   *Weather Fair*

Took my lesson today but Mrs. French was so late home from the dress-maker's that she called it a half lesson.[17] Am to play in a recital soon.

Fri. Jan. 7

Letter from Raingald today. He sent me the "Moonlight Sonata" which I have always loved and have been crazy to play since I heard Grace Follett play it at Mrs. French's recital.[18] Went to CHS [Camden High School] dance.

Sat. Jan. 8

Abbie's first class letter came tonight. We are to call for it every Sat. so that I can have it to read to the girls Sunday. She is going to have the S.S. [Sunday School] Times sent to me.[19]

Sun. Jan. 9

Went to Sunday School. Martha, Mildred and I were alone again. I'll be glad when the girls get back from Boston. They have all seen Abbie I believe. I wish I could. I miss her already. What'll it be by April?

Mon. Jan. 10

Mama cashed [illegible] $41.00 check from Rockland and paid lots of bills. Mr. Frye [storekeeper] had to cash it to get out the price of a quart of milk. He shouldn't carry so much money around in his pockets. In Camden it isn't healthy.

Tues. Jan. 11

Received from Maine Music Co. receipt for $3.00 paid on piano. Corrine called. Made a much needed muslin bag for my reserve stock and linen and stuff. It is very gay—red with green strings.

Wed., Jan. 12   Weather Fair

Mama went up to Mrs. Stearns on a case of indefinite length. Mrs. Stearns has a 14½ lb. Boy to add to Raymond who is a geometric problem all by his lonely. Raymond asked me if I wouldn't like to have a "nice little boy about my size."

Thurs. Jan. 13

Took my lesson today. Paid Mrs. French $3.00 on lesson account. I believe I like the second "Studies in Phrasing" better than the first. Bach and I are getting acquainted and I find him fascinating.

Fri. Jan. 14

Mama brought Raymond down for a call this afternoon. He raised everything possible and nearly sent me into nervous prostration, asking to see the hole in my tooth where the filling worked out. "Enfant terrible!"

Sat. Jan. 15

Letter from Abbie, as usual. I don't answer promptly, sad to say. Somehow my pens always scratch or sputter, and my ink comes either in blots or not at all.

[Sunday] Jan. 16   Weather Fair

Went to church to hear Mr. Evans' last sermon before he leaves for Egypt. I asked Mrs. Evans to bring me some sand from near the Sphinx. Was deathly sick in S.S. and had to come home without bidding him good-bye.

Mon. Jan. 17

Sick abed all day. Norma stayed home from school and doctored me. I don't know what I should have done without her. Perhaps I shall be better tomorrow.

Tues. Jan. 18

Feel a little better but as weak as if I was getting over a fever. If church going has such an effect on me I shall most certainly stay at home.

Wed. Jan. 19

Mama came down today with Raymond who gymnasticated around worse than a three-ring circus. If his eyes weren't so brown I couldn't endure it but a person with brown eyes has to be forgiven. My own are green.

Thurs. Jan. 20

Have been sick abed all week and couldn't take my lesson today. Mrs. French says she's going to find out what I do to get sick so often. Possibly she wants to try it but she wouldn't if she felt as I do.

Sat. Jan. 22   Weather Rainy

Will call in office before S.S. and get Abbie's letter as it stormed too hard tonight. Would like to be out slopping around but mama is like a hen with one duckling.

Sun. Jan. 23

Ethel has returned from Boston and was at S.S. today. Mildred and I made the rest of the class. It's against the law for us to have more than three, I guess. Of course Ethel and I had a heated discussion and nearly kicked over the pulpit.

Tues. Jan. 25   Weather Fair

Called on Ethel today. Had chocolate from her new set and ate delicious cookies which she calls "Hard Rocks." I embroidered a quarter-inch on a butterfly's wing.

Wed. Jan. 26   Weather Uncertain

Not pleasant enough for Ethel to have her photographs taken so we called on Corinne.

Found to my joy that she has "The Flatterer," which I read of in "Dr. Bryson."[20] I didn't rest until I got it myself. Am having it for a lesson.

Fri. Jan. 28

Stella called today and stayed to supper. Fred called for her after Moving Pictures, and made fun of my embroidery.[21] Boys don't know anything anyway. Stella makes one exception but so far I don't.

Sat. January 29

Letter from Abbie.

Sun. Jan 30

Went to S.S. today. Florence was there for a wonder, and became highly enraged because I refused to believe the Jonah & Whale yarn.

Mon. Jan. 31   Weather Fair

Called on Stella. Stayed to supper. Norma came over to show her new coat she and mama had just bought in Rockland. Bliss Mariner called. S. and I went to the pictures and Dick came home with me.

Thurs. February 3

Took my lesson.

Thurs. Feb. 17   Weather Fair

Took my lesson today and called on Stella. Stayed to supper and brought her home with me to stay all night. Had an indigestible but delicious spread and talked all night. S. can't talk as fast as I but she can talk as much and does somehow.

Fri. Feb. 18   Weather Fair

We didn't get up till noon. What's the use? Finally arose and waded through the drifts into Bay Street to get a loaf of bread for toasting. Were having a nice breakfast when the girls got home from school. We didn't say but that it was dinner.

Tues. Feb. 22   Weather Snow

Went to Fireman's Ball tonight as a birthday dissipation. I am eighteen today. This diary was a present—and M[endelssohn].'s "Songs Without Words," stationery, hair-ribbon, ring, handkerchiefs, Rubaiyat.[22]

Wed. Feb. 23   *Weather Snowy*

Winnie G. stayed all night after the ball because of the drifts. Wrote a long letter to Abbie and played some of the "Songs Without Words."[23] They are beautiful and I fear I shall neglect my lessons for them. Evening clear. Full moon.

Thurs. Feb. 24   *Weather Fair*

"God makes sech nights." Tonight was made for sleigh-riding. Was sick this morning and canceled my music lesson over the phone. It is time for Halley's comet to appear but I haven't seen it yet. Mama has been home since Tuesday.

Memorandum

Mama said today that if she dies before we do Kathleen is to have her wedding ring and I her mother's wedding ring though she formerly expressed a wish to have that buried with her. I['m] to have a wide band on my 18th birthday, and Norma her engagement ring when she graduates if not before.

Fri. Feb. 25   *Weather Fair*

Norma, A.D., and I went to the Senior dance tonight and had a nice time. Did my hair coronet for the first time.[24] I must write Alma and Clara tomorrow without fail.

Sat. Feb. 26   *Weather Snowy*

Uneventful, except for Abbie's letter which is always an event. Prepared tomorrow's lesson. N. and K. have gone to a social at our church. I've written to Alma, to Clara and to papa.

Sun. Feb. 27   *Weather Rainy*

Sunday School. Jess, Ethel, Martha and Mildred came. First news of Mrs. Cyrus Curtis's death. How terribly Abbie must feel. After Norma and Madolin went to church tonight Uncle Bert and Aunt Rose came and made a nice call.[25] I let her have "Leuseton [?] King" to read. They have just got a copy in the library.

Mon. Feb. 28   *Weather Rainy*

Last day of February. Almost spring? Mama was going up to Mrs. Stearns tonight but she must have got cold while doing the washing for she is quite sick tonight couldn't go. Practised quite a lot today. Embroidered quite a lot on my corset cover.[26] Corinne is working in Cleveland's now and I must take my sewing over some day soon.

Tues. Mar. 1   *Weather Rain*

Stella [Derry] called and stayed to supper. Mama is sick tonight. She's tired all out with the washing. Got a lot done on my corset-cover and had a good practise. Norma didn't go to the dance tonight. Mrs. Frye's cat has a little yellow kitten with which I am very much in love. I must have it.

Wed. Mar. 2   *Weather Drizzly*

Corrine called in a minute to invite me to a party Friday evening. All the girls in C.H.S. '09 who are in town will be there. Tomorrow one of the greatest joys of my life so far is coming to me. I am to hear Mme. Freida Langendorff sing in Rockland; Margaret Wilson, violinist; and Chapman, accompanist. I shall make a memorandum of this tomorrow.[27]

Thurs. Mar. 3   *Weather Fair*

I went, heard, and was conquered. It was grand. I am more wild than ever to go to the Maine Music Festival in Portland next fall. Lots of the girls are going. Took my lesson today and got an O.K. on the "Raindrop Prelude."[28] Am getting more and more fascinated by Bach.

Memorandum

Lagendorff Concert Mme. L. is the first great singer I have ever heard; Miss Wilson the first great violinist; and Mr. Chapman the first great pianist. I liked best Mme. L's "The Cry of Rachel."[29] I can never express the way it affected me. It was tremendous. The violin's "Spanish Dance" was beautiful and Miss Wilson is a perfect dear.[30] When I remarked that she was dressed in exquisite taste Martha said it was easy to see she was a Maine girl. Mme. L.'s "Habanera" from "Carmen" was great.[31] I couldn't understand a word but her face expressed it all.

Fri. Mar. 4   Weather Fair

Sick abed all day. Read "The Alley Cat's Kitten."[32] Crawled out at five and wobbled around till time to get ready for the party. Was bound to go if I had to be carried up and was afraid I should have to be carried home, but I felt better after I got up there and had a perfectly delightful time.

Memorandum

Corinne's Party. Corinne entertained all the girls in our class who were in town. Mary is home from Castine so all but Margaret Cripps were there.[33] Stella Derry, Marian Payson, Maud Fuller, Martha Knight, Mary Pendleton, Corrine and myself. Corrine invited Ethel Knight to make the eighth at table. We had creamed chicken and olives, peaches and cream, with whipped cream chocolate and little cream cookies. I might have suggested crème de menthe but didn't for fear of horrifying the company.[34] Got home at twelve after a very delightful evening. Forgot to say that Corinne painted the dearest little place-cards with our class pins done in black and gold.

Sat. Mar. 5   Weather Fair

Raingald Carter is home from Boston for a week. He and Tyrrell and Earl Patterson called this afternoon while Norma was at basketball. We played all the time and Raingald sang. They are coming down again. Letter from Abbie tonight. Mr. and Mrs. Evans are crossing from Cairo to Athens.[35]

Sun. Mar. 6   Weather Fair

The lesson today was on miracles and Martha, Jess, and I had a heated argument just as I knew we would. The girls are thinking of a masked surprise party on Mary. Norma & Madolin went to meeting tonight. I embroidered. I am to have the yellow kitten as soon as he is weaned and I am thinking of naming him "Muffin."

Mon. Mar. 7   Weather Rain

Today came the first thunder shower of the year. Dull, dreary, damp, dead, dolorous day. How many "demmed cold and uncomfortable" words begin with "d." Also "decorous" and "dowdy." I would about as soon be one as the other. I'm dying for that cuddly yellow kitten.

Tues. Mar. 8   Weather Fair

Norma's team played basketball with the Rockland Juniors in Rockport tonight. The score was 7–6 in favor of Rockland; a hard, rough game. Called on Jess, Corinne and Ethel today. We may have a sheet-and-pillow-case surprise party on Mary tomorrow. Worked on my corset-cover and practiced.

Wed. Mar. 9   Weather Fair

Had the surprise party tonight. Splendid time! Mary was really surprised. Mrs. Pendleton has promised a luncheon to the first girl of us who becomes engaged. I don't know who it will be, but I know right well who it won't be. Got into bed at 1. Corinne stayed up with Martha.

Thurs. Mar. 10   Weather Fair

Took my lesson today. Got O.K. on the "Flatterer." Called on Martha at the news-stand and walked up with her. Stopped a minute in Jess' on the way home and she painted me all red chalk. Why doesn't Abbie write?

Fri. Mar. 11   Weather Fair

Uneventful and tiresome. Embroidered a little, ironed a little, played a little, ate a little, and slept a little. Mrs. Frye's cat was cross and wouldn't let me take Muffin. Cats don't know anything. Why do dear little kittens have to grow up?

Sat. Mar. 12   Weather Fair

This makes nine days of beautiful weather with one rainy day sandwiched in between. Class letter from Abbie. Glad to hear she'll be home in a month. "Then come what may. What matter if I back-slide? I shall have served my term." Apologies to Lord Alfred.[36] Fire at "Red Market" tonight.

Sun. Mar. 13   Weather Sulky

Sabbath School today. Avoided a discussion by the skin of my teeth. Kathleen saw a man on the street today who looked like Uncle Bert, but wasn't. Wrote to papa tonight. Read "The New Sophomore," a fine and very exciting college boy story.[37]

Rainy this morning. Town meeting day. Awful fuss lately about some Armenians whom Mr. Hanley has called in to take the place of the Camden Mill strikers. They have got to leave town. Dick gave me one of his photographs tonight. It is fine of him. Quite serious, for a wonder.

Tues. Mar. 15 Weather Fair

Practised stupendously today. Mrs. F. will be alarmed. Got cold from my shampoo yesterday and am deaf in one ear. Unromantic but annoying. Read some of the "Sonnets from the Portuguese," which are very beautiful, especially to one who is acquainted with the Brownings.[38] Miller's house, Union St., burned to the ground last night.

Wed. Mar. 16 Weather Fair

Got out my green check suit today. It is disgracefully short and gives me a tiny hope that I have grown since Commencement. A sixteenth of an inch would be gratefully received. Called on Martha a few minutes and on Uncle Bert in the store.

Thurs. Mar. 17 Weather Fair

Took my lesson today. Had a good lesson and got O.K. on one of Devil's Inventions which has an unholy fascination for me. My right ear is so deaf it bothers me awfully about playing. When I think I'm playing soft Mrs. F. doesn't. Poor Beethoven!

Fri. Mar. 18 Weather Fair

Mama went to the G.A.R. [Grand Army of the Republic] meeting tonight.[39] I ironed about all day. My trunk and bureau drawers are filled with clean clothes. Too tired to read, write, play, or embroider. I just must write to papa and Clara.

Sat. Mar. 19 Weather Fair

Dead tired. Took my black serge up to Mrs. Barker's to get her started on my skirt.[40] Looked at samples for Norma's dress next Commencement and picked out a lovely sprigged lavender organdie for a shirtwaist for myself.[41] Letter from A.H.E. [Abbie Evans]

Sun. Mar. 20   *Weather Fair*

Sabbath School. Next Sunday is my last one, thank the Fates. Read Abbie's letter and our verses, avoiding the quarterly lesson by general consent. I am trying to persuade Jess to take the class next quarter. My ear is all right tonight.

Mon. Mar 21   *Weather Fair*

Mama is engaged for a case in May. I ironed some of her things today. Isn't that a neat little rhyme? Getting our summer sewing around. Going to get some pretty things of Miss Hall. Norma has picked out her dress for commencement.

Tues. Mar 22   *Weather Fair*

High old time tonight! Here it is twenty minutes to one and mama and I are still getting her ready for a case in Rockland tomorrow. Lots to be done before she goes. Wish this book was bigger.

Wed. Mar. 23

Practised a lot today. Pretty Easter card from Mrs. Bryan. Mama hasn't had to leave yet and has about given up on the R[ockland]. case. Expects to go to Mr. Paysons's in a day or two. Norma has got her Basketball pictures and they are fine. Mrs. Leighton called today. Seniors start [on a field trip] for Washington tomorrow.

Thurs. Mar. 24   *Weather Fair*

Mama went up to Mr. Payson's today. His wife is ill and delirious. The Seniors started for Washington today. From my window I saw the big "Camden" [ferry] go out and I felt bad enough to cry. We tried so hard [to win] last year, and if the anathematized boys hadn't been so lazy we would have gone, too. I may go with Norma's class.

Fri. Mar. 25   *Weather Fair*

Hot as summer today. I took "Bella Donna"—the book, I mean—and Norma took "Stradella" and we went down on the beach.[42] So hot we had to shed our coats and roll our sleeves up. Walked almost to Rockport on the beach till we found some enticing rocks. Lay there and read until sunset. Bonnie went. He thinks he has to take care of us.

Sat. Mar. 26   Weather Fair

Mrs. Payson is better. Letter from Abbie. Read "Aladdin" to the girls.[43] I shall never grow too old to enjoy it. Clyde Groves called today. He is home from college on vacation. Wants to know if I'll help him with "The Mill on the Floss."[44] I thought I was through with all that at graduation. It seems not. Why am I so good-natured?

Sun. Mar. 27   Weather Fair

Easter Sunday. My last lesson [as teacher] today. I've gone every Sunday this year. Jess is to take the class next. Finished my corset-cover all but the eyelets for the ribbon. It's lovely. I'm going to give it to mama.

Mon. Mar. 28   Weather Freakish

We had a storm today. Thunder and big hail-stones! Then the sun came out and ducked back again at irregular intervals. I did the whole washing today for the first time in my life and scraped the skin all off my knuckles. So warm I've taken the blanket off my bed. Madolin was here all morning.

Tues. Mar. 29   Weather Fair

Had a shampoo today. The little yellow kitten has come home to stay. I'm going to call him "Yaller Katt."[45] He's the smartest kitten I ever saw and I love him. Mrs. Payson is getting better all the time.

Wed. Mar. 30   Weather Fair

Norma went maying and brought home one bud.[46] Practised like everything today to make up for a week of indolence. Yaller Katt is perfectly contented and laps milk from a saucer in a very fastidious style.

Thur. Mar. 31   Weather Rainy

Had a fine lesson. Went up to Aunt Rose's and stayed till K. and Stella came up for me in the evening. Aunt R. gave me a little begonia she had potted for me. Clyde came over today and is coming again tomorrow.

Fri. April 1   *Weather Fair*

Clyde came over and we got through "The Mill on the Floss" after a fashion. He is going to send me a U. of M. [University of Maine] Banner. If Yaller Katt grows much cuter I shall squeeze him to death. I am studying the Dvorak "Humoreske."[47] It is dear.

Sat. April 2   *Weather Fair*

Did a lot of baking; bread, cake, cookies, doughnuts, pies, turnovers, and beans. Madolin over to supper. Mr. Joe Simonton, an old friend of mama's called and wanted me to play and sing for him which I graciously did. Gershorn Rollins is home from Colby. Saw him today a few minutes. He is going to call.

Sun, April 3   *Weather Fair*

Had a row in S.S. today and I've decided not to go anymore—only till Abbie gets home so as not to be a quitter. It was all about fatalism which is a tommy-rot idea. Jess & Florence & Edith Avery are obsessed with it. There's no sense in my going any longer. I don't believe as they do and we can't agree.

Mon. April 4   *Weather Fair*

Washed again. Was all done at 11. The soap makes my wrists so sore I can hardly practise.

    Yaller Katt is the biggest devil I ever saw in the shape of a kitten. He tears through the house at a rate of 49 knots a minutes and upsets everything in his way. We took down the sitting-room stove and carried it into the cellar.

Tues. April 5   *Weather Fair*

Norma and I cleaned the sitting room today; took the big rug out and the portieres and the sofa throw and the piano scarf, and whacked them till they must have felt black and blue.[48] Washed the floor and all the woodwork and the lace curtains. We've put the piano back where the sun strikes it and I shall have to dust it oftener. Farves [spelling?] was down.

Wed. April 6   *Weather Fair*

Gershorn called today while I was giving my sore wrists a cold cream massage. I didn't wash it off either. If he can't stand a little cold cream he can stay away. Winnie was down and she and Norma went to the dressmakers. Norma is having a suit and I a skirt.

Thurs. April 7   Weather Foggy

Sick abed all day. Norma stayed home from school. Couldn't take my lesson of course but I don't care because I didn't have a good lesson. Norma, Kathleen, Winnie, Madolin, Farves and Carleta Porter have been having a circus in the sitting room. Hope I'll be well enough for the Junior play tomorrow. Stella called.

Fri. April 8   Weather Rainy

Went to the Junior play tonight; good except for the last act which dragged fearfully. Had a good time at the dance. F.C. came home with me. He is going to call Tuesday. Norma christened her new dress, as she always does, by falling down in it in a mud puddle.

Sat. April 9   Weather Fair

Dead tired. Amy called this morning before I was up. Had breakfast at dinner time. I'm not satisfied with my skirt and shall take it back tomorrow. Winnie was down a little while. Haven't practiced, haven't done anything. Feel like the day after the 4th.

Sun. April 10   Weather Aprilly

Went to S.S. Martha is back from Portland. She has the sweetest hat I've seen this season. May change my mind about S.S. Wrote a long letter to Abbie but am undecided about sending it. It would seem funny to drop right out of S.S.

Mon. April 11   Weather Fair

Arose at 5:15 A.M. and took a sunrise walk along the beach with Bonnie. Took my skirt up to be re-modeled. Practised a lot on one of the Bach Three Part Inventions; the hard fingered one in E minor.[49] The girls got a lot of may flowers up on the mountain. They are worse than dandelion greens to pick over.

Tues. April 12   Weather Fair

Hail this morning. Fred called. Norma and Farves went to the rehearsal and after they got back we had fudge and played whist. Can do my hair with a coronet braid now. Some night we are going to have a barn dance in the kitchen. Didn't get time to go up to Mrs. Baker's today.

Wed. April 13   Weather Fair

My skirt is turning out all right. It will be done tomorrow. Went maying tonight with Norma and Farves. Got almost a bushel I guess. Corinne was out superintending a bon fire and I gave her a handful. Little Arthur Knight is home from the hospital. I saw him and Martha in the window this afternoon.

Tues. April 14   Weather Fair

Took my lesson. Ethel, Norma and I went maying this afternoon. Got lost and crawled up Spring Brook a long way like John Kidd in "Lorna Doone."[50] Had supper with Ethel and stayed the evening. They are right in the middle of house-cleaning.

Fri. April 15   Weather Fair

Stella called tonight. We all went to the moving pictures. They were fine. My kitten is getting to be so cross I hate him. He scratches and bites every chance he gets.

Sat. April 16

Ethel called up and told me I had been awarded a Cash prize in the last St. Nicholas!

Called on Ethel a minute. Spent the afternoon with Martha. Had a delightful walk right into the sunset. Wrote papa tonight. Shall see Abbie tomorrow!

Memorandum

Ethel called me up today and asked if I had seen the last St. Nicholas. Words can not express my feelings when she told me I had been awarded a cash prize of $5 for the best verse on the subject "Friends." One can not contribute to the League after his 18th birthday and this was the last poem I had ever sent in. I had given up all hope of ever getting a cash prize, which is the hardest of all to get. Imagine my state of mind. It was printed at the very head of the League and half of the editorial was spent praising it. Never before have I seen in the League an individual criticism of anything. I am simply crazed with delight. I think I shall get a beautifully bound "Browning" with my prize.[51]

Sun. April 17   Weather Fair

So good to see Abbie again! We three walked up to Melvin Heights to see mama. Forrest Burguette was visiting there and he came down to meet us. Had a lovely time. He came down with us in the evening. Lent him "Tueston [spelling?] King."

Mon. April 18   Weather Rainy

Washed all day. Put them out between showers. Norma & I went over to Jess' in the evening. Have decided to get a "Browning" with my prize money. We talked books. I want a brown "Browning." I should have "Tennyson" bound in a beautiful royal wine-color.

Tues. April 19   Weather Rainy

Got cold last night traveling around without a hat. Ethel & Martha called tonight. Wanted me to go over and get an ice cream but I didn't dare go out. So they went over and brought them back. We talked over the menu for tomorrow's spree in honor of Abbie. Hope I shall be able to go.

Wed. April 20   Weather Rainy

Sick abed all day. Awful cold. Couldn't take my lesson. Mrs. F. is all out of patience with me. Forgot to say that Tue. Night Ethel gave me the dearest little hand-bound book of "Nature Themes" by Thoreau.[52] They are as invigorating as a salt sea-wind.

Fri. April 22   Weather Rainy

U. of M. concert & ball tonight [in Camden]. The time of my life. Account in my journal [below]. Winthrop Wilson, a junior in the U. of M. came home with me. He is very nice and very interesting. I danced every dance—eight with the towns and eight with the gowns. Mr. Wilson has my order, plague take it.

Sat. April 23   Weather Rainy

"Nothin' doin'!" Marion Bucklin was here all the morning. She played the piano and we had a three ring circus. When I said "nothin' doin'" I meant nothing in the shape of house-cleaning. Marion is the cutest rag-time player I ever heard.

[Later, same day]

The devil is in the polka-dots on my brown satin dress. I never wear it but I bound to the height of ecstasy or fall into the Slough of Despond. Other influences seem to determine which it shall be.

The first time I wore it was at a dance just before Frank Ryan went back to Connecticut. I don't know whether the determining factor that night was my bracelet, which continually came unfastened and had to be carefully clasped; or my little tan pumps with the big silk bows. There is no doubt that they were bewitched. My tan silk stockings may have had something to do with it. There is something exhilarating about silk stockings. Then there was that night in Lowell—that terrible night when I cried myself to sleep, stretched out across the bed in a foolish story-book attitude. I don't know what turned the scales that night—unless it was the hammock. I should beware of hammocks. It is always the Slough of Despond where they are concerned.

Last night I think it was the rain,—a fine, foggy drizzle that blew into our faces just enough to curl the hair on my forehead. It fairly sizzled in my veins and beat my blood into a froth. If it hadn't been for the rain I think I should have come in as soon as we reached home after the concert, instead of walking right past.

I think we were both insane. Never had I talked to anyone before as I talked to him. Perhaps the almost certainty that I should never see him again made me reckless.

Principal Gardner, with whom he was to stay, introduced him to me. Poor Mr. Gardner! How was he to know? Anyway, it is too bad he knows I live so near the Opera House. Perhaps, though, Mr. Gardner was asleep and didn't hear him when he came in.

I am truly amazed at myself. I had been stolid and impulse-less so long that I imagined I had strangled my reckless love of adventure the last time I let myself down from the High School office window, onto the top of the front portico and stayed there all afternoon with a French romance, while Mr. Gardner and the assistants in the office wondered where I might be. It must be that I kept too quiet lately or it couldn't have happened. And then there is something interesting about a college man.

He asked me to let him know if I ever came to Bangor, and gave me a queer frat. Address which I promptly declared I could never remember, so that he said that—University of Maine—would be enough. There is another in the college with the same surname whose initials are W.D. So he told me his name, Winthrop F. W——, that I might not get them confused. I shall probably never go to Bangor and shall probably never see him again, though he says he may be here next summer. Anyway, "If I've done anything I'm sorry for, I'm glad of it!"

Sun. April 24   Weather Rain

Got a puff about my cash prize in the Bangor News yesterday.[53] Went up with Mr. Payson to see Mama and come home with her tomorrow. Had an open fire in my room tonight. It was lovely. When I have my house, I shall have it full of fire-places. Dele and Hugh are here.

Mon. April 25   Weather Rain

Rain, rain, rain! I wonder if we shall ever see the sun again. Went up in the rain and came back in the rain. Walked back because I was determined to come. Drizzle, drizzle, drizzle, drizzle! We shall all be mildewed! Mama didn't come home, plague take it.

Tues. April 26   Weather Sulky

Went to moving pictures last night with Stella. Shall not go again unless I am pretty sure what the pictures are to be. Never was so disgusted in my life. Mama is coming home Thursday.

April 26

Of course I'm not in love with him! It's ridiculous. But I think of him all the time and it makes me nervous. I don't want to think of anyone all the time, just yet. I've always expected it to come but now that there seems to be a possibility of it I'm beginning to be afraid. If I'm in love it isn't with his beauty, for I can't remember his face,—I've tried to so much that it has become a blur in my mind. Somehow I seem to see the look of his eyes, and then again the curve of his mouth when he smiled, but it's gone in a flash. I can remember, and feel, all over again, the way I felt when he looked at me,—but I can't remember how he looked. It is very singular. But sometimes his presence seems to envelop me—and I can't get away from it. "I gang like a ghaist an' I carena to spin." I feel restless and hysterical and horrid, like going off somewhere and crying—miserably and luxuriously.

It seems to me I shall never go out on a misty, drizzly night without feeling an emptiness beside me, without missing something—sorrowfully and, in an unaccountable way, resentfully. It is too lonesome almost to be borne. And yet I don't want anyone to come with me; I should be hateful, I know, to anyone who persisted in coming. To be lonesome is awful, but if I can't be happy I want to be lonesome. On a pleasant night I wouldn't resent the presence of someone else but in the rain I just couldn't bear it. It's foolish but it's true. And every night since that night it has rained. I shall have to stay in the house, that's all, for if I go out I shall be rude to someone, or too gloriously unhappy for safety. I go around the house restless and purposeless. If I start to sweep, in a few minutes I forget all about it, leave the broom leaning against the table and drift into the sitting room, where,—the piano stool being directly in my path—I sit down and begin to play, listlessly and with no technique apparent. Soon with a nervous and exasperated discord, I push back the stool and rise.

Reading won't do. Love stories make me worse than ever and my head is too unsettled for anything else. Embroidery would drive me raving crazy. All I can do is sit at the window and watch the rain until I can hardly keep from screaming. Am I in love with him? Or am I simply in love with love? Whatever it is I wish it would get either worse or better right off, for one thing is certain I can't stand this long. If this be love, I've had enough of it!

(September 22, 1911. Now you know better, don't you? It wasn't with him you were in love all the time, was it dear?)

Wed. April 27   Weather!!! Fair!!!

The sun is out again. All I could do this morning was sit on the steps and sun myself. This afternoon I practiced diligently for my lesson tomorrow.

I am in love with the Schumann "Polonaise in D Major."[54] The third movement is fascinating.

Thurs. April 28   Weather Fair

Took my lesson today. Had a good one, too. May have the "Polonaise" for No. 8 at the recital. Mama came home tonight. Seems as if she'd been gone a year.

Fri. April 29   Weather Fair

Went over town and payed some bills. Picked out a beautiful green silk for a dress. Just the color of my eyes. Bought a pretty pair of gray gloves. My check from St. Nicholas came Wednesday night. Adelyn called on N[orma]. tonight.

Sat. April 30   Weather Rainy

Didn't do anything today except a little cooking. Ethel & Martha called up. They want me to go to church with them tomorrow. I will if I get up in time.

Sun. May 1   Weather Fair

Church & Sunday School. I wish our church would take some of the heathen missionary money and put some pews that wouldn't cut my back in two. Went to walk with E. and M. Spent the evening with them. Lovely time. Mrs. K. is home.

Mon. May 2   Weather Nasty

Nothin' doin'. I wish the weather didn't change its mind so often. It's quite disconcerting. Mama is sick tonight. This rain is enough to make anyone sick. The Huckleberry Finners [girls' Mark Twain reading club] meet Tuesday at Ethel's.

Tues. May 3   Weather Rain

Went to and returned from Ethel's in a thunder storm. "Huckleberry Finn" is great.[55] We meet here next Tuesday. We had a lovely candle-lighted lunch and the dearest place cards. They made me read all evening while they embroidered.

Wed. May 4   *Weather Horrid*

Just like any other old day. Awfully tired after my spree last night. Practised like all J. S. Bach for my lesson tomorrow. Am going to have my lesson changed to Tuesday.

Thurs. May 5   *Weather Winterish*

Chas. Dunton called. Had a snow storm today. Went over to see Jess on urgent invitation. She says she'll give me a beautifully illustrated, fine edition of the "Rubaiyat" if I'll teach Sunday School class in her place this term. Oh, what a cinch!

Fri. May 6   *Weather Fair*

The Grammar School fair and concert today. Perfectly great. I think they made about $200. The operetta was "an unqualified success." Raingald is home from Boston. He and Earl V. called today.

Sat. May 7   *Weather Fair*

A beautiful day. Did a little of everything. Wrote to St. Nicholas, clean[ed] out my bureau, ironed a little, played a little un-classical rag-times and did nothing much that amounted to any thing.

Sun. May 8   *Weather Fair*

Went to Sunday School. Jess was not there. Ethel, Martha, Corinne and I took some magazines and went down on Sherman's Point. Walked across the bar to Mouse Island and stayed there so long that the tide came in and we had to wade ashore. Oh it was great! Saw the comet this morning.

Mon. May 9   *Weather Nasty*

Mama washed today but they didn't get dry. I'm going to have my green suit and my green silk shirtwaist done for tomorrow night. Someone got "Huckleberry" out of the library ahead of us, so I had to hunt her up and borrow it for tomorrow. Wrote to St. Nicholas. Mailed it today. Sent a postal to C.

Tues. May 10   *Weather Fair*

Loveliest day this year. Had a lovely time tonight. Read eight more chapters. Funniest thing I ever read. Am embroidering a little tie in yellow. My green suit is a dear. Didn't have any idea I'd like it so well. Next Tuesday at Corinne's.

Wed. May 11   Weather Fair

Sick today. Read "The Trail of the Lonesome Pine." It's a lovely story. The girls went over to the quarries after greens tonight and got a lot. Shampooed my hair and can't do anything with it. Earl P. and R.C. here in a minute, separately.

Thurs. May 12   Weather Fair

A little showery. Played a lot. Ran on to a lovely quartet of Mozart in D minor.[56] Arthur Foote's Pierrot & Pierrette are in the same book.[57] I must get it. Read a lot. Aunt Clara was down with Isabel H. last night.

Fri. May 13   Weather Fair

Played all day. Have two new songs—new, that is, to me—"In Old Madrid" and "Anchored." I think sometime I must have danced the Bolero and played a guitar, the guitar accompaniment in "Old Madrid" simply sets me wild.[58] Someday I shall get a guitar and I shall play it all the time.

Sat. May 14   Weather Fair

Didn't do much of anything. Nothing much to do. Jess called up to say she isn't coming to S.S. tomorrow. She's making the most of her hard-earned freedom.

Sun. May 15   Weather Fair

A little showery. All four of us spent the day at Aunt Clara's. There was a Mr. Greaves there who has a beautiful voice. He's coming down some night with the Carter boys and I shall keep him singing all evening.

Mon. May 16   Weather Fair

Am dead tired tonight. Have been cleaning the pantry. I'd rather clean Don Quixote's study.[59] We're going to have the kitchen and pantry floors painted Thursday.

Tues. May 17   *Weather Fair*

Helen Ritterbush called up from the High School to see if I could take Miss Purinton's place in Latin and Ancient History while she is out sick. Fancy me among the High School Faculty! Can't go to Corinne's tonight. Must study.

Wed. May 18   *Weather Fair*

Got along splendidly, wasn't a bit nervous. I guess I must be a born teacher. I have all four years in Latin and the Sophomores and Freshmen in History. Wonder how long she'll be sick.

Thurs. May 19   *Weather Rainy*

Taught today with equal success. I feel quite pedagogic. It is hard work, though. It seems funny for me to be teaching pupils as old and older than myself.

Fri. May 20   *Weather Fair*

Awfully tired tonight. Taught today. Mama left for Rockland on a case. We went to see the "festival of a Thousand Lanterns." The house was so packed that they had to put in an extra row of seats.

Sat. May 21   *Weather Rainy*

Nothing in particular. Slept till noon. Winnie is waiting on tables at Mrs. Thomas's. She was in a long time today. I'm dead tired.

Sun. May 22   *Weather Fair*

Went to Sunday School. Mr. & Mrs. Evans are home from Europe. Nobody was at S.S. but Mildred and myself. The others should be ashamed.

Mon. May 23   *Weather Fair*

Miss Purinton was back at school today so I didn't have to go. Seems to me she recovered from the measles mighty quick. "Huckleberry Finn" tomorrow at Ethel's.

Tues. May 24   *Weather Fair*

We dressed like little girls at Ethel's tonight and had a little girl lunch. Shall finish "Huckleberry Finn" next week at my house. Martha and I are going to read "Tom Sawyer." Took my lesson.

Wed. May 25   *Weather Fair*

Going to have the sewing room border painted tomorrow; also the front hall. Called on Mr. Packard at the Select Men's Office to get my teaching money. He's going to send it. . . . is a mess. The piano's stranded in the middle of the floor and I can't practise. Made a bridge of the ironing board so we can get into the kitchen.

Fri. May 27

Mr. Packard hasn't sent my money yet. Wish he'd hurry up. I want it more than he does.
If I were a man I'd not be so everlasting slow.

Sat. May 28

Am going to Rockland tomorrow after Sunday School. Wonder how long 'twill be before Abbie gets home. Must be almost vacation time. Must take my green silk up to Mrs. Barker.

Sun. May 29   *Weather Fair*

Looking back a little I notice we haven't had any weather for two days so today will be a change. Ethel & Martha went down with me and we each had an ice at Mrs. Thurlow's. Called on Mrs. Healy and Aunt Net.

Mon. May 30   *Weather Fair*

Didn't take my lesson because I haven't been able to practise. Finished "Huckleberry" tonight. Martha & I begin "Tom Sawyer" Thursday. Finished my corset cover tonight and Martha finished a yard of ruffle.

Wed. June 1   *Weather Fair*

Went to the ball game. Camden beat Rockland 16–1. Rah! Rah! Rah! We'll get the championship yet. See if we don't.

Thurs. June 2   *Weather Fair*

Began "Innocents Abroad" at Martha's today. Shall read it at our leisure.[60] "Tom Sawyer" isn't in the library. Great Library, I must say.

Fri. June 3   *Weather Rainy*

Ironed a lot. Mama was up a little while. She may be there a long while. Dorothy Bird is at Bowdoin for Ivy Day. Wish I was there. She has a pink satin dress for the occasion.

Sat. June 4   *Weather Fair*

Norma's coat's done. It's a dear. Got some tan pumps. Am going to have a blue linen suit. Haven't practiced a note this week. *Must* write Aunt Clem! She'll cut me out of her will if I don't.

Sun., June 5   *Weather Cold for June*

"Made Norma's little waist today. It is awfully cute." Norma just wrote that in there.

Went to Sunday School but didn't stay because I didn't think there was any.

Mon. June 6   *Weather Bum*

"Wrote Aunt Clem and the book-store man today." This is Norma's preface. Awfully cold and rainy day. Just like November. Am going to Hazel Hall's recital tomorrow evening.

Tues. June 7   *Weather Cloudy*

Went to recital tonight. Hazel Hall played beautifully. Earl Dickens sang twice; the first wasn't very good but the second was lovely. Cashed my check. Called on Ethel. Had a fine lesson.

Wed. June 8   *Weather Fair*

Washed all day. Martha & Ethel were down a few minutes. Have promised myself to practise at least an hour a day. I got in almost two hours today. Worked on Mama's corset cover this evening.

Thurs. June 9   *Weather April-ly*

Washed all day and finished everything. Finished mama's c.c. It's her birthday tomorrow and I'm going to send it down. Got a second letter from that Fall River book man, Edwin Champlin, about my prize poem.

Fri. June 10   *Weather Rainy*

Went to the circus in Rockland with Ethel, Martha and Marion Knight and Kathleen Fiske. Had a great lark in the mud and rain. Supper with Marion; moving pictures in the evening with the Knights and Anna Cobb, who is home from Smith [College] on her vacation.

Sat. June 11   *Weather Rain*

Nasty weather. Didn't do much of anything except cut and half-make a shirt-waist. Practised quite a lot. Mama was in yesterday while I was gone. Saw Helena Blethen yesterday. She is going to Bates [College] next fall.

Sun. June 12   *Weather Rain*

Rain! Rain! Rain! I'm going to build an ark. Baccalaureate Sunday and the weather couldn't even be polite to the graduates. Didn't go to S.S. Stayed at home and finished my shirt-waist instead. It's a dear.

Mon. June 13   *Weather !!! Fair !!!*

Just think of it! It has stopped raining. Norma and I went up to see about her dress for commencement. It's lovely. Mrs. B. is going to try and get my green silk done for the graduation ball. Did up six starched shirt-waists and lots of other things.

Tues. June 14   *Weather Fair*

Took my lesson. Mrs. French is going to Canada for a short vacation and I shall have no lesson for two weeks, probably. Called on Martha.

Wed. June 15   *Weather Fair*

I didn't go to the Alumni Banquet tonight. I don't know why. Probably because I didn't think much about it till it was all over. Tiresome affair anyway.

Thurs. June 16   *Weather Uncertain*

The Seniors went on their picnic today and had a great time. Kathleen's class has a picnic tomorrow if it doesn't rain. It probably will.

Fri. June 17

It did and they didn't. Went to Graduation tonight. Hope my dress will be done for the graduation ball Monday.

Sat. June 18   *Weather Rainy*

Went to Bangor today on an excursion. Our boys played the B.'s and beat them 16–5. Rah! For us! Saw "St. Elmo" at the Bangor Theatre.[61] It was great. Dinner at "Frey's." Moonlight coming home.

Sun. June 19

Didn't go to Sunday School. Abbie'll be here next Sunday and then I'll go.

Mon. June 20

Sick abed all day and couldn't go to the ball. "Curse the luck!" Norma went and had a great time. It makes me mad.

Tues. June 21   *Weather Rain*

Mama came home. Gwen & Helen Perry, Edna Simmons, Helena Blethen and Kathleen Fiske were up from Rockland today to climb Mt. Megunticook with Ethel, Martha, Marion, Corinne, Norma & I. Couldn't go on account of the shower. Stayed at Ethel's and had a jamboree.

Wed. June 22

Mama's going to Boston tomorrow. Worked all day getting her ready.

Thurs. June 23   *Weather Fair*

A beautiful day for mama's journey. She'll probably stay in Newburyport two or three weeks.

Fri. June 24

Tired to death. Norma went to Silas Heale's dance in the Cleveland Hall.

Sat. June 25   Weather Fair

Got up at six and washed all day. We're going to take time while mama's gone in sewing, washing, and ironing. Abbie just called up. I must be sure and go tomorrow. The "New Bedford Standard" I sent for has come.

Memorandum

There's an awful puff about my "Friends" in the "New Bedford Evening Standard" for May 26. Mr. Champlin sent it in. There is two-thirds of a column about it.

Sun. June 26   Weather Fair

Went to S.S. today. It seems good to see Abbie. The S.S. goes on a picnic Tuesday if it is fair. I think I will go. Ethel, Martha and I all happened to wear our graduation dresses today.

Mon. June 27   Weather Rainy-Fair

We ironed from five in the morning to one at night, or rather, one in the morning—taking turns and resting in between. That awful three weeks ironing is all done but for two or three of Kathleen's things. Letter from mama.

Tues. June 28   Weather Rain

Didn't have the pic-nic. Cleared off beautifully this afternoon. The girls have gone in bathing with Dorothy and Constance Simonton. I've the house almost cleaned up after the ironing spree.

Wed. June 29   Weather Fair

Didn't go to the picnic today for which Ethel & Martha will be "mad with me all summer." But what care I? Verd & Nan were down. Called on Aunt Rose.

Thurs. June 30   Weather Fair

Norma & Dot went strawberrying today. Got quite a lot.

Fri. July 1   Weather Fair

Had tea with Jess out in the orchard. Lovely time. Went to the dance with Gladys Gilbey. Check from Rockland.

Sat. July 2   Weather Hot

Money from Kingman [from her father] and check from mama. Didn't do much of anything. The girls went out sailing. I went down on the beach this afternoon.

Sun. July 3   Weather Fair

Started in to cut out a shirt waist but Hazel Dearborn came down and wanted me to canoe up the river with her, so I went. Charlie Swan took us up. Went in swimming. Dinner at the camp. Paddled all over the lake.

Mon. July 4   Weather Fair

Went to the ball at Lincolnville tonight. Lots of Camden people went. Had a great time. Didn't get home till 3:30. Wore my pink silk muslin. I was the only red-headed girl in pink, at which I was not surprised. Red-heads are supposed to wear blue.

Tues. July 5   Weather Fair

Lay abed almost all day. Have to go to Rockland tomorrow and hate to take time.

Perhaps I can bribe Norma to go instead.

Wed. July 6   Weather Fair

Norma went to R. for me. Stayed all day, called on everybody and had a great time. Russell Avery called this evening. He is the only man I know who is as Rubaiyat-mad as I am.

Thurs. July 7   Weather Fair

Went down to the beach with some magazines this afternoon. Saw R.A.

Fri. July 8   Weather Fair

Went to the dance. Had a bum time and am never going again to a Friday night dance. See if I do.

Sat. July 9   Weather Fair

Went riding with Linda McKanne down on Beauchamp Point.[62] Winnie is down. Russell and Fred came over this afternoon.

Sun., July 10   *Weather Fair*

Went to Oakland with Uncle Bert & Aunt Rose. Stayed with them the evening. Had a nice time.

Mon. July 11   *Weather Fair*

Went canoeing with Russell today. Took the "Golden Treasury" with us. Went ashore on the beach and read.

Tues. July 12

Went to bed early tonight. Winnie and Madolin were down and talked so I couldn't get to sleep until later.

Wed. July 13   *Weather Hot*

Music lesson today. Pretty good. Too hot to practise. Went up to see Mrs. Barker. Have to get a third pattern for my silk dress. Nothing suits me after I get it. Went up to Win's a few minutes.

Thurs. July 14

Sick headache all day. Russell called tonight.
(B & I.)[63]
Slept on the roof last night with Dot & Kathleen. Salt plunge this morning at 4.

Fri. July 15   *Weather Fair*

R.A. over this afternoon. Went riding with Guy Grey as soon as he was out of sight. Alden Allen over a few minutes this evening. Gershorn called and brought me some cherries.
    (B. & I.)
Norma and Win went to a dance.

Sat. July 16   *Weather Fair*

Cooked a lot. Winnie down. Russell called again. Made him wipe the dishes. My bread turned out fine.

Sun. July 17   *Weather Fair*

Norma & I canoed up the river with Charlie Swan. Had a great time. Went swimming. Dinner at the camp. Paddled all over the lake. Went blueberrying. Came home by moonlight. Fred, Russell, and Dill Munro were down.

Mon. July 18   *Weather Almost Fair*

Lay abed till noon enterprising creature that I am. Made up for it, however, by darning a pair of stockings, setting bread to rise, and practising quite a lot.

Tues. July 19   *Weather Fair*

Didn't do anything but bake bread, shampoo my head and read. Norma and Win found a letter all torn up under the bridge on High Street. We pieced it together and it is a perfectly scandalous love-letter from a married woman. It is awful.

Wed. July 20   *Weather Fair*

Took my lesson. Met Guy just as I was starting out and went riding with him so was a half hour late. Mrs. French has sworn to spank me if I do it again. Russell called. (B.)

July 20, 1910 Wednesday Night

Journal of a Little Girl Grown-Up

I'm tired of being grown-up! Tired of dresses that kick around my feet, tired of high-heeled shoes; tired of conventions and proprieties; tired, tired and sick of hairpins! I want to be a little girl again. It seems to me, looking back over my jump-rope and hop-scotch days, that I never played half hard enough, always came in a little too soon, lay abed a little too long. If I had only known, and had climbed enough trees and made enough mud-pies to last me through the awful days when I should want to and couldn't! And the awfullest thing about it is that I haven't forgotten how. It wouldn't be so bad if I just couldn't remember; but to know how so well—to want to so bad—and not to be able to!

It seems to me I can remember everything I ever did, every place I was ever in. My mind is a labyrinthian picture-gallery in which every painting is some scene from my life—vivid and distinct, even in its most trivial details. It takes but the tiniest thing, the faintest sound or scent, often-times imagination—to bring such a scene before my eyes. There is a little spicy-smelling yellow flower growing in clusters on a bush, in old-fashioned gardens—I think they call it "clove" or a "flowering currant." The smell of it inevitably never fails to take me back into a little playhouse I made once under such a bush, just this side of the church-yard fence. It is a hot summer afternoon. The air is drowsy with the sweetness of the tiny trumpet-shaped flowers above my head and, save for the monotonous droning of many bees, there is no sound anywhere. I am painstakingly trimming a rhubarb leaf hat with white-clover and buttercups with which my lap is filled. Beside me are two long, slender white wands from which I have been peeling the bark for ribbons, with primitive implements of sharp teeth and nails. I can taste again the sweetness of the smooth round stick in my mouth. I see again the moist, delicate green of the bark's living. And into my nostrils I breathe the hot spicy fragrance until my soul is steeped in it.

Then on and on into picture after picture after picture, through a meadow where, at every step, I had to pick the violets to clear a place for my feet; over the short stubble of a wide level field to the place where a friendly grapevine climbed a tree and, with its own weight bent the branches to the ground, bringing forth grapes and apples into easy reach; up the side of a woody hill and [wandered] a winding path to a secret spot where fox berries grew bigger, sweeter, and more plentifully than anywhere else in the world.

Hundreds of places, each one as dear as these—each one so distinct that I know I could find now if it is still there. If I could just go back like a little girl and revisit each scene alone. Who would there be to say "Go away, you can't come here, for you are a little girl no longer,"?

July 21, 1910 Thursday morning

I couldn't get to sleep last night for thinking of it. I twisted and I turned until the sheet beneath me was rough with wrinkles. My shoulders felt cold and I tried to pull the bed cloths up under my chin. They seemed to be nailed to the bed. I set my teeth and pulled stubbornly until at last they gave way (with disconcerting suddenness) and settled unpleasantly about my ankles leaving my feet exposed. The room was so dark that I could not see myself but I know they must have looked very startled and indignant. As a last resort I reached for a match. My groping hand struck the tray and sent it spilling to the floor; and for a minute I was too enraged to move. Then I slid out of bed and began to crawl about on my knees feeling carefully over the rug. Every match I found had already been struck.

And suddenly, from sheer vexation and discomfort, I began to cry; sitting back on my heels, my hands hanging limply beside me and my face disconsolately upthrust into the dark—for all the world like a lonesome puppy—until I had cried down into the tears of a strange, resentful grief which had grown bitter from lying in my heart so long. And the hurt of those tears left me huddled beside the bed weak and quivering. After a while following an impulse I had often had in childhood, I reached up and pulled the cloths in armfuls from the bed, sheets, blanket, spread and pillows, heaping them into a big soft mound on the floor. Then with a sigh of utter heaviness I wriggled down into this grateful warmth and went to sleep.

July 22, 1910 Friday Morning

I wonder if I have really found the way. The idea came so suddenly that I hardly dare trust it, and yet—indeed, indeed, I don't see why not! I may have dreamed it, for I must have been asleep,—but I am not sure. I only know that all at once I sat straight up in bed and stared out into the darkness, and that the darkness rolled up like a curtain and left it there, clear and perfect in every detail like the setting of a play. And as I gazed, fascinated, the broad low house clung easily to the slope of the hill. It seemed to fit there, somehow, as if under the measured hammering of the years it had relaxed, unresistingly to become at last a part of the soil on which it stood.

Its whiteness, surrounded by the wonderful green of the grass, was fairly dazzling. Where did the grass grow green like that? Where suddenly the old house opened its eyes and blinked sleepily at the setting sun and I caught my breath in an ecstasy of recognition. I know it now! The sunset on the window panes, the snowy washing spread on the short grass. The wilderness of blackberry bushes behind the house. I knew it now, a wave of tender memory came flooding over my heart and my eyes were heavy with tears. When the mist cleared and I could see once more, the big front door had opened and The Little-Girl-I-Used-To-Be was standing on the step, her small face upthrust into the sunlight—silent and adoring.

Why not? Why not? I say it over and over to myself. I am home-sick for that little girl on the step. Perhaps she would let me play with her, for indeed I have not forgotten how. I loved the old white house and the wild grass around it. I loved the blackberries on the hill—and Auntie Bines![64] Why, I was Auntie Bines' little girl! O, Auntie Bines, if I might just come back and be your little girl again! Indeed I have not forgotten how. You would know me, you would love me just the same, Auntie Bines, and we would both forget that I have ever been away. I would pick the blackberries for supper and set the table, and I would wipe the dishes afterward, just the same. Why not? Oh, why not?

Thurs. July 21

Nothing in particular.

Fri, July 22

Russell was in a little while before the dance.

Sat. July 23

Didn't do anything.

Sun. July 24   Weather Fair

Couldn't go up to the lake for mama has written forbidding us to step into a canoe again until she returns.

Mon. July 25   Weather Fair

Russell and I went to walk down by the Lily Pond, and had a falling out. "Oh, what a fall was there, my country-men!"[65]

Tues. July 26   Weather Fair

Gershorn was down a little while. Norma has gone rowing. Stella called.

Wed. July 27   Weather Fair

Took my last music lesson for this summer. Recital next Wednesday. I play Dvorak's "Humoresque" and [Ethelbert] Nevin's "Twas a Lover and His Lass."[66]

Thurs. July 28   Weather Rainy & Fair

Called on Stella. Have got Dr. Sheckley treating my ding-busted warts. Gershorn called this evening and brought down the "Colby Oracle."

Fri. July 29   Weather Fair

Sick abed most all day. Couldn't go on the class picnic.

Wed. Aug. 3   Weather Fair

Recital today. Wore my green silk for the first time. I didn't make a single mistake but am glad it's over. Walked up with Martha and met Marion Hatch.

Thurs. Aug. 4   Weather Fair

Went to the theatre, "Romeo & Juliet." It was great. Madame Marie Rappold of the Metropolitan Opera Co., Rudolf Berger of the Berlin Royal Opera Co, Orville Harrold of the Manhattan Opera Co. and Lucien di Vannos of New York sang the wedding music. It was beautiful.

Sat. Aug. 13

Saw the Klark Urban Co. in "Sold into Slavery." Pretty good for a melodrama. Went with Winnie & Kathleen.

Mon. Aug. 22

Mama and I called on the Derrys tonight. Eliza & I went down on the wharf and put our feet in the ice-cold salt water. Norma went too. Norma stayed with Dot and Kathleen on the roof tonight. I'm going to stay with Stella.

Tues. Aug. 23

Stayed all night with Stella last nigt [*sic*]. Was allowed to read some rather interesting letters she received while in Bangor. It seems funny for Stella to be having love-letters. I don't think I'd let any body read mine. But I like to read hers.

Tues. Sept. 6   Weather Rainy

Saw "The Man on the Box" tonight.[67] It was perfectly great. I'd like to see it right over again.

Thurs. Sept. 15   Weather Rainy

Ethel Warren and I went on a tramp of about 10 miles up over Mt. Battie across the table-lands to the top of Megunticook. I'm going walking at lot this winter.

Sun. Sept. 18   Weather Sultry

Went on a tramp about 14 miles up Megunticook to Maiden Cliff and home by the Turnpike. Warren Coombs was the guide. Ethel, Norma & I went. Perfectly beautiful view from the cliff. Warren goes back to Bowdoin tomorrow.

Tues. Sept. 20   Weather Cloudy

Had a corn-roast down on the shore at Oakland tonight—3 Knights, 2 Sawyers, 2 Millays, Given Derry, Jess Hosmer, Sadie Easton and Katherine Johnson.

Wed. Sept. 21

Stella called up to see if I can finish out the week playing at the Dreamland Moving Picture Theatre in Rockland. I think I will. It will be something new, at least. Shall stay to supper with Aunt Net or Mrs. Healy. Began music lessons again today.

Thurs. Sept. 22   Weather Fair

Played at Dreamland today. Rather amusing, but tiresome. There's a big fat vaudeville man whose accompaniments I have to play from dirty manuscripts. It's awful. Had supper at Mrs. Healy's. Didn't get home till 11. Alden Allen came up in the car [streetcar] with me.

Fri. Sept. 23   Weather Fair

Played again today. Awfully monotonous. Glad I haven't got to do it right along. I should die. Had supper at Aunt Net's. Haze was just getting ready to go on a corn-roast. Jess was on the car coming up.

Sat. Sept. 24   Weather Fair

Got through today, thank the Fates. Never so sick of anything in my life. I never shall earn my living that way. Supper at Mrs. Healy's. Saw Alice W. and Katherine in the car station. We came up together.

Sun. Sept. 25

Abbie's last Sunday before she goes back to Radcliffe. I should have gone but I was dead tired.

Mon. Sept. 26   *Weather Fair*

Went over town and bought me the sweater I had seen in Haskell's window and admired so much—$6.00. It is a beautiful shade of gray, has two deep pockets in front and a little breast-pocket—all lined; a collar that can lie down or stand up—with a strap that buttons across the throat. Just right for snow shoeing this winter.

Tues. Sept. 27   *Weather Fair*

Ethel, Martha and I went walking tonight up Elm Street, through pasture and woods & under barbed-wire fences until we struck Pearl St. and then home. Met Abbie and said goodbye to her. Awfully glad I saw her, especially since I didn't go to Sunday School.

Wed. Sept. 28   *Weather Fair*

Came down "like the wolf on the fold" on Mrs. French today, only to get sent home. It seems I should have gone at 2:30 instead of ten, and it's a sure bet no-one knows how I got mixed. We are going to walk to Rockland and back this afternoon so I had to put off till tomorrow at 1:30.

Thurs. Sept. 29   *Weather Fair*

Thunderation! Ethel couldn't go yesterday and has to go today. I've got to take my lesson so I shall have to ride down. I did want to walk both ways. Ethel is going to the M.M. Festival in Portland. Wish I was going. Dot went back to New York tonight on the boat.

Fri. Sept. 30   *Weather Fair*

Norma & Kathleen went to the Freshman reception tonight. I made up K's new petticoat today. It's a beauty. Had a lovely time yesterday. Had a good nine-mile walk, as it was, but did want to go both ways.

Sat. Oct. 1   Weather Showery

Had a thunder storm this afternoon and the glorious rain-bows. After that it cleared off lovely. Went over town this evening. Called on Jess. My good-bye letter is in this month's St. Nicholas. Embroidered this evening.

Sun. Oct. 2   Weather Fair

Didn't do much of anything. Embroidered this evening while mama read aloud "Anne of Green Gables."[68] It's the dearest story.

Mon. Oct. 31   Weather Fair

Hallowe'en Party at Ethel's tonight. Martha, Corinne, Jess, Gladys and I. Have the dearest Witch Costume which I wore. Lovely time. I met my Fate and everything is satisfactorily settled.

Tues. Nov. 1   Weather Fair

Called on Ethel today. She is taking advantage of her father's absence from the store and is abusing Jake awfully.

Wed. Nov. 2   Weather Fair

Took my lesson today. Am studying the Chopin Scherzo in E [B] flat Minor.[69] Called on Martha and stayed to supper. Went to moving pictures with G. & M. Stella is back from Boston.

Thurs. Nov. 3   Weather Fair

Called on Corrine. Went to see Jess & Ethel a few minutes. Have begun my Christmas sewing.

Memorandum

Things to Remember

> Gold Badge in St. Nicholas League for poem, "The Land of Romance"—March, 1907.

> Silver Badge in St. Nicholas League for poem, "Young Mother Hubbard"—August, 1909.

Prize of $10 in a competition for the best girls' composition for poem, "La Joie de Vivre"—at my graduation from the Camden High School June 16, 1909.

Lagendorff Concert in Rockland, Mar. 3, 1910.

"Willowdale" in Fairfield, myself as "Milly"—Nov. 2, 1909.

Cash prize of $5 in St. Nicholas for poem, "Friends"—May 1910.

Vigils with Imaginary Lover
(1911)

I n April of 1911, when Edna was nineteen, a second confidant entered the world of her diary. He would serve a purpose more complex and far-reaching than Mammy Hush-Chile, whom she had summoned in order to comfort her in her physical and emotional distress.

Now she demanded more than comfort. She needed to be rescued from her life of withering and demoralizing toil, loneliness, anxiety—and perhaps worst of all, her own flaws and frailties, her lack of perfection. Mammy is maternal and asexual. What Millay wanted now was a man, the perfect man, the perfect lover, to sweep down upon the wretched house in Camden where she worked herself to exhaustion. She wanted him to carry her away. To where? She doesn't tell us exactly. But what is wonderful about this part of the story is that the conjuring of the sorceress actually succeeds. And dreams really do come true.

"The Imaginary Lover," Millay's phrase, is apt. The imagined knight errant is an embodiment of the life of her imagination, and a sort of intermediate "mage" who will assist in effecting her deliverance. There is a charming photograph of the girl in the lee of Mount Battie, dressed for Halloween in a witch's costume: a wide-brimmed black hat with a pointed crown, black robes; she is leaning pensively upon a broom. Glowering, grim, she looks the part.

Millay knew a good deal about the black arts from reading Sir Walter Scott's *Demonology and Witchcraft;* her diary from April of 1911 until January 1913 records not only her yearning monologues to the spirit lover; in addition she describes magic rituals involving candles, incantations, rings, secret codes, needles, and blood-letting. In her desperation the young woman will go to any length to get her man—if he is a man of flesh and blood—or to engage the empowering spirit, if that is what he is in truth.

ℬ

Jan. 3, 1911

This isn't a diary. I don't know exactly what to call it, but it isn't a diary, that I'm sure of. I've tried to keep a diary and it doesn't work. I always forget it for two or three weeks and then, with the aid of dance orders and programs and newspapers and a memory not very strong on dates, I go back and fill in. A diary of this kind is neither authentic nor satisfactory. This is to be more after the fashion of a journal. In a journal you can write whenever and whatever you please, and it's nobody's business. Journal really means daily, too, of course, but no one ever thinks of it that way. I'm too spasmodic to do anything daily so I'm going to keep a book the very inspiration of which shall be my spasmodic temperament. Cut and dried accounts are all right in their place but here isn't it.

Spasm the First

[A blank space]

April 12, 1911

I've just been looking this thing over and it struck me as being laughably— though unconsciously—consistent, that my first "Spasm" should be the most spasmodic thing I could possibly do—nothing! I wonder what happened just then to start me off on something else. For I remember I was going to make a long entry and had a lot to say. I may remember it sometime. If I do I'll try and keep my mind on it long enough to write it.

Spasm the Second

"Intellect is but half of the man: the will is the driving wheel."[1] I've seen that somewhere and it sticks in my head. It's just what's the matter with me. I've brains enough but I haven't any stick-to-it-ivity. I'm one of those comfortable people whom you can't depend on. I'll promise most anything just to be agreeable and keep people from crying, and then I promptly forget all about it. A very nice person to have around. I always make a hit with strangers, because they don't know me. If I never met anyone more than once I would have hosts of friends.

One commendable thing about me is that I have no bad habits: which virtue is more than canceled by the fact that I have no good habits. I never do anything the same way twice—excepting rarebits.[2] I always make them exactly the same, but it isn't a habit. I do it consciously, and because I don't dare do it any other way. With this single exception I don't "always" anything. I don't always brush my teeth before breakfast; I don't always brush my hair before I go to bed; I don't always leave my window up. If you should ask me right now I should tell you that salmon is nasty stuff and that I hate it. Tomorrow I would very likely say that I'm very fond of it, especially in a "wiggle." Sometimes I wear my hat on the back of my head; sometimes I wear it down over my eyes; sometimes I don't wear it at all. Sometimes I wear heavy underclothes clear into May. Sometimes I wear thin ones all winter. Sometimes I sleep with two pillows; sometimes with no pillow. I don't coincide with myself.

Sometimes I finish things and sometimes I don't. I'm pretty sure to get sick of it before I'm half-way through. I have made shirt-waists with innumerable button-holes and a tape stitched on to tie around the waist. I have made shirt-waists with no button holes, that had to be fastened up the front with beauty-pins.

I have had freaks of washing the dishes after every meal, and scalding the towels after every dish-washing. I have let them go until you couldn't find a clean one with the aid of a whole detective agency, and had to wash a cup for coffee. I wake in the morning with ambitious plans for getting the house in order for Mother's return in the evening. Mother arrives. The beds aren't made, the lamps aren't cleaned, the dishes aren't washed, the floors aren't swept. There's nothing to eat in the house, and the stores are closed! But I have blacked the stove! Oh, yes. From an unsightly object covered with dust, grease and ashes it has been transformed into an immaculate, shining advertisement for the hardware store whence it came. I have taken it all apart. I have taken every door from its hinges, unscrewed every screw I could find, and washed the whole thing, inside and out. I have blacked every inch of iron and scoured the nickel-work with Bon-ami.[3] I have polished the entire surface,—first with a brush and then with a flannel cloth, and the affect [*sic*] is hard on the eyes unless one wears smoked glasses. The hind legs do not shine because no light strikes them, but they have been rubbed as conscientiously as the others; and there is a high-light on the tip end of the poker. It is not a stove, it is an ornament: and we shall not have bacon for breakfast.

There now! That's the kind of person I am. Wouldn't you like to have me around?

Sometimes I make me laugh; sometimes I make me cry; frequently I make me sick.

But I have never been in a position where I would consider it an honor to shake hands with myself. I'm a "liberal education," I am!

May 3, 1911

Beloved,—I am alone with you again tonight. One month ago tonight we were betrothed, and I made-believe the ring on my finger. Tonight I have a real ring,—a ring not accepted as a gift, nor bought, nor stolen, nor yet borrowed for the occasion. It came to me in a fortune-cake; just the sort of ring to link me to a Love-o'-Dreams, like you. I shall wear it every time we are together. It is a cheap little thing in imitation of a solitaire, but I love it with a passion that is painful. It is the symbol of all earthly happiness to me. No costly stone could be more than that. And I should love it for its symbolism no matter what it might be.

Beloved—I have been true to you in thought and deed. I have been saving up for you my month's allowance of Hearts' Adoration. I have been right miserly about it, but tonight I give it all to you. There is more than you can have imagined possible, I know; for it grows most abundantly of all the flowers in my Heart-Garden, and it is the most beautiful of all; more beautiful even than Heart's Delight or Heart's Surrender or Bleeding Heart or even Heart's Ease.

I have been nearer happiness in the last month than I have been before since I can remember. I have felt a sense of security that is quite new to me. The thought of you steadies me. After this when I feel the need of your strength I will kiss my ring and I know it will come to me. I will try not to be lonely for you; not to grow weary with waiting.

Good night, Beloved. I shall lie down and think of you. I shall sleep and dream of you. My love for you is infinite and eternal; for it is my very soul, and the soul is boundless and cannot die.

Spasm the Third

May 25

It is funny how different people do the same thing. I suppose everybody gets mad, but no two people get mad in the same way. Now Norma, when the atmosphere gets congested, storms around and shouts insulting remarks about everybody that gets underfoot. The madder she becomes the louder she shouts and the worse she storms. That's her way. Kathleen stamps, slams the door, and howls. That's her way.

I knew there would be a fight sometime today. I felt it coming. Everybody was irritable, no one had a bit of patience, and family relations became strained. The clouds began to gather early in the morning. At noon they were close overhead and waiting for a good place to burst.

It came soon enough. I was eating my dinner without waiting for the others because I was in a hurry to take my music lesson. I was filling a saucer with strawberries when I heard the preliminary shouts and stamps from the sitting-room, and I didn't pay much attention because it wasn't my fight and I was hungry. Besides, I had heard millions of others just like it, and—well, as I said before, it wasn't my fight. But after a while it began to grow monotonous. Everybody seemed to have something very important to say and nobody seemed to want to listen. So they all stuck their noses into each other's faces and tried to out-drown the rest of the conversation. Then everybody began to get mad in their own particular way. Norma began to call people names, Kathleen began to slam. Mother became violently hysterical and flapped around the room in all directions at once, insisting that she should do as she pleased in her own house and nobody cared anything about her anyway.

Well, as I said before, it began to grow monotonous. It seemed to me that people had been shouting ever since I could remember and there seemed not the slightest possibility of the noise ever subsiding. And after a while I began to get mad myself. I hardly dared lift a strawberry to my mouth for fear it would get jarred into my lap; and when at last I got it safely deposited, something would happen and I'd bite my tongue instead.

And at last I decided I'd had about enough. So I just sat back in my chair, took a deep breath, and screamed, piercingly but dispassionately; not the cry of one who is being murdered or even robbed, but just a good technical scream, as if I were trying to see if I could do it.

For fully a quarter-minute afterward everything was absolutely still. You can't imagine how funny it seemed. Then it began again worse than ever, only this time it was mostly directed at me, which was a change at least. But there was so little fun in that, since I continued to go calmly on with my dinner and paid no attention to anyone, that they were forced to turn back to each other. And after a while I did another scream, louder and more prolonged than the first.

Then I began to mash my strawberries. Now, if there is anything in this world that can set my teeth on edge quicker than anything else, it is to see someone lap ice-cream from a spoon. But next to that comes mashing strawberries. So I mashed 'em. I had just dipped me out some more so I had a nice lot to work with, and it was really lovely. They made a little scrunching noise that is very pleasant and soothing to the nerves. Sometimes they squirt which adds to the excitement. Occasionally one shoots out from under and goes reeling across the cloth leaving a gory trail behind it. That is because it is only slightly wounded. If you slash 'em right in two at the first whack they can do nothing but writhe while you finish 'em. It was very murderous and enjoyable. But after a while, I'd killed every one. Then was the time to eat them but I couldn't, they were so messy and wet. I could think of nothing else to do so I pushed back my saucer and listened. It was like the noise that bursts from the chest where the little boy is supposed to be hidden when the ventriloquist lifts the cover. For a minute or two I sat there and let it rattle against my ears, and then all at once I jumped to my feet, seized a dinner-plate, smashed it down onto the floor, turned and cut for the beach, bare headed in the rain.

That's my way.

Spasm the Fourth

I have just laid down for myself ten commandments. See that you obey them Vincent, you old back-slider you.

These are They.

1. Thou shalt not sit on thy foot.

2. Thou shalt not cross thy knees.

3. Thou shalt not twist thy legs the one about the other.

4. Thou shalt not slump thy shoulders.

5. Thou shalt not bite thy lips.

6. Thou shalt not wrinkle thy forehead.

7. Thou shalt not fold thine arms.

8. Thou shalt not lay thy hands upon thy hips.

9. Thou shalt not speak in a loud voice.

10. Thou shalt not speak rapidly nor run thy words together in a verbal hash.

June 3, 1911

Sweetheart, I am so very tired that I am going straight to bed. I am too tired even for our little tea-party. But I have kissed your ring and I will light our candle a minute before I go. I can scarcely hold the funny little stub pencil with which I am writing this, I am so very, very tired. But I love you just the same. I shall never grow tired of loving you, sweetheart, oh darling! Oh, I do love you. I kiss my ring, my foolish little ring, and I could weep with the love that does so hurt my heart. Oh, I adore you!

The thought of you even is the loveliest thing that has ever come into my life. Sometimes I let myself think for a minute what it will be when you really come, the sweet things that we will say and do. Sweetheart, come soon! Think of the time that we might have together and that we are wasting apart. The love of you lies on my heart now like a sunbeam and I could laugh with the joy of it. Oh, darling! Goodnight. Goodnight, sweetheart! Beloved. If there was a word more beautiful than "Beloved" I would call you it. When I have found a way to express the inexpressible then will I tell you how I love you. Goodnight, oh wonderful thing that has come into my life. If you were here I would say it over and over to you: Beloved, oh Beloved, Beloved!

June 27
Spasm the Fifth

I'm darned lonesome. That's all there is about it. I'm just *darned lonesome.* Mother's in Rockland on a case. Kathleen is visiting Dorothy Simonton. Norma is away all the time; this particular night at Emma Ritterbush's where she is taking supper. Nobody's taking supper here nor me there. It's no fun to eat supper alone. I've just got through. And there's not the slightest chance of anyone's calling up to take me out for a spin, or a drive, or even an ice-cream soda. Boys don't like me because I won't let them kiss me. It's just like this: let boys kiss you and they'll like you but you won't. And as long as I have to spend so much of my time with myself, I'd rather be on good terms with myself than with anyone else I know of. If I'm not on good terms with Ethel I can have a perfectly splendid time with Corinne; and if I'm not on good terms with Norma I can have a very pleasant time with Kathleen, but if I'm not on good terms with myself I can't have even a decent time with anybody. But I'd almost be willing to be engaged if I thought it would keep me from being lonesome. Even being engaged would have its compensations. For instance: if I was engaged I would be going to the play tonight instead of sitting humped up on the steps in a drizzle that keeps my pencil point sticky. I'd be going out paddling tomorrow instead of practicing the Beethoven Funeral March Sonata. And I'd have something to do besides write in an old book. I'd like to have something happen to give me a jolt, something that would rattle my teeth and shake my hairpins out. That's like saying, "Won't you come in?" to an earthquake, isn't it? I'd like to talk to someone I don't know; I'm too well acquainted with myself to make it very interesting. I'm going in and sing "Flow Gently Sweet Afton," and then I'm going over to the Public Library for a book.[4] Perhaps I'll meet my fate.

June 27

Good evening, Dear! I know this is not my "night" and of course you're not expecting me, but here I am. But I'm not going to stay very long. Just long enough to say that we'll have to find some other place to meet in. For people have moved in on the other side [of] the partition and we would be in danger of interruption if we met here again. So we'll have to find another place. And I'm going place-hunting tomorrow. I'll be sure and find an attractive and a capacious place, and I shall live there all by myself and let no one in but you. But you will be welcome at all hours. The third of every month shall be sacred to you, but if you wish to come at any other time, come; and your coming will make that day sacred, too.

I'm going now. I don't feel free to talk with you here with people so near us. I don't want to go a bit but I'm going right now, this minute, before I have time to think. Goodnight! I'll blow you a kiss from the door. Goodnight! Goodnight, Dear!

June 27, 1911

Mammy Hush Chile! I have come to say goodbye. For I am going away where I shall never see you again. You dear old brown Mammy Hush-Chile. I have loved you for a long time and I shall always love you. Your heart is so filled with my griefs and delights that it is like my own heart.

I shall have other friends but they will not be Mammy Hush-Chile's. For you have been the friend of my little-girlhood and I shall never have another little-girlhood. But when I go back in memory to it I shall find you there and love you just the same.

I am very sad at parting with you and doubly sad because it means and makes me realize that I am leaving my little-girlhood forever behind. Wish me Good-Luck, Mammy, in my big-girlhood. Say a charm for me that cannot fail to bring me happiness, and that will keep me a little girl at heart, through everything.

Goodnight, Mammy Hush-Chile, and Goodbye. I will kiss you and leave you. May God bless you and our friendship.

July, 1911

Vigils With Imaginary Lover

"He who myne heart would keep for long
 Shall be a gentil-man and strong."

72

"And if he come not by the road,
  And come not by the hill,
  And come not by the far sea-way,
  Yet come he surely will.
  Close all the roads of all the world,
  Love's road is open still."

My life is but a seeking after life;
I live but in a great desire to live;
And this the motive of my every deed,
The undercurrent of my every thought:—
To seek you, find you, have you for my own
Who are my purpose and my destiny.
For me, the things that are do not exist;
The things that are for me are yet to be:
And so my waking hours are as a dream;
And so in dreams I wake and am with you,
A shadow figure and a myth, and yet
More real than reality, to me.
O love! Must I grow old with waiting?
Grow, Tho of the search unweary, weary with it?
And follow stumbling where my thoughts have flown,
And drag my fainting body after me,
While ever more reluctant goes my blood
Till life be but a crutch whereon to lean?
No, love, not that! Oh, love, I that should be! If it must be I do not
    wish to know. For I would rather seek you all my life,
Finding in each false hope a transient gleam,
And die at last alone and seeking still;
Than live unseeking, knowing search in vain.
No, love, not that! No, love! Oh, love, I know
That our two souls will not be long apart.
And when we meet—I love to say the words:
There is a benediction in the sound—
And when we meet 'twill be as tho the years
Had never been that each has fared alone.

And not as strangers meet, with curious eyes
And furtive glances each one at the other,
Nor will we meet as meet long-absent friends,
With outstretched hands and eager questionings,
Scanning each other's face with frank regard;
Not yet like them who last night were betrothed,
With close embrace, and sign, and passionate kiss,
All interspersed with vows of constancy;
And not as in our dreams twin souls do meet,
Slowly advancing toward each other's eyes
With parted lips and fascinated gaze
As to a magnet, irresistibly.
For love will seem so much the natural thing
To us, who have loved constantly and long,
That when you hear my step you will not start,
Nor turn, not leave your chair, but only smile
And reaching back your hand await my touch.
And, moving with the sweet security
Of one whose love and trust is absolute,
In perfect understanding I shall come
And lay my hand in yours, and at your feet
Sit, silent, with my head against your knee.

July 3, 1911

Tonight, Dearest-Of-All, is the night before the 4th. It is also your night, Dearest-Of-All, and as I shall be kept awake all night I shall have all night to think of you. It is eleven o'clock now—and hot? Keep us a'! I have been out all by ourselves a-hunting a breeze, and failed to find it,—even on the fire-escape of my old High School, where there's always a wind if there's a wind at all.

It's strange how little I find to say to you when we at last are alone. I just want to sit and think of you, and love you, and never say a word.

Sometimes I don't mind so much the uncertainty which envelops you, but tonight I wish we were quite, quite sure of each other, and I knew all your nicknames, and what kind of pipe you smoke. It would give me such a feeling of security and comfort just to know what kind of pipe you smoke.

Does it seem strange to you, Dearest-Of-All, that I love you so much, knowing you so little? Why, I have loved you since I knew women could love. And I know your heart. It doesn't matter what kind of pipe you smoke. But it makes me very wistful when I think that I don't know.

I think you'd better hurry up and come, Dearest-Of-All; there's a very lonely little girl a-waiting for you.

July 13, 1911

I have just been reading a dear little story called "The Golden Heart."[5] In one place it says, when Paul and Natalie find that they love each other, "her lips meet his very bravely and sweetly." Bravely and sweetly. I think that is very, very beautiful,—bravely and sweetly. Those are the two things that women should always be, I think,—brave and sweet—, the two things I know you would want me most to be. Natalie has a little heart-shaped gold locket in which she has kept Paul's picture for years.

It has kept her safe, she says;—safe for him,—the little golden heart. It will help to keep it golden, I think; and keep me safe for you, and brave and sweet. I must remember always that my heart is gold, and that your face is in it.

July 27, 1911

Beloved, I need your strength tonight. Keep me more with you and away from myself. Don't let me be a bundle of nerves and emotions, now up and upright at the top of the world, and now lying face-down at the bottom of everything. O, I am sick of myself! If I might have another self—more governable, more temperate. To think that even now I don't know my own self, that I do things I never thought to do and go right against my intention and will in a dreadful breathless sort of way. Oh, I need your strength. I need calmness and restraint, I need a balance wheel. I wish you would come now and get me and take me away from everyone I ever saw. I am not really brave I think. I just pretend to be brave while I'm alone with myself and then something happens and I forget everything almost except my great desire of you. I wonder how much longer it will last. I think it gets worse all the time. I depend more on you. I look to you for help and you don't see. I lean on you for support and you aren't there. It's a dreadful feeling, you know, dear, to lean on something which isn't there.

It makes you think for a minute that the bottom has dropped out of the world. But there has never been a bottom in the world for me, nor anything but a seeking and a breathlessness.

Never all the time I have wanted you, have I wanted you as I do tonight. It is not true that souls call to one another, or you would come. Nothing in life could keep me from you if you knew. But you don't know and sometimes I think I will die before you know and come. It is not happiness to love as I love. It is nothing but longing and grief and utter weariness. I am so tired, so tired all the time I ache for you! It is as if I had been cut in two and ached for the rest of me. I wanted the feel of your arms around me. I am too tired to stand alone. I crave the feel of your coat-sleeve. I need the touch of your hand. I am not brave. I am afraid. I am not strong; I am all tired out and I have no strength to fall back on. I am so many different things. There is everything in me and I never know what to expect next. I tire myself with my restlessness. I am all feelings. My emotions are wearing my body thin.

Beloved,—Oh, my love! It is my soul that needs you. If I might wake tomorrow and find you here. O, sweet quiet and calm. O, wonderful strength that would go through me like new blood. O my heart, it is worth it all, but the waiting is killing me. Oh, beloved, beloved. There's nothing else to the world and until you come my world I am empty.

Aug. 3

It is hard work being brave when you're lonesome. I've tried to be brave and I've done pretty well, but I've had to cry just a little tonight. It's no fun being in love with a shadow. But then, it's no fun being in love with anyone. And it's shadow or nothing with me until you come. God keep it so! And don't let me make any more mistakes.

I pray that my happiness when it comes will make up for the unhappiness of this waiting. Sometimes I am afraid that I love too much and expect too much in return. May be men can't love as I want to be loved. But I mustn't let myself think that. If all I can do is wait I must at least have something to wait for. But—"What are we waiting for, O, my heart?"! You must be somewhere in this world. God could not have made a heart like mine and not made its mate. It would be too cruel. O, I know you are not very far away.

I know you would be proud of me if you knew how well I'm doing without you,—outwardly, that is. I'm trying to make myself into a normal, methodical person. It is no easy task. —I'm going to get into my night-dress and braid down my hair now. Then I'll come back for a minute— Dear! —I didn't go at all. It is as if you were really here and I couldn't bear to leave you. But I'm really going now—for a minute.

'Lo, dear! Back again! —I had the funniest feeling just now that you were in a sort of brownish room, reading by the light of a study-lamp, and I parted the curtains and peeped through, in night-dress and pigtails. I can see you just as plain. I wonder if you can see me. How do you like my hair, sir? All you can see is my head now for I'm hiding in the curtain. Wait just a minute and I'll come out. —Now! I'm coming out to see you. I am wear-ing a fluffy lavender thing over my night-dress. It is very soft and long and trails on the rug behind me. My bare feet sink into the rug. My hair is in two wavy, red braids over my shoulders. My eyes are very sweet and serious. My mouth is wistful.

You watch me from your chair.

I come slowly to you over the rug.

I drop at your feet and lay my head on your knee. My braids touch the floor. You lift my head in your two hands and look deep into my se-rious eyes.

You lift me from the floor in your two arms. You rise to your feet and hold me straight before you, flat across your arms. The lavender thing falls soft about my feet. My braids sway slightly. My eyes are closed.

You kiss my wistful mouth.

Oh, Love! I feel your arms about me. I feel ——————!

Good night, sweet-heart!

Sept.

At last! To be alone and quiet! I have grown so tired of noise, so tired of talking and confusion. Sometimes I think that silence is the most beauti-ful thing in the world. To sit quite still, to listen and hear no sound—it is so restful. I am tired tonight, all tired out; and you rest me, you and your silent companionship. There is too much talking in the world and repetition is the curse of conversation. God teach me when to be silent, and God kill me if I ever I become a nag! I am so tired of noise! I long for you and the silence of a perfect understanding. May the day never dawn when you will hate the sound of my voice. God helping me, I shall not be like that.

My own wonderful dream! I will believe in you as long as my soul exists, though all other beliefs crash about me till I stand buried in dead illusions. You will be with me through it all, indestructible as my soul itself, undying till the death of my soul—for in your death would my soul be annihilated. There are no words for this! My heart can not be translated. It speaks in its own language through infinity and eternity to you. There is no time, no distance in my love. It is the supreme element. There is nothing else. But it is too great to bear alone and the weight of it is crushing me. It is too big, too terrible! I need your hand to cling to, your face to look at; something tangible, something to touch! My soul is a spirit and communes with yours, but with my arms, my eyes, my heart, I want you—and you do not come! Oh, Sweet-heart! Sweet-heart! How long will you leave me alone?

September 19, 1911

[This long entry was likely composed over several days.]

ESSAY ON FAITH.

1. Things are real only as we believe them. Just as surely as each is the center of his universe, just so surely is his universe bounded by the circumference of his life. His believings are the radii he sends out the edge of things, and on the edge of things does each find his corresponding belief. Starvation or atheism may be on his side but as yet he has sent out no radii to either, so he still eats heartily and believes in God.

The universe is made up of a million universes, each one as big as itself, for all infinities are equal. My soul is as deathless as God's soul, for there is no degree in eternity. But this is true only because I believe it, and if in this my belief is no stronger than your disbelief, then it is as false as it is true, for nothing is except as we see it.

2. Faith is all that keeps the world alive. If Faith were all at once to be

78

taken away, the tide which is now high would forget how to fall, birds flying fearless across the sky would drop in terror to the Earth, fishes would drown in the sea; I should die forgetting how to take my breath; and the reins of the universe would fall tangled from the nerveless hands of God and the worlds would gallop headlong to destruction. For when god loses faith everything will die. The future is nothing more nor less than what we expect and as long as we look forward there will be something ahead of us for our eyes to see. It matters not that the sorrows of today are greater than those of yesterday, that our burdens this year seem heavier than ever before; though the future grows in proportion as the present devours it and is still rosy if we still see roses there. Better die firm in the faith of immortality, than live, dreading an ultimate death. Better be burdened by the present than by the future. For the thought of grief to come shadows every joy. And sweet is but bitter-sweet when we dine with [Fore-]Warning.

A man's future is his own and he is its creator. Would you be a king? Only believe—and your future is your kingdom and all your days will you go crowned. Would you be a gardener? Only believe,—and your future is your garden and you will walk among flowers forever. What though you "believe" be to others but "make-believe"! Their reality is not yours. Their words can not disturb your royalty nor blight the blossom of your faith. Keep faith in the future, be the last to go, for after the future there is nothing. [4.] Ghosts are as real as starvation, for what you see is not more real to you than what you think you see, and if a man die from terror, he is as surely dead as if he had starved. Santa Claus is not a fib he is a creation. He lives in the hearts of a million children. He is more real than Columbus for Columbus is dead. [3.] To the fearless there is no such thing as fear, but to those who are afraid of cows a cow is a fearful object, and to those who are afraid of the dark shadows are terrible. The majesty of fear brings everything to life, and Hell is as real as Heaven for those who are afraid of Hell. God is very real to the man whose prayer has just been answered, but He is not so real as cabbages to the Atheist who raises vegetables for a living.

A man may believe in signs. You know he is a fool. He knows better [illegible] A man may tell you that Bohemians _____ And for you Bohemia may be merely another name for Utopia. Each of you has marked off a little [time? Illegible] the land of his imagination and named it Bohemia. You are both right. You have no cause for quarrel. Everything is forever what you believe it to be. 8. The future is nothing more nor less than what we expected _____ Have faith in the future be the last to go, for after the future there is nothing. And faith is all that keeps the world alive

Only Believe! Believe in anything rather than in nothing. If you cannot worship God whom you have not seen, worship the Sun, and no matter what the object is always the same. It is the believing which counts, not the belief. The man who believes in something greater than himself cannot be annihilated. And to lose faith in everything is to kill one's soul. For to have faith at all is to have faith in God. Since faith is the link which binds us to Him.

Believe all that is necessary to your happiness. Build about yourself a wall of faith that neither doubt nor fear can batter down, and live within surrounded by all the beauties your soul can create. Take into your heart every beautiful belief you can find. Believe in God. If there is no God a life of unbelief will not help make one. Believe in immortality, and if in the end it befall your soul [to] die with your body, at least you will not have known. And annihilation will surely be bad enough without having had the fear of it.

That soul is blessed which, through pain and adversity, still sends its believings out to the edge of things. Tendrils of faith will always find something to which to cling.

*

They are there, but he does not know it, and until he does they are not there for him. Nothing is a fact until [we] believe it.

Oct. 2, instead of 3

You don't mind coming tonight instead of tomorrow night do you? I may not have time to explain now for my sister is coming right back and then I'll have to hide you, but I'll let you out whenever I can and then we'll talk. I shall have to wear my ring very surreptitiously, too, and put it in my middy blouse pocket when I hear her coming. Won't it be exciting? I am going to embroider all evening on something white and soft and dear— just the sort of thing I shall be working on many sweet evenings when you are here; when you are really here, I mean, not just make-believe here. And I shall have a really-truly ring then, instead of a make-believe ring—almost a ghost ring. What would the girls think if they knew to what use I put the fortune-cake ring?

It is on account of the girls that I wanted you to come a night early. The crowd is planning some sort of a hike for tomorrow and I couldn't make them understand without being rude, for, of course, they don't know about you. So I thought this would be best. Sometime it won't have to be like this. I am going to embroider now; I think Norma is coming.

Oct. 3

I didn't have a chance to see you again last night, and, as the plan for tonight didn't materialize, you can have your own special day after all. The soft white thing I was working on is all done. It is very lovely. Perhaps I'll show it to you sometime if you only come quick enough.

We have been betrothed just half a year tonight. I have been very faithful to you. I have loved you more and better every day. Six months is quite a long engagement, I think. It seems to me you might come before long. I am very lonely. There doesn't seem to be much of anything in the world. And I am very tired. I wish I might go to sleep tonight with my head on your arm. Or if I might only know just where you are this minute. You would seem very near to me even tho you were way across the world. Oh, you have done so much for me. You have been everything to me for half a year. There was no room for anything else. It has been full of you. I start in tomorrow on the second half and I am going to try and make it better than the first. I will try very hard and what is there I cannot do with you to help me? I must keep always before my mind, as I have tried before, the thought of what you want me to be. I will try harder than ever before. But I am so tired! I am always tired. It is the waiting, I think. I shall be tired as long as I wait, I know. But when you come I shall rest. All the weariness and anxiety and hurry will be over, and I shall rest. You will take good care of me, won't you, dear? I do so ache to be taken care of. How I shall glory in your strength—I who am not strong. You will have to be strong enough for both, I think. The shadow of your spirit over mine is all the strength I have. All that I am, all that I have is yours. With you I shall be complete and wonderful, but without you I am nothing.

I hope you will never be as lonely for me as I am for you. You wouldn't know what to do, dear, being a man. You would be frightened and think you were dying, dear, being just a man; but I, being a woman, know it for loneliness. I have walked and slept with loneliness so long. How strange it will seem to find you beside me instead. Oh, I do want you so! If you would only come sometime in the next half-year. If you would only gather to your heart the love I send so lavishly out to you, blindly, because I do not know where you are. I will send out my love over the whole earth tonight—there is enough, Oh, love! There is enough—and wherever you are it will reach you. And, dear, if I might but get a thought from you to start the waiting right again tomorrow. I will believe—that is all I have to do—believe and wait. O, my dear love, my dear love!

Friday evening, Oct. 6

I can't help coming to you tonight for I have something very sweet to tell you,—something very sweet and pleasant and wholesome and comfortable. Our meetings have always been so tense and passionate, and often so black with the gloom of my unhappiness, that it would be wicked of me not to let you know when I feel as I do tonight. For the weariness and the restlessness have left my heart—for a time at least—and in their stead is a wonderful feeling of calmness, confidence, and constancy, all in one. They go well together, don't they! I love you differently tonight;—not more, perhaps, but differently.

You are my boy tonight—my own dear, dear boy, whom I "do utterly love and adore." (I wonder who said that. It is beautiful.) I do not need your strength tonight. I have enough of my own. The mother-heart in my breast beats steadily, and sends healthy blood through all my quiet body. The mother-heart: there is no strength like it. You are my boy tonight. I want not to be comforted, but to comfort;—to hold your head in my lap, and love you, and fuss with your hair, and cry over you; not stormily, not hysterically, but tenderly; and quietly, lest you see and be grieved. I want to find things for you, to pick up things after you, to straighten your tie and brush your coat, to fill your pipe,—all the little things so many women have done and that I long to do.

I seem to feel that this is the love that will last me through the years.

It is a most beautiful and holy feeling. It explains everything, it is the how and why of everything.

Do you know, you extremely nice person, you,—I am actually becoming domestic. Actually. I keep house; not just do the work, but keep house. There's a difference. (And that reminds me,—as soon as I get through talking to you I must pick over my beans and put them to soak.

Tomorrow is Saturday, you know.) I have tried to keep house before, tried it so often that you might think I would be discouraged by now for it never worked. I did too much when I did anything and didn't do anything half often enough. That's something of an equation,—I think things can be canceled and make something equal to something else. But I'm not going to bother because I can easily get the answer by doing it in my head. Here it is.

X = equilibrium

Do you get the same answer?

It's correct, I know, for I have proved it,—under the stern eye of experience, that "hard teacher." —All of which would sound rather hashy to one who didn't know what I was talking about.

Now I must tell you how it is to feel so confident of success in this, my last attempt. It is because I am doing it to please you, whom, of all people I strive to please. I am being moderate and temperate yet industrious withal. I don't try to clean house in a day nor do I think to get a start on the day's work by scribbling till two the night before. Believe me, I know better. I am being sensible. And always before me, I keep this thought: I must so keep my house that I should be proud at any time to have you go through it, and so keep myself that my perfect house shall be a setting for me, rather than a foil. That is the whole thing. It is for you. And it shall not fail. I swear to you by our love, than which no oath can be more sacred, that I shall not fail. Tho the reins become tangled, tho they strain and tug at my arms, yet will I keep them in my hands. I will not let go again. I will not let go.

The depth of my purpose has underscored these words more heavily than anyone else could possibly understand.

Be these my fairies: Strong-Heart, Clean-Hand, Clear-Eye, Brave-Soul,

Sweet-Tongue, and Thou,—my Robin Good-Fellow, who will come unseen, unheard, unqueried by all but me, and with thy "shadowy flail" thresh for me

> "In one night, ere glimpse of morn . . .
> What ten day-laborers could not end."[6]

Monday night, Oct. 9

My own Man; I have sent for you tonight because I wish you to be with me. That's the only reason. I haven't anything special to tell you but I just want to talk with you. I've received you sitting up in bed, which doesn't mean that I'm sick—only tired. It is very early to be going to bed but I am very tired indeed. I've worked almost ten hours—no, almost twelve hours today, from seven to seven, almost, with just time out to eat. I've been washing,—Oh such a washing! My poor hands are blistered in a dozen places. But the washing is done. There was a barrel of old skirts and things that had been left from week to week because no one felt inclined in their direction. O, it was awful! But it's all caught up now. Next Monday will be easy; just the weeks' washing. But before then I must catch up on the ironing. It's an awful ironing and it will blister the insides of my hands in a dozen places and by that time the outside blisters will be all healed and I shall be ready for more. How providential everything is.

—My sister just came in and made me cry. I don't like her very well. It's mean to make me cry when I'm so tired. I sha'n't always scrub her old clothes for her. No, darling, I didn't say that to her. I didn't say a cross thing to her. I haven't said a cross word all day. But if you were here you wouldn't let her be so hateful to me. Perhaps you'd tell her what you think of her.

Oh, dear! If you were really here now instead of just in effigy, so to speak, I'm afraid I should be weeping on you. I'm having a spasm of self-pity and I feel like crying all night and sobbing out at intervals, "O—O, dear—Why is everybody—so mean—I wasn't ever meant—to work so hard—and I only—weigh 109 anyhow!"

You aren't my boy tonight. You're my man. I don't want any boy when I'm so tired. Two girls are enough for me. And I wouldn't pick up your collar-button if you did lose it, and I wouldn't get out of bed for you, but

I'd just lie around and howl till you came in and got me and carried me away somewhere where there wasn't anybody but us and where it was dark and warm and fire lit, and you would wrap me in something soft and sit [in] a big rocker and rock me to sleep. And I don't care if you are a man and don't like rocking-chairs. If you can't rock me to sleep just once you aren't my man. —Oh, yes, you are my man and you would be gentle to me if I was very tired and you would do most anything for me if I was tired as I am tonight.

I wish your name might be Robin. I just love people named Robin;— Robin Adair, and Robin Hood, and Robin Red-breast, and Auld Robin Gray, and Robin Good-Fellow—of course—, and oh wouldn't it be nice if your name was Robin?[7]

You must go now for I must go to sleep. I hope I will rest at the rate of an ache a minute tonight so that I won't feel tired in the morning. I am so anxious to get the work all caught up. You are my reward, you know, and I'm trying very hard to earn you. Oh, dear, I would like so to be rocked to sleep tonight!

"Friday the Thirteenth" [October 1911]

What an awful scrawler I am! Oh, dear! I shall always write like a third-grader. I came this morning to tell you of the dearest thing I found in a book. It is—oh, it is just dear! I didn't know men felt that way or even thought that way and wrote such things. I am glad I found it. I say it to you while my starch is cooling. (I am *so* domestic.)

[Here Millay transcribed a sentimental poem, "Amaturus" by W. Johnson Cory.][8]

I stuttered three times, didn't I? I always stutter when I get to talking too fast. I haven't time to talk it over with you now for I must do my starching and get dinner. But I'll come back as soon as I can and see how you like it. You can be thinking it over.

Monday,—16th Oct 1911

Oh, my dear love, if you would only come and get me! I am so tired. It isn't right. And what is it all for? Everybody works, everybody gets so tired that when he finds a minute to enjoy things he is too tired to enjoy. I looked out of the window a minute ago and saw a mountain. I "lifted up mine eyes unto the hills," you know. They are so beautiful they almost kill me. The color—oh—there is never any thing like their color in the fall! And I want to climb Megunticook before the leaves are all gone. But I can't. I've got to work—work all the time. And for what? What shall I get out of it? What does anyone ever get out of it?

I can see the men at work now in the coal-yard. A man just went by on a bicycle, his cap and over-alls covered with paint. I saw a boy going up the road carrying a window-frame. Whistles blow, and smoke pours out. I can hear hammering now. Hammering, and shoveling, and digging, and dredging; and trams going past filled with windows and barrels; tired men and tired horses, everybody tired, and no one with a minute to call his very own. No time to lift your eyes to the hills. Go in and get to work. Get into the house and scrub the dirty clothes till you rub the skin off your fingers. Sweep the floor, and sweep it again tomorrow and the day after that and every day of your life;—if not that floor, why then—some other floor. And bake beans Saturday and bake beans next Saturday and every Saturday, and make bread and pies and stir and beat and whip and butter and bake, and then eat it all up and get hungry again and stir and beat and whip and butter and bake; and keep yourself alive from day to day feeling every day more tired and crushed and driven than ever before, and yet keep on eating and living.

What is the good of it all? I might as well be a pile of lime or rocks or windows or barrels, for all the good it does anyone. What is the good of music. I love it—I—oh, I love it?! And I can't get a minute to practice my beautiful sonatas. I might sometime have a beautiful sonata all my own come into my head. But what of it? What good would that do? I couldn't take my hands out of the wash-tub long enough to play it over. I couldn't get my mind off my baking long enough to write it down. What's the good of books and poems? I don't get any time to read. If I should stop for awhile everything would go to smash; things would boil over and burn on and mildew and sour and mould. Dust and dirt and clutter would take possession of everything and I would have to start it all over again to catch up.

I'm getting old and ugly. My hands are stiff and rough and stained and blistered. I can feel my face dragging down. I can feel the lines coming underneath my skin. They don't show yet but I can feel a hundred of them underneath. I love beauty more than anything else in the world and I can't take time to be pretty. Wash and iron! What time do I have to wear the pretty things I work over. Gingham dresses and aprons are good enough for me. Crawl into bed at night too tired to brush my hair—my beautiful hair—all autumn-colored like Megunticook. Why do so many people take so many pains to keep in a world they don't care about, and that doesn't care a snap about them. People work hard enough for something to be gained. There must be some enjoyment somewhere. But who gets it? Rich people don't. They have to work, too. Work to get more than they have already. The world is civilized to death. What's the sense of flying across the Atlantic? What's the sense of going to Europe anyhow? We have enough at home to keep us alive and happy—happy! Think of it! —if we would only stay at home and mind our own business. Camden is just as pretty as Venice, only I'm more used to it. What's the sense of discovering and inventing things? We don't either understand or appreciate those we already have. Everyone is working his life out and sweating and hustling himself to death, doing something he thought to be very important and—Good Lord—what good comes from his industry? He keeps alive! Pouf! Why not keep dead? You wouldn't have to work half so hard. Keep alive, indeed! Now if we might only live, that would be worth while, that would be something, but it seems so comical to think of a world full of people flapping around in all directions, hunting for something. Nobody knows what he's hunting for and nobody ever finds it, but he keeps flapping. Well! That's over! And I'm going back to work. I happen to know what I'm hunting for, which helps a little, I suppose. Or perhaps if I didn't know—didn't even know that I was hunting—I should be happier. You're never coming any way, I guess, and perhaps it's just as well. I'd be so worn out and homely by the time you got here that you wouldn't care anything about me anyhow.

Darling: I just remembered how I promised you I would never let go again. You think I have broken my promise, but I haven't. No one else knows how I feel. I am keeping up before everybody else. But I can't pretend to you. And perhaps you will come after all, and perhaps you will love me if my hands are this tired. God knows, God knows that I would love you anyway. My husband. My husband, I am ashamed to think I didn't know why Megunticook is there! It is to look at! That's why! And to think that I didn't understand! To look at, to lift your eyes to! While I am hanging out clothes and shaking rugs—right there before my eyes! What a privilege! And I didn't appreciate. To think—it mightn't be there. There mightn't be any beauty anywhere. It is something to know that the world is full of beauty even if we don't have time to look at it. But I can see it from my back yard, from my back door-step. My husband, I am ashamed. Forgive me.

All Hallowe'en

Hi, you! Guess what I'm doin'! I'm celebratin' Hallowe'en, I am! I'm talkin' with a spook! Boo-oo! Hi, spook! I'm a witch, I am!

I don't look a fit witch, tho. I'm at my old trick of receiving in night-dress and kimona [*sic*]. It isn't exactly conventional, but it's decidedly comfortable. And of course I don't mind you. It doesn't feel a bit like Hallowe'en. There hasn't been a groan or a shriek or a Jack-o-Lantern. It's awful 'scouragin'. A year ago tonight I blew out a candle in seven breaths which meant I was to be married at twenty-five. And I'm only nineteen now. That gives me six more years. But you needn't think it gives you six more years. No such thing! You'll have to come before that or I won't speak to you when you do come. Honest! And I won't love you so much as an achorn-[*sic*]shell full. No, I won't. And I'll say hateful things to you and then I'll tell you some of the nice things I'd say to you if I did love you. And you'll gnash your breast and beat your hair and tear your teeth until you're an awfully funny-looking thing, and then I'll just sit down and howl with demonic laughter at the spectacle you present which won't tend to make you any more pacific, you know.

I've almost been asleep and now I'm going to really do it. So go-'way, now, which means—clear out, please. I'll take it all back though about not—you know. If only you'll promise not to do all those dreadful things to your anatomy, I'll—well I'll speak to you anyway. —Never mind what I'll say. Good-night spook!

Nov. 3

I am going to bed. I am so tired that I cannot sit comfortably and I'm going to bed. Believe I sha'n't lie comfortably but I'm going to try it. I have been sitting alone with you a long time in firelight. I was too tired to talk, but it was lovely. I am sitting now in the light of that candle which tonight I have lighted for the seventh time. I shall light it five times more, and on the fifth night I shall let it burn out. Then, if you have not come by that time, I shall get another and begin again.

You are my own sweetheart and I do love you. I am too tired to talk but I do love you just the same. Good-night.

Dec. 3

It's colder than a polar expedition right here in this room. We've been having a racket on "James," my chafing-dish, but now everybody's gone and I'm all alone and ready for bed. The clock has just struck twelve. The racket I spoke of wasn't of my desire. It was in honour of a Rockland friend of Norma's. Norma has callers and I have to entertain them. Always! I have to concoct menus on "James" and I have to strum the piano and be "general utility" so to speak. It gets monotonous. Why don't you come over some evening and have something on "James"—doesn't that sound dreadful:—"have something on James!" —But really, I'll make a delicious rarebit for you. Better think about it! I'm going to bed now. Tomorrow is wash-day. And I'm not going to think about you until I get into bed, because it always tires me all out to think about you. But after I get into bed I'll think about you, and I'll kiss you seven kisses.

Wait until I get all tucked in and then if you want to be kissed seven times you may come in and kneel on the rug beside me and put your arm beneath my head, and I will love you ten minutes and then I will send you out and go to sleep. Now! I will light my candle and kiss my ring and then I'll go to bed.

Good-night! (This is the good-night I shall say when I send you out.)

Sweet and Twenty
(1912)

illay wrote to her imaginary lover on January 6, 1912: "Although I loathe the position I am in, although my need for you is terrible . . . yet I must exert every atom of my will and lift myself body and soul—above my situation and my surroundings. I must . . . And if there is so much as an atom in all this universe that understands and desires to help me, let that atom come forth . . ."

The atoms that would come forth to save the young woman are the words of her poems. Never in Millay's diaries is the dialogue between the diarist and the poet as evident and crucial as in this period. Entries such as the philosophical "Essay on Faith" (September 19, 1911) serve as groundwork for the great poem "Renascence," which Millay began composing, in a state of psychic terror, in the dead of winter, January 1912.

> All I could see from where I stood
> Was three long mountains and a wood;
> I turned and looked another way
> And saw three islands in a bay . . .
> And all at once things seemed so small
> My breath came short, and scarce at all.

The first half of the narrative, which she referred to as her "underground poem," was composed in the dark tenement on the ground floor of 40 Chestnut Street, where the family had moved in the fall of 1908. During the weeks she was writing the poem she would have little time for her diary.

In the heat of composition, she got word that her father was ill, perhaps on his deathbed, in Kingman, Maine. She had finished half of the 214 verses of the poem by February 22, her birthday; a week later she took the train to Bangor. Her reconciliation with her father ("he didn't die after all . . .") and a month's sojourn in Kingman, where she stayed with Dr. Beverly Somerville, her father's physician, had a marked effect in lifting the young poet's spirits. Her new friendship with the doctor's daughter Ella, a twenty-four-year-old painter and pianist—as celebrated in Millay's diary and their letters that spring—was Millay's first sustained erotic encounter. The experience of paternal love, and a strong dose of erotic love, had restored Vincent. Then she returned to Camden in April to learn that the family would be moving to a new address on Washington Street, a spacious free-standing two-story clapboard house. There, in a light-filled aerie on the second floor she completed her great poem, and it was fit to present to the world by the end of May.

On May 27 Millay entered "Renascence" in a national verse competition sponsored by the New York publisher Mitchell Kennerley. In July the poem was accepted into the anthology of poems that was to present the hundred best entries and the prize-winners; and Millay's flirtatious correspondence with Ferdinand Earle, the man she began to call "my editor," commenced—at the same time her attentions to the "Imaginary Lover" dwindled. Earle shamelessly encouraged her belief that she would win the $500 first prize, delivering her family from poverty. She formally concluded her "Vigil" on January 10, 1913. Perhaps the ghost had served his purpose.

In any case, the fortunes of the oppressed schoolgirl shifted magically that summer as she began to recite the new poem for wealthy New York socialites vacationing at Camden's fashionable Whitehall Inn.

Soon she would have not only an editor and a publisher. She would have patrons eager to send her to college.

꧁

Jan, 3 [1912]

Honey, I don't feel good a bit. I've a tooth-ache and I think I'm going to have a cold. I've been freezing all day and now my nose feels all squizzled up. Does your nose squizzle up when you're about to have a cold? Mine does, and my conscience with it.

I know a girl that's engaged to be married and she doesn't seem to realize it. It seems funny.

I'm dissatisfied with everything,—myself first of all, I'm egoistic and self-analytical. I suffer from inflammation of the imagination and a bad attack of ingrowing temperament. I don't believe in anything. I am morbid and miserable. My mind must be rotten, I think. I need a man who has been somewhere and done things to graft his healthy ideas into my silly brain.

Truly, my head is in a dreadful condition. I don't know what to do.

Anyway, I can go to bed. Perhaps I'll feel better in the morning. Come to me in a dream and teach me a truth. Good-night.

Saturday, Jan. 6

Just at this instant I am passionately endeavoring to be self-controlled and absolutely unshaken by any exterior unpleasantness. As a matter of fact, I have never been more nervous and irritated in soul than I am right now, and everything has combined and is combining to keep me in this state. Just at this instant—now—things, little things are happening that are almost driving me crazy inside. But none must know. And I must find some way to stop it. I will not any longer allow little things to ride over me. I will be mistress of something, it doesn't make much difference what. I can not go on as I have been going on. I can not bear much longer such acute unhappiness as I suffer. Whether or not you come to me in a dream Wednesday night I do not know, but I have learned a truth. And this is it. Although I loathe the position in which I now am, although my need of you is terrible and my desire of you almost annihilating, yet must I exert every atom of my will and lift myself body and soul—above my situation and my surroundings. I must—it has to be. There is no other way. I have tried everything, it seems to me, and everything has failed. It will be almost impossible, this uprooting of myself and everything in me, and it will be disastrous, maybe, to everything which now seems biggest to me. Perhaps when I have done I will no longer love you—though at this instant my love for you shakes my throat, and is at once a sob and a scream and a rushing like that of a night wind—yet this thing must be and I know it. I am not fit for you now, and though by the process of fitting myself for you I may lose you entirely, yet this thing must be. I have looked for help longingly and have received none.

Now is the time for me to help myself. I will take each part of myself that I find faulty and twist it in my hands until it moves back into place. Never in my life has anything so terrible as this dawned on me. I do not even now quite understand the nature of the thing I must do, but its enormity I feel on my shoulders like the hands of Fate. I have always been dissatisfied and unsatisfied with myself. Now I will make of myself a person whom I can admire. I will drop into the midst of the housekeeping which I detest and I will get at the heart of it. Where I have been extravagant I will be thrifty. Where I have been careless I will be thorough. And I will be systematic and not begin by tiring myself all out. I will forget myself in the condition of others. I will forget myself as much as I can and you as often as I can. I will grow up. I will make of myself the woman necessary to the place in which I am. If it does not kill me at first I shall be wonderful for having lived through it. I will be a slave, as I have always been, to my personality, but I will have a different personality. This I mean to do though it tear me in pieces. And if there is so much as an atom in all this universe that understands and desires to help me, let that atom come forth and stand by me now in this my last, desperate war against futility!

Wednesday, Jan. 24

I have something to say. It isn't the right time to say it, I know, for I am cold and uncomfortable and sleepy; but when anyone has to say the thing I have to say it doesn't much matter when he says it.

It must be about one o'clock. I've just finished reading a book, "Robert Kimberly."[1] It's about a woman who dies on her wedding-day and a man who goes to nurse the lepers. To me the whole situation seemed disastrous, hopeless. And I realized then how thoroughly wrapped up in this earth I am. I have none of the "faith that looks through death." Indeed, I have no faith of any kind. It cannot be that I have lost it. I don't think that real faith is ever lost. It must be that I never had it. Up to a few years ago I believed just as I heard at home; God was real, there was a hereafter, Christ was a human being, there were no miracles, there were no Angels, the Bethlehem star was a comet. Then I began to grow sick of the fights I got into by standing up for beliefs which really were not mine and I thought, "How do I know there are no Angels? How do I know Christ wasn't divine? How do I know anything?" Picking up the pieces I saw that faith in God and faith in immortality were all that was left. But I didn't really believe in God. I only believed in some power that made the world go round. And as for the other, why, I just couldn't imagine a soul dying. But after awhile I began to wonder if the world wasn't just going by its own momentum, and as for the other, well—I just couldn't conceive of a soul living forever.

And tonight I found myself in the words of Robert Kimberly: I do not know what I believe; I believe nothing.

I am frightened. I do not know of what I am afraid. The thought of the universe makes me sick. It is dread that I feel, an intangible, fatalistic feeling. There is so little left of my winnowing on which to build a faith.

By careful weighing I find that all I am actually sure of are—doubt, suffering, and the "hot-in-the-chest" feeling I have for you. Certainly I shall get no faith from doubt. But then, I might. There! You see I am not sure of that. What the "soothing thoughts that spring out of human suffering" are, is more than I can tell. But if it is true that from doubt and suffering I shall get no faith, then it rests with you. You are responsible for me, then, body and soul. But Robert Kimberly's faith died on his wedding day. And it doesn't say whether he found her again at Molokai.[2]

This I know, my mind is in a dreadful condition. I have been doing as I promised last time, working for the good of others and keeping myself in the background; and this is what I have reaped. My head is like a child of whom people say "You never can tell what will drop out in him. Nobody knows who his folks were."

I love you. At least, I think it's love. But it seems to me I'm drowning.

Feb. 3

I have a lot of things to say but this is another death—this night. I've lighted my candle and I'm going to wear my ring all night. Perhaps I will tell you the things tomorrow.

Feb. 11

I do not know what will become of me. I do not see how I can go living from day to day as I have lived for the last few months. I know that I am in a dreadful condition. I know that the thoughts that fill my mind are fearful thoughts. I realize acutely the full horror of the thing that has come over me. Having no religion, no faith of any kind for an outlet, all the terrible intensity of myself is forced into one channel, the one possible channel, adoration of you. There is something hideous in the situation— perhaps no one could understand that I love you as deeply as if you were here, that I miss you as keenly as if you had been here and gone, and that under it all is the awful fear of never finding you, of never having you,— even for an hour. People read "The Garden of Allah" and think the end is sad.[3] Sad! They don't know anything about it. Domini finds her Man; she has him all to herself for a little while, and in that little while she lives all a woman can live. Then she loses him, and what has she left? Faith in God, the memory of a wonderful passion, and the child. They might have lived together longer, but not more. And what have I? No faith in anything, no real hope of our ever meeting, and not so much as an old pipe for a token of you. It seems to me that what you have had is always yours, that nothing can take it away from you. She had everything.

I do not think there is a woman in whom the roots of passion shoot deeper than in me. "The two elements of passion arc rapture and melancholy." It seems to me I am that incarnate—rapture and melancholy. I can not recall a time when either one or the other was not the dominant feeling in me. I am and always have been intense. I feel intensely every little thing. The most insignificant action is to me symbolic of something tremendous. I have made myself sick regretting things. Sometimes I think that I have experienced, in an abstract way, every emotion, that is, the emotions I have not physically felt I have imagined so vividly as to make them real to me. Indifference is the only feeling I have neither experienced nor imagined, which only goes to prove that for not one minute of my life have I been without keen feeling, for indifference can not rightly be called a feeling, it seems to me. It is rather an absence of feeling, a negative sensation, I have never been indifferent to anything. And what life I have lived I have lived doubly, actually and symbolically. When I am so tired in the morning that I dread to get up, I see in my mind a whole world-full of tired people filled with the same dread, and it seems to me that it is not right for people to be so tired, that something is the matter, and then I wonder what the matter is. My love for you is something more than just thought, it is the love of Everywoman for Everyman. It is all primitive female life desiring its mate, it is all hunger crying for food, all weariness sighing for rest, it is the instinctive reaching out of the universal soul. What life I have lived I have lived hard. And so, although I know I shall not have lived twenty years until two weeks from Thursday, I wonder tonight how old I am. Someone has said that no woman really loves until she is thirty, so that it seems to me I must be at least thirty. But if I am wrong, and the feeling I have for you now is nothing to that which I shall have ten years from now, then may you be with me then to share it; I have all now that I can bear alone. I pity you, whoever you are, wherever you are, if you live out your life without having known the love I could give you. I think there is in me as great a capacity for loving as there has ever been in any woman. My heart is bigger than I, I do not understand it, it terrifies me, but with the whole of my heart I adore you, and I am sorry for you if you do not find it out.

I am leaving you as I always do, physically all tired out but mentally a little rested. I do not know why this is. I simply record my feelings as they come without presuming to understand them. I shall begin tomorrow not quite so hopelessly as if I had not been with you tonight.

I need you. And I want you, with an ever increasing, terrible passion of longing. I do not dare to think what will become of me if you do not find me soon. I don't know what I shall do.

Good-night, dear.

Washington's birthday, & Mine [February 22]

Good-morning! I am twenty years old this minute—half-past nine—and you are the very first person I've spoken to. Just think! Not in my teens any more and never again. It seems so funny. I usually make resolutions on my birthday, and I usually keep them pretty well—one made on my sixteenth birthday I kept two years and a half—but I think I'll not make any today, or perhaps just one, the one Elbert Hubbard suggested in 1909; something like this—suppose that during the next year I try to be fairly decent.[4] I am really not at all well lately and I can't do what I'd like to do but I guess if I try I can be fairly decent.

Isn't it funny that today I should happen to begin the second half of this book? I really didn't notice it until just now.

Now I'm going out and be fairly decent to somebody. Good-bye!

March the 4th, not the 3rd

Because

I forgot all about you

My beloved;—I don't love you any more. No, I don't care a snap about you. I don't even think of you. No, these are lies, I adore you, but yesterday was the 3rd and I didn't know. I am in Kingman, called here by the news that my father was dying. He is better now, was better yesterday, but I didn't think of you. I would have had no opportunity to be with you if I had thought—but I didn't think. It's the first time the 3rd has ever gone by without my knowing it. I have been so mixed up that I didn't know one day from another and not till tonight did I look up the date and then [get] sick at the sight of it.

I don't feel like talking to you tonight! I adore you but you make me tired. Why don't you come get me? You don't love me the way I love you, I'll bet. A man told me today that all men are naturally polygamists. Nasty speech! Nasty world! Nasty things, men, anyhow. I'd hate to be a man. If you ever love anybody but me—if, after you have known me, you ever want to kiss another woman—then;—I shall not curse you nor kill you nor cry, but I shall stand one instant looking at you, fully realizing at last the futility, the horror, the hysterical face of this world; and I shall laugh such a laugh as you have never dreamed, I shall thrust my fists up into the sky and laugh at God. Perhaps then I shall fall dead at your feet, striking you with my dead hands as I fall, perhaps I shall simply go insane and laugh and scream all day, perhaps I shall just drop my arms and turn and leave you.

I mustn't talk like this any more. I mustn't even imagine such things. They make me hate the Creator; never you, for I could never hate a human being; if I should ever hate, really hate, it would be God.

I shall love you forever, no matter what you do. I should not be able to help it. If you should be false to me I should not cease to love you but I should die.

You are not God but you are the one being on earth who can make me believe that—make me be sure God lives and loves his creation. Perhaps together we could find Him. I shall not find Him save with you. If I alone should meet Him face to face I should not know Him.

Hyacinthus + One + 8

*(I must date this cryptically, lest you
sometime find who the man was)*

I have sinned unspeakably. I have sinned against you, against myself, and against another man. I have sinned for a week steadily, in thought, in speech, and in deed. And now my sin so sickens me that I could die. There is no sickness, I think, like nausea of the soul. I sit here and try to realize what I have done and what I am. I go over in my mind every chapter of my sin and I could die with the shame of it.

I worship you utterly, and yet I have irrevocably cheapened our love.

———————————

I have been trying to put into words the feeling that I have, and when I would write something, all I can think to say is, "Oh, my God! Oh, my God! Oh, my God!" over and over in a sort of dry expressionless tone, all the while twisting my head from side to side, as if I were trying to free my throat from a constricting hand. Always terrible agony so expresses itself with me, my head strained back and turned slowly from side to side.

———————————

Well, I have been away for an hour and my convulsion is past. I will try to forget my sin and to win back by some means my self-respect. Perhaps I shall yet live to be happy with you if you still want me after what I have done. For I am all through. It will not happen again. If I were not so sick of it I could not be so sure. I am not good—actively, that is; I am only negatively good henceforth. Because one must be either good or bad, and I am sick of sinning.

I do not know if what I have done would be a sin if the man had been you. It would be scarcely virtuous, I think, anyway, but I wish you had shared it with me; for our love would have lifted it to dignity at least.

I must go. You *dear, dear thing. I could hurt you in my arms.*

SWEET AND TWENTY

Being
The Extraordinary Adventures
Of Me
In My Twenty-first Year

In Two Volumes

Volume One Being
The adventures occurring before
September the nineteenth—as recalled
And recorded on that date—;
Volume Two Being
The adventures occurring after that date
And up to February the twenty-second—
As entered on the date of occurrence.

1912–1913

Sept. 19, 1912

I was twenty the twenty-second of last February. If I had known then how much was to happen to me this year I would have started a diary that night. But I didn't. And since then things have happened so quick I haven't had time to write them down; at least—to be truthful—very little time, and then I haven't felt like it. But I feel now that I shall someday want very much a record of this year; so, with the aid of my memory, letters, newspapers and souvenirs, I will try to fill in the most important happenings to date, and after that go from day to day.
D Vincent Millay

Thursday, Feb. 29

Long-distance call from Kingman [Maine]. I shall never forget the message, as it came over the wire in a faint, squeaky voice: "Miss Millay, your father is very ill; and may not recover." I knew there were a lot of things I ought to say, but I couldn't think of a word; so I just stood there. After a minute she asked me if there was any message, and I couldn't think of anything then; but I managed to stutter something and to say that I would send a telegram. Then she said, "Is that all?" And I said, "Yes" and hung up the receiver.

Mother was in Rockland at Mrs. Merrill's nursing. I called her up and made arrangements to start for Kingman the next morning. Then I called up Mr. Chas. R. Dunton in Bangor—an old friend of the family—and arranged to stay with his people the next night, it being impossible to get to Kingman until Saturday morning. Borrowed Aunt Rose's suit-case—Mother had hers with her—and got some clothes together after a fashion.

Mar. 1

Took the noon boat to Bucksport;—from there to Bangor by train. Mr. Dunton met me and took me home with him. Met his wife and grand-daughter, Gladys Niles, who attends law school and is very interesting. Mrs. Dunton is a perfect old dear.

Mar. 2nd

Arose at two in order to catch the 2:45 out. Mr. Dunton went up with me. Got into Kingman about six and was met by Ella Somerville, the daughter of Papa's doctor, with whom arrangements had been made for me to stay. Had breakfast, or rather, had a cup of coffee as I had already breakfasted before leaving Bangor. Then the doctor took me down to the place where my father was boarding—at the home of a man named Gannas Boyd; it was a pale-blue house—. The minute we came in I heard from upstairs the sound of a man coughing, and it was then, for the first time, that I realized how long it had been since I had seen my father—eleven years! The nurse, for whom they had sent to Bangor, a tall strong-looking girl with an odd Irish name that I can't recall, said Papa was awake and expecting me.

Mr. and Mrs. Boyd and their two sons, Ralph and Earle, and the nurse, and the doctor, and Ella,—it seemed to me they did nothing but stand around and watch me! They kept telling me to brace up, and be calm, and things like that, which was really funny, as I was not in the least bit nervous and everybody else seemed very much upset. Isn't that always the way? Perhaps I wasn't so calm tho, as I was numb. I know now that I went through the whole thing impersonally, hearing myself say things and watching myself do things as if myself were an altogether different being and I not in the least concerned.

The doctor took me upstairs and left, telling me to stay only a few minutes.

It didn't seem to me that the man on the bed was my father, but I went over and stood beside him and said, "Hello, Papa, dear," just as I had planned to say only that my voice seemed higher than usual; and when he heard me he opened his eyes—the bluest eyes I ever saw—and cried out "Vincent! My little girl!" and struggled up in bed and held out his arms to me. (It was pitiful to see a man so sick. I thought that morning that he had very little longer to live and later, when I asked him, the doctor said so too.) But I put my arms around him and made him lie down again. Then I sat on the side of the bed and talked to him a little, not of anything in particular; I remember saying that I wished my eyes were blue, too, so they'd match my hat and that he whispered back—he couldn't speak at all—"You can't very well change your eyes, Vincent, but you might have got a green hat." Then I laughed, and he smiled a little, with his eyes closed. He had difficulty, I noticed, in keeping them open, and somehow that made me all the more certain he was going to die; I had never in my life seen anyone so sick.

But he didn't die after all. In spite of everything he got well; and my sojourn in Kingman turned out to be a visit to Ella Somerville whom I grew to like very much. I stayed there almost a month (I will stick dates in the margin), while Papa grew steadily better and Ella and I grew steadily better friends until, by the time I came away, Papa was up and dressed and Ella was ready to cry to think of my leaving her.

The Somervilles are Newfoundland people. There are the doctor, whose name is Beverly and who is the "spit'n' image" of Andrew Carnegie, one of the jolliest and best men that ever were; his wife a short and stout woman who speaks with a decided accent and bakes all sorts of strange and delicious dishes, many of which (English puddings) were much too heavy for me, possessing a great deal of child-like credulity and almost no sense of humor tho she would laugh herself weak at Ella's and my fantastic celebrations; and Ella herself, who is twenty-four, a graduate of Kent's Hill, and very clever with the brush and palette. One painting, a big copy of sad *Landseer* dog was simply fine.

Ella asked me the first night I was there if I wanted to stay in her room or come in and sleep with me, and I told her I should much rather have her with me. After that we slept together every night,—at least we spent the nights together; (we used to talk sometimes till the cocks crowed). Sometimes we'd keep the light burning after we went to bed and I'd read aloud to her,—Burns most always, she loved to hear me read Burns because I rolled my tongue so easily around the words; told her, conscientiously, when she first praised my accent, that it was very likely not correct at all, but she said she didn't care whether or not it was correct so long as there was plenty of it! She used to bother me at first by asking me what the words meant, until I told her not to mind the meanings if they only sounded well, that probably we'd both be disgusted if we did know what they meant and that, anyway, it spoiled the metre to stop and translate. So after that we got on capitally, I wallowed about through *amours* and epitaphs until the burr around us grew as thick as Scotch mist and we couldn't talk straight Yankee to save our lives.[5] Then we'd put out the light and turn our respective backs on temptation, as represented for each in the other, lest we find ourselves whispering still while the window-panes grew gray.

The nights were cold then and Ella used to beg me to sleep inside the blankets, but I was immutably in favor of sheets and, as it was my bed we were bunking in, Ella had to succumb. But one night, just to astonish and delight her, I announced that we would try the blankets. Ella was like to weep for joy. She was so glad that she became hysterically loquacious, and we both got to giggling. After a few minutes we found that we couldn't stop giggling and the thought of our powerlessness was so amusing that we giggled all the more. After a while the bed got to giggling, and we all lay and shook together,—but silently, for we didn't dare make a noise.

It was about that time that the blankets turned into burdocks and began to prick us all over. After a few minutes I became so uncomfortable that I forgot what the joke was and stopped laughing. Ella stopped to find out what made me stop, and I enlightened her by throwing down the clothes and getting out of bed.

"What's the matter?" she asked fearfully, knowing only too well what I would say.

"It's them satin sheets," said I, "Pile out!" and poor Ella piled.

We made up the bed in the old way and crawled back into it; after that she never begged over the blankets, tho she eyed them lovingly sometimes at bed-time, when I turned them down.

––––––––––––––––

There was a funny little clock in my room that had to be wound whenever you thought of it. It was customary, in passing, to give it a turn or two by way of perfunctory greeting. But at night the task would always fall to me, as would also the raising of the window—that always let in a shivery gust—, and, if we weren't to read in bed, the "dousing" o' the "glim." For Ella was always ahead of me in turning in; she didn't do so many things to herself before the mirror.

But one night, when we had talked ourselves tired and were almost asleep, Ella stuck her elbows into my back and asked me if I'd wound the clock.

"No," said I; "I ain't. And I ain't a-go'n' ter!"

"Oh, dear," said Ellen. "That clock has got to be wound."

"*That's* true," said I.

There was a heavy silence. I knew she was thinking how she hated to get up; I was thinking how glad I was I didn't need to.

After a minute or two the bed creaked, and a minute after that I heard Ella ploughing around over by the bureau. It was pitch-dark but she didn't want to strike a light because the shades were up, and she didn't want to put down the shades because then she'd only have them to put up again. If Ella hadn't been so disinclined to exert herself more than was necessary, I should never have mentioned the clock at all. (In other words, "This story would never have been written.")

"Where's the stand?" asked Ella, in a startled voice, after a futile five minutes of scratching and pawing about the other end of the room.

"Where's the stand?" I repeated.

"Where's the wall? You want to find that first. You're drunk, Ella."

Now the truth of the matter is this:—the stand, whereon the clock was wont to rest, habitually stood half-way between the bureau and the little wood-stove. In fact, it had never been moved from that position while I was there,—except once; and that "once" was the night before.

We had been intending to write a letter after we went to bed; that is—we were to compose it together, but I, who slept on the front side, was to do the writing. So we wheeled the stand over to the bed,—and the little funny clock came too! Ella had forgotten all about its having been changed, but I—I could have reached up one hand and wound it without turning in bed. But I was sick of winding it. It was Ella's turn.

"Well I can't find that—are you laughing?!!"

In the ominous silence that followed her discovery of my unreasonable mirth, the little clock ticked with incredible vigor,—and unmistakably from the direction of the bed! And Ella, regardless of the windows, groped for the shelf above the stove, and struck a match.

It must have looked funny to Ella. I can see now just how funny it must have looked. But then all I could do was laugh. And after a minute Ella laughed, too. And after a while we both laughed, "fit to die."

"It serves you right," I said when I could get my breath.

"I know it," Ella agreed, when she could get hers.

But the real joke of the matter was this:—I didn't know where the stand was, either, until I heard the clock tick. Ella had had to crawl out over me, and stumble across the room in the dark, and feel along the furniture, and bump her elbow, and bang her ankle, and get cold and mad all over,—only to come back to bed and wind the clock that I could have attended to without the slightest trouble; it was the best joke Ella ever had played on her,—but I didn't play it!

But did I let on to Ella? Guess not! 'Twas too good just as it was for me to go spoil it. So when Ella told her father about it at breakfast, and concluded by saying, "And the little sinner knew it all along!" I didn't say a word;—jist laughed!

Home about March last.

April 1st

Began moving to 82 Washington [in Camden]. Dear place. Moved in the 8th.

Through April and May helped Norma with her studies.

About May 27

Sent *Renascence* into verse competition. —(Held by Mitchell Kennerly, New York, Publisher of *Forum*.[6] 100 poems by different American poets to be chosen and brought out Nov. 1st in a book called "The Lyric Year"; $1000 to be awarded in three prizes. Judges;—William Stanley Braithwaite of Boston, and Edward J. Wheeler of *Current Literature*, who has in March, 1907, reviewed my "Land of Romance" with the following criticism:—"The poem which follows seems to us to be phenomenal." It was encouraging to find him one of the judges.)[7]

June 13

Norma was graduated from the Camden High School. Sang my "Humoresque," and I accompanied her.[8]

Sometime the last of June

Announcement of Ethel Knight's engagement to Lerois Hodge, and Marion Knight's marriage.

July 19

Letter from Editor of "Lyric Year":—*Renascence* accepted, liked "tremendously," biographical data requested.

Aug 7

Letter from Editor.

Aug 15

Letter from the Editor and (I think) shower on Ethel at Corinne's.

Aug 17

Shower at Pleasant Beach.

Aug 20

Tin shower here (at my house). —Ethel, Marth, Corinne, Hazel, Abbie, Gladys, Pearl, Jess, Norma, Wump & I.

Aug 21

Shower (linen) at Alice Wadsworth's.

Aug. 21   [From the "Vigils with Imaginary Lover" diary]

Somehow I love you just the same always. In spite of mis-steps and slippings—which are really only the results of gropings for you—in spite of everything my constancy, my constancy of purpose and of thought, is unswerving. I do love you so; oh, I do love you. I have lit the candle for a minute tonight. I can't wait for it to burn out, but I will some night soon. I really can't write much tonight because my arms are tired from swimming. But I feel just like writing to you. Oh, if that other man had never come!

Why am I as I am,—my ideals higher than those of any of the other girls, yet a something in me that makes me do things they would turn white to think of? Never untrue to you for an instant in thought, but—Oh, I'm not going to speak of it.

Perhaps I think too much of mistakes I have made. Perhaps they only serve to keep before my eyes the knowledge of that weakness which I try so hard to overcome. But do I really try? I can remember now one, two, three times at least when I could have come out victor if I had only held out an instant longer. If it had been my life—oh, this is awful! But I know that this afternoon when I stopped at the black rock, too tired almost, it seemed, to take another stroke, if it had been five strokes away I could have done it,—rather than drown! Oh, why do I give up and go under. I must try and think of myself as one who can't go under, forgetting the times when I have. Then,—then, perhaps I can shake myself free, and rise unhampered, out of my other self. I must go.

God love you, love. I do

Sunday morning, September 8

Awful early—'bout half-past five

Why on earth, pray tell, should I have dreamed last night of velvet?—Pink velvet garters and white velvet Teddy bear! Never before, it seems to me, did I dream of velvet, and whether or not it presages a calico future is more than I can tell. It was very crumpled velvet; the poor Teddy bear looked abused, and the garters might seem to have been carelessly kicked off, except for the fact that they were not the kick-off kind. Long ones, they were, and very pretty—tho I dislike pink garters only next to pink stationery.

I didn't jump out of bed to write this. I am actually all dressed, at this unearthly hour. "Is't murder?" you ask, "or a pic-nic?" Neither, my friend; or, as Helbert Uffard would say—*Terese*. Neither, Terese. I'm up simply because I can't stay abed. And I'm going out-door. It's too *early* to stay inside. My, how very funny!

Sept. 12

When I came in Sunday morning I had written a little verse. Want to hear it?

Here 'tis.

I never knew that honey bees got up so very early!
Here in the morning-glory flow'rs all pink and
mother-of-pearly,
A-climbin' up my porch on little ladders crisp and curly,
Already are they so intent they never think to knock;
Did anyone know that honey-bees are up at five o'clock?
Luffingly Dedicated at You!
Ain't it cute?

I ought to write some letters—three at least—; I ought to tell you the
volumes and volumes of things that have been happening to me lately; I
ought to keep a almost diary; but I can't start in tonight. Maybe, tho, I
could start my diary tonight. I'll see if I have a book. —Yep. I'll start it now.
Good-night, you! I wouldn't kiss you good-night if you were here.

Sunday 22—Sept. 1912   [Also from the "Vigils with Imaginary Lover" diary]

I have been trying to think why it is that I feel so *physically* lonely and I
have about decided that it is the coldness of the room. Ah, but I love
warmth! It is such a friendly thing. I wonder if I shall ever realize my
dream of firelight and me on a big rug before it and you in a big arm-chair
and my head on your knee; storm outside, windows rattling, but inside
the roaring fire and you and I. Always the room is fire-lit, always the storm
and always my head on your knee. It won't be when I kiss you that I love
you most, or when I think how strong you are, or when I hold your coat
for you; it will be when I sit with my head on your knee. —If my dream
ever comes true! Doesn't it seem strange to you that, at my age and with
my temperament, peace should seem to me the most blessed thing that
love could possibly bring? It astonishes me.

It is when I am cold that I want you most. I wonder just what that fact
means. Don't ever, whatever you do, after we are married, let the fire go
out! I might find out that after all it is the fire and not you that I love. Do
keep me warm! Buy me furs and things—big soft cuddly bath-robes,—a
tan one and a yellow one and a red one. (The red I can't wear, but I can
look at it.) And awfully soft little bedroom slippers to match. Don't laugh
at me for saying "little." Diminutives are very often indeed—as you must

know—terms of endearment. And, anyway, they'd have to be small,—"to match"! Can I have lots of rugs and blankets? Part of the time I shall want to be rolled up like a papoose, very likely. *Dear, have* you good warm hands! Oh, please! I love warm hands. People who have warm hands can almost always hold mine—yes, isn't it shameful? But really it is actual physical hurt for me to draw away from warmth,—provided, of course, that their accompanying personalities are not in the least distasteful to me. I hate to be kissed—unless I love to be!—there is no indecision about that. But hands are different. You shake them when you meet and when you part; why not hold them, if you like, in between?

If I kissed a man a little kiss when he came, wouldn't he be likely to expect a big kiss when he went? There are enough distinctions; the trouble is that they are not distinct enough. Hands should be for friends, lips for lovers, laps for children, heads for business associates. Then you would know what you were about. Now you don't. You don't know really whether you may or whether you may not, but it's a pretty safe bet that you'd better not. That's certain. And it's mighty tiresome. Duty and conscience! The one to tell you that you must,—the other to remind you that you mustn't. Needless to say they're not speaking of the same thing. And most of the musts and mustn'ts are observances of form and would-be *variations*—not *disregardings*—of proprieties. There must always be conventions, of course, but can't there ever be different ones?

—Oh, drivel! If only this rant would warm me up! What do I care for conventions and proprieties, anyway? It seems to me I am very little governed by them as it is. And yet—yes—if I went bare-headed to church it would be in defiance of, not in indifference to, the custom. So that, if not governed, I am influenced,—which is usually only a subtler form of government! How very odd! Oh dear, is it this English language that is so pliable, or are these things really true? Search *me!*

Aug 29 (?) 1912

Masquerade dance at Whitehall. Went as Pierrette.[9] Summer guests interested in my songs, verses, etc. Mrs. Louise Geier and brother, Frederick, spoke of taking some of them back to Cincinnati. Met Miss Jean Conrad & mother, Mr. & Mrs. _____ Kent, Mrs. Rutherford, Mrs. Ezra Grant Stearns, Mrs. Elisha Dillingham Bangs, Mrs. Francis Carpenter, Mrs.

_____ Gibson, Miss Foss & "Mary"; Mr. and Mrs. Blanchard, Mr. Day Allen Willey, Mr. Walter Geier, Misses Helen & Virginia Geier, Miss Margaret Louise Langermain,—and others. Mrs. Stearns, leaving Saturday, wished me to come up again Friday,—the next night. Met (I forgot to say) Mrs. Frederick Geier.

I sang *The Circus Rag, Humoresque,* and several others, and then "Sun's Comin' Out" which they liked best of all and made me sing over and over.[10] Sang a few lines—which was all I had done—of *Who'll Go A-Maying?*— Mrs. Geier said "We all will!" Mr. Walter Geier asked me about my verse-writing and I told him about *Renascence.* Then they made me say it aloud to them. Then they made me say others.

Left, to come up the next night.

The next night—Fri. 30

Met Mrs. Esselborne (Julius), Miss Lake (?), Miss King (a fairy-tale princess girl, with the Kents), Miss _____ Donahue and Miss Tate (?), Mrs. Fogg.

Same programme repeated, save that I sang the whole of *Who'll Go A-Maying?* Which I had finished in the meantime. Mrs. Stearns left the next morning for Bangor (she lives at *The Colonial*) after asking me to come up and stay a week with her.

Friday morning Mr. Wiley called a *literary agent,* wishing to take some of my work back with him to New York.

Tues Sept. 3

Went up again. Met Mrs. Crane, Miss Dow, Mr & Mrs. ____, friends of the Geiers; Mrs. _____ a first cousin of Ethelbert Nevin. Miss Dow asked to call on Mother and me the next day.[11] Walter Geier (sub rosa) presented to me the "little gift"—game of *Poets,* etc.

Wed. morning

Miss Dow (Caroline B.) called;—dean of New York Y.W.C.A. Training School. Wealthy friends in New York now might send me to *Vassar.*[12]

I can't begin to tell how wonderfully kind and charming they all were to me. I just am all too enthused out to tell it. It was the most wonderful thing that ever happened to anybody, I think. When I get time to breathe (for things are *still,* Oct 25, happening) I will try and tell more in detail the wonderful things that happened in that short time at *Whitehall.*

Wed. Sept. 4th

Ethel & Lerois Married. Met Elizabeth Bromell (not spelt right, probably), and Margaret Longfellow.

Letter (afternoon mail while I was in Mr. Montgomery's office) from Editor "The Lyric Year."

Mart [Ethel's sister Martha] spent the night with me.

Sept. 17

Letter from the Editor.

Sept. 21

Proof of *Renascence* sent for correction.

Sept. 26

Letter from the Editor.
His own name signed;—
                    Ferdinand Earle
I am invited to visit "Vindenholm."

Oct. 1

Correspondence card and snapshots from *my Editor.*

Oct. 14

Letter, postal, and copies of other "Lyric Year" poems.

Forgot to say that from Tues. oct. 8, to Tues. Oct 15, I did type-writing for the Rockport Y.M.C.A. campaign, and earned $22.00.

Oct. 15

Postal from my Editor.[13]

Oct. 17

Letter from Miss Dow, "Be ready to study for Vassar."!
Letter from my Editor and postal.

Oct. 19

Sent telegram.

Oct. 24

Letter from Miss Geier.

I wish I had written things down as they happened; they were—and are—so wonderful! The bare facts of course call up to my mind all the wonder of it, but I'm just too tired to write it down. I must, after this, keep some sort of journal. I'm too tired now to more than mention Mrs. Esselborne's scheme to get me into Smith [College] and Miss Bannon, her friend, who wrote me, and how mother went to nurse Miss Geier, and how Norma and I went sailing with them and motoring with them, and how they all called to see us before returning to Cincinnati, and all the cards left by people who want me to come see them if I ever should go where they lived. I have all the letters and all the cards and all the souvenirs, and I shall never forget a bit of it,—so what's the sense in scratching it all down?

It will be easier after this, telling it as it happens, and there promises to be enough to tell.

VOL. II

Oct. 25, 1912 (Friday night)

Uncle Charlie Hemingway is downstairs talking to mother. He lives in Mt. Vernon (N.Y.) and I shall visit him just before I visit my Editor, who lives I [*sic*] Monroe, which is only about twenty-five miles below Poughkeepsie, where Vassar is. (!!!!!!!!) Those are the ways I ought to feel about it; and do, too, when I'm not so tired.

"The Lyric Year" is to come out in a week, and I'm almost dead with impatience and nervousness and wariness and anxiety. (I'll explain later why the "anxiety.") Not a word from my Editor since night before last and then only a word (silver crested envelope and paper) saying that he and Edward Wheeler had been "gossiping about me." —Fancy!!! And two sketches of heads, one he and one I, dreadful caricatures—he has studied with Whistler—been abroad all his life anyway, has a [Aemora?], and plays it, too;—read a poem of his in the last February Forum.[14] . . . . I don't care if this entry is a mess.

If I don't get word from him tomorrow I shall crawl into a hole and die!!!!!!!!!!!

Oct. 26

Letter from Mr. Earle.

Oct. 29

Letter from Miss Geier.

Oct. 31

Kathleen's club had a Hallowe'en party here; masked. *Such* noise! I went to bed, but couldn't stay. I just *had* to dress and go down and see what they all wore. The costumes were really awfully cute. They all stayed till twelve, so as to go home in November.

Nov. 4

Two letters and a card from my Editor. Miss Rittenhouse, secretary of the Poetry Society of America, says, "*Renascence* is far the best thing in the book. If it doesn't get the prize I pity your judges." —But it didn't get the prize! Everything but money!

Nov 15

Letter from Miss Bannon. My poems had been shown to Miss Jordan, head of the English epartment [*sic*] at Smith, who said lovely things and "If she can get admitted to Smith (i.e. pass the exams) we can manage to take care of her
after she gets here."[15] !!!!!!!!!!!!!!!!!!!!!!!!!!

Now what do you think about that!

Nov. 18

Letter from Mr. Carpenter. Interested in Vassar.

[Continued later] Wrote right off to Miss Dow who was trying to get me into Vassar, and told her about the people who were trying to get me into Smith.

Nov. 26

Letter from my Editor.   (Lavender crested!)

Nov. 27 Late in the afternoon, night before Thanksgiving

The Book! And a letter from one of the contributors, Herman Montagu Donner. No need of detailing, for I have the letter and his biography in the back of *The Lyric Year.* But I *will* say that it was a *very* nice letter.

Nov. 28 (Thanksgiving morning)

Letter from Papa—(long-expected, much-neglected, soon-detected, close-inspected). That isn't true, tho. For it was an immediate answer.

Dec. 4 afternoon mail

Letter from Witter Bynner (!) and Arthur Davison Ficke, whom I have since found he visited over Thanksgiving.[16] Both contributors to *The Lyric Year;*—

> "Dear Miss Millay—
> This is Thanksgiving day; we thank you. If we had a thousand dollars, we would send it to you. You should have unquestion-ably had the prize.
> > All three prizes!
> > > Very truly yours, etc."

(I shall never emerge!)

———————————

Also a letter from Louis Untermeyer, another contributor:—

> "Allow me to congratulate you upon your splendid poem in *The Lyric Year.*[17] It makes nine-tenths of the volume look like the pale, pink-tea poetry that most of it is . . . If Floyd Dell does not re-view the volume (as, being one of the contributors, I have asked

him to) I shall "do" it myself in the Chicago Evening Post—at which time I shall say more things about your eloquent verses."[18]

. . . I answered his letter and asked him to send me a copy of the paper in which the review appeared . . .

Dec. 3

Two postals from my Editor.

One—"33 lines in the *N.Y. Sunday Times Book Review* about *Renascence* (Dec. 1st 1912). Read it and get a life-long swell-head! Review by Miss Rittenhouse!"

The other—"William Marion Reedy (editor of) in the *St. Louis Mirror,* Thursday, Nov. 28, 1912.[19] 'The Lyric Year contains other poems of wonderful poignancy and power, notably to me *Renascence* (etc.) with a finer virility than even the over-virilized Masefield.'"[20]

Evening

Letter from Miss Dow. Nothing definite enough to write Miss Bannon. I was just about crazy, and wrote right back asking for more information. (I have been a perfect *bear* to Miss Dow.)

About Dec. 5

Letter from my Editor. Mr. Ficke had written him, on behalf of himself and Witter Bynner, to try and find out my identity. They thought I was a man! The extract Mr. Earle sent me is too long to give here,—but the whole idea is killing!

Also, from my Editor, some darling snaps of him, and her, and it!

Miss Dow sent Vassar application to be filled out and returned.

Dec. 8

Letter from Ella. She is going to get the book. Wants me to visit her. Wish I could.

Dec. 9

Letter from A.F. Monroe, which I shall not answer for approximately one hundred years. A.F. has owed me a letter since, I think, last February, maybe longer even, and he *must* be disciplined. He is studying journalism at Columbia and happens to be living on the same street with Ridgely Tovener [?]—no, I guess it's William Stanley Brainwaite [*sic*]—, tho he probably doesn't know it, and he's working on the New York City News staff. Smart kid! But—gr-r-r-r!

Dec. 12 morning
Letter from Mr. Ficke . . . Lovely letter, and a copy of his "The Earth Passion," which I love.[21]

Afternoon
Enclosure from my Editor of a letter which contained something nice about *Renascence*.

Evening
Letter from the Poetry Society of America, asking for some unpublished (save the mark!) poems, to be read aloud at the next meeting. I sent some stuff,—of which more anon!

Dec. 13
Letter from Mr. Donner. Letter from Columbia University, through the secretary. Miss Dow's name was mentioned; I was completely at sea.

Dec. 14
Letter from Papa.

December 16
Letter from Hazel.

Dec. 17
Letter from the Poetry Society:

> "I have the honor to inform you that you have been elected to membership." The next meeting Dec. 27. O, my heart! O my wetched wymes!

Dec. 18

Letter from Hazel.

Dec. 19

Letter from Miss Bannon. (I had written her a desperate confessional of my wiles and strategies.) She wrote me the *dearest* letter, everything all right, understood *perfectly,* would *always* understand perfectly, asked me to come and see her soon and talk things over. She lives in Northampton where Smith is.

   Also a letter from President Burton of Smith, offering me a full tuition scholarship.

Dec. 20 (I think)

Letter from Mrs. Carpenter, with enclosure of a letter to her from Miss Dow which explains everything. Letter from Gladys N.

   Letter from Mrs. Ficke and "The Happy Princess."[22]

Dec. 22

Lovely letter from Miss Dow, which I answered by return mail.

Dec. 23

Enclosure from Mr. Ficke* from Springfield, Ill., of a Nicholas Vachel Lindsay pamphlet of poems.[23] Mr. Ficke must have gone up to hear him lecture. (Mr. Ficke lives in Iowa,—Davenport.)
*[Entered later] Have since found that Mr. Lindsay himself sent the verses. Mr. Ficke wrote and asked him to. There was an unmistakable thumb-mark on the envelope,—Mr. Lindsay is a tramp!

Dec. 25

Had a fountain pen, three boxes of Crane's Linen Lawn [?] different kinds, a paper-knife, books and things, oh a lovely Christmas![24] Mr. Ficke's "Breaking of Bonds" came the day before I think.[25]

Dec. 26 (I think)

Mr. Ficke sent me a copy of William Blake, of whom he has been astonished to learn that I had never heard. Mr. Ficke is a dear!

Dec. 28

Letter from Papa.

Letter from an autograph-collector in Chicago, who wants the name of each Lyric Year contributor signed to his own poem on its particular page in the A.C.'s own copy. I hope that's clear. It sounds sort of funny. I wrote Mr. Ficke asking him what to do. He's a lawyer besides being a poet, and knows an *awful* lot! Also wrote Mr. Donner, Hazel and Aunt Rose.

Norma's birthday. Planned a spread for the next night, Sunday.

Dec. 29

Spread. During the festivities my yellow chiffon, gradually but inexorably, fell from me, in ribbons. Poor Cinderella! How she must have felt when the clock struck twelve! My yellow chiffon is now but a souvenir.

Dec. 30

Bought a diary for 1913, whose rites I shall religiously observe.

Dec. 31

The long-looked for newspaper clipping from Louis Untermeyer! He *did* write the review, but it didn't come out until Dec. 27, which is why! He has said about *Renascence* the very loveliest things that have been said. Also clippings of a few of his own poems, which I am crazy about. The last mail of the year! Wasn't it *lovely!*

December 31, 1912

Oh dear! *What's* the use! I never shall be able to write regularly, and yet,— tomorrow I begin a diary, a *daily, diurnal* diary. (I don't just know what that last adjective means. Shouldn't be surprised if it meant "every two days.") But never mind. The question is,—how shall I be able to *keep* that diary? And the answer is,—I've *got* to!

All I can do now, I suppose, is to hunt up my letters and give their dates in here. Perhaps I can remember a few other things, too. Later I think I will paste souvenirs in the back of this book. That will be a great help. I'm dreadfully sorry I haven't kept a diary this year. Next year nothing may happen,—oh, but something is going to happen, something I know about now! I guess I shall have something to write.

But there! I must catch up! It is almost next year.

[Here she recorded the dates of her recent correspondence, and details of other events from October 26 to November 15. They have been placed in chronological order above.]

December 31, 1912

(Mother has just brought up the mail, the evening mail, the last mail of the year and something indescribably unspeakable came in it, but I can't tell about it now because I've got to wait until I catch up to it and there is a lot between, and, anyway, I'm going to the movies with Norma and [her boyfriend] Kenneth, so I can't write any longer now. I'll sit up and watch the New Year in, and finish this record. There's a lot to tell. I hope I shan't have to lap over. But I shall probably get all caught up before tomorrow night, when I shall have to write the first New Year's entry. I think I'll make a resolution to write in my diary every day. No, I guess I won't.)

"Lest We Forget"
College in New York
(1913)

T he combination of literary genius and personal charm embodied in the petite form of the small-town girl from the coast of Maine was more than many socialites, and most literary folk, could resist. She soon found distinguished strangers vying for opportunities to help the budding poet to the advantages she so clearly deserved. These included Miss Caroline Dow, a wealthy woman who was the dean of the YWCA Training School in Manhattan and wanted Vincent to attend Vassar; and Mrs. Julius Esselbourne, an heiress with connections at Smith College. Both women had heard Millay read her poetry at Whitehall, and they were amazed that the twenty-year-old author of "Renascence" had never been to college.

In December 1912 she received a letter from the president of Smith offering her a full scholarship. She would have to weigh this opportunity against the attractions of attending Vassar, near New York City, as well as Miss Dow's practical plan to send the girl first to Barnard in Manhattan. There she would do remedial study for a semester in preparation for the rigorous course work at the prestigious college in Poughkeepsie.

She looked like a princess in a fairy tale. And now her life would begin to take on the character of a fairy tale dream come true.

Her performances in Camden had gotten the attention of wealthy patrons. Then "Renascence," appearing in the widely circulated and reviewed anthology *The Lyric Year,* with all the controversy swirling around the ill-judged prize itself, brought her to the attention of most of the famous poets of the era. Several of these poets and critics, including Witter Bynner,

Arthur Ficke, Louis Untermeyer, and Sara Teasdale, became lifelong friends, lovers, and cheerleaders during the poet's meteoric career.

On March 9, scarcely a month after Millay arrived in New York, the Poetry Society of America hosted a literary evening in her honor. The attendees included Edwin Markham (author of the famous poem "The Man with the Hoe"), the groundbreaking older New York poet Edith M. Thomas, and Witter Bynner, who read all of "Renascence" aloud to the company. And on March 21 she dined with the illustrious Sara Teasdale.

In April, Kennerley, the publisher of *The Lyric Year,* began publishing Millay's poems in his prominent literary magazine *The Forum.* As poets come and go in America, she was already famous in literary and intellectual circles. Upon meeting the wunderkind on April 18, he proposed bringing out a volume of her poems, an idea that flattered and frightened her, as even she realized her body of work was not equal to such a production.

The excitements in Millay's life during her half-year in New York were not solely literary and academic. She records in fascinating detail the streets and business establishments of the great metropolis in 1913; attending the famous Armory Show of modern art; a performance of Sarah Bernhardt in *Camille;* and a baseball game between the New York Giants and the Philadelphia Phillies.

Jan. 1, 1913

(The first time I've written "1913." Seems so funny.)

Now full speed ahead!—over the never-sailed sea of this new year. 1913, with your hands behind you,—"which hand will I have?"? Please, the right one!

Shall I go to Vassar? Or to Smith? Or to neither? Shall I visit my Editor? Miss Bannon? Ella? Shall I be present at any meeting of the Poetry Society? Shall I have a poem printed in any magazine?

I wonder how many of these things will have happened, a year from today.

Letter from my Editor. He suggests my sending a manuscript or two to Mitchell Kennerley, for the Forum.[1] As soon as they are returned from the Poetry Society I will send in one of the best ones.

Lest we forget
To

The New Year This little volume Is Fearlessly dedicated.

E.St.V.M.

Jan. 1, 1913

Camden, Maine

Wednesday, January 1, 1913

Letter tonight from Ferdinand Earle, "my Editor." New year cards from Clara and Aunt Rose, Doctor Hanscom called up from Rockland to get Mother to do night work in his hospital for a few weeks. Called up Abbie and told her of my last night's letter from Louis Untermeyer. Abbie goes back to Radcliff tomorrow.

Thursday, January 2, 1913

Letter this morning from Mr. Ficke. Enclosure of the same review of the Chicago Evening Post that Mr. Untermeyer sent me. Letter tonight from Ella. Wrote Ella & papa. Mother went to Rockland this afternoon. Kathleen's club met here today. She is staying all night with Hope. Norma is at the dance with Kenneth. Called up Mr. Champney; Norma can have her proofs tomorrow.

Jan 2

Letter from Mr. Ficke. Thinking I would not be likely to see the *Chicago Evening Post* he enclosed a copy of the one which contained *The Lyric Year* review by Louis Untermeyer; so now I have two copies, which was just what I wished. Nevertheless I must not forget to tell Mr. Ficke that I had already received a copy from Mr. Untermeyer himself. It's quite too good a chance.

Letter from Ella. I hadn't more than hinted to her about college and everything, and she's wild!

Friday, January 3, 1913 [New diary]

Not one scrap of mail all day! Even the proofs didn't come. I didn't get my letters mailed until tonight about seven. Read "The Moth" today.[2] It seems to me a particularly uninspiring book. Must tell Kathleen that Polly Follett called up. The telephone has been ringing all evening.

There is a fiendish wind out. The night is actually noisey with it. I'd like to be out in a hammock under a tree. Wouldn't we swing, tho! I should have to be strapped in. If I slept, I bet I'd dream!

Jan. 4

The Vassar *Bulletin* came.

Saturday, January 4, 1913

Letter from Mother tonight. I have answered it, but will leave my letter open and add something tomorrow perhaps. The *Vassar Bulletin* came this afternoon. I must hunt up the things I need and begin to study. Forgot to say yesterday that I wrote a sonnet in the afternoon. —I must go down and shut up the fires. It's quite cold tonight. —Norma & Kathleen have been to the moving-pictures. Tonight,—no, yesterday was the monthly-versary of an old vigil, I notice.

Sunday, January 5, 1913

Took a little walk in search of adventure today; found three little boys a-skatin' on a flooded field, and stopped to talk with them,—or rather, watch them skate and let them talk to me, which they did. Oh, aren't little boys the *dearest.* They told me all about themselves and all their folks, and they did exhibition stunts on the ice just as if they *weren't,* and when I came away they told me to come again and bring skates and they'd teach me how. —Norma had Kenneth up tonight. We all popped corn over the furnace-fire. Saw Mart & Corrine a minute.

Monday, January 6, 1913

Card from Corinne this morning; her book has come. And the January *Forum,* with a very gratifying review of *The Lyric Year* in it. I think Mr. Kennerley himself must have sent it. And Norma's proofs,—at last! This afternoon a letter from Gladys. Tonight a letter from Miss Bannon. She is *determined* to have me go to Smith. Didn't post Mother's letter till 5. Wrote Louis Untermeyer, Miss Dow, Gladys, and Aunt Sue. Kathleen went to basket-ball practice this afternoon (Norma's proofs are perfectly lovely . . . We can't decide *which to drown!*)

Jan. 6

Someone (I think it *may* be Mr. Kennerly) sent me a copy of the January *Forum.* When I first caught sight of it I thought that it might be a sample copy, and then wondered if there *could* be anything about my poem in it. So I looked down the index—and *there* was a review of *The Lyric Year* by one Charles Vale.[3] So I hunted up the page (mit hands vot zhook) and happened to strike the end of the article first so that I caught a fleeting glimpse of a whole page of my poem. After which, very calmly (!), I proceeded to hunt up my beginning and find out what was said about me. Almost all of *Renascence* was quoted and the comments were *quite* satisfactory. I wonder if any other of the January magazines will have mention of the book. I must look them up.

Afternoon
Letter from Gladys.

Evening
Letter from Miss Bannon.

Tuesday, January 7, 1913

I suppose that until I am twenty-one (Feb. 22) I ought to put down all the nice happenings in this Sweet-and-Twenty book,—even tho I have to give up the idea of souvenirs in the back, and even tho I am keeping a regular diary, too. So I'll go back and put in the dates and principal characteristics of my nicest letters for the past week.

Tuesday, January 7, 1913

[Regular new diary as mentioned above]

Just a postal from Mother tonight. Found out from Supt. Packard that Smith is on the Camden High entrance-without-examination list. Wrote

Miss Bannon and told her. Mailed the letter at eight tonight. Called on Corinne in the news-stand. Saw Gladys a long time and Martha a little time. We planned a little birthday spread for Corinne tomorrow. I'm to make a chocolate cake. Kathleen is spending the night with Hope. Kenneth has been up. He really kills me, he's so comical. Don't I love a funny man! There are too few of them. I'd rather laugh than anything.

Jan 8
Card from my Editor.

Wednesday, January 8, 1913 (B.&M.)[4]
Card from my Editor; I must write him. Lovely letter from Mother tonight. Corinne is twenty-three today. We had a supper and general old-time-joy-fest for her at Mart's tonight. I got the money in the cake. As I made the cake and stuck in things myself the girls are a little inclined to look upon my sudden wealth as "ill-gotten gains,"—thus are the virtuous slandered! We are going to meet at Jess' next Wednesday. It's time we did something. We haven't seen anything of each other in ages.

Jan. 9
Letter from Miss Bannon & Mr. Ficke.

Tuesday, January 9, 1913
Letters from Mr. Ficke and Miss Bannon this afternoon. She sent me a Smith application blank. I'd give that cent I got last night to know where I'm going to college! Answered Mr. Seymour's letter today and asserted my willingness to comply with his request.[5] Went down town for the mail tonight and didn't get a thing.

I'm glad this day's over; I've hated myself all day long.

Friday January 10, 1913
Twice today the postman marched right straight by, and I didn't go down after the mail tonight, so didn't get a thing all day.

Kathleen's team, or rather the C.H.S. Girls' Basket Ball team played

Rockport and beat them, I believe—15:3. K. made 8 of the points and the other forward 7. Kenneth & Norma went to the pictures.

T.T.M.M.

Friday night—Jan 10, 1913

I'm so cross tonight, and my pen spills and everything! —I'm burning my candle out. When it's gone it seems to me you'll be gone—and I've *loved* you so while that little candle burned! —I'm so lonesome tonight that I cry and I cry. Everyone else has someone to love her,—and I can't be *satisfied* with the little loves! I want *you.*

My little ring is all tarnished now, my candle is almost gone, and I never come to you as I used to do on the third of the month,—but I love you. Some people think I'm going to be a great poet, and I'm going to be sent to college so that I may have a chance to be great,—but I don't know—I'm afraid—afraid I'm too—too *little,* I guess, to be very much, after all. I'm not joking a bit. I don't want to disappoint people and perhaps tomorrow I won't feel like this, but it seems to me that all I am really good for is to love you,—and that doesn't do any good. Perhaps I could be a great poet or nearer to it—if I had you and if you wanted me to. I have some big thoughts.

But then, it doesn't matter, I suppose. I've got to try, anyway. —I can't write any more now. I'm just going to watch my candle a minute. It's getting low.—

Darling, Darling, Darling. I could *kiss* you *now,*—and now I could kiss you,—and *now,* and *now!*

I wish you would have been the one to kiss me first. —But you couldn't be and you weren't,—and now I only wish that you might kiss me *soon,*— not *first,* but *soon,* and *again,* and *soon again,* and *last.*

Will you love me all the time, I wonder?—Even when I can't get my hair up? Even *I* don't love me then. —Dear, I think if I once saw you I could write and write and write! If I could just *hear* you over the phone wire— and know it was you—I could work and work and write and write! Do you suppose I could?—I thought once that I saw your *name,* and hoped it might be,—but I guess it isn't going to be

Next to having you I'd like to have some pretty clothes. I haven't *any*. I'm a sight all the time. I can't go *anywhere* unless it's in a snow-storm, because all the hat I have is just a monkey-cap.⁶ I haven't any shoes or any dress or anything. —I hope you'll have lots of money. —I'll *blow* it!

How do you like my new writing?—Fountain-pen *did* it! It won't let me write in the old way,—but I love it. It disciplines me. It makes me do something that I don't like to do but which is for my good

My candle is almost gone.

I'm going to pigtail my hair

Now I'm going to take my ring and a drop from the candle and seal them up together in a little white box,—and never open it perhaps,—perhaps not open it till I get my real ring.

I did it. And I pricked my ring-finger and dropped in a drop of red, red blood. (I shall always have to do things like that. It is my *self* that does it.)

When my candle is quite gone I will write you a word in the dark. And then I don't know what I'll do. Perhaps I will not write again until I think, until I am almost sure that I have found you. And perhaps I will write much as I have done. But we will have no more vigils. This is the last. —I wonder if you are thinking of me now. —the first vigil was April the third, nineteen-eleven. This is January the tenth, nineteen-thirteen.

Goodbye

Jan. 11

Letter from Miss Dow.

Saturday, January 11, (P.S.)

Letter from Miss Dow. It has come at last to the place where I shall have to sit right down and *decide* between Smith and Vassar. There are so many reasons why I want to go to each that I wish I could go to both! Have made an appointment with Mr. Dwinal to help me with my Smith certificates and things. Rehearsal tomorrow at 3:30 in the H.S. Building. (There's more than one farce in this production.) Went to the theatre, "Freckles,"— enjoyed it immensely.[7]

Jan. 12

Got my Smith application filled out.

Sunday, January 12

Saw Mr. Dwinal and got the Smith application filled out. Wrote Miss Bannon, Miss Dow, Mr. Ficke and my Editor. Mother was up this afternoon. It seems so good to see her. She's going to try to come up every Sunday. Kenneth is up. There was no rehearsal on account of the howling blizzard which has been pleased to visit us today.

Jan. 13

Letters from Miss Dow and Mr. Donner.

Monday, January 13,

Letter from Miss Dow this afternoon. Answered by return mail.

Delightful letter from Mr. Donner tonight. Baked today,—it being wash day. Norma went to Rockland to get some clothes and things. Kathleen had Vera over to supper and afterwards went to dancing school with her. First lines of "The Dead Path."[8]

Tuesday, January 14 (T.)

Nothing happened today. No mail, no anything. Doc [?] and Madolin were up a few minutes this afternoon hunting for sun enough to take a picture in. Went to the moving pictures with Norma and Kenneth. Mother sent up by Kenneth some little scruffy straw slippers for all us girls and Madolin. I must go try mine on.

Wednesday, January 15

Club meeting tonight. Seemed *warm,* somehow, to be together again. Couldn't stay long because of a rehearsal for the play. All of us there at last, and it went off fine. Another Friday at seven. The little slippers are darling. I can't bear to take them off even when I go to bed.

Thursday, January 16 (T.)

Heard from R. Seymour again this morning,—and "signed the page." He says that the January *Poetry* has a very *unusual* review of my poem.[9] That wasn't the word he *used*. —Went to the pictures with Mart. Norma & Kenneth went to the dance.

Friday, January 17

Heard from Mother tonight—telephone. Harold & Kenneth & Madolin have been up all evening. The boys brought up steak & onions & a whole armful of stuff and we concocted several delicious messes for supper. Harold brought up that song I've been so crazy about. Didn't rehearse tonight. Norma was too hoarse.

Saturday, January 18

Norma got a new hat today, brown, and a beauty. Went to Rockland and got her suite. Nothing happened to me. I had such a cold that I couldn't go to Mildred's to supper. Norma stayed overnight with Madolin.

Sunday, January 19

Mrs. Tufts called.[10] Rehearsal today at the High School building. Mother came up this afternoon. My cold so bad I couldn't go over to Gladys'.[11] She served tea. Kenneth was up tonight. We four, Kathleen, Norma, Kenneth and I all played poker till eleven, when he has to go to get the last car.

Monday, January 20

Letter tonight from Mr. Untermeyer. He is going to send me a copy of the volume *First Love*. I didn't exactly *ask* him to but—oh I'm *so glad!* Norma has a vacation this week. She & Kenneth are at dance. My cold is *hateful!* Am working on "The Dead Path." Have some more beautiful ideas for it. If only I can get it somewhere near the way I *see* it!

Tuesday, January 21

Letter this morning from Miss Bannon. Went to the movies tonight with N. & K.

Wednesday, January 21 [22]

Went to rehearsal tonight. 'Nother one Sunday,—Opera House, I think. No mail at *all!*

Thursday, January 23

Mr. Untermeyer's book came this morning. I *love* it! —And he wrote the dearest thing on the fly-leaf. —Letter from mother. Kathleen's team plays basket-ball tonight. Norma and Kenneth are at the dance. —K's girls beat— 18:14.

Friday, January 24

Announcement of the Poetry Society dinner to be given, I think, next Tuesday.[12] Wish I could go! Wrote Mother. Kenneth was up and we all played poker. We have rigged the study up sporty and re-christened it "The Poker Joint."[13] Norma tacked a great big and awfully cute Velvet Tobacco ad up on the wall. Mary Emery called with a friend Mrs. Getchell of Waterville.[14]

Saturday, January 25   (T.)

Letter from Mr. Ficke and Mr. Seymour.
Spent most of the day desk-cleaning and looking over manuscripts, etc. Kathleen went to the club. —Norma to the movies with Madolin.

Sunday, January 26

Very good rehearsal today.
Mother was up, and K. [Kenneth].
I *must* get that typewriting done.

Monday, January 27

The January *Poetry* which Mr. Seymour sent me came today. Did a little type-writing. Norma went to the dance with Madoline. Mother came home. Started a letter to Mr. Donner, but got sleepy in the middle of it and had to go to bed. Wrote Mr. Seymour.

Tuesday, January 28

Letter from Miss Dow: must be ready to go to New York next week to study at Columbia the rest of this school year. Went to Rockland and "purchased a few necessary articles." Letter from Mr. Monroe. K. [Kenneth] was up.

Wednesday, January 29

Letter from Mr. Donner this morning, and the poem I asked him to send. Rehearsal.

Thursday, January 30

Rehearsal at 6. Went to the dance with Norma & Kenneth. First dance I've attended for ages.

Friday, January 31

Took down to Mrs. Barker the material for my tan dress and two shirtwaists. The farce, "A Pair of Burglars," went off without a hitch.[15] Mother went. We may put it on in Rockland. If I go to New York next week we will have to hurry up about it, tho.

Saturday, February 1

Am spending the night with Aunt Rose and Uncle Bert. Went to Rockland this afternoon & brought home my suit, my hat, a brown leather traveling bag, and a pair of tan rubbers. An express package from Miss Dow came tonight. It doesn't seem possible the things are really for me. Letters from Miss Dow & Ella.

Sunday, February 2

Tea at Mart's. Wrote Mr. Untermeyer and Mr. Donner. Did a lot of typing. K. [Kenneth] was up.

Monday, February 3

Got a telegram to come to New York tomorrow (!).
Party at Corinne's tonight.

Tuesday, February 4

(About one o'clock A.M. I guess.)
Am in a berth, in a sleeper, on a train, somewhere between Lowell and New York. Have just made the alarming discovery that my comb is not in my

bag. And I did my hair without side-combs or back-comb. Fancy! After all these years, to strike New York in pigtails!

Wednesday, February 5   NEW YORK

I don't realize it and I can't and I'm not going to try.

Got in about seven. Registered at Barnard. Met crowds of girls here at the national Training School, and am tired to death.

Could find my way lone if I had to from East 52nd Street to 116th St.— subway and all. Shall have a chance to try it tomorrow.

Must go to bed now.

Wrote Mother.

Thursday, February 6

Chaperoned again today except on one voyage which I made alone from the School of Journalism to Milbank Hall and around the corner to Union Seminary.[16] Wrote Louis Untermeyer and Mr. Monroe. Went to the Philharmonic concert in Carnegie Hall.[17] Walked up Fifth Avenue for the first time. Had luncheon at Milbank Hall. Wish they'd send up my trunk; I haven't a *thing* to wear.

Feb. 7, 1913 [Old diary]

Well, here I am in New York! At last! I have heard a Philharmonic concert, I have ridden in the subway, I have bought a tie on Fifth Avenue. I am going to study at Barnard for the rest of this [school] year and try to get into Vassar in the fall. I am at the home of the National Training School of the Y.W.C.A.'s of America, Lexington Avenue and 52nd Street.[18] I have met scores of charming girls, and I'm having a glorious time.

I can't bother to go back and fill in letters and dates now,—suffice it to say that I got in on the sleeper Wednesday morning, the fifth, (my first sleeper!) after having tipped two porters and that I have been so very good that I haven't yet been sent home. Tonight at a reception thing here in the building I met a Mr. and a Miss B [*sic*] who are, I think, among those interested in my Vassar prospects.[19] They are fine and *dears,* both. And I think Miss Dow may have been pleased with what they have said of me after we had talked a little while,—for, later she let me have two cups of tea, Russian tea, lemon tea, samovar tea. He, the man, told Miss Dow to bring me over to their place some day, and when I said, "May I?" something, I've forgotten what, he said "You may do anything you like"! —O, everything is *lovely* here. It's wonderful to *be* here!

Friday, February 7, 1913 [New diary]

Lots of things have happened today. —I went down to the station and had my trunk sent up, purchased two collars, two collar-buttons, a tie, and a bottle of ink, unpacked and put on some *different* clothes, attended a lecture given by Dr. King, Pres. of Oberlin, attended a sort of reception here in the building and met a Mr. and Miss Babbott, who are *charming,* saw a man in the Grand Central station whom I hadn't seen for ages and who was, when last I knew, in Milwaukee.[20]

Saturday, February 8, [New diary]   (T.)

Went to the movies today. Had notes from Mrs. Louis Untermeyer, Mr. Louis Untermeyer, and *Sara Teasdale!* Inviting me to "take tea" with her![21] Had a lovely long talk with Miss Dow. Wrote Mother.

Sunday, February 9, [New diary]

Met Mr. and Mrs. Fellows Morgan at dinner. Went to the Madison Avenue Presbyterian Church with Miss Dow and heard Dr. Coffin.[22] He's fine. Wrote Mr. Donner & Mr. Ficke.

Monday, February 10 [New diary]

Letters from Mother, Mr. Boehler, and a California reader of *The Lyric Year.* Mr. Donner called tonight. Went with Miss Dow & Dr. Talcott Williams to see Annie Russell in "She Stoops to Conquer";—Dr. Williams took us behind the scenes to see her.[23] It was wonderful.

Had my first experience alone in the subway,—and I flatter myself that not even the conductor knew it.

February 10, 1913

O, today has been wonderful! I wish I had more room here to tell about it. I can only summarize. This morning I had three letters and two packets in the mail;—letters from Mother, Mr. Boehler, and a California woman who has seen my poem. One packet was the February *Poetry* from Mr.

Ficke, the other a hand-illuminated (for want of a better expression) poem that Mr. Boehler had promised to send me. This morning I had my first experience alone in the subway,—from 42nd St. to 116th St., all around the college buildings, lunch in Milbank Hall, interview with Dr. Talcott Williams, then home again,—I even had the temerity to board a local at 116th and change to an express at 96th. Tonight Mr. Donner came to see me right after dinner. I had only a few minutes' talk with him before it was time to go to the theatre with Miss Dow and Dr. Talcott Williams. Annie Russell in "She Stoops to Conquer," —and afterwards we went behind the scenes and met her, Her, *Her!,* and also him, Him, *Him,* for he's a dear, just as she is,—Oswald Yorke.[24] I'd like awfully much to know him. Still, as it might just as well be a nice person as a horrid person. ——— (The thought has just occurred to me that it might be a great deal better.)

I *must* go to bed,—but oh, it was wonderful, wonderful!

Feb. 11 [Old diary]

At the Macdowell Club with Miss Dow. Met Edward J. Wheeler, Parker H. Fillmore, Mr. Maurice (I think) of the Bookman (I guess) and several others.[25] Disgraced myself during a speech of S. S. Mcclure by fainting, or near it, and having to be assisted out.[26] Still,—I don't know. I had a lovely time later out in the other room.

Tuesday, February 11

Shopped all afternoon. Went to the Macdowell Club in the evening with Miss Dow. Met Edward J. Wheeler, and Mr. Maurice (?), and Parker Fillmore. Wonderful evening. Fainted in the middle of it and had to be toted out, and all the lovely men were so sorry! Not sorry I went out, 'cause *they* came out later, but sorry I didn't feel well.

Wednesday, February 12 (T.)

Pretty well settled at Barnard. Went up twice today. Three letters [illegible] home with an enclosure from Aunt Clem, express package; and box sent up from Lord & Taylor's.[27] Wrote Mother fifteen great pages of note. At least, I hope so.

Thursday, February 13 (B & M)

Little letter from Mother. Went to college this morning. Valentine celebration tonight at dinner. Don't see why they didn't wait till tomorrow. Sent dues to P.S. of A. [Poetry Society of America]. Mrs. Trowbridge visited me tonight in my room.[28] She's a dear.

Friday, February 14

Sick abed most all day. Went up to dinner. Letters from Hazel & Aunt Clem.

Saturday, February 15

Went up to college this morning. Went to see Miss Teasdale this afternoon. We rode on a Fifth Avenue bus,—my first. It was simply great. Stayed at a hotel to dinner. Came home & wrote "I brought my little song."

Feb. 15

Went down to Martha Washington Hotel to meet Sara Teasdale. Had dinner there after riding up and down Fifth Avenue on a bustop, the most exhiliarating sport ever heard of.[29] She gave me a copy of her "Helen of Troy & Other Poems."[30]

Sunday, February 16

Nothing.

Feb. 17

Letters from Mr. Ficke and Ferdinand Earle, who is going to Europe, or rather, to start for Europe, or rather, to sail for Europe on the 27th. Shall perhaps see him before he goes, at the meeting of the Poetry Society, which is, I think, the 25th.

Monday, February 17

Went up to Barnard and had luncheon there. Letters from Norma, Mr. Ficke, Mr. Earle, and a review from Mr. Untermeyer. Hateful, *hateful*, cold. Hate everybody.

Tuesday, February 18

Cold a little better. Hate most everybody; like a few people. Abed all day. Went to college today. Had a terrible spell of nerves and cut class to go for a walk,—up Riverside Drive.[31] My first peek; glad I was alone. Went to a piano recital in Aeolian Hall.[32] (Norman Wilks).[33] More music here tonight, a Miss Merrill (I think) and A. M. Parker (whom I wouldn't like *awfully* well, but who is good-looking and,—oh well—and knows what to talk about). Mr. Untermeyer called up while I was gone.

Feb. 19

Walked up Riverside Drive for the first time, all alone,—from 119th to 135th. Saw two men riding down the muddy part marked "Equestrian Only" and all at once realized with a sickening thud, that here was the place, the very exact Riverside Drive, where the heroines of so many books I have read went riding with the heros. (Is there, I mean might there be an "e" in that word?)

Went to recital at Aeolian hall, Norman Wilks.

Tonight here at the building a girl in a pale satin dress trimmed with vivid red chiffon played the violin and did Canadian dialect readings.

Feb. 20

Went to walk this afternoon with Mrs. Untermeyer. Went to a dear little tea room "Vanity Fair."[34] But I can't say that I like those black velvet suits that button up the front and are always partly unbuttoned. She talks very interestingly.

Tonight saw & heard my first grand opera, "Madame Butterfly," at the Metropolitan Opera House. Geraldine Farrar sang Butterfly and other big ones did the other big parts.[35] Wish I could hear it again *tonight* (am getting this mixed, this being really the 21st, you know)—wish I could hear it again tomorrow night & the next night. Truly. I really ought to hear it three times right off. It is the most *wonderful* thing. But there! —Mem. I did not weep. The lady who accompanied me and whom Miss Dow warned that I *might* weep, *did* weep! Well, well! I never cry at the theatre. It seems to me that I feel things far too deeply, too deep down in my heart, to splash on top!

Thursday, February 20   (T.)

This morning at Barnard. Paid for the *Horace* which I had charged yesterday. This afternoon went to walk with Mrs. Untermeyer, and went to the dearest little tea-room, off Fifth Avenue, "Vanity Fair." This evening saw & heard my first grand opera, Farrar in "Madame Butterfly." Went with Mrs. Trowbridge. No need of making further notes about that, for I shall never forget.

Friday, February 21

Went up to College. Had an awfully interesting French conversation class. Am twenty-one tomorrow, my first birthday away from home. Have finished up my *Sweet & Twenty* book. Miss Dow has gone to Atlantic City for a short vacation. Paid my tuition fees to Mrs. Liggett. Letters from Mr. Ficke and Ferdinand Earle, who is going to Europe, or rather, to start for Europe, or rather, to sail for Europe on the 27th. Shall perhaps see him before he goes, at the meeting of the Poetry Society, which is, I think, the 25th.

Feb. 21

Shall be grown-up tomorrow, oh, dear! I *loved* being twenty! Good bye to this beautiful year. I somehow feel that twenty-one will be different. (Just got my mail,—five letters & no postals. Birthdays have *some* compensations. But still,—oh, well!)

February 21 Evening [Last entry in old diary]

Twenty one tomorrow, so I must finish this up. Tonight I have so little space that I will have to cramp considerably. With the aid of my diary I will go back and fill in.

Saturday, February 22, 1913

Twenty-one today. And my first birthday away from home. Last night & this morning had twelve letters & twenty-six cards. And some of my presents came, too, but some of them are in the office now, I know, and will have to wait until Monday. Still it will be lovely Monday. Tonight at dinner one of the girls as George Washington (stunning!) and I as Martha (—!)

went in together, and I had a big surprise birthday cake, and afterward we danced the minuet. Loveliest time! I wonder what will come Monday.

Sunday, February 23

Nothing much, except that I wrote two letters and eleven, I mean nine, one cent postals. Wore my hair down in a curl into the dining room to-night. I won't be grown-up even if I am twenty-one. I *love* my little black satin slippers with the rhine-stone buckles. Wonder if Witter Bynner will be at the Poetry Society meeting Tuesday night. I hope so, but I don't believe so;—he's too *mean*. I *must* get a book and begin to read up. Lecture courses aren't as innocent as they look, when exam time comes.

Monday, February 24

This morning six letters, five cards, and my *darling* bed-room slippers. Wrote Mother tonight. Luncheon at the college today. Met Grace White & went to walk with her up Riverside Drive.

Tuesday, February 25

Went to Barnard. Sewed all afternoon on my yellow chiffon and now is the meeting of the Poetry Society. Met Miss Rittenhouse, Miss Anna Branch, Mrs. Edwin Markham, and some others.[36] Mrs. Trowbridge went with me.

Wednesday, February 26

Went to Barnard. Haven't done anything but have worked every minute. I don't know what I shall do. I *can't* work any harder or I shall be sick. I'm just about sick now.

Thursday, February 27

Mrs. Fellows Morgan was here today and introduced me to Mrs. Douglas Robinson. Wasn't up to breakfast,—didn't *wake!*—and had to go and beg a biscuit of black Nancy in the kitchen. She's awfully good to me. I hear that she baked my birthday cake herself,—very great honor.

Went to Barnard for Eng. Comp. But had to cut Horace.[37] Poor thing. "This is the most unkindest cut—." —There, there! But is, tho, for I think it is my last. Sent "Honey-Bee" thing to St. Nicholas.[38]

Friday, February 28

Today has been wonderful. I have done so many things. Wasn't late to breakfast. Did a big washing in the laundriette. Translated about ten pages of French on the roof (glorious!), dressed, and wasn't late to luncheon. Started for Barnard about quarter to two, and wasn't late to French (translated the rest of my lesson on the subway), went over to Morningside Drive and had tea and a delightful talk with Miss Rittenhouse, her mother, and Mrs. Kendall (?). Got home at ten minutes past six, dressed, and wasn't late to dinner. Had another birthday party (all the Jan. & Feb. birthday girls) and a lovely carnation. Mrs. Trowbridge asked me to read some of my poems aloud after dinner, and I did. Later translated 2½ pages of Horace.

Saturday, March 1

Lovely day. Very satisfactory talk about Horace with Miss Goodale.[39] Ironed. Wrote part of my theme for next Tuesday. Met two nice young men to-night whom Miss Jacobs had to dinner.[40] Miss J., coming home late from the theatre, saw the light over my door and enticed me in to the Kitchen to have a mug o' malted milk and some Educators.[41] The thought that they were both good for me did not spoil my enjoyment of them.

Sunday, March 2

Miss Dow is home. Went with her to a reception given at Prof. Trent's to Dr. Euhen (or is it Euchen?) Met him, his wife, and daughter, and Mrs. Forbes Robertson.[42] Later went to the Untermeyers' to tea and spent the evening. Had a lovely time. He plays beautifully.

Monday, March 3

Went to college. Went in the evening to see "Die Walkure."[43] Grand. Gadski, Homer, and Matzenany.[44]

Tuesday, March 4   (T.)

Didn't go to college. Went to the Poetry Society luncheon for Alfred Noyes.[45] Met him, Witter Bynner, Chas. Hansom Towne, Edwin Markham, Rose Cecil O'Neill; saw Hildegarde Hawthorne, Florence Earl Coates, and, oh, it was lovely![46]

Wednesday, March 5

Luncheon at Barnard. Wrote the girls and Mother.　(One letter only.) Sent in four pages of execrable French as a critical review of "Mlle de la Leigliere."[47] Poor, long-suffering M. Muller! Took out a library card at Columbia.

Thursday, March 6

Went to college. Had tea this afternoon with Anna Hempstead Branch.[48] And a delightful call. She talks a great deal about Dugal Walker whom she is *very* anxious to have me meet.[49] Who *is* he? An artist or something. I am sort of anxious myself. Wrote Mrs. Bryan, a Mr. Munroe, Mr. Ficke and Mr. Donner. Card to girls. Mr. Munroe called me up.

Friday, March 7

Went to college. Had tea with Miss Hubbard. Met Miss Mary Miller. Borrowed two books—Alfred Noyes' *Drake* and Miss Branch's *The Heart of the Road and Other Poems.*[50]

Saturday, March 8

Went to college. Went shopping, i.e., bought a pair of long white gloves and a bottle of hair tonic. Went to International Art Exhibit.[51] Saw the most beautiful and also the most hideous pictures I ever saw. Miss Finney went with me.

Sunday, March 9

Party at Miss Rittenhouse's. *Lovely* time. Mr. & Mrs. Edwin Markham, Mr & Mrs. Louis Ledoux, Dr. & Mrs Rolf-Wheeler, Sara Teasdale, Anna H. Branch, Edith M. Thomas, Gertrude Hall, three or four others, Witter Bynner, and Dugal Walker.[52] Yes, I met him. I don't think he loves me *yet*. But then! Witter Bynner is delightful. Talked with him a long time. He read my poem "Renascence" aloud, beautifully. Mrs. Trowbridge went with me.

Monday, March 10

Went to Barnard. Had luncheon & went to walk & over to Brooks Hall with Florence Harris.[53] Did my Horace with Miss Ludlow. I didn't suppose anybody could do Horace at sight, but she is very, very quick indeed. Sat in the Barnard Library and wrote "If we should die tomorrow" which is not so bad as it sounds and "I'll keep a little tavern below the high hill's crest, Wherein all gray-eyed people may set them down to rest." —Sent some laundry. Letter from a crazy kid in Texas.

Tuesday, March 11

Went to college. Had a page more of Horace than anyone else had done. Perhaps I wasn't tickled![54]

Got B on my theme in English 2. They say that's pretty good. It says on it "Full of feeling, verging on sentimentality, but with some pathos. Not particularly healthy. Technically good."

Lots of mail today. Worked hard on theme (other one) and English— 26 notes.

Wednesday, March 12 (S.)

Rode up to college on a Riverside bus. Glorious. Will do it again some day. What you call riotous living. Just twice as much as it costs in the subway.

Got A on a critical review written in French & four pages long. Wore my new brown tie for the first time. Washed my hair & dried it on the roof. Am not trying to keep account of letters. Can't possibly.

Thursday, March 13

Barnard. Slept all afternoon. Mr. Caldwell's nephew at dinner [tonight]. Also Mr. Finney and a Mr. Norton. All at our table. It really looked piggish. The only men in the room and about fifty women. Wrote home. Pretty well up to date, I think, in my home accounts. Laundry came. Looks lovely.

Friday, March 14   (T.)

Washed a big wash & had a lovely time. Went up to Barnard in the afternoon for French. Went over to Morningside & was lucky enough to find Miss Rittenhouse. Made a little call, and we came together on the subway. After dinner played the pianola thing a long while.[55] First time I ever tried it. Wrote Mr. Ficke. Miss R. says that Witter Bynner said some very nice things about me. I didn't ask what they were, tho I'm dying to know.

Saturday, March 15

College. Went all alone to Bloomingdale's palatial emporium and spent seventy-five cents for scribble paper & pencils, etc.[56] Mr. Munroe called tonight. Just as much of a kid as I knew he would be, but a nice kid I think, and a smart kid I know. Conductor fell over my umbrella today & broke it in two. I said, "It doesn't matter. I don't think I'll need it this morning." How did I happen to say that?

Sunday, March 16

Went to church with Miss Dow. Grubbed over French irregular verbs for a while. Examination tomorrow.

Monday, March 17

French quiz. —Don't ask *me*.
Concert here. Prof. Eucken's daughter. Everything was in German, so I couldn't understand a word, but some of the things were very pretty. She hasn't much voice. Met an awfully nice woman who has had three daughters in Wellesley [College] and her husband who has been in Camden and whose voice sounds exactly like that man I saw in the station that day that it's startling. You'd think he *must* be his father.

Tuesday, March 18   (T.)

Saw & heard stereopticon lecture on Livingstone; the first time I knew he was a missionary.[57] I don't think I've had a letter for a week. Wasn't late to my nine o'clock class.

Wednesday, March 19 (B & M)

Sick abed all day. Everybody has been lovely to me. Alice Jacob brought me in a cup of tea while they were serving in the little alcove this afternoon. One sugar in the saucer, one lemon in the saucer, three crackers, and—*one sugar already in!* Bless her heart! I drank it, too. Grace Henley has had a box of fruit sent her from Florida. She brought me in a great juicy *wonderful* grape-fruit & two oranges. It is "Jakie's" birthday tomorrow. We eighth floor girls chipped to get her a fat Easter Br'er Rabbit with a basket on his back who *stands up on his hind legs & walks! —I want him myself!*[58]

Thursday, March 20

Did a lot of easy mending & read about 120 pages of Paradise Lost. Called up Sara Teasdale and she's coming to dinner tomorrow night. Wrote Dean of Vassar. Letters from home; wrote Norma.

Friday, March 21

Sara up to dinner. (It sounds lovely not to say "Miss Teasdale." And I don't have to any more because we're really truly friends.) We had a wonderful time. Served tea with Jeanne Grotard [?] this afternoon on the eighth floor here. Dear letter from Mother. Wrote her.

Must do—no, I *won't* write any musts on this lovely page. *Must do nothing.*

Saturday, March 22

Conference here today. A great many conventional people. (Don't anybody laugh.) Finished reading *Paradise Lost* at three gulps makes one long to spring hysterical puns. I say "one." The one is I. I can't answer for anybody else. Wrote Martha.

Sunday, March 23   (T.)
Easter

Beautiful day in every way. Went to three churches. First to Trinity Chapel, which is almost Catholic.[59] The service there was dreadfully oppressive & Miss Barnwell & I got out as soon as possible & went over to Dr. Parker's church, Madison Square.[60] This evening to Calvary Church, Organ Recital, beautiful, and *wonderful* choral & all kinds of singing by men & boys.[61] They sang the *Hallelujah Chorus.* I honestly believe, as truly as I believe in fairies, that *angels always join in that.* They always sing the *"Hallelujahs."* I'm sure of it.

Monday, March 24   (T.)

Am tired to death. Went with Mrs. Trowbridge to look at dresses. Everything that is pretty is too expensive. I am *cursed,* and I know it, with a love for beautiful things. I can't *bear* anything that looks cheap or feels cheap or is over-trimmed or coarse. I hate myself all the time because I'm all the time wearing things I don't like. It's wicked & it's ungrateful, but I can't help it. I wish I had one *graceful dress.*

Tuesday, March 25

I've got it. O, my heart! The *sweetest* thing. Makes you think of summer & iced tea on the lawn & men & girls & once in a while a breeze. I am— I am *languorous* in it. I have to be. It's that kind of a dress. Went to Macdowell Club with Miss Dow & Sara Teasdale & Mrs. Helena Knox, whom I like immensely. I was the least bit disappointed because Parker Fillmore was not there.

Wednesday, March 26

Went to college. Terribly hot & sultry. Saw an open car. Had to pay *seventy cents* fine on some anathematized old Milton books that I'd kept out a week longer than I was supposed to and hadn't looked into it once.[62]

A Miss Hoburn played the violin here last night, beautifully.

Read "The Cardinal's Snuff Box." I *love.* Henry Harland.[63] He has as true a sense of nonsense as Lewis Carroll.[64]

Thursday, March 27

Moved from room 860 to room 863, just around the corner. I love my room & my wonderful down-town view. But room 863 has one peculiarity which sets it apart from every other room in the building, one advantage which more than offsets every deficiency, and I am looking forward to a joyful sojourn here. For in this my new room the hot water comes out of the cold water faucet. Such a feeling of comradeship as it give[s] me! Here I am at home. The room is surely mine,—made for me.

Caught in the rain today. Rain is so unbecoming unless one appears to be enjoying oneself in it! How blissfully I paddled along! Sans rubbers, sans umbrella, sans friend, sans everything.

Friday, March 28   (T.)

Did a lot today. Washed & ironed, studies, and went to college, & made a call on the fifth floor here, and, oh, did a lot of things. Letter from Norma yesterday. Today letter from Mother & Kathleen. Sent two cards home cramped full of important things. Letter from Gilbert Patten.[65]

Saturday, March 29

Ironed this afternoon and read a lot of Andrew Marvell.[66] Got two more books from the Columbia Library.

March 30

Read a merciless amount of Milton and Marvell. All caught up now. Went to the Calvary Church tonight. Miss Finney had *two* rather nice men here tonight at dinner.

Monday, March 31

Same old thing. (Heaven forgive me!)
I mean that I went to college & attended a lecture here, Mr. Trowbridge on Balkan affairs & intensely interesting & studied meters & scansion of Horace.[67]

Tuesday, April 1

Saw Dr. Williams a minute today at the Columbia Library. To get a book out of the Columbia Library does me up for the day. Splitting headache. Read my prescribed chapter of Mackail.[68] Slept this afternoon. It's wonderful to be able to lie right down any time and go to sleep like a baby. That's the only thing that keeps me alive.

Wednesday, April 2   (T.)

Luncheon with Miss Hubbard at Barnard. Wore my new dress to dinner tonight.
Everybody loves it.

Thursday, April 3

Got my scansion paper back with something awfully nice written on it.
   Tonight the girls had what they call a Millinery Show on the 9th floor.[69] Set a chair before the long glass, brought out some little tables, and then all the girls brought in their new hats & everybody tried them all on. Great fun. But when you consider that I am expecting to wear a felt hat all

summer you can understand that my pleasure in it was a rather whimsical one.

Friday, April 4   Cut French.

8 P.M. I'm crying because while I was studying my Horace like a good girl, it got later & later and I didn't know it because I haven't any clock, and the bell didn't ring and nobody called me and so I didn't get any dinner. You can talk all you want to about virtue being its own reward, but it's darned unsatisfying when you're hungry. And I think my tooth is ulcerating. And I want a hat. And I want my mother.

Saturday, April 5

Went up to Barnard and wasn't late to my nine o'clock class. Mr. Wilhelm Bachenheimer, baritone, sang here this afternoon.[70] I am *crazy* to learn German. I can sing one line of one of his songs just as if I knew what it meant.

Sunday, April 6 1st C.B.

It snowed two or three times today, rather heavily for a few minutes about five o'clock. Went to Dr. Coffin's church with Miss Deane, but it was a communion service and I came out. Miss D & I stayed up on the roof a long time. Miss Sescholtz (?) came to see me in my room.

Monday, April 7

I feel awfully funny today. Made up the last of that seventy cents by going without luncheon at Barnard. But that isn't why I feel funny. I don't know why I feel funny, and I can't explain how funny I feel.

Tuesday, April 8

This morning—I actually had to look at it again before I dared to write it down as truth—this morning I got a check from Mitchell Kennerley for two little poems I had sent him - - $25.00 !!! O, girls!!!!

He is "delighted" to have them. They are to appear "in early numbers of The Forum." I wrote write [*sic*] straight home & told Mother. After I look at it a day or two I'm going to endorse it and send it to her. O, —— glory!

Wednesday, April 9

Didn't do much besides college. Prof. Trent called on me to answer a question right in the middle of his lecture! Horrors!

Thursday, April 10

Got a hat today. (Ain't yer shamed, Bincent?)—a dear, too.

My tooth didn't ulcerate, either. Saw something about me today in the April Bookman.

Friday, April 11

I Iad the nicest lesson in French. Talked a while with M. Muller after class. *Such* Fun! Rainy & I didn't wear my new hat.

Sat up late doing Horace. Translated two odes so as to be sure & get the right one.

Saturday, April 12

Found that we skipped both those odes.

Went to Columbia Library, gave back the Songs of Sappho & took out Alice in Wonderland.[71]

Sunday, April 13

Went to Jerry McAuley Mission down at 316 Water St.[72] Way, way down. It was wonderful.

Monday, April 14

Party here tonight. Had the first really *hectic* time I've had since I've been here. Have fallen in love again,—thank goodness! I won't feel so lost, like now—with the red-headed boy who sat next to me at dinner. He's not really red-headed, not nearly so much as I am, and I'm not so very myself. A kid, graduated from Yale last year, and a—a *darned sweet kid.* And it's fun to talk just plain nonsense to him because he is sure to understand & answer back. He has a *real* sense of humor, and he loves music. I—I think I honestly hope I'll never see him again, because I'd be awfully likely to spoil him. I wish I were a really *nice* girl!

Tuesday, April 15

Have had a wretched day. Didn't go to college. Didn't do anything. Couldn't do anything. Tried to write, and got off *two lines,* and rather middle-class lines at that. Couldn't *study—Lord!* Couldn't play. Such a wretched, wretched day as I've had.

Note from Mr. Kennerley with the proof of one poem. Am to see him Friday. Mr. Caldwell is to call Sunday.

Had dinner sent down. Mrs. Trowbridge & Mrs. Caldwell came in to see me tonight. We talked about the red-headed boy.

Wednesday, April 16

Went to hear *Cyrano* with Heloise Hedges.[73] *Great.* Most beautiful effects & wonderful music. When he said, "My dearest love, I love you not," I almost died & so did Heloise. Rained so I didn't go up to college this morning. Afternoon French. Mr. Ficke has sent me his last book, "Twelve Japanese Painters" beautiful inside & out.[74] It came some time last week but I neglected to put it down & now I've forgotten the day.

Thursday, April 17

Have felt sort of seasick all day. Told Miss Reinheimer, editor of the *Barnard Beat,* that I simply cannot get time to write anything for that estimable periodical. Stayed with [illegible] Miss Alene Stern to a lecture on Whitman by Miss Hubbard. Miss Hubbard has a tea to which I am invited one week from tomorrow.

Cleaned the net collar of my brown silk waist with a towel & a soapy toothbrush. It's wonderful. The girls here told me how.

Friday, April 18   (B & M)

Interview with Mitchell Kennerley. Very pleasant. He has invited me out some Sunday to see him & her & the kiddies. They are in the country! —I can eat grass!

He wants me to bring out a little volume of my stuff, but I don't think it feasible.

Saturday, April 19

Barnard.

Sunday, April 20

Didn't go to church. Mr. Caldwell & I rode up to 135th St. back on a bus. *Cold,*—my stars!—and *windy,*—my garters!

Monday, April 21

Barnard. Lunched at the Copper Kettle with Miss Stern.

On the way back met Grace Maxwell going up to Bronx Park.[75] Turned around and went up to Bronx Park. More fun. Ate apples & milk chocolate & devoured the landscape. Did some typewriting for Miss Adams. (3 hrs.). *O, how I hate it.*

Tuesday, April 22

Am dead tired. Did a whole lot of things today. Washed & shopped, and went to college.

O, I'm dead tired. I quote a little verse which I've just learned.

> "I wish I was a little stone
> A-settin' on a hill,
> I wouldn't do a single thing
> But just set still.
> I wouldn't eat, I wouldn't sleep,
> I wouldn't even wash;
> I'd jest set still a million years
> And rest myself, by gosh."[76]

Wednesday, April 23

Lovely letters from Mother, Aunt Clem, Norma & Mr. Ficke. And *arbutus* from the *Maine Woods!*

I wonder if my hair grows prettier. So many people have spoken of it lately. One of the Barnard girls said today, "Haven't you gorgeous hair! —Simply wonderful!"

I'm *so* glad I have red hair. That's *one* thing I don't have to envy. (How ungrateful I sound, and what a little beast I am!)

Thursday, April 24

Had a very interesting meeting tonight at the Poetry Society. Elizabeth Dean went with me. Arthur Pease Ginterman was there, and Burton Braley, too.[77] Celebs, more or less. Went to a ball game with Mr. Caldwell this afternoon. We (the Giants—while I am in New York) beat them, the Phillies, 7–0. If the Red Sox should come out here I bet I'd go right back on the Giants. I know I would. Of course I would.

Friday, April 25   (S.)

Went down all alone this morning to look for opera cloaks for Norma. Went to Wanamaker's in the subway & then came out on the street & asked a policeman where was Broadway & then found my way up to Lord & Taylor's, getting nervous but not stumped at 14th St., when Union Square butted in.[78] I knew that Broadway runs up town from East to West so I picked up the scent again all right. Did some more work for Miss Adams. 2 hours.

Saturday, April 26

Went to Staten Island with some of the girls here. Saw the Goddess of Liberty.[79] Saw Sailors Snug Harbor.[80] Walked around in the grass & got homesick.

Sunday, April 27

Made out a list of studies & then got mixed up in a poem & couldn't do anything. What shall I do with four years of college if this one semester is turning out like this? Here register I my first doubt.

Monday, April 28

Went to Miss Rittenhouse's after classes this afternoon. Had a lovely call. *The Anthology,* in which I am, is all ready to go to the press.[81]

Tuesday, April 29

Worked on a poem. I am going crazy with the poems that I simply can't get time to write. It isn't a joke. I can't study now; I'm too old; I ought to be through college at my age, and I know it, and I have other things to think about, and *I can't study.*

Wednesday, April 30

Had tea with Elizabeth Dean & Elsie Gervis [?] at Women's Exchange Tea Room.[82] They have *delicious* grapefruit salad.

A little box from home. Norma sent it. A little bag of salted peanuts, a tiny box of chocolates, one round apple, and a bunch of may flowers. I hope I shall never be so old but that reading this paragraph will make me want to cry. That little box was a wonderful thing.

Thursday, May 1

Luncheon with Miss Janet Kissell. *Two butlers.* I shall never do it again. *I was announced.* I should rather be *de*nounced any day. 'Evins [   ] [   ]!"

Friday, May 2

Crammed for Horace quiz.

Saturday, May 3

Saw suffrage parade. Two hours going by. You couldn't help being impressed by the mere numbers of them if by nothing else.

Sunday, May 4

Was up till the wee hours writing a French theme. I hope he'll like it. I got *A* on my last.

A reputation is a merciless thing.

Monday, May 5

Cut French to go to Ellis Island.[83] The most interesting place I was ever in. It would have been too terribly bad if I hadn't gone. My soul, what do they *do* with all those people?

Tuesday, May 6

Awfully hot. I'm glad I'm not going to be here all summer. There's a little—not so very little—Russian girl here just learning to speak English. She is very bright & very interesting. I am thrilled to hear that she has a brother named Boris. His name might so easily have been unknownski.

Wednesday, May 7

Luncheon at college. Had strawberries. Had a good French lesson. He's got so he pronounces my name in a tone of voice different from that he uses to the other girls. He doesn't realize it, but, it's so. And the reason is that he recognizes my sense of humor, and that makes a tie between us. You see, I can't talk French, but I insist on doing so, and on making jokes in French, and the result is that someday I *shall* be able to talk French, and that he pronounces my name in a different tone of voice.

Thursday, May 8

Very elated about the success of two themes of mine which Mr. Brewster read aloud among other things in the class this morning.

_____

A little Hungarian girl sang & played here tonight beautifully. Two or three of Hazel's old songs—made me homesick for her,—and the sixth Hungarian Rhapsodie, Lizst, (or Liszt, I guess) which Norman Wilks played in his recital I liked especially.[84]

Friday, May 9 Cut French.

Today (I wish I had red ink to write in) I saw Sarah Bernhardt in *Camille*.[85] It was only the last act (she is in vaudeville here) but the last act is the best, and it was the most wonderful thing I ever saw, heard, or imagined. —Ever since I can remember I have cut out pictures of her, and longed terribly, and hopelessly, to see her. And now, I cannot express my happiness or gratitude to the people who, with quite another end in view, have made this thing possible. *I have seen Bernhardt. Seen & heard her.*

Saturday, May 10

Went with some of the girls to the Bohemian church on 72nd between 1st and 2nd Avenue & heard an operetta given in their own tongue by children.[86] Lots of fun & very pretty & some of them, one little girl especially, had lovely voices.

Sunday, May 11

Horrible day, tho my hair went up beautifully. Did a little bit of Latin, and that's all. Couldn't get my mind on anything. Talked French with Joanne

Liotard [?] this evening & felt myself improving even as I talked. That *one* thing I did today. And I really did learn a lot & improve a lot. Perhaps—if I work hard tomorrow—

Monday, May 12

Got *A* on my English theme and *A* on my French theme today.
Prof. Brewster told me some awfully nice things about my short story work.

Mr. Ficke sent me the photographs of the two portraits he's been having painted.

Tuesday, May 13

Elise Lewis' engagement was announced tonight. She is one of the girls here. Goodness, it's so *thrilling!* He's a doctor, and very nice-looking.

Saw Dr. Talcott Williams today. Am to lunch with them Friday.

Did some typing for Miss Adams. One hour.

Wednesday, May 14

Nothing very special. Did quite a lot of typing tonight on my back English theme work, am all caught up now in that. (That last sentence reads awfully funny if it happens to hit you that way. I could never have got an effect like that if I'd tried for it. I've just read it again. It is really killing funny. "Did quite a lot of typing tonight on my back.")

Thursday, May 15

Wrote out & typed an old Horace Epode I was back on.[87] Last Theme class today. Wrote Corinne & Ethel. Letter (spec. deliv.) from Mrs. Mitchell Kennerley asking me out there Sunday,—*I'm so glad!* Witter Bynner is going to be there, she thinks, and Bliss Carman.[88] I hope they *will* be.

Friday, May 16

Last French class. Lunched with Dr. Williams. Am to dine there tomorrow night. Met a Scotch girl, a Miss Brown, a reporter on the New York City News. Filled out my application for Credits. Bought a pair of tan walking shoes, ties. Edith Caniff had a party here tonight and all the ice cream that was left she let us eighth-floor girls go into the kitchenette & eat. Little cakes, too.

Saturday, May 17

Went with the Training School girls out to Miss Grace Hodge's place at Riverdale. Had pleasant time, lovely things to eat,—all I talk about lately is eating—. Was fierce tired & went to sleep on a sofa.

Sunday, May 18

Went out to the Kennerley's. Lovely place in Mamaroneck.[89] Witter Bynner came in on the train with me. (Whereby hangs a tale.) Bliss Carman didn't come out but I don't care. It's the other one I was anxious about. Met another man, Mrs. Kennerley's cousin, I think. Motored down to Manursing Island beach where there's a club they belong to.[90] Had a "Poet's Evening"—horrid phrase.

Monday, May 19

Stayed all night. Mrs. K. brought me in the machine this morning & called for me this afternoon to take me out again. Wonderful ride both ways. Saw the other man again. Came home this morning just in time to go with the girls on a picnic to Coney Island.[91] Rode on the flying horses. Nobody would ride with me. They just stood around to chaperone & I did it all alone. All all alone, because there wasn't a single soul but me on any horse. For five cents I had the music & the ride & two men & all the horses.

Wednesday, May 21

Examination in English 29. Think I got through it all right. Training School commencement exercises. Madam Souberiane (I guess) whom I met Monday came & I showed her all around & we talked French. I mean that she did and so did I.

Thursday, May 22

Latin Exam.
Had Dinner with Dr. Williams & his niece.

Friday, May 23

Dinner with Alene Stern. Got lost in Central Park on my way there, pouring rain, no umbrella, getting dark,—it was wonderful.

Saturday, May 24

French exam. Came out to the Kennerley's. Dance at their country club house.

Sunday, May 25   (B & M)

It must be about one o'clock. I have not yet begun to regret this day & night, but I shall be sick about it in the morning. I have been intemperate in three ways, I have failed to keep, or rather to fulfill an obligation, and I have deliberately broken my word of honor.

_____

The cocks are crowing. It's later than I thought. I must get to sleep before I get to thinking.

Monday, May 26

Went back to the city. It must be I am getting terribly calloused in soul. I don't seem to be regretting very much. Packed some.

Tuesday, May 27

Finished packing. Mrs. Kennerley called up. She was in, and insisted on taking me back with her. She really did insist and I came. *Fool! Fool! Fool!*

Wednesday, May 28

Mrs. Thorp, a friend of Mrs. Kennerley's, sang here tonight. Her voice is almost too beautiful.

Thursday, May 29

Tonight—oh, dear, what's going to come of it all?

Nothing ever does, so I suppose nothing really will this time. I don't really care, and he doesn't really care, but we seem to have had an unexplainable, tacit falling-out which is rather interesting.[92] Mr. and Mrs. Drake at dinner tonight. Beatrice Howe here.

Friday, May 30

(Today is the 16th of June. I haven't written anything in this for over three weeks. I'm going to fill in what I can from memory.)

Went to Manursing and went swimming. Borrowed a black silk bathing suit which made me glad I'm red-headed. Stretched out on the beach and talked to Him. We are made up. He says I have been damned nasty. I suppose I have. I *hope* I have.

Saturday, May 31

Went motoring to Briarcliffe and back, through Sleepy Hollow.[93] It was beautiful, but stupid. He didn't go, and there were five women of us. Went to New York this afternoon. Didn't catch Miss Dow but saw Dr. Williams and Miss Hubbard. Left word for Miss Dow to call me up. Took the train at 125th St. Went all alone and never had been there before.

Tonight was lovely. I wore my white dreamy dress and walked under the trees with Him.

Sunday, June 1

Muriel Price here today. We all went down to Manursing. Herbert Kaufman here too.[94] Went in swimming again. Gave Mr. Kennerley my signet ring to hold and he lost it. Miss Dow called up. She's heard some new cursedness about me is about heart-broken. Damn 'em. I wish they'd keep their mouths shut.

Monday, June 2

Didn't rest much last night. Came down to breakfast looking like a ghost. Felt like dying and couldn't do anything. He came over this afternoon. He felt like dying and couldn't do anything. So we went off into the woods together.

Tuesday, June 3

Tea at Miss Strecker's. Delicious sandwiches. Wish I had one now. They found my ring in the sand. Isn't that wonderful?

Wednesday, June 4

Today he's dying to be in England at the Derby races. Been walking the floor with his watch in his hand, poor fellow.

Left Mamaroneck forever. They all came down with me in the machine. He stayed until I started.

O, well!

Thursday, June 5

At Uncle Charlie's in Bristol, Connecticut.[95] There are four boys here, boarders. I see where I have a picnic. Went over to Mrs. Jenkins!

Friday, June 6

Went down to another place, Spoor, I think the name is.

Saturday, June 7

As Torchy says "Nothin' doin'. . ." Torchy is one of the four, a little red-headed Jew, with beautiful brown eyes and an instant feeling of liking and fellowship for me.

Sunday, June 8

Went down to Lake Compounce.[96] Jimmy wanted me to go with him but I told him I'd promised to go with my aunt and uncle. Jimmy brought me a bunch of roses today.

Monday, June 9

Went up to Merrills'.

Tuesday, June 10

Went car-riding, something I detest, with the little Merrill girl. Later went to a Rebecca social with Aunt Jennie, who belongs. It was deadly. (But don't think I'm not having a good time. There are always the boys.)

Wednesday, June 11

Think this is the day we went out and took Henry with us.[97] Henry is the nicest of the four. He is engaged to a girl in Minnesota. I don't remember just where Minnesota is but it seems to me it's a long way off. *However.*

Thursday, June 12

Think this is the night we went car-riding to Plainville terminus and got so effusively iced and soda'd.[98] Wish I could remember what day it was Harry (the fourth) brought me up the ice-cream.

Friday, June 13

Don't remember.

Saturday, June 14

Party at the Spoor's. Torchy and Bill—oh, he's the fifth and I'd forgotten him. He works nights—Torchy and Bill each wanted me to go to a dance at the lake. Henry wanted me to go out home with him for the week-end.

Sunday, June 15

Henry waited till this morning and I *did* go out home with him. To Collinsville.[99] Rather unconventional even for me, I suppose. We went canoeing for about four hours. It was simply perfect. Henry is a nice boy, and I was a nice girl. I made him talk about the girl in Minnesota.

Monday, June 16

Torchy wants me to go out to Hartford with him tonight. Can't do it. Letter from New York. Back to see Miss Dow tomorrow.

Tuesday, June 17

Came in town this morning. Miss Dow called away by the death of a friend. Can't see her till tomorrow night. Came out to Mamaroneck with Mr. Kennerley for the night. Went to Manursing and in swimming. The water was great.

Wednesday, June 18

Back in New York. Lovely long talk with Miss Dow. Everything's going to be all right. Rather hard up for clothes as I didn't intend to stay more than an afternoon. Did a washing tonight and hung it in the window between the curtains.

Thursday, June 19

Ironed before breakfast. Went to Public Library and Metropolitan Museum and prowled around by myself. I hate the guide. Back to Bristol tonight.

Friday, June 20

Had our last sing tonight. Said goodnight and goodbye to all the boys. Henry gave me a lovely pound box of chocolates to take with me tomorrow.

Saturday, June 21

At Aunt Clem's in Newburyport. Got across Boston all alone—the first time I ever was there, since I can remember. I'm getting to be so self-reliant and resourceful!

Sunday, June 22

Went 100 miles in The Magic Carpet, Aunt Clem's automobile. Went to Gloucester, and all around,—to Beverly Farms. Had a lovely time, but I've got to get home. *I wan' my Mama!*

Monday, June 23

Came home. Long, long trip. Am tired to death. Surprised them all. Saw everybody I ever knew.

Tuesday, June 24

Corinne was up to supper. Bless her. Have a hateful cold. They say everybody does when they first get home. Mart was up in the evening.

Wednesday, June 25

Sick with my cold. Kenneth up. Mother went on a case for Dr. Wasgatt in Rockland.

Thursday, June 26

Went to "Thursday Night Dance" with Hunkus [Norma]. She and I did the tango and were afraid of getting put out of the hall, but weren't. I love those disreputable dances.

Friday, June 27

Kathleen went to Rockland to see Mother and do some errands, and stayed all night. Terribly hot. Went for a little walk with Mart. Kenneth got caught in a pouring thunder-storm after having brought up from down-town a whole lot of things to eat and drink. We sat on the porch all through the storm and feasted and then we three, K, Norma and I just sat and talked—and talked—and talked—.

Saturday, June 28

Sunday School Picnic. Norm & I went, just to see Abbie, Ethel and the old crowd. My cold kept getting worse and worse and I wept and sniffled all the way home.

Sunday, June 29

Went driving with Kenneth & Norma. Should feel as if I were sticking around a bit if I didn't remember how she used to tease one of my beaux to take her with us to dances up in the country.

Monday, June 30

Nothing much. Polly Follett played for the show and lost the last car so she stayed all night with Kathleen.

Mr. Boehler called up. He's here again this summer. Will be up to-morrow evening.

Tuesday, July 1

Mr. Boehler called. It's nice to have him here this summer and he makes another man. Norma & Kenneth went to the play.

Wednesday, July 2

Party at Clara's. Went down and went with Mart.

Thursday, July 3

Went to the dance with Mr. Boehler. I wish he could dance.

Friday, July 4

"The Glorious 4th."

Kenneth up to dinner. We four went paddling in the afternoon.

Saturday, July 5

Aunt Sue down from Portland, motored down, unexpectedly. Cleaned up the house from garret to cellar as soon as Mother called up to let us know she was on her way. Great to see her.

Sunday, July 6

Picnic,—Kathleen, Norma, Kenneth, Mr. Boehler, and myself. Perfectly great time. Went in a big canoe. Gone all day. Built fires and took snaps and got our feet wet and everything.

Monday, July 7

Went to "Brewster's Millions."[100] Awfully funny.

Tuesday, July 8

Did a lot of tiresome little duties I've been putting off and putting off for ages. Went down town. —How I hate to! Kenneth and Norma are fighting about going to the pictures. She wants to go and he doesn't.

There's the sweetest rain just beginning. Coming straight down.

Wednesday, July 9

Mr. Boehler was up. After this it is to be "Fritz." Jenness Thomas and Kathleen went stealing cherries.

Thursday, July 10

Didn't go to the dance. Too tired. Went to bed. Norma & Kenneth went.

Friday, July 11

Kathleen & I did a terrific ironing. Fritz was up.

Saturday, July 12

Washed all the morning, "Sent[?] indeed!"

Went up to Aunt Rose's in the afternoon & stayed all night. Saw Mr. Tufts, Gladys,—and my darling Mrs. Carpenter from Providence.

Sunday, July 13

Kathleen & I went down where Mother is and spent the day. I got the loveliest letter from—guess who!—Fannie Stearns Davis![101] Mm-mm! About my poem in the July Forum. I'm *so* glad to get a letter from her.

Monday, July 14

Awfully tired. Didn't do much of anything. Wrote Miss Davis, Sara Teasdale, Miss Dow, and Robert Shafer. Hazel was up a minute. Bless her!

Tuesday, July 15

Fritz & I went down to the boat-house to try & get a canoe but the man was gone—just because it was drizzling a little! So we went to the stupid moving-pictures. I won't go again.

Wednesday, July 16

Norma & Kenneth & Doc & Madolin have gone to a dance in Hope in Doc's machine. I'm not doing anything.

Thursday, July 17

Did a lot of geometry. Mart up in the evening. We lay in the hammock and giggled until eleven o'clock.

Friday, July 18

Fritz up. He says it's down.

Saturday, July 19

Washed again.

Sunday, July 20

Had the grandest time. Went sailing, Norma, Kenneth, Mother, Kathleen, Fritz & I. There were showers and we got soaked. Went ashore at Oakland Park, to get something to eat.

Perfectly lovely time.

Monday, July 21

Washed. Went down town in the evening to get some lemons for Kathleen's cold. Saw Mart a minute.

Tuesday, July 22

Awfully bad day. Just puttered. I guess I'm not very well. Kenneth brought up something nice and cold to drink.

Wednesday, July 23

Kathleen went to Dark Harbor with mother & Mrs. Young.[102] To be gone a week or so. Norma home sick. Bacon Bat at Oakland.[103] Big crowd of girls. Did all the kid stunts.

Thursday, July 24

Kenneth up. Norma still sick.

Friday, July 25   (B. & M.)

Norma & I went paddling with Fritz.

Saturday, July 26

Must have washed.

Sunday, July 27

Fritz & Kenneth up. Fritz has a gray suit that exactly matches his eyes.

Most delicious sandwiches for luncheon, chicken with lettuce. Fritz & I stole the lettuce.

Monday, July 28

Norm & I cleaned up the house.

Tuesday, July 29

Went in swimming with Hazel over at Negro Island.[104]

Wednesday, July 30

Kathleen & her Cap'n from the Light at Kindle Point over to dinner. Brought us some crabs and other salty sea things. Norma, Hazel & I went swimming over at the island.

Thursday, July 31

Norma & I went to the Comique [?]. Kenneth came up when he was told not to, so we left him to sleep in the hammock.

Friday, August 1

Saw Mildred Perry & Marian Prescott. They want us to go swimming with them from their bath-house.

Saturday, August 2

Went swimming with the Perrys. Hazel went too.

Sunday, August 3

Mother, Kathleen, Mrs. Young & the baby came home. They'll be with us a while.

Norma & I and the boys went paddling.

Monday, August 4

Norma & I went in swimming all alone. Gray cold day. Water cold but lovely.

Norma went to work at Whitehall.

Tuesday, August 5

We three girls went in swimming with a whole crowd. Swam out to the float. Pretty good swim. I guess we can really swim.

Went sailing with the Perrys.

Wednesday, August 6

Kathleen, Hazel, & I went in swimming. George Perry was there and went too[?]. We tried to learn the crawl.

Big sea in swimming.

Thursday, August 7

Sick abed all day. Thought I was going to die. Sent for Fritz. (Tee, hee!)

Dressed all up in a red kimono and red blankets & things. He likes me in red—in the evening.

Friday, August 8

Still sick. Hazel, Kathleen & Corinne's cousin Lillian went in swimming.

Saturday, August 9

Studied all day. Norma brought up Stewart Cottman and a Mr. Neil. Men are an awful bother. They interfere with my studies. It's got to stop.

Sunday, August 10

Fritz & Kenneth were up. Fritz & I went driving. Told Fritz he can't come up any more. He's dreadfully cut up about it. I wonder if I've done anything terrible. I didn't mean to. I think it would kill me to know I had hurt anyone like that.

Monday, August 11

Studied all day.

Wednesday, August 13

Went on a bacon bat with the Perry's & a whole crowd to Big Spruce Head.[105] Didn't get in till after midnight.

Thursday, August 14

Algebra.

Saturday, August 16

Algebra.

Sunday, August 17

Kenneth & Norma have had another bust-up. They make me ache. I've told her to be sure to get another man before he gets another girl.

Monday, August 18

She has followed my advice, I guess. Out motor-boating with the Cott-man boy and that Neil man the first thing. Hazel stayed to supper tonight. I mean came.

Stewart goes tomorrow, he says.

Tuesday, August 19

Norma & Mr. Neil went to Rockland in his little runabout. Wanted me to go but I was studying.

Wednesday, August 20

Joe Neil & I motored around all day. Had dinner in Belfast, a blow out in Searsport, and a collision with a motor cycle in Northport. Glorious time. Lobster supper here. Hazel, Norma, Kathleen & I, Joe Neil & *Fritz!* — Yes, I did.

Thursday, August 21

Mr. Neil & I went on a little spin to Rockland.

Friday, August 22

Norma & Mr. Neil, & Mother & Ellen & Wump [Kathleen] went to the theatre, while I stayed home with Gwendolyn.[106] She was awfully good. Seemed to realize I didn't know anything about it.

Saturday, August 23

Joe & Norma & Fritz & I went down to Rockland to see *The Pink Lady*.[107] It was awfully good. And awfully bad, Norma says. Wore my tan satin with the little train. Hit's hawful helegant.

Sunday, August 24

We four & Wump paddled over to Sherman Point in the evening. Made coffee & had a late supper on the rocks. Put out for home at about eleven in a pretty stiff wind, Fritz & I paddling. Couldn't get her more around into the wind to save our lives and had to turn back and haul her up for the night in a little cove, & walk home. About three miles.

Mother was crazy. Never no more.

165

Monday, August 25   (B. & M.)

Joe took Fritz & me down to the point in the machine. We two paddled her home, the canoe home, I mean and Joe met us at the slip and took us back again, back home, I mean—O, Lord!

There was quite a wind this morning but it was glorious.

Letter from a girl on the Vassar receiving committee (I guess). She has seen all about me in the papers. It's no use.

(Sick & almost died.)

Tuesday, August 26

Wrote a few letters. It's colder than anything you can think of. I have a new sweater that I love, sort of green & orange mix, and I wore it all day. Gwendolyn saw her fist today for the first time and hit herself in the eye with it. Then she looked at me as if I'd done it, and howled. I'm sore yet from laughing.

[Note by Norma Millay: Gwendolyn is Ellen Young's baby. They are staying with us. Vincent has a snapshot holding this baby in her arms—very sweet.]

Wednesday, August 27

Joe & Norm went to the movies. Joe brought up some samps we took Sunday that have just been developed.[108]

Thursday, August 28

Lil' weeny party.

Joe & Hazel up. Fritz went to Augusta in Mr. Chatfield's machine with Mr. Chatfield on business. Had to go. I don' care.

Friday, August 29

Joe & Norm & Fritz & I went down with Hazel on the boat as far as Rockland. Had a little supper at the *Copper Kettle*. Awful time with Fritz afterwards. Not a fight. Just an awful time.

Kenneth called up Norma!

Saturday, August 30

Norm & I scoured out our burrow. Put up some yellow curtains.

Millay at Halloween in Camden, Maine, standing in front of Mount Battie, 1910 (Courtesy of the Edna St. Vincent Millay Society)

Millay at twenty in Camden, 1912 (Library of Congress)

Steepletop, Millay's home in Austerlitz, New York, 2021
(Courtesy of the Edna St. Vincent Millay Society)

Arthur Ficke (left), Millay, and Eugen Boissevain, spring
1923, before her marriage to Eugen on July 18
(Library of Congress)

Millay (left) with her sisters, Norma and Kathleen, around 1930
(Library of Congress)

Millay's mother Cora in her nurse's uniform, about 1910 (Courtesy of the Edna St. Vincent Millay Society)

Millay (left) and her Vassar classmate Elaine Ralli, 1914 or 1915
(Library of Congress)

Millay in Albania in 1921, wearing a traditional Albanian costume
(Library of Congress)

Millay and Eugen on their belated honeymoon trip around the world, 1924
(Courtesy of the Edna St. Vincent Millay Society)

Millay picketing in Boston in April 1927 during a march
supporting the reprieve of Nicola Sacco and Bartolomeo Vanzetti
(Courtesy of the Edna St. Vincent Millay Society)

Millay at Steepletop in the late 1940s, the last decade of her life
(Courtesy of the Edna St. Vincent Millay Society)

Vassar
(1913)

I n the annals of higher education, few college careers ever matched the
spectacle and melodrama of Edna St. Vincent Millay's four years at
Vassar.

After finishing her Latin and French preparations at Barnard in late
May, the poet spent much of the spring with the Kennerleys at their cottage in Mamaroneck before going home to Camden. The summer of swimming, picnics, sailing, and flirting with the boys of the coastal villages came
to a close in August as she began teaching herself algebra in anticipation
of the dreaded math requirement in Poughkeepsie.

Vassar College, founded in 1861 in the Hudson River valley seventy
miles north of New York City, was the most prestigious (and perhaps the
most rigorous) college for women of its day. There were about seven hundred students when Millay enrolled, in September 1913. At twenty-one
years of age she was three years older than her classmates, about the age of
the returning seniors. In this small academic community Millay's Cinderella story preceded her and produced great excitement. Her celebrity in
the highest literary society in New York was a matter of wonder, admiration, and envy. She was famous, and the aura of fame that attended her
every movement affected her self-regard as well as the impression she made
upon the students and professors who surrounded her.

With her flame of red hair, those green eyes, and the natural grace of
her figure, the young poet possessed not only a rare charm of personality,
but erotic power as well. On October 23, 1913, she wrote, with what was
left of her innocence, "I wonder why people love me so." It is an endlessly

fascinating question. As we shall learn from the diary entries that follow, she was not above using that power to confuse, dazzle, and captivate her classmates.

Millay's college diary ends, abruptly, and quite dramatically, on January 19, 1914, with a concise description of an erotic affair with one of her classmates with whom she had been flirting for months. After this there is blank space, silence. This silence falls so suddenly that here and now, as in few other places in Millay's diaries, we cannot help but wonder if a notebook or two, or more, has been hidden from posterity, either by the writer herself or by family members who believed that such censorship was in Millay's best interest. There seems to be no winding down, and no particular reason why she would have been less interested in recording her thoughts and impressions in 1914 than in 1913.

One must turn to Millay's excellent letters to her family and friends to discover her feelings about the events of the rest of the decade. We do not get to hear directly from the famous undergraduate about her triumphs and misadventures at Vassar, which she called, dismissively, "this pink and grey college," and a "hell-hole," while laboring to excel, and to honor a course of study she desperately needed in order to become the writer she wanted to be. At Vassar she became a superb scholar of Latin, French, and mathematics. She was a beloved outlaw. She smoked cigarettes in the cemetery, drank gin in the dormitory, cut attendance at chapel, showed up late to classes when she was not absent without leave. Edna broke all the rules. But her papers and exams were so brilliant the teachers were obliged to reward her with good grades, and her extracurricular fame was so conspicuous that the college president repeatedly commuted sentences that the faculty passed against her. Her talent and experience as an actress won her starring roles in campus plays; and of course if her classmates wanted an anthem, a marching song, or a poem for the literary magazine she was happy to provide them.

But in June of 1917, a week before commencement, the faculty voted to suspend the wayward student for going off campus, denying her the right to graduate with her classmates. They in turn got up a petition which they sent to the college president, Henry McCracken. An eleventh-hour reprieve from that beleaguered official allowed Miss Millay's suspension to be ended on the eve of the graduation, so that the campus heroine could cross the stage with her fellow students.

🝆

Tuesday, September 16 [1913]
Started this morning by train for New York again.

Wednesday, September 17
Got in New York this morning. Saw Miss Dow, breakfast at the Training School, went down to see Mr. Kennerley, & Sara Teasdale, who got in town yesterday, and came up to Poughkeepsie tonight. Dinner at Main Hall.

Thursday, September 18
Am to be off campus a while, at Mrs. McGlynn's cottage, with a lot of Freshmen.

Saturday, September 20
Trying to get settled and to get word to the girls & noise [*sic*].

Sunday, September 21
A wild time in room. About fifteen of us, planning a spread for Friday. Adele & Dorothea Campbell, Kim Tyler from *Bal'more,* Annic Hope Smith from Tennessee, Bianca Scheuer, Harry [Harriett] Wiefenbach, Olive Burke, (my room-mate) and I can't remember the rest.

Saw Miss Fiske in the morning & arranged my Sophomore English course,—*Old English! Joy!*

Monday, September 22
At Vassar

Almost a month since I have even opened this book. But I couldn't help it. Too busy, too tired, too confused, to even write or even think of it.

It is wonderful but I am tired, tired, tired. (*Today first classes at Vassar.*)

I am going back to fill in.

Tuesday, September 23

(10 P.M. Monday con[tinued].)

Just went down stairs to the kitchen & begged for a plate of cake. —Poor little hungry Olivers![1] —She gave it to me, too, and we all had a bite.

Tuesday

Dead Tired. The girls make it hard for me in my official capacity [as dorm proctor].

Two or three seem to understand & they help a lot but somehow to-night I realize more than ever before how very young they all are.

Wednesday, September 24

My room-mate upset her ink bottle tonight all over everything, after which she had a crying fit and "wanted her mother." Poor kid! I have done just the right things & said just the right things, (somehow, I must have been inspired) and got her quiet again.

Thursday, September 25

Olive has been called up on campus.[2] She is broken-hearted. I am not. I wanted a lonesome room in the first place. I'm "goin on" twenty-two and Olive is seventeen, and a common room is difficult. She is extremely so-cial, and when not actively so, humidly homesick. Dinner at the — with my senior, Katharine Pratt.

Friday, September 26   B. & M.

Went up for a history class in the morning and then came home and went to bed. Cut German and English.

Had the spread here tonight. The girls fixed me up an invalid chair and I went in for a while.

Saturday, September 27

The — something or other reception on campus. I had four invitations to go. Accepted the first, Agnes Rogers, and then was sick and couldn't go. However, recovered sufficiently to go see Ruth Stanley-Brown and Agnes in Ruth's room and to stay to dinner. (That sounds horrid. I really was invited to dinner.) Letter from Mother.

Sunday, September 28

Went to church on campus. Was delighted to hear my old friend Dr. Coffin of the Madison Avenue Presbyterian Church.

Some girls called for a poem for the *Miscellany*.[3] Oh, for a bushel that I might hide my light![4]

Monday, September 29

Lovely letters from Norma and Miss Dow. Miss Dow is coming up to see me!

Am awfully tired. Wish I could go to bed now instead of doing Geometry.

Tuesday, September 30

Got my table home from the gymn [*sic*]. Terrible time getting it in my room. Had to be all taken apart. I'm glad to have it. Perhaps now I can do some work.

Letter from Miss Dow with my allowance. Sent books home and to Ellen Hovey.

Wednesday, October 1

Miss Fiske, my instructor in Old English has advised me to sit up till two o'clock tonight over my Anglo-Saxon verbs. I couldn't get any book at first and so I got a little back in them. Her advice doesn't fit in with the Hygiene Lectures we're having.[5]

Friday, October 3

Got a *Forum* today from Mr. Kennerley, and in it I found a picture of Witter Bynner I'd wanted. The last I heard Miss Anthony Comstock of New York had put Mr. Kennerley in jail for something or other.[6] The envelope was in his writing so he must be out.

Wednesday, October 8

Heard Schumann-Heink tonight for the first time, and fell in love with her, as everybody does, they say.[7]

Saturday, October 11

Katharine Tilt is in Albany, Loraine Schultz in New York, Grace Hedley & Grace Roper have their fathers here, or coming tomorrow.[8]

Wednesday, October 15

Tonight I got my first real insight into German. I *love* the grammar book we have. Bierwirth seems to *want* us to learn German. I think he must be nice to pour tea for.

Saturday, October 18

Just home from the sophomore party. Very clever. But what a heap of work it must have meant. —And I am tired to death. And no studying done.

Sunday, October 19

Have to go to chapel. Therefore:—went to Chapel.

Monday, October 20

Mademoiselle asked me after class this morning, "est-ce que vous savez trop pour cette classe?"[9] —which means that henceforth I am a Sophomore in French as well as in English.

Tuesday, October 21

Was physically examined. Am five feet one, and weight one hundred and one. Blew 160, whatever that means, and I guess it means not much;—also my feet are mates.[10]

Friday, October 31

Halloween Ball here at McGlynn's. Some of the girls met the dearest boys. They all sent flowers and we really dressed. I had a perfectly lovely time. I wouldn't have believed it possible.

Saturday, November 1

Didn't go to the Junior Party. Too tired. Just about sick.

Sunday, November 2   B & M

Stayed in bed all day.

The book agent girl came to see me. Her number is *444 Main.*

Wednesday, November 5

Letter from Miss Dow and my allowance. She is coming to see me tomorrow. I must have my bureau drawers in order in case she should wish to inquire into my personal habits.

God bless her!

Thursday, November 6

Sat up until about two, I guess, digging at a history outline.

Friday, November 7, 1913

Dead to the world.

Came home from German—cut it and went to bed. Too tired to go to the first Hall Play.[11]

Geometry test. Didn't pretend to do it. Instead spent the time writing a letter to Miss Cummings. Hope she's pleased with it. Perhaps I'll be expelled.

Saturday, November 8

Washed this morning. Studied History in the library all afternoon. Miss Conrow, my French instructor, told somebody that I am a very brilliant girl who probably won't stay the year out. She doesn't know that there's nothing else for me to do.

Thursday, November 27

Beginning of Thanksgiving recess. Had boxes from Aunt Sue, Mrs. Carpenter, and Home, and a present from Aunt Clem. Am Head Proctor while Katharine Tilt is gone.[12] Only a name because we can all make all the noise we like.

Wednesday, December 3

First meeting of the French Club. Only two Freshmen were admitted, and I was one of them.

Read a little French poem I made up because Miss Conrow wanted me to. I mean "said it." Had the most wonderful time talking French every minute.

Friday, December 5

Haven't written a word here for ages. Am ashamed. Am going to write every day now and fill in all I can in back.

Saw Miss Sexton in the library today and she planned out a way for me to like history. I am going to try it. I love her.

People, my friends & hers, are very much interested in a seemingly new friendship which has sprung up between Catherine Filene & me.[13] Handsome great big child!

Kim & Margaret made candy for us. Catherine & I came in together. People are very much disturbed.

Made proctor of my wing.

Saturday, December 6

Went down town with Katharine Tilt to get stuff for tomorrow's tea. Told her about Catherine Filene purposely to make her jealous, because she's been telling me how much she likes somebody else. It worked beautifully. Met Josephine Preston Peabody (Mrs. Marks) who read at college today.[14] She knew my name & remembered my poem & gave me *The Singing Leaves* with both ourselves written in the front of it.[15] It was very wonderful. But she has awfully rovy eyes, and I wish she hadn't.

Sunday, December 7

Horrible day. Katharine & I gave our tea tonight to Agnes Rogers, Phoebe Briggs, Dorothy Bailey & Estelle Bonnell. Everything turned out all right, but I just came home & howled over a little thing Katharine did.

However, Catherine Filene came in & consoled me beautifully.

Spent the whole afternoon shelling shrimps, and my hands are sore. After this we have 'em canned.

Monday, December 8

Katharine feels nervous about what she did last night. She will feel nervouser before it's over. And it will be good for her.

Mr. Ficke has sent me his last book, "Mr. Faust."[16] Saw the manuscript of it last spring at the Kennerley's. Shan't have time to read it for a month.

Tuesday, December 9
Cut two classes today. Feeling pretty ragged.

Wednesday, December 10
Letter from home. Can go to the Kennerley's Christmas then home. Ought I to go? What train.

Thursday, December 11
Yesterday I got a letter from Henry. They want me to spend Xmas there. Sorry.

Friday, December 12
The old McGlyn girls had a reunion & dance here tonight & invited us. Can't *tell* what a good time I had! Wore my tan satin with the train & not much of anything else & felt just like dancing. Danced with Catherine Filene most of the time. Katharine Tilt came upstairs with me & asked to unhook me. I let her. It's all working wonderfully.
    Did 10 theorems in my math note book.

Saturday, December 13
Did 12 in my math note book. Had a nice call on Miss Coggeshall. Was invited to & attended a very exclusive dance in Catherine Filene's room. She & Adele & Harry & I, and the Victor. And some eats. Heaps of fun. Love to dance. And Catherine makes a wonderful man. She was *swell*-looking & swell-*feeling* last night.

Friday, December 19
"Lower 3, please," the conductor just said and I handed out my tickets through the slit in the green curtain. —I am on my way home. Had "seven hours in New York" this afternoon & spent them at the Training School.[17] —I am going to write a story about a girl in a sleeper who pins her skirt to the curtain & pins a man's back right in with it. His coat, I mean. —Well, when I wake up I can say, "Today I'll see them."

Saturday, December 20

Five hours with Aunt Sue in Portland. George took me down to the train & introduced me to a college chum who was going as far as Newcastle,— almost all the way. Which made it very pleasant, especially so, as it turned out. For the bridge was down at Wiscasset & we had all to pile into automobiles & be toted across the other bridge to So. Newcastle (I guess) where another train was waiting for us. And with all my luggage it wouldn't have been much fun alone. In Rockland all the electric power was off and no cars running but the girls had met me and we found a friend in a machine who took us home. So here I am.

Sunday, December 21

Rested a little. Kenneth was up. Found out that Fritz left last night just before I got in. Well, never mind.

Monday, December 22

Nothing much.

Tuesday, December 23

Went up to Uncle Bert's & stayed all night with them. I wonder why people love me so.

Wednesday, December 24

Went to the Knights of Pythias dance with Norma & Wumps,—and drew the turkey![18] Didn't even know there was a turkey till they handed around the little slips. But, oh, what fun to bring it home to Mother! —Christmas dinner! & we hadn't really known what we were going to have.

Thursday, December 25

Went to a swell ball in Rockland with Norma & Kenneth. Wore my tan satin with the train. And Kenneth brought me pink roses & Norma violets for her yellow. Had a lovely time. Love to rag with Kenneth.[19] Had some lovely dances with him & other people. Love to dance anyway.

Friday, December 26

Had a little party for the old crowd but it stormed terribly & only Mart & Jesse who live near came.

Fritz sent me a book that we had talked about last summer & I hadn't read. Good old Fritz. So he doesn't forget.

Saturday, December 27

Came on to Portland to stay a day or so with Aunt Sue. Met George's Gladys. Awfully cute.

Sunday, December 28

Am back again in a berth on a train. Decided to go on tonight. Too restless to sit still for long anywhere & there was nothing much doing in Portland. Went to hear a recital on the lovely big organ, tho, which was beautiful. There is a young man asleep up over me. He breathes awfully boyishly somehow. Not heavily, but regularly & softly. Guess I'll go to sleep & see how I breathe.

January 19, 1914   Memoranda

Tonight Katharine and I came together with a crash that smashed us all up, and when we picked up the pieces we put them together as they should be and now everything is quite wonderful. God, if you are looking, bless her, please

Europe
(1920–1921)

From 1907 until 1914, Edna St. Vincent Millay succeeded, intermittently, in keeping a conventional diary, more than a hundred and fifty pages of notes, descriptions, meditations, and anecdotes that amount to an autobiographical narrative. Carefully studied, those pages chart the life of an extraordinary young woman and writer from adolescence to adulthood.

The diary as such ends in 1914, as far as anyone knows. She picks it up occasionally during trips abroad, to Europe and Japan in the years 1920–1924, and those entries are preserved in the following pages. The next period of sustained diary writing covers the years 1927–1930, after she and her husband, Eugen Boissevain, had moved to a farm in upstate New York.

More information about the poet's life during the years missing from the journals after 1914 can be found in other sources about her, including biographical works. Many letters, reviews, press clippings, and the memoirs of contemporaries survive that chronicle the events of a very eventful life lived to the hilt during years of World War I and the Roaring Twenties.

It is certainly worthy of note that the ten years from the time she left Vassar College for Manhattan in June of 1917 until she resumed her diary writing in 1927 spanned the era of her greatest productivity as a lyric poet, dramatist, actress, and writer of popular fiction. Her labor was incessant and seemingly tireless, and the more she produced, the greater was the demand for her poems, plays, and stories.

In December 1917, Kennerley published Millay's first book, *Renascence, and Other Poems.* It was an immediate sensation. And in the same season she became a leading actress in the famed Provincetown Players, where she was constantly in the public eye. When her mother and sisters came to live with her in Greenwich Village in June 1918, young Edna supported the family by writing humorous fiction for *Ainslee's* magazine under the pen name of Nancy Boyd. At the same time she was publishing her greatest lyric poems in magazines like *Poetry, The Dial,* and *Reedy's Mirror.* In December 1919 her antiwar play *Aria da Capo* opened at Provincetown, assuring her place in history as a playwright. In November 1920 Kennerley published her second book of poems, *A Few Figs from Thistles,* which included the immortal verse, "My candle burns at both ends / It will not last the night; / But ah my foes and oh my friends— / It gives a lovely light!" Her name was, by then, a household word, and scandalous, as she carried on well-publicized affairs with literary figures including Edmund Wilson, Floyd Dell, Arthur Davison Ficke, John Peale Bishop, and others.

Her third book of poems, *Second April,* was published in the summer of 1921 while she was writing "The Ballad of the Harp Weaver." In 1923 she was awarded the Pulitzer Prize for that poem, eight sonnets that appeared in an annual anthology, and her collection *A Few Figs from Thistles. The Harp-Weaver and Other Poems* (1923) was the focus of worldwide acclaim. In American literary history, there have been few, if any, serious reputations that have so quickly arisen and burned so brightly as Millay's did during that decade. Not surprisingly, the workload weighed upon her health. In her late twenties she developed gastritis, and probably ulcerative colitis, requiring emergency surgery in the summer of 1923. Biographers have credited her fiancé and husband, the Dutch businessman Eugen Boissevain, with saving Millay's life.

In any case Boissevain rescued Millay from the chaos of her personal life, and took charge of her health care, which had become a full-time job for someone other than herself, as we shall see.

And so, assuming that none of Millay's diaries or journals have been lost, it would appear that during that extraordinary decade, 1914–1924, she did not keep a diary because she had neither the time nor the energy to devote to it. The entries that we have, from 1920–1921 and from 1924 are meager but fascinating, making us wish for more, particularly about her time in Paris and Albania. I suspect that more exists or existed somewhere recording her time in Europe, but efforts to turn up other journals have been fruitless. The few Paris entries display a quantum leap in terms of her narrative powers, after years of writing short stories for popular magazines. Her account of the American girls chattering in the room next door to hers in the Hôtel des Saints Pères is very funny, and her descriptions of the cafes on the Left Bank are vivid pictures of a scene that has not changed much in a century.

One of the most extraordinary sequences in all of Millay's diaries consists of several thousand words written during October of 1921. The American Embassy in Rome, upon the advice of Millay's friend and lover John Carter, an attaché there, had decided it would be a good idea to send the famous writer to Albania, recently opened to Western tourism. Carter, a young poet who had roomed with Stephen Benét at Yale, offered to escort Millay on the difficult journey by sea and horseback. Millay's account of the trip, the poor people of Albania, the difficulty with customs officials, and finally the hospital that was clearly the chief destination of the Americans, is first-rate modern journalism. Few if any Americans had witnessed, in the twentieth century, what Millay saw in Albania; it is likely that these diary entries, transcribed here for the first time, were meant to serve as groundwork for a full-length magazine article that never saw the light of day.

Finally, a brief and sketchy travelogue of the married couple's trip to Japan has survived; but it is of little interest and will only be mentioned here in passing. Millay married Eugen Boissevain on July 18, 1923, the day before she was to undergo the surgery that would save her life. When she recovered, she began, in November of that year, a lecture tour, more than thirty poetry readings in twenty American cities. The voyage to Japan via Honolulu in April 1924 was one leg of what was intended to be a round-the-world honeymoon. Neither of the two was strong enough for such an ambitious journey, but Millay's notes on the Japan adventure give us an idea of how much the newlyweds enjoyed each other. The first entry is April 29, 1924: "Meridian Day—Lost Day—Day that never dawned," and the last May 21. There will be no more diaries until 1927.

It has been said, half ironically, that Millay fled to France in 1920 to escape the too-tangled web of her love life. It might be said, more accurately, that she went there to perfect her French and find lovers who had a better sense of humor. In any case her fame pursued her, and she was soon the toast of Paris as she had been of New York.

PARIS, 1920

Tuesday, Jan. 18, 1920
Hotel des Saint Peres, Paris

They told me it would be damp in Paris. It is so damp this afternoon, & it has been for two days, that the wallpaper of my room is dark & bubbly with it. I have given orders that my breakfast be brought me at eight o'clock after this, it being my notion to work in bed until noon; I can write much better in bed, think much better, that is,—tho the typewriter is a little awkward. But there are a couple of American school-girls in the room next to me, & the wall is very thin. From nine to ten in the morning they have a French lesson,—if only they could have arranged to go to the tutor instead of having the tutor come here! How casually one arrives at such decisions never realizing—but that has been said before. The vocabulary of one of these young women consists entirely of connectives; the other has a set of five polite idioms, a little pompous to the ear, with which she brings herself airily about, no matter what the conversational task may be.

(It has begun to rain in earnest now; it is pouring. I see it shine on the iron fleur-de-lys of the grating outside my window & hear it splashing in the little court.)

They are amusing, however, these two girls. Immediately the tutor departs, ushered out in their most restrained & idiomatic manner, they turn upon each other a despairing torrent of American slang, all in a rather pleasant drawl which might mean Memphis.[1] I feel a certain friendship for them. One of them has bought a cloak, at no inconsiderable outlay, I gather, which is not by one-half so engaging in Number 14, Hotel des Saint Peres as it was in the Rue de la Paix.[2] Every evening there takes place the following rather pathetic conversation:

1st: Y'know, Angela, the more I see of that cloak the more I think maybe I'm going to like it *after* all.

2nd: Oh, sure, I think you like it, Shrimp, all right, after *w'ile.*

1st: O' course, it doesn't look the same here as it did in the shop, *that's* certain. I'm mighty glad you-all didn't get yours. I don't think you'd a' liked it much.

2nd: Yes, I'm glad I decided not to. I just sort of had a hunch it was a terrible impulsive thing to do. Still, yours was *much* the better-lookin' o' the two.

1st: I dunno. They were pretty much alike, y'know, Angela, when you come right down to it. Anyhow, I'm crazy about my kimono.

2nd: Oh, sure. An' I think you'll get to like the cloak all right, Shrimp, after *while*.

1st: Oh, I reckon so. O'course, you have to sort of get accustomed to a thing by degrees, especially when it's so sort a' different from what you bin wearin'. I think I'll get to like it all right.

I see them in the dining-room sometimes. Their mother is with them then, & a little brother, about eight. The three topics of conversation among the women are: Clothes; How many Francs does one get for a Dollar; and How well one has done in a week to see all one has seen. Yesterday, the little boy remarked plaintively, "I'm goin' home, that's what. I got too much on my mind."

He has taken to smiling at me lately, after leaving the table, through the crack of the dining room door.

Last night I had dinner with Van at the Taverne de Pantheon, down in the old Quartier Latin.[3] He tells me that the artists are moving to the right bank now, & that the Latin Quarter is now in Montmartre.[4] Probably they have been forced to by sight-seers, much as in New York the Greenwich Villagers are being forced out of the Village.

There is in this tavern an orchestra of perhaps four pieces, with an unusually mellow & sensitive first violin, which plays Mozart as he himself would have liked to hear it. I realized as I listened that I had heard no music for a long time & that, after all, it is music that I like more than anything.

They brought us for dessert a bowl of brown pears, rouge-skinned, big as pumpkins, almost as squat & twisted as quinces. I had never seen any like them before. I wondered if they had not ripened near a wall, maybe, in a thorny garden, where in the summer-time go walking of an afternoon an old blind woman & a little boy in bright blue apron. But probably they had not. However, I will not thank you at all for telling me where they grew.

Jan. 19, 1920

I was told last night that today they were coming to take the mattress out from under me, & do something to it which I couldn't understand very well, but which is done every year or two, & which would make it more bumpy, but in the end very superior. —It is very well as it is, in fact I think it is the best mattress in the world, but perhaps that is just because every year or two they do something to it which makes it bumpy for a time.

The *femme de chamber* has just come in with hot water. She informs me that I needn't press myself, because the mattress-man can't come until tomorrow.

Last night I walked along the banks of the Seine alone, close, close down by the parapet, where people drown themselves. There was a high wind blowing, dripping rain.

The river, flowing broken from around the piles of the bridge, in the high wind, is crumpled on the surface like dead leaves. And in flowing it makes a sound not like a river, but like a forest, a leafy rustling, an articulate sound, ancient and mysterious to the ear.

After all, it is a French river, and it is to be expected it would speak in a different tongue.

After all, it is a French river. It speaks no English.

With the best of my French, I cannot catch what it is saying.

I think it speaks an old French yet, that is why. Its "s"s are all "f"s, and its "aussi" still "auxi."[5] I doubt if all these modern Parisians understand it much better than I do. One thing is certain, they do not give it so much thought.

Jan. 29, 1920

Twenty-five days without a decent cup of coffee,—twenty-five days, three hours & forty-six minutes, to be exact,—an honest calculation, too, allowing for the difference in Paris time. I am becoming [irritable] to children. Ten days more & I shan't even like dogs. —Oh, Napoleon! —Poor Boy! —I know, I know. You *couldn't* conquer the world on *café au lait!* Naturally! And there forces itself upon me the unwelcome reflection that maybe neither can I.

My "friends & other enemies," as someone who lives in my memory only for that pleasure once put it, advised me on the eve of my departure, & not without a certain gouty satisfaction, that I would get no cream in France. I smiled at them kindly. They would have their little jest.

But, do you know, it's true. It's as true as the prohibition of spirituous liquors in America,—truer. You simply can't get it. There isn't any. The milk doesn't "jell." They use a different kind of cow. If you order cream they bring you either an emerald-green liqueur or a platter of artist's-paste with sugar on it. You can't even get cold-cream. The nearest they come to it is mutton-tallow, which, I am told, is very healing. All right; fine, say I. Long may it heal. But if you have the kind of complexion which requires not to be healed, but to be [fostered], you'd rather have cold-cream.

(The hysterical title of the preceding dignified paragraph is "The Cream of the Jest.")

Every morning at eight o'clock I am awakened by a solemn tapping at my door. "Come!" I shout,—because I still wake up in English. And there enters a pink-faced baby in a swallow-tail coat, bearing like a crown on a cushion, my *café au lait.*

Darn it all! What a way to be awakened in the morning.

I sit for some moments with the tray on my knees, considering it, carefully keeping one eye open and the other shut so that I may even now go back to sleep if I should decide to.

Two elliptical brown rolls, two medallions of butter, two small [illegible] apples, & two white pitchers! Of the two white pitchers one contains a steaming black fluid, one a steaming white fluid. They sit side by side on the tray, brought together by force, sullen partners & a nefarious deed. They hate each other. —I pour them into a cup, & stir them angrily. They mix, but they do not communicate. They are incompatible.

There results from this union a dull grey fluid, which I drink. It is not the dove-grey of absinthe, nor the _____ grey of clam broth. It is puddle-grey,—the grey of despair.

[Undated. Paris 1920]

Spent most of the day at the café that is named the Café Brasserie de la Rotonde. Went back to my hotel and got a book,—a French book with a yellow paper cover. It was exciting to be reading a French book in a French café!

I had luncheon upstairs in the grill room.

I spent all the afternoon looking at the pictures on the café walls—wonderful pictures, many of them painted by artists who were right there in that café with me! Oh, it is all too thrilling!

Had dinner upstairs in the café grill room. Later went down into the café and ordered one lemonade after another and watched the people. I couldn't *believe* it when they began putting out the lights & everybody began to leave. Two o'clock!

Sunday afternoon

Such a surprise! At the café de la Rotonde today I ran into a lot of boys I know in New York, Harrison Dowd, the beautiful young poet, who plays better jazz than any three n***s together, & Dougie [Allan Ross Macdougall], who is running a funny column in a Paris paper, & [illegible], the artist, who has just done a portrait of James Joyce, author of Ulysses, & is going to do one of Henri Barbusse and Anatole France.[6] What fun to have these kids here to play around with!

I find that the thing to drink here in Paris is something they call *fin a l'eau.* It is rather strong.

I forgot all about the Louvre today until it was too late to go. I could have cried with disappointment!

[Undated fragment]

I had them send me up some coffee, but it was so grey & luke-warm & terrible & all full of pieces of blotting paper I couldn't stand it. I decided right then & there I would have to go out for my breakfasts.

The only place I knew to go was that café where Van & Chloe took me last night. I remembered that it was right on the street where I live & not far from my hotel. So I went there. I had no difficulty at all in finding it. There were very few people there, but the chairs were [illegible] on the sidewalk cute little cane chairs, thousands of them, all empty, and little round, marble-topped tables; and [illegible] running over there to keep out of the rain.

I took a table under the awning, & ordered a *café au lait,* and I saw somebody eating some muffins, so I made them bring me some. He called them something that sounded like *Boche,* but I don't suppose it could be.

The coffee was terribly good. That girl [illegible] came along, & I was so glad to see her. She pointed out to me a man sitting just inside the door & said it was James Stephens, who wrote *The Crock of Gold.*

April 30
Versailles

The palace was too big; there was no doubt about that. It took me an hour & a half to walk through it, one floor of it. And if you were a queen it would take you longer, because everybody would be looking at you, & you would not be wearing low-heeled Oxfords & a short tweed skirt.

—I became very tired after a while of the big rooms, one just like another except for a different battle or a different death among the paintings on the ceilings & walls, and when the guard was out of sight I skidded the polished floors like a child [on] the first frozen puddle. But it was far too big, & the guide was too much with us.

We resented the presence of the guide in the first place because he made us feel like tourists, which, obviously, we were not, I having been in Paris half a year & my friend half his life. We felt it nobler, considering our position, to remain in ignorance, than to be instructed by a guide. The villain had us by the nose, however, & fed us forcibly. Of what he told us, in a manner sinister but possessive,—as if he were at least a bastard offspring of these kings—I heard every other sentence twice, once in French, and once in English—& the following sentence not at all. For my friend, with the pig-headed enthusiasm of the person who knows something a little better than you do, insisted upon translating it all to me in a kind paternal voice, thus confusing my hearing, filling me with shame in the presence of the other tourists in the room, & altogether nearly ruining my day. So that if in the course of these remarks I set down boldly what any scholar, with half an eye-glass, will know to be fake, it is not because I do not understand, to say nothing of speaking fluently, dozens of foreign languages,—it is because I have a surly & stubborn insistence that they be spoken at me one at a time.

The palace was all very well for a palace. But palaces, after all, were made to be turned into museums & opened to the public from 12 to 6,—not to be lived in.

There's a fellow in Paris named Kervais,
Who is nothing, my dear, if not nervais,
    He makes, if you please,
    All the cream into cheese,—
A trick which I call rather scurvais.

*

ITALY AND ALBANIA, 1921

Sunday October 16

Left Rome at half-past eight in the evening—night train to Brindisi—Italian sleeping car much more comfortable & infinitely more private than the American compartments with doors—not curtains—two compartments separated by a small dressing room [illegible] hardly room to stand up when dressing—trying to set up a little table to write at—chair to sit on—coffee brought in in the morning—no sound of snoring from other passengers through the thin curtains—might have been alone on the train—neither saw nor heard a sound from other persons in the train until we got off at Brindisi.[7]

Monday October 17

Morning—We have crossed the Italian peninsula from west to east during the night & are traveling down the eastern coast along the Adriatic—orchard after orchard of olive trees grey with dust—trunks of the old trees incredibly gnarled & twisted—houses of chalk-white dazzling stone—two different kinds of cactus—thick padded round leaves—long spikey leaves along the walls & by the houses—white houses set on red soil—arrived Brindisi about noon—Taken at once to hotel on the waterfront—wind blows so we can't have the dining room windows open—bright blue day—get some rest in—boat not sailing until night.

Saw for the first time hotel beds with canopies of mosquito netting over them—malaria!—well, we are bound to a country full of it—plenty of quinine along—There's a Greek destroyer in, just across the road—and the boat we are to take rides at anchor within a stone's throw of the hotel.

—At dinner a Table-ful of Greeks, deputies from the Greek government on their way to London, the waiter tells us. Four of them are middle-aged men, very fine-looking.

Night—On board *The Molfetta*—a small and apparently very dear Italian boat—only about a dozen first class passengers—two Frenchmen, a Greek, several Italians, a couple of Albanians—and only two women besides Mrs. Carpenter and myself—Americans probably, bound for the Red Cross at Durazzo—very calm crossing on the Adriatic![8] —I hope, as Horace, or was it Catullus wished for his friend Arrius [?] that it will not prove to be the (H)Adriatic—a stormy sea—blonde Frenchman complaining that we needed a pr[illegible] aboard—I was very glad there was none, being in no mood for the monotonous Apache bewailing of *Bon Homme.*

Tuesday October 18

Wakened very early—boat passing a big barren island—slept again—wakened later, boat coming into harbor of Vlore to remain at anchor until tomorrow morning—boat rowed by men wearing wide white trousers & fezzes put out [from] shore to meet us—we go ashore making room, are to come back on board at five for supper—passport looked at, apparently official cannot read them at all; bystander, Albanian, comes to our rescue with a mixture of the smattering of German, French & Italian, & through him we are able to spell out our names—official in despair however suggests that we leave our passports with him & collect them later, thus giving him half a day to conn & decipher them—a horrifying idea, to give up our passport, even for a moment—we cling to them desperately, & finally are permitted to keep them, provided only we will write our names and addresses in a book full of unintelligible dots and scratches which he holds out to us—

Go to see Kokoshi [their native guide]—entertained by his mother & family while a child is sent to fetch him—curious conversation—mother speaks nothing but Albanian & Turkish, also the older girls—younger girl speaks Italian, when she is present conversation progresses, but she goes out to get coffee, & the conversation becomes a series of dead calms interspersed by smiles, awkward inexpressive signs, & frustrated giggles. Old woman very handsome—large eyes that give the impression of being[?] strips of black & grey—white cloth over head—high bodice, loose under trousers of calico, shoes with turned up points—children dressed in European fashion—they bring us our first Turkish coffee in Albania—tiny cups of black fluid with a brown foam on top, excessively sweet. I, who never take sugar in my coffee, tell myself that I must learn to like it—drink it smilingly. Our host returns & offers us gold-tipped cigarettes—very good tobacco—Albania is a tobacco-producing country—the old woman motions to the child—bring her a cigarette—she smokes it in expressionless calm—

Kokoshi, who wears a fez, but is otherwise dressed as a European, takes us to see the town—terribly dusty, thick with dust—there has been no rain for six months, & will be none for a few weeks more—mountains all about—one mountain where a handful of Albanians, we are told, captured a whole company of Italians together with all their guns—they are still contending over the island of Cezani, at the mouth of the harbor which we passed early this morning—from the town this island looks like nothing but a great rock,—wondered why they should make such a fuss over a barren rock where nothing could grow and nobody could live, not realizing until I was told that with this rock as a fortress on the Albanian coast and Brindisi on the Italian coast opposite the Italians would control the entire mouth of the Adriatic.

We are taken to have coffee & sweets before luncheon.

Beautiful fruit on table looks like reddish yellow cherries [illegible] clusters of them but is hard and thorny to the touch as chestnut burrs— they call it *salvatigo,* [probably litchee] though they may not spell it in this way—proprietor shows me a bowl of dark jam, what they make of it— gramaphone plays arias from Carmen & Rigoletto—La Donna e mobile—

My sweet in the other café where we have luncheon, a kind of cottage pudding-cake with a sauce poured over it—I take one taste, & all my passed life moves before me as in the moment of death, the most horrible taste I ever tasted. Tastes exactly as goats smell—pushed it away & drank the coffee, to save my life I could not have eaten it—or perhaps to save my life I could have done, but that would merely have substituted one form of

death for another—I am sick in my stomach all day as the result of it &
go to bed at night feeling very sick—

Luncheon—Italian food—risotto & some kind of meat but all cooked
with a curious taste which is most disagreeable to me—more sweetened
coffee—

We are accosted—our host hails a curious kind of carriage with seats
covered with red cloth facing one another—we are [illegible] through the
dust to see the hospital—Dr. Cesar Shom (?) enveloped in a long-sleeved
white apron, dark-skinned, very alert-looking, had studied in Constantino-
ple, two young doctors with him, took us through the hospital—one ward
after another, men, women, & children—no attempt as yet to get them
out of their own clothes and into white nightgowns—they lie for the most
part swaddled in bright-colored tatters, or sitting up in bed looking very
bewildered, having very little idea what it is all about—a woman whose leg
had been amputated the day before—a man about to be operated on for
some abdominal trouble, probably appendicitis—the man from whose leg
the tumor had been extracted which [illegible] had seen before, apparently
doing very well—(Doctor converses with us in French, knows no English)—
very likely the operation for appendicitis was postponed an hour or so by
our visit & would take place immediately upon our departure

—I carried through the wards the flowers that the doctor had gathered
for me in the hospital gardens—autumn flowers, dahlias, snap-dragons,
etc., very lovely in dark colors—it did not occur to me until afterwards that
people who bring flowers into hospitals usually distrust [crossed out and
illegible]—this many patients, & I was glad that it had not occurred to me,
for I should not have known what to do—a couple of asters to these people,
so distressed, so horribly suffering—it would have been an impertinence—

We saw a whole family suffering from some dreadful skin disease, two
little boys & a little girl—We stopped at the foot of their beds. The doctor
would speak to each of them & the patient would dumbly pull back the
covers or shyly lift a bandage to show us what it was that had brought him
there—the little girl was very beautiful—even in bed she was wearing a
head-dress which hung prettily about her dark hair—she turned down the
covers & showed us her left leg, a leg as foreign to a human body as if it
had been the branch of a tree she showed us! Covered with small leeches—
a sight such as I had never seen before—from the foot to the thigh, shrunken

& covered with round scabs the size of a dime, drying, apparently, & perhaps healing, though it seems impossible she will ever be well.

Syphlitic mother & child—great deal of syphilis, hereditary syphilis, he told us. There were a great many patients, brought in from miles around—perhaps seventy-five patients in all, though I am not sure. He took us afterwards through a store-room full of dry goods boxes & supplies of different kinds, but the operating room, a small room, with the table & instruments, very clean & efficient-looking—showed us a bath-tub, real bath-tub, but rather a narrow[?] one, which had apparently just been put in, signs of recent carpentry and plumbing about the room—Here every patient is washed as he is brought in, we were told. —Kitchen, two middle-aged Albanian women—whose husbands had been killed I think by the Turks. (Go back & describe tumor in paper bag & enlarged artery that had been taken out after the man half dead.)

[October 1921, no date]

Rain on the Adriatic and on the Moslem tower & in the empty chambers of houses gutted by earthquakes, and on the warped and mossy red or yellow house tops of Durazzo—From the white minaret the dark muezzin leans a moment over the roof—Sleepily from the chalk-white minaret an hour before daybreak the dark young muezzin calls the town to prayer—Only you and I, alarmed from slumber, listen, staring into the darkness, Ah—Ah—Ah—husky & shrill the bodiless voice in the sky climbs/mounts the wide uneven steps to the folded feet of Allah

Sounds of day rising from the [illegible] street—ducks scolding thirstily —wooden shoes clattering over cobbles—& in this room the thick pink walls are hot with sunlight—

Let us tear apart the tough thick skin of the ripe pomegranate & split the seedy fruit in two—ah, how wet & good to the love-parched mouth— how cool on the naked breast and knees drips now the clear bright blood of the crushed pomegranate—suck up & split—wipe the wet mouth & chin on the warm smooth shoulder—there are six pomegranates in this basket—shall we eat them all—hurl now the empty shells in the corner of the room—Ah, how stained & drenched we are! —Let the wind dry us if it will.

Steepletop
(March to May 1927)

Lawrence Tibbett (1896–1960) was one of the greatest American baritones ever to command the stage at the Metropolitan Opera in New York City. Early in his career Tibbett originated the role of King Eadgar in the original opera *The King's Henchman,* composed by Deems Taylor (1885–1966) for a libretto by Edna St. Vincent Millay. This opera, a huge success from the night of its premiere in 1927, was accorded a headline on the front page of the *New York Times:* "King's Henchman Hailed as Best American Opera." It was staged seventeen times over the next three seasons, while touring companies gave ninety more performances in forty-six cities.

As a token of his undying gratitude and admiration, the young baritone gave his librettist a beautiful diary with gold-leaf edged pages bound in white calf. His dedication is preserved at the head of the diary: "This is the day of the first "King's Henchman" / And this just a small remembrance . . ." It was February 17, 1927, the night of the world premiere of the opera in New York.

It was a lucky little book. Millay, who had not kept a diary with any regularity since she was in college, began writing in this one at the beginning of March, and kept at it for years, health permitting. And so once more, as in the early years of the century, we have a window with a clear view upon the poet's world, and her thoughts and feelings. How different this world is from the scenes the young woman described in her ragged diaries in Camden and New York! And how different, indeed, is the writer herself. Fortune acts upon each of us differently; this dynamic is one of the measures of character. Some people appear little changed by great prosperity or calamity; others come unhinged, or seem warped by events.

It would appear, by every objective measure, that the girl from Camden had gotten everything she had hoped and prayed for. It is fair to say that as of March 1927 Millay had succeeded beyond her wildest dreams. She was rich—apart from the fact she had married a wealthy Dutch merchant. Her husband was devoted to her, as he had been to his late wife, the great suffrage leader Inez Milholland. It is perhaps too easy to idealize someone else's marriage from a distance; but from all accounts, Eugen (whose name is sometimes spelled "Ugin") and Edna were a match made in heaven. He came into her life when she was physically frail, and we are tempted to regard Eugen as the "Love of Dreams" she imagined when she was a girl struggling in Camden. She had become one of the most famous and admired women in America, and he was content to stand in her shadow. Her circle of friends included many of the most distinguished writers, musicians, actors, and visual artists in the world, and her husband was delighted to entertain them.

What Millay would make of all this good fortune is as fascinating and surprising as what she made of her youthful poverty and adversity.

After more than a year of living in a tiny house in Manhattan, the Boissevains purchased the berry farm near Austerlitz, New York, and moved there in June of 1925. The seven-hundred-acre property, on a hillside encircled by wooded mountains, was called "Steepletop" after the steeplebush (hardhack) flowers that grow there.

The two-story wood frame house with its steep roof and central chimney had been built soon after the Civil War. An iron gate guarded the circular driveway. The main entrance to the house—with its sidelights and semicircular transom—was covered by an arched porch with a gabled roof. This door led into a stair hall with a stone floor. Ahead was the dining room, and to the right was the parlor, which ran the length of the house, and enjoyed the southern light through a side door and long windows. The room was large enough to accommodate Millay's two pianos; a bust of Sappho stood in the corner. Linen curtains with a floral pattern softened the light. The couple often took their meals in this room before the fire.

On the other side of the entrance hall was the kitchen, and beyond the kitchen was another small room with a wood-burning stove.

Up a narrow staircase from the front door was the poet's library, a long room that extended across the front of the house. Her vast book collection crammed the shelves on all four walls: dictionaries and grammars in many languages, law books, volumes on nature and horse-racing, as well as her personal library of poetry, fiction, and philosophy. She kept every book she and her mother had ever owned, and many of these were annotated. Next to the library was a large room Millay used for her study, one door of which led to her bedroom and another to the bath. Through a short hallway at the stair landing was the main entrance to Edna's bedroom. Eugen's bedroom lay on the other side of the stairway, in an ell-shaped recent addition, above the kitchen.

The house overlooks a terrace where the couple planted a splendid rose garden. This slopes to a clearing where they installed a wet bar and a swimming pool, a small park and an amphitheater, some benches, and statues of nymphs and fauns. Features and outbuildings included a guest-house, a barn, a cabin Edna used as a writing studio, and a tennis court.

Steepletop would serve as Millay's home and sanctuary for the rest of her life. Mr. and Mrs. Boissevain entertained magnificently, and their gracious estate was a magnet for New Yorkers who took the train up from the city. Frequent house guests mentioned in these pages are the poet Arthur Davison Ficke (1883–1945) and his wife Gladys. Arthur and Edna had been friends since the discovery of "Renascence," and subsequently became lovers. He remained so devoted to Millay that he eventually purchased a farm near Steepletop to be near her. Other visitors included Cora Millay, Edna's mother, the great poet Elinor Wylie (1885–1928) and her husband, also a poet, William Rose Benét (1886–1950). The novelist Floyd Dell (1887–1969), another lifelong friend and lover of Millay's, was a welcome guest whose attentions to the married Elinor Wylie created a tension that was not quite welcome even during the freewheeling 1920s.

[The opera star Lawrence Tibbett inscribes this gift diary to Millay, 1927]

This is the day of the first
"King's Henchman"

And this just a small remembrance
Of a great pleasure—
that of meeting and knowing you.
with the admiration of
Lawrence Tibbett

New York City—February 17, 1927

March 1

Back in Steepletop, & Gladys [Ficke] with us. Everybody worn out & dead for a little sleep. We are all retiring at nine o'clock. Our little Elsie [a housemaid] has learned to cook in our absence, as we directed her to do, & served us a sparse but well-seasoned dinner. All the way up from New York the roads seen from the train windows were muddy and black,— everybody going on wheels; but here the drifts still so deep Stanley could hardly get us through with a sled & two horses.[1]

March 2

8 o'clock, and I'm already in bed. We all went to West Stockbridge today to get provisions, taking the two horses & the front runners only of the big wood-sled.[2] The snow is very deep. In many places we were obliged to leave the road & go over the fields. Everybody is tired tonight, & sleeping,—I most of all. Wore my funny belt for the first time today, that Dr. Bache says I must wear continuously until I get a little fat on my bones to help hold up my innards.[3] Very tight & uncomfortable, and yet in a way pleasant, a support for my back, something to lean against. But I don't like it much, & I'm drinking milk & cream all day long, in order to get fat in a hurry & be able to leave it off. Ugin [Eugen] was all dressed up today in his plus fours & a new sweater & looked very handsome. My boy's knickers don't look so nice on me with my belt on as they did before.

March 3

Nine o'clock. I am sitting up in bed drinking my milk & cream * milk-sugar night-cap. It has been a bitter cold blustery day, with high wind and snow flying. Gene [Eugen] & Gladys walked over the hills to the ruined house on Pearson's land. Gladys is mad about the place & wants to buy it.

I suggested to Elsie today that she warm the dinner plates, and a few minutes later she told Gene she was going to leave on Saturday. I hope to Heaven she'll think better of it,—things are going so smoothly now.

It's a pleasure to write in this beautiful book. Lawrence Tibbett is a great darling to have given it me. I feel a little lonely at moments for the Metropolitan [Opera]—the little crowded back-entrance—the enormous dark house—& the singers in their street clothes, all so simple & friendly & sweet. I miss the Henchman.[4] And so does Ugin.

March 4

Elsie left this morning,—too lonely, she said. I connect her loneliness with the fact that Gene discharged the hired boy yesterday. Such a dreadful little boy,—but apparently both women liked him a lot. It is so funny—we installed her here the day we left for New York, that she might get used to the place during our absence. We return, & she promptly leaves, taking with her her full four weeks' wages—earned by cooking her own meals & those of the other servant!

Gene & Gladys went to Austerlitz to see Frank Wolfe about Pearson's land, only to find that it is sold.[5] They spent some time going over the little old house between us & Austerlitz. Gladys & Arthur [Ficke] may buy that. Prices are going up enormously even in the two years since we bought Steepletop. —Eggert of the *Columbia Inn* found a long piece about the *Henchman* in his German newspaper & was very thrilled.

March 5

A little too much cream & butter today, in my zeal to get fat quick. So I was very sick in my stomach and stayed in bed & had no dinner at all—lovely baked beans, too, that I made myself! . . . . Gene, Gladys & I went over the old house on the road to Austerlitz. Gladys is keen about the place. Most lovely view from here. —Brooks & his wife from Austerlitz happened to be in the old house when we arrived, also looking it over. Life is a scream. Why should they be just there just then?—We talked about chickens. Stanley went to Pittsfield by the 1 o'clock [train].[6]

March 6, Sunday

Ugin made the world's best cocktails for dinner tonight. —I played the Henchman all afternoon. Ugin came forward with the monstrous proposal that we go down to New York on the 11th to hear it again.

I gave Madeleine [house servant] a copy of the book. —Gladys read her play "Papa Was Right"—started by her & Ugin in Sante [*sic*] Fe just as a joke—but somehow very interesting & full of good lines & laughs.

March 7

Gladys left for Santa Fe today. Gene & I took her to the train. Lovely soft weather. Stanley didn't come in all this morning, so Gene had to milk the cow & harness the horses. He was furious. —On the way back from State Line we stopped to see Bailey, & Gene engaged him to work for us in Stanley's place.[7] When we got home we heard Stanley roaring & singing to himself in Tamarack [a cottage across the road from the main house], dead drunk. He had "clinned the steebles," he informed us. He milked the cow, & on the way up from the barn fell twice in the snow, & the milk with him.

March 8

Rain—& thaw. The brooks are raging torrents. The horses are standing in water in the stables. . . .

Gene had a talk with Stanley—but he's so in love with the graceless drunken bum that he never scolds him properly.

"That's right boss," says Stanley. "Gimme the devil, boss. I deserve it." —And Gene comes back grinning sheepishly, & says, "Oh hell, what's the use. He's no good, but I can't help liking him."

Some of the little lilac bushes Mother raped from the House of the Swallow & transplanted here are putting out leaf-buds already.

"That's right, boss," said Stanley, "a man hadn't ought to work when he's drunk. He don't enjoy his work, & he don't enjoy his drunk."

March 9

Today on the front page of the [New York] *World* we came upon "$100 a day for Poet of King's Henchman" and an article telling how my book has already sold 10,000 copies.[8] Sometimes I get a kick out of things like that—oftener I don't. But this time I did. I was thrilled to death. That the amount of royalties I get for a book of poems should be of front page interest to the great New York public—well, I just sat for ten minutes with my eyes sticking out, drinking it in. —Oh, what a thrilling winter this has been! Ugin & I—what fun we've had!—how happy we are!

March 10

This is really the first day of spring. All I wanted to do was sit in the sun. And Ugin & the dog & the cat & the cows & the horses & the pigs all felt the same. We went to Austerlitz for the mail with Brownie [one of the horses] & the red sled. The snow was so nearly gone on much of the road that I believe the next time will be on wheels, though on East Hill the drifts are still so deep we had to go over the field as usual. Received from Bunny today his book of dialogues and plays "Discordant Encounters," & nearly went blind reading it, I found it so fascinating.[9] I had no idea he could create living characters as he does, or write dialogue so marvelously. I had thought of him as an essayist purely. Great thrill. Ugin & I go tomorrow to New York for one night only, to hear the *Henchman*—if we can get seats. —Four at least of the baby pines Mother pulled up by the roots & Harry & I transplanted are alive & growing; the fifth may be under the snow. —

Apple-sauce for dinner tonight—put up in August or September—just as if it had been made today—I never get used to this—it is much more wonderful than the telephone—well, I don't know—the telephone is wonderful, too—Stanley dead drunk today when Bailey called for him, and didn't come.

March 11
420 Park Avenue

Here we are chez Mr. & Mrs. Mabon. We have just come back from *The King's Henchman*. Most lovely performance tonight. Easton went up in her lines terribly in the second act, but nobody noticed & it didn't matter at all. Mrs. Mabon was crazy about it. —They made us take curtain calls again tonight. . . .

House for Henchman sold out again to standing room. Couldn't get a thing. But Mrs. Mabon has seats in Opera Club, so it was all right. Saw Deems & Mary [Taylor] in between entre acte. Deems looks sick. He is tired out, I think. Mrs. Tibbett told Ugin that everybody has told him he is known as The Sheik of New York. He is pleased as anything.

March 12 (written March 23)

Took 3:20 from New York. Bailey met us at State Line with wagon. Changed at Stanley's for sleigh. Left Bailey at Stanley's & Ugin & I started on alone. In the dark, going over the field to avoid deep snow, we mistook the gap in the hedge & turned into the road too early. Horses in snow up to their bellies, foundered, became frightened, reared, & plunged aside into thicket. I was struck smartly across the left eye by a branch of a tree. Incredible pain, million constellations, very sick for a few minutes. But said nothing, not considering it very serious, & went back to fetch Stanley while Ugin held the horses. Stanley & Bailey came with ax & cut us out of the thicket. —When we arrived home my eye frightfully swollen, discolored & disfigured, & extremely painful.

March 13 (written March 23)

My eye very bad. The slightest increase of light, causing the pupil to contract, is like the stab of a sword. The sudden striking of a match in the room, untold agony. Cannot open my eyes at all—to open the right, brings on a loathsome, surging pain in the left as well. Ugin has to feed me all day, & give me dreadfully big mouthfuls of cold meat & potato, that roll off my fork. —I feel very mizzy indeed!

March 14 Monday (written April 8)

Went to Pittsfield to see oculist. Long drive by wagon to Bailey's house, my eyes heavily bandaged so that Gene has to lift me in & out, from there telephoned for motor from Troy's in W. Stockbridge. Finally got to P. Man very serious about my eyes, much to my surprise. I had supposed he would only say "tut, tut," or "Life is like that," or something like that. But he didn't. He was terribly serious. Abrasion of the cornea. If inflammation set in, might be troublesome. I felt frightened, odd & not a little important. He gave me belladonna drops to put in three times a day till it heals.[10] This is supposed to stop the horrid sharp pain when the lights go on. Also, it must be bathed with very hot water for twenty minutes stretches five times a day.

Ugin saw a red-winged blackbird.

March 16 Wednesday

Auction. —Beautiful day. Eugen went to auction of Judge McClellann's things. I couldn't go, my eye was so bad. The belladonna distends the pupil about ten times the size of the other, it gives me a crazy look, besides being very painful still.

March 23 Wednesday

This is the day of the fourth "King's Henchman," and we are not there to hear it. —I have not written in my diary since a week ago Saturday, when I nearly had my eye put out. Apparently I am going to pull through, and see as well as at any time during the past two years, which is damn poorly. —Today we dug up around the rhubarb, and put manure and coal-ashes (which we thought were wood ashes) around the roots. —If our egregious Madeleine, whom I have long since christened "The Countess Gruffanuff," becomes much more sulky & uncivil, I shall *have* to fire her. —Stanley, Bailey, McCagg & John Pinney are all working for us now . . .[11]

The delphinium is up. —In the last week or so, bluebirds, song-sparrows, & robins have all returned.

March 24

Today, sitting in the living-room, we heard suddenly the incredible but unmistakable sound of a motor-car on the road,—a road closed by snow for more than three months to everything but ourselves & our two horses. It was a tiny little Ford, & it was coming to our house. In it was a young woman from the other side of Austerlitz, her mother & her brother-in-law. The young woman is named Elsie Shutfelt, she is an experienced cook, prefers the country to the city, and wants to cook for us. So we engaged her, for twelve weeks.

Gene & I went down for the mail. —Stanley not here today. We paid him off yesterday, so he'll probably be drunk for a few days. —Frightfully cold day. Water frozen in the glass beside my bed last night. . . .

March 25

Very cold. This morning, hearing certain birds, I looked out & saw Frank
Wolfe standing in the road. He had motored over as far as the post-office
& walked up the hill to bring us news that the land next door to us is Arthur's for the buying. There is a very *complicated* business including Hall the
coal-man of Chatham who was buying the property but couldn't pay off
the mortgage before the time of foreclosure, April 1st. We pay Hall, which
enables him to pay off the mortgage, thus saving his face, & he turns over
the property to us, for Arthur & Gladys. —Hooray!

March 27 Sunday

Well, my wonderful cook can't cook. And that's that. She can't cook even
as well as I can. In fact, she's pretty awful. She is a sweet little girl. I wish
to God she could cook. —And if that were all. I had to ask her to serve at
the table, because Madeleine swore she wouldn't do it, & I was too soft or
too tired to kick her out. And apparently they think they're running a 60
cent blue-plate restaurant,—everything is brought on all slopped together
on one plate, & cold at that. And to cap it all, at dinner I notice to my pity
& horror that the poor child has malformed hands & arms & is so awkward she seems about to drop every dish she handles.

Young Moran sent his two sows over to visit our young boar. They put
them into the pen with ours, & a marvelous fight ensued, in which one of
our sows had an ear half torn off, so that John Pinney had to stalk her
around the pen for an hour with a smoking puff-ball to staunch the blood.
—This morning ground white with snow. —But it melts in the daytime.
—More snow tonight.

March 28 Monday

On this day several things happened. Ugin & I spent the morning burning the old bean & potato vines. Velvet Paw [the cat] had a dreadful fit
under an apple-tree & suffered frightfully. Ugin fetched some milk but she
refused it. I wrapped her in my woolen scarf & she lay in the sun for a long
time, complaining most pitifully, & following us with her eyes if we made
a step to leave her. Our cook baked some wonderful cakes with two kinds
of icing, & we felt quite cheered up.

Mrs. Tanner came to do the washing, & it was fun to see the white sheets flapping on the line, the first time of this year.[12] —Ugin & I drove down for the mail & stopped in the Columbia Inn to phone Frank Wolfe about Arthur's property. Sat at the table in the jolly bar-room & got tight on Muscatel. Came home roaring & laughing & nudging & shouting obscenities.

Arrived home to hear from Madeleine that Elsie was lying in her room sick with an attack of appendicitis. I went up to her. She begged to be taken home, saying her mother knew what to do. So Ugin had to harness the horses again all by himself in the dark & drive her home. I am sorry she is ill, but heartily glad she is gone. It made me nervous, feeling she was not strong enough for the work, but I hated to discharge her for fear of hurting her feelings. She was more comfortable when he left her. Apparently nothing acute.

March 29

Today Ugin & I sawed down the rotted pear-tree & the twisted young maple on the lawn, & now the snow-ball bush stands alone & very impressive. We transplanted two little snow-ball bushes that had budded themselves from the big one. . . . Bailey, Pinney & McCagg shoveled the plaster out of Tamarack onto the wagon & dragged load after load to our driveway & dumped it on the road. Mrs. Tanner washed & ironed all day. The beautiful new towels we got at the Maison de Blanc are all done up & look nothing less than ducal . . .[13]

—I weigh 103, as against 96 I weighed in Dr. Bache's office before he left town about March 1. . . . Stanley hasn't come back since Saturday. Gene says he is poisoned by the Italian liquor-dispenser of West Stockbridge, the descendents of Catherine de Medici.

March 30

Horrid raw wind. Nasty day. Transplanted two big snow-ball bushes. All the plaster is out of Tamarack & the house looks almost fit to live in, now that it stands lately-washed, shorn of its incestuous Polish tenants & their unimaginable filth. I say incestuous advisedly, Stanley having intimated that that was about all they had to do to amuse themselves in the winter, not being fond of reading. "That why they're all so pale," he said. Dear me, I must read again, "Tis Pity She's a Whore," to get the unpleasant taste out of my mouth.[14]

We drove down for the mail & went hunting for Mrs. Quigg's cook, who is apparently free now. She's in New York for a few days. —Mrs. Tanner here again today, doing the ironing. Elinor [Wylie] writes that she will come this Friday. And Madeleine has requested just this week-end to go to Pittsfield. But never mind. If it will only just get a little warmer I don't care.

March 31 Thursday [Eugen's entry]

Vincie felt terribly bad today. Awful head & indis.—therefore washed hair cleaned bathroom & autographed 200 pages for the 3rd special edition of the Henchman, when Ugin stopped her doing more. . . .

—Artie's money had not arrived & I paid with our money. Deed will finally be turned over to us next Saturday. Wolfe & Ugin got drunk at inn. Vincent saw poor Stanley visiting the cows & looking for horses. . . .

Madeleine is worried that house won't be nice enough in order for Elinor.

Lots of coal left for furnace & stoves.

Goodnight all. Please stand by. Ugin announcer.

April 1 Friday

Went to the station to fetch Elinor, but again she didn't come. We were desolate, & furious, & cold & ready to cry. On the way home we turned into a grass road by mistake & had to turn. I was off hunting for the road & saw Gene turning the horses on a steep embankment & thought he was going to be killed. —Madeleine wanted to go to Pittsfield for a few days, so we took her down when we went to meet Elinor. When Elinor didn't come we vowed we'd never go to meet anybody again, especially a night train, so dark & nervous & dangerous.

Borrowed fifteen cents from a man named Murphy in the station to telephone to Chatham. But the hateful man said there was a wire but he had already mailed it & wouldn't read us the copy. We hated him. We hated everybody.

April 2

Tonight they really came, Bill [William Rose Benét] & Elinor.[15] We sent Bailey to meet them, because we couldn't believe they would really come. It was too wonderful to have them here—dear Bill—my beautiful Elinor! —Today Gene went to Chatham with Wolfe to finish paying for Arthur's land—Arthur's money had come—all fixed up now—and think! —Arthur & Gladys own the land right next to ours—and will build there!—and tonight Elinor was talking of getting a place near here.

Bailey & Harry went down to Auster[litz]—two trips—& got the auction furniture from Grant's—all here but the mirrors. Gene & I tried to get things in shape before Elinor got here & got nervous & tired—but we did save just enough time to get a bath & dress. I dumped a lot of the bath-salts Gene got in Chatham into my bath, & it left a mauve line around the tub, & the whole place smelled like a whore-house.

Ugin & I had a lovely row about Shelley—a long lovely gentle jeering row.[16]

April 3

This morning Mrs. Tanner came bringing the first mayflowers—the very first flowers we have seen this year. Elinor, Bill, Gene & I walked up to the top of the hill & looked at the Catskills & all the beautiful hills spread out. I found a spruce tree, the only one, I believe, on our place. I was so happy to see it. There were several babies standing around it, clinging to its skirts. We shall adopt two or three & bring them nearer the house.

Tonight Elinor read us, or rather Bill read us, Elinor's new short story, "A Birthday Cake for Lionel"—the most delightful story imaginable.

I read aloud—which I shouldn't do, because it strains my eyes so, but never mind—two or three poems from *The White Rooster* by George O'Neill— some lovely things in this book.

April 4

Had to take Bill to the station today—we all drove down—such a lovely drive in the day-time—so perilous & terrifying at night with nothing to light the road.

Coming home we saw a crow driving a hawk from its neighborhood, swooping at it & rising & swooping,—the hawk sailing steadily off—but *off!*

This afternoon I lay on the couch before the living room fire & Elinor read me from [Robert] Browning things we both used to love & half know by heart—*Love Among the Ruins*—& *The Spanish Cloister,*—and other things—such fun. —Gene sent Stanley home drunk & Mrs. Tanner followed him to see that he didn't set fire to the house—so we were without a cook & Gene got a beautiful dinner.

—Tonight Elinor told Gene & me from beginning to end the story of her strange & wonderful life up to the present moment, a most engrossing tale, full of tragedy. —She is the most lovely creature. Gene is crazy about her. If he weren't, I'd be furious.

April 5

Ugin brought up breakfast to Elinor & me in my bed & made a lovely fire in my fireplace.

Elinor, Gene & I drove down to Austerlitz in a snow-storm, Gene on the seat & Elinor & I tucked in on the floor, facing back. Went to Columbia Inn & drank muscatel & read mail. Elinor loved it. —In the evening we discussed relative weight of *St. Agnes' Eve & Epipsychidion*—not as poems— but as love-poems, Elinor holding that the last twenty lines or so of it are highly sensuous & impassioned, I insisting that, except for a phrase or two, they are so much rhetorical hot air.[17] —Later she read aloud from Shelley—the lovely little, "if thou couldn't be as thou hast been" once, & "Less oft is peace in Shelley's mind" & "Listening to my sweet piping." Finally she read the *West Wind*.[18] "The Best Poem Ever Written!" she cried when she finished. I did not dispute her. I do not think naturally in terms of best—next-best. I think I love the *Grecian Urn* better.[19] But I am not sure.

This morning Elinor read to herself from *Mortal Image,* while I played first Chopin, then Bach, then Beethoven on the piano.[20] I play so badly. But not too badly, I think, to be allowed to play them. And sometimes, for a few minutes, I know that I am playing well. It is fun, Elinor there reading,—& listening, too.

April 6 Wednesday

Madeleine returned yesterday afternoon.

Today warm & springlike. . . .

Madeleine doesn't do the chores now that she does the cooking—the cooking consisting chiefly of frying a few potatoes & opening a couple of cans, but never mind. Anyway, his [Eugen's] bed is never made, & I hate it. However, we all dress for dinner, & that helps a lot. —When we drove back this afternoon, Altair [their German shepherd] was in the driveway waiting for us, crouching with his head on his paws all ready to spring up & leap about us, the cutest attitude & the most darling little figure I ever saw. He must know the sound of the Maxwell for he barks at strange cars.

April 7 Thursday

Elinor has gone. We brought her to the train in the Maxwell. As we drew near the station a train pulled in, going in the right direction. We were frantic. We swung up to the platform, leapt from the car waving & shrieking. The train had started again. The engineer, the brakeman, a porter, lots of passengers & the conductor looked out & saw us, and the train stopped again. We ran to the steps, dragging Elinor's big bag & the bundle of autographed sheets for the new special edition of the Henchman. And came the conductor to the platform to let us aboard. "Is this the New York train?" we gasped. "Albany!" he snapped. And the train pulled out again.

This morning Elinor said she had read Kathleen's "Wayfarer" & didn't like it.[21] I asked if she hadn't liked the second part; she didn't remember—I gave it her & made her sit down & read the part about Mother's life on the Maine farm, which is so beautifully treated. "Why, this is lovely!" she said after a little while. "I never read this." She had confused it with something else. —I am very tired. All this strenuous reading & discussing is bad for my head & bad for my eyes. But Lord! What fun it is! —She is such a delight, my wonderful friend. And Gene enjoys it all as much as I do.

April 8 Friday

Gave Up Smoking

I think it possible that cigarettes may make my headache worse. And Gene has been getting a thumping heart, so he has given it up, too. But he's suffering pitifully & making the most awful fuss already, though we've only given it up for about six hours.

Read in the World that Janet Mabon made a very good impression at her recital, & sang well & everybody loved it. So very glad for them all.

April 9 Saturday

Heard a phoebe this morning. Heard also for the first time this year Sebastian, one of last year's song-sparrows. Eugen & I worked all day digging & transplanting the snow-ball bushes that had budded themselves from the old tree, & raked & burned the driveway circle & other odd jobs. Most lovely day. —Ugin is kicking & screaming terribly about not having cigarettes. I don't see how he can stick it out if he goes on like this. —Tonight I discovered in an old book of sonatas the most lovely thing of Mozart which I had never seen before & never heard. Played it over all evening, over & over—it is a splendid thing—thrilling from beginning to end. I had the most gorgeous time playing it. I believe I will try to learn it by heart.

A man came bringing five gallons of excellent applejack—fourteen dollars per gallon—an *awful* lot of money. But what's a fellow to do if he mayn't smoke? He's gotta poison himself somehow. . . .

April 10 Sunday

Last night got into bed to write up the day's events in this book & found my pen empty. Not ink enough to write the word Sunday—only ink enough to make a big horrid blob on one of the beautiful new towels from the Grande Maison de Blanc that was on my night table in place of a runner. Thank God the first spot has been made, & it was I who made it.

Weighed in at 104. Man came from Albany to see about surveying Arthur's property. —Drove down for the mail. Received furious letter from mother in answer to my note in which I said, regarding the W. K. Stevedore motif, "Gee, what of it?—It isn't true—but, hell it might have been. Who cares?"—or words to that effect. She's raging, snorting flames, poor old girl, & high-hatting me something wicked.[22]

Heard—just once—the song of Sebastian, one of last year's song-sparrows. —Finished transplanting snow-ball bushes—put wood ashes on lawn. —The Countess is getting a bit out of hand. Pretends not to understand, & does things wrong, or sulks. However, I'm not afraid of her anymore. "Madeleine, are you ill?" I say: "Then why isn't the chamber-work done?"—I'll learn her, the vaporous poetic bitch.

April 11

Clock stopped this morning. Wound again.

Bailey & Pinney cut down the beautiful unknown bush with the big round buds that we were going to transplant when we should become sufficiently expert. It was in the way of their fence, so they whacked it down. I cried, when I found it all cut off. Great flat-footed, fat-headed galumphing dumb-bells.

Mrs. Tanner here all day ironing. Madeleine made her do the chamberwork, so she might sit on her tail all afternoon & make herself a brassiere. Consequence is the bath-tub has not been scrubbed out all day. I believe I shall fire the Countess tomorrow. Why should I pay her fifteen iron kisses per week for giving me indigestion all the time, I have just now begun to ask myself.

—Me & Ugin motored to Great Barrington & got us each a hair-cut. Had mine shingled.[23] I look very funny & skun [*sic*].—but I'll wash it tomorrow, & then it will look cute. Anyway, it did last summer.

April 12

This morning got up early, both, at about 7:30,—Altair found a nest of baby moles. They must just have been born, three of them, all red & grey, with their ugly mouths opening & shutting & this little claw moving up and down. We remembered that they were moles, and that we are farmers, so we killed them. It made me really sick. And I cried. It is true that my tears come easily, at times. But life is cruel, & on a farm very cruel—there's no getting around that. It was thinking of their mother that made me cry. She had just given birth to them, strange little blind creatures—smelled smoke & saw pillar of smoke over hill—thought it on Arthur's land— further away—forest fire set by burning off a field. Gene & I went & helped fight it with shovels—man came with tractor—big International 10-20, & plowed in a hour [*sic*] an enormous piece up the side of a steep hill. We have bought it. It is wonderful. But it gave me a little chill of apprehension seeing it there on the sky-line. I wonder, shall we make a success of it here—so very many have failed.

Sweet cable from Drafna, thanking me for the little flowers sent Gene's father.

April 13

Distressed tonight reading the case of Francesco Caruso, found guilty of murder in the first degree for killing the doctor who he thought had killed his child—poor dark brain in tumult.[24] And now they will execute him—but that will teach him nothing. Whom will it teach?—whom will his death instruct to be good & wise, that would not learn as much from a ten year prison term?—a slovenly school, this capital punishment, hysterical & lazy & afraid.

———————————

Went to Chatham to do some shopping. Have put Madeleine back on her old job & Gene & I are doing the cooking. —Autographed a good many books—Gene helping me to wrap, tie & stamp them—& got them off. . . .

April 14

Wound big clock at 10 p.m. It had stopped at 7.

Demonstrator of electric washer & ironer came again from Pittsfield, but must come tomorrow to show the washer. Tried the iron, really very exciting, very simple, too. If it will do sheets properly I must have it. . . .

—Sent back the Conning Tower watch to Betteridge today & told them they know what they could do with it, or words to that effect.[25] It is the world's worst watch, & no damn good whatsoever, so they can keep it.

April 15 Friday [Eugen's entry]

Electric washer demonstrator came. He & Vincie worked all day. We are crazy about washer & ironer. —Whole wash done & ironed in one day. —(Including 12 sheets).

Lime mixer machine arrived.

Vincie got letter from Thomas Hardy.[26]—

Stanley came & is coming to work Monday.—

Mrs. Tanner and a [illegible] pie & cake.

Ugin saw a downy woodpecker.

The Countess is going to enter church next Sunday. (I hope she stays till Xmas.)

Put sweet peas in soak. Will plant them Easter Sunday. Vincie says, it proves we believe in resurrection.

We both are furious about a letter which the pen women of A. [America] have sent to Elinor. Vincie is going to give them the devil.

Peterson really sent the men to work on the road.

April 16 Saturday

Bought a pink hyacinth for Easter.

Last day of school! —I mean to say, Countess Gruffanuff has given notice! All day long I've been busting out in song—can't contain myself, I'm so happy —She says she's leaving Tuesday; if you ask me, I think she's leaving tomorrow. —Freddy [Eugen's nephew, a landscape gardener] threatening to descend on us any moment like a plague of locusts, but not yet arrived.

—Gene's bootlegger is at the door. We are getting a five-gallon keg of apple-jack to keep in the wood for a year. (At least, that's the big talk we're making now.) —Took one cigarette tonight & smoked it between us, gravely, calumet-fashion. It tasted awful—made Ugin giddy, & light & dirty feeling on my tongue. We had no desire for another. —Mrs. Tanner did some mending & baking. She's so nice & human & friendly after that Gruffanuff! —Soon the house will be ours again, & we won't have to take a deep breath & square our shoulders before diving into the kitchen. Saw a yellow-bellied sapsucker & a flicker.

April 17

The Countess has gone. —I told her she needn't wait till Tuesday on *my* account. But her gloomy presence still is felt—though chicken dinner in the kitchen tonight displaced it somewhat. Saw a beautiful bird—about 5 in. blueish green back or greenish blue, with some black & white stripes (suggested a blue jay)—yellow spot on head—yellow breast with some black—very active, never still. Cannot find in my bird-book. Found another lollipop-bush across the road, though not as beautiful as the one the man cut down. Transplanted it. Terribly long central root. Am afraid it hasn't much chance. —Planted about half the sweet peas. The ends of our fingers are so rough from this garden work that they made a scratchy noise when we turned back the silk cover of my bed. —Gynie the white horse was shut in the pasture & wanted to get out. We were watching him & we actually saw him lift the top bar of the gate with his teeth, drop it on the ground & begin on the next one. We stopped him just in time!

[Insert at top of the page from May 8:] *Max was here and I told him about Gynie & he was shocked that we stopped him.*[27] *"Why didn't you watch him," said Max, "& see what he would do?"—and I was shocked at myself when I considered the incident.*

20 of the rhubarb we transplanted last year have come up.

Weight 106.

Heard hill-frog from swamp tonight.

April 18

The loveliest day that ever dawned. A soft warm, really caressing breeze. And so wonderful to have that woman away! —Gene went down to A[uster-litz] & rescued the Mercer from Ferry's barn, where she's been since three days before Christmas when we got stuck in the snow at 2 a.m. on our way home from Santa Fe [New Mexico] via N.Y. —She looks so beautiful in her new coat of paint that Robert gave her—such a beautiful car. —I almost finished the sweet-peas. —The boy who sold us the barbecue last year called this evening & we ordered a lot of shrubs & roses & things. Terribly exciting. I wrote a letter to the League of American Penwomen, telling them where to get off—for inviting Elinor to be Guest of Honor & then writing her canceling the invitation on the grounds that she is not a respectable person.[28] The sanctified flatfooted gadgets. —I wish I had been a Fifth Avenue street sparrow yesterday—or in other words:

> I wish to God I might have shat
> On Mrs. Grundy's Easter hat.

April 19

Warm as summer. Stayed in bed all day—nearly—with some thirst, but no fever. —Tractor man came—plowed with tractor—got out of gas. — Planted some sweet-peas —I sitting in deck-chair wrapped in rugs. House is nearly all scraped—soon painting begins. —Ugin smokes pipe now,—no cigarettes—& loves it! I don't crave smoking now—except very seldom. — The delphiniums are marvelous—but most of the foxgloves & holly-hocks died.

April 20 Wednesday

Stayed in bed all day with a sore throat. Very dirty-looking right tonsil, but no fever. Gene went to Chatham, & did a thousand errands. Got some nasty medicine, comprised, I believe, of equal part creosote, varnish & old pipe stems—from Dr. Stacks for my throat. —Heard the first tree-toads & peepers tonight. —A flock of those little red birds were here again that came for a day or two last April, feeding among the dead leaves & singing a most lovely warbling song. I am not sure what they are—purple finches, perhaps. —Mrs. Tanner brought me up such a nice luncheon of mush-room soup & cold chicken, &, for my poor throat, lemonade & red currant jelly. —Received from Harper's a special presentation copy of the *Henchman,* all bound in the most beautiful red morocco with hand-tooled edges—"leather tooled fair," to quote a recent popular success.

April 21

The pasture fence is finished & the cows have been turned into the pasture. They look beautiful—especially Dolly, the white one, rubbing her head against a wild apple-tree, with the yellow willows on the left.

Saw from the bathroom window a meadow-lark sitting in the top of the tallest maple & singing. Saw very plainly his big yellow breast & the black mark on his throat. A great many flickers about, making that strange little sound like a whiskey-drinking dove.

> That strange little sound like a whiskey-drinking dove
> That the yellow-hammer makes when he's very much in love.

First thunder-shower this evening.

Harry worked with tractor. Some trouble getting the disks in front of the plows adjusted. Very hot all day—delicious—a thrilling day—every plant grew at least six inches between 7 a.m. & 7 p.m. . . . .

April 22

Saw a barn-swallow this morning. Saw also a new bird I had never seen before, but identified it immediately as a ruby-throated kinglet—which it was.

Rained all day—very foggy. Went out only for a few minutes—afraid for my throat which is little bit better but still bad. Gene goes to Pough-

keepsie tomorrow to fetch Max Eastman & his Russian wife Eliena. —
Spent all afternoon making up my seed & plant list for Dreer—it comes
to $77—less than I expected.[29] —Had a sweet fire in my bedroom, & a big
fire downstairs. —My throat still sore & hateful . . .

Weight 109!

April 23

This morning the ground white with snow. Gene went to Poughkeepsie to
fetch Max & Eliena. Altair & I took a walk to the blue-bird pasture. I gathered yellow pussy-willows & red maple flowers, & a few may flowers. . . .

April 24 Sunday

Cold. Snowed a little. Gene took Max & Eliena up to the top of High
Hill. They got some lovely may flowers.

The fattest woman in the world called here, having seen my ad in the
Chatham Courier, seeking to become a combination house-maid, & stenographer. We've taken her on for a fortnight, to begin Wednesday. But I
don't see how she can be a stenographer, for I'm sure she can't cross her
knees. Had beautiful roast chicken which Mrs. T prepared before she
left,—but while we were talking with Max about the value, if any, of anthologies of verse, the onions burned on. Max doesn't mind anthologies,
as such. I hate 'em.

Opened one of the last jars of raspberries—incredibly fresh & delicious.

April 25

Stayed in bed most all day, feeling mizzy. But got up in the afternoon &
motored to Albany with Ugin, to take M & E to the train. —Several
howling blizzards of snow during the day, but cleared before sunset, beautiful for the drive.

Opened one of the last jars of red strawberries—so good, so good!
Max says if I get fatter, I'll feel better. He did.

April 26

This was the day of my encounter with the Juggernaut.[30] From the on-
rushing wheels of the tractor I save, for the present, at least, my favorite
patch of wild strawberries—covering an area not quite so big as my bath-

room. But everybody was very much upset, because I was interfering with the straight line from X to Y. —And I knew that soon that day would come when all the wild strawberries, & all the daisies & hawkweed would be ploughed under to make a straight line for the tractor. —So I went down into the clearing below the blueberry pasture, & cried & cried & cried. —The most dreadful day, physically, that ever dawned, icy cold & the wind blowing a gale, deafening & confounding.

April 27

Ugin & I decided to take it a little easier, & not try to do much farming till we get a few decent servants in the house. We have to watch ourselves, apparently, just like the other city fellers, or we'll do too much & get worn out, & chuck it & go to Madrid to visit Velvet [?].[31]

The Fat Lady arrived—she is really too darned fat for anything but a circus, I'm afraid. —Took John Pinney to C[hatham] to buy harness—got a beautiful double harness all babied up with brass, & we have ordered plumes.

The house is getting its first coat of paint now & is dazzling.

April 28

We are buying the two handsomely blackish horses—they look like a million dollars in the new harness. —Man came with 160 Japanese blackberries & we set all hands to putting them along the drive.

Grace (her name is Grace!) won't do, I'm afraid, except, perhaps as a stenographer; we'll try her on that tomorrow. Motoring to Chatham to see a person who answered our ad. —house-maid, liked her & engaged her on the spot for a week from Monday. —Got stuck in the Mercer & had to leave it in Spencertown. Bander brought us up in his Ford—ignominy!

April 29 Friday

Gene went with team to fetch Mercer. It has a loose chain somewhere & we can't get it till next week. However, the Maxwell battery is charged again, so all is well. Ugin saw a big red fox in a field. I transplanted some hollyhocks. Gene dictated some letters to the Three Graces (my new name for our mountainous stenographer). She is pretty good at that.

At eleven o'clock this morning The Three Graces had not descended from her bower. —We thought she was dead, but decided to have our breakfast before finding out. I went up & knocked. "Grace," said I, "are you ill?" "No," she responded benignly, "just tired out." —So that's that as far as the housework is concerned.

April 30 Saturday

Saw chipping-sparrow, & downy wood-pecker & cherwink. —The shrub & perennials, millions of them, came from Red Hook, & we had two of the men helping us all day setting them out. They are going to be gorgeous. — The cottage is being jacked up & has been raised two inches.

The painting of the house goes steadily forward. —Gene took the Three Graces to Chatham & fetched Mother from the train.

Stanley has not been to work for several days. Mrs. Tanner is sick.

My wonderful new maid I had engaged for Monday week saw Gene & says she's changed her mind—too lonesome out here. —We had forgotten to tell her we have six hired men.

May 1 Sunday

Gene & Mother & I dug up all the woodbine from around the stump in front of Tamarack & set it out around my shanty. Also transplanted a lot of hibiscus & Iceland poppy & Achillea.[32] Ugin did all the cooking & washing dishes today & was a perfect angel. I had a splitting headache, but it was such a lovely day I played around in the garden & strawberries & didn't mind at all. One of my pine geraniums is all ready to bloom. I shall set them out soon. —and my carnations, too. —I have to give a reading in Rochester Friday, & it's such a bore. I don't know what to wear—it's at *noon!* But I get five hundred bucks, so I shouldn't have a nervous breakdown.

May 2 Monday

We gotta cook! We gotta cook! We gotta cook! —Old Mrs. Schaefer of Spencertown, and she's cooked in the Copake Inn, and everybody says she's good! —And maybe her grand-daughter will come and be the house-maid.[33] —All the perennials look lusty & thriving. —The Three Graces came & took some letters. Mrs. Tanner is back. —Also Stanley (this afternoon). —

Somebody has taken the bulb from the cellar-fixture—a mystery. Mrs. T brought me some hepaticas to set out. —Mrs. Eggert gave me some clips from her English Ivy. I put them in water. My seeds & garden tools came from Dreer, but so far no shrubs or roses. —Thunder-storm this p.m. — New moon tonight (I believe) so thin & pretty.

May 3 Tuesday

She's come! She's come! She's come! —And she's lovely—& old-fashioned— & good-natured!

Did all the washing today—Mrs. Tanner, Mrs. Schaefer, & I with the new washing-machine. —Mother went may-flowering & then she went dandelion-greening, just as I knew she would. —I transplanted a lot of Golden-glow into the ruins & some hepaticas Mrs. Tanner brought me. The blood-root is in blossom that I set out last year, & one of the clintonia is up, and the maidenhair fern & the trumpet-honeysuckle & all the little swamp flowers Harrison [Dowd] & I set out last year, ten big marsh marigolds among them. —It pays to transplant. Almost everything lives.

Heard a white-throat sparrow yesterday & today.

May 4

Transplanted some golden-glow into the ruins, & had Stanley put out a lot of day lilies. Day-lilies are very dull company, as flowers go, but they will look bright by the wall.

May 5 Thursday (written May 8)

Motored to Albany to take the train for Rochester where I was to give a reading for the Women's Union. Gene came too. Stenographer here in the morning—got quite some letters off.

On the way to Albany we stopped for the mail & there was a cable from Gene's Mother saying that his old father died this morning. He has been blind for some time & confined to bed & failing. Arrived in R & went to the *Sagamore*.

May 6 Friday

Gave my reading before a dense audience in what seemed like a banquet-hall of the Sagamore. Horrible place to read. Awful acoustics, & people sitting out through the doors into other rooms, & people standing. Hard to make myself heard. Never worked so hard in my life. —But they seemed to like it all right. It was one of the worst readings I ever gave, but Gene says it was not bad, that they liked it a lot. I feel it was awful. Have not read for two years,—since Bowdoin. Out of practice, I imagine. And it was at 2:30, & I had to wear an ordinary dress. —Caught a train immediately after back to Albany. Worn out. —The Maxwell got stuck in the middle of Albany & the starter went dead & Gene had to push & I had to put her in gear & start her that way. Dismal. —We were glad to get home.

May 7 Saturday

Never want to leave Steepletop again. Perfect day. Did a lot of transplanting of perennials. —This afternoon a car drove up & it was Harrison [Dowd].— Great excitement. We knew he was coming but didn't know when.— I put him in charge at once of all the annuals. Saw a cat bird. Saw two white-throat sparrows. They were eating up the grass-seed where we have sown the old driveway to grass, I hadn't the heart to shoo them off.

Burnt up some dry stalks on the ploughed land, & sat around the fire like Navajos, Ugin, Altair & I. Most beautiful evening sky, a long twilight. . . .

May 8 Sunday

Motored to Green River & engaged a housemaid, named Lockwood, to come a week from Monday. Looks capable, but neither of us loved her at first sight.— However.

—Had a flat tire.—

Transplanted two syringa bushes from the old syringa behind the house. Ugin calls it mock-orange,—(Dreer calls it Philadelphus.) What I call lilac, Ugin calls syringes.— Still we manage to get along very well.

Heard a whippoorwill.

One month today since I smoked a cigarette.

May 10 Tuesday

Got a wire that Uncle Fred is dead.[34] So strange. A little while ago Gene got a letter from him all about the blueberries.

Heard & then saw four bobolinks in the big maple in front of the house.

Saw a pair of (possibly) Baltimore orioles & the most brilliant thing in flight I ever saw—red-orange with black and a lot of quivering white—marvelous—breath-taking on a misty day like this. —Ugin & I transplanted a young pine. This p.m. took Molly and Tom hitched to the big wagon, & Bailey to help, & went to the old Hamlin place back on the hill.[35] —such avenues of maples & avenues of giant pines & avenues of tamaracks & elms as were never matched elsewhere, all leading to a heap of boards & laths & a clutter of wheels & potshards. What a house must once have been there! It did not burn down—it was abandoned & fell to pieces years & years ago. —Hundreds of young tamarack crowding each other in a big field—sown from the tall trees. We brought home several and set them out, also a couple of mountain ashes. If only they will grow! They look so beautiful, and add so much to the place.

Wednesday May 11

Saw a pair of gold finches.

Ugin & I went to Chatham—bought pansies, tomatoes & cabbage—& ten crimson geraniums which we set out in a row in the ruins—magnificent.—

Stanley worked on the front stoop, Bailey moving the heavy stones about with Tom & Molly & stone boat. —The town of Austerlitz has begun to repair our road, and it is something terrible. . . . Mrs. Tanner said Velvet caught a bird.[36] I can't bear it. But don't know what to do. —She catches mice, too! —I shall try to keep her shut up for a couple of months. I might put a bell on her, too.

May 12 Thursday

Saw a kingbird. The plants arrived from Dreer—the roses all standing up in little pots so fresh & green & thriving. Bailey went to fetch them with the horses. —Planted some honeysuckles & weigelias & lavender.[37] (The Virginia creeper we dug up & transplanted from the other side of the road, is doing beautifully.) A great deal done in the garden today.

Man & girl got stuck in their car, & Ugin got them out. The man offered him money, & when he wouldn't take it, just turned & went, without a thank-you. —Ugin & I saw a red fox, a vixen with one of her cubs. She was beautiful, pure gold, like a flame moving through the bushes.

May 13 Friday

Darling letter from Elinor, just in sight of England. —Letter from Deems, enclosing my half of the Henchman royalties—$525—this with the $480 or so for the libretto makes an even thousand already, and the royalties from the book sales not due till November. Not so bad.—

May 14 Saturday

Saw in the crabapple tree, all at the same time, a black & white warbler, a black throated blue warbler, & a Blackburnian warbler. Mumbles [her mother], Harrison, Ugin & I all motored to Pittsfield to buy a window for the pantry that's being built. —Saw some lovely models & pictures of doors & garden furniture, too,—& corner cupboards. —Had a lovely drive. Came back a new road, through Lenox & Stockbridge—longer but lovelier.

Bailey & Harry worked on the rose-garden. Ugin saw a thrush—and then I saw it. I think it was a Wilson thrush—but not sure. The shad-blow is in blossom everywhere, & so pretty.[38]

May 15 Sunday

Planted twenty roses in the new garden. It will be charming. The stone walls & steps are sweet. And we are going to have arches & trellises.

The new house-maid came & said she needed a week longer at home before coming here.

May 16

Funny day. Sun—& then showers—& then cold—& then warm—& then thunder-shower—& then hail-storm—& then sun. Mrs. Tanner came & did the wash. Got it dry, between showers. Harrison & I worked all day on the rock garden, slaved on it—& it is about the darlingest thing I ever saw.

The peas are up.

May 17 Tuesday

Raked the new rose-garden, & laid a path of pink & blue slate. . . .

Went to see Mrs. Quigg, a former employer of our imminent house-maid, & learned that she is "lazy, impudent & dirty." So that's that. Dirt I can stand if I must, & laziness grows about us on all sides like the blossoming tansy, but impudence I've had enough of.

May 18 Wednesday

Loathsome disagreeable day. Told Harrison we'd sell him Steepletop for a dollar & forty-six cents. —But in the afternoon the wind died a bit & the sun came out, so took it back. —Took Mother to the train at State Line— for New York. —Saw Mr. Moran who was perfectly pleasant, but his wife turned her back on us. I so much prefer men to women—they are much more civilized. He hates us quite as much as she does, but doesn't get sour & uncivil about it.

Planted four roses on the south side of the house.

Wrote Lockwood, telling her we've changed our plan.

May 19 Thursday

Kathleen's birthday.

Gene went to State Line to fetch Three Graces.

Cook got a pain in her side & had to be taken to her daughter's in Chatham. Gene took her in. So that's that. She won't come back. They don't come back. Well,—that's that.

Put beans in soak tonight by mistake & by mistake paid the cook two dollars extra, thinking it was Friday.

May 20 Friday

Ugin's birthday. Had a lovely cocktail. Got lovely tight—almost.

Went down in the Mercer for the mail, & the right rear wheel came off the Mercer. This being the last of the Mercer's four wheels that have come off, & we still being alive, we voted to sell the Mercer & there was no dissenting voice, so we are going to sell the beautiful faithless Mercer & get a horrid little Nash.

Had baked beans tonight, by mistake.

Mrs. Tanner is here every day doing the work. We do nothing but work in the garden.

Bailey is making beautiful flag-stone paths for us.

Altair had a fight with a woodchuck, & killed it. Ugin & Harrison saw the fight. Altair's mouth is pretty badly cut up, but he's terribly proud.

Lindbergh hopped off this morning for France.[39]

May 21 Saturday

Mrs. Tanner bakes us lovely sweeties, so we shouldn't feel lonesome for Mrs. Schaefer. And it was hot today. So we had lemonade instead of tea.

Gene received from Holland a sheaf of copies of the *Handelsblat* telling all about his father's death & burial, & full of eulogies. His photograph was in one, just as I had seen him. It seems so strange.

Death is a funny business.

Harrison saw a rose-breasted grosbeak. —I want to see it too.

Picked some rhubarb from the Tamarack garden.

All our thoughts with "Lucky Lindberg,—the Flying Fool."

May 22 Sunday

Lovely day, mild & beautiful; with soft wind; Nobody here—no hired men, no servants—lovely. We all worked in the garden all day. Harrison planted lots of annuals. Ugin & I planted a hundred gladiolas (-i—ae)—damnedest word in the whole damned horticultural vocabulary—damned silly, pompous, unwieldy, pretentious, ignorant word. Anyhow, we planted 'em—& the sweet-briers, & the wisteria.

Saw two chipping-sparrows making love.

May 23 Monday

Disagreeable. Rainy. —Gene went down & brought home the Mercer. We've *got* to keep it, anyway, till we get the Maxwell back. Got stuck on the top of East Hill in the mud, & Tom & Molly had to pull him out.

Went to State Line to meet Robert & Anne [Eugen's brother & sister-in-law] & brought them here for the night. Everybody drank quite a lot of applejack. Harrison got more than a little tight. Robert brought us two bottles of sherry.

Great excitement at mail time. Got the Sunday paper & learned that Lindbergh had made Paris. We were frantic with excitement. Norma, also frantic with excitement, had sent us a wire which came in the same mail.

May 24 Tuesday

The baby's-breath is up.

Stayed in bed all day. Horrible head-ache, among other things. Rained all day long, loathsome day.

Had a sweet cheerful fire in my bedroom.

The little brook is swollen, just like the Mississippi, and is washing away the homes of forgetmenots & irises that were just getting settled there.

May 25 Wednesday

Poured all day—till late afternoon. —Harrison planted the dahlias that Mrs. Tanner brought us. I pruned some raspberries & a lot of shrubs. Ugin had to go to Austerlitz with the horses—road too slippery for the car.

The new pantry is all finished but the milk shelves & the painting.

Bailey shingled one of the dormer-windows.

The English ivy slips I got from the Columbia Inn proprietor are beginning to root.

Poor Velvet had the most dreadful fit today. I don't know what to do about it.

The green peas are way up—eight long green rows of them. Treated my sweet-peas today by the secret process the Chatham florist told me about.

Altair is a sight. His back is all white paint & his tail is all green paint.

May 26 Thursday

Poured all day. Horrible. Roads so terribly muddy Ugin & I got stuck in the mud with the Mercer coming back from the post office. Walked back. Weather cleared & became warm & sultry.

Thunder-shower—wind-storm.

Can think of nothing but the weather—horrible—horrible.

May 27 Friday

Cloudy & cold—horrible.

Took Tom & Molly to haul the Mercer out of the ditch. They were marvelous—just one long pull, & out she came. Broke the whiffle-tree.[40]

Gene went to Chatham. Harry [Harrison] & I walked home by Ar-

thur's hill & past our sheep-barn. Blossom was put in the barn with Buttercup tonight & Dolly was all alone.[41] She followed us along the fence &
mooed most plaintively.

Harrison & I found a lot of frogs' eggs in a flat pool, strings & strings
of them, all coiled like the small intestine.

Got both my watches back from Betteridge, in spite of what I said to
them in my letter. And they both behave as if they had really been opened
up & looked at this time.

May 28 Saturday

Ugin & I climbed the ridge-pole of the roof of Tamarack, where the men
are shingling, & looking down into the tamarack tree we saw a robin's nest
with four blue eggs in it.

Went down for the mail, & the wheel came off the Mercer again, &
this time the ring was right on the wheel! The thread is entirely worn out.
You can screw the ring on, & then pick it right off with your fingers.

Gene took Tom & Molly to the train to meet Margaret Cuthbert.[42]
Margaret brought me "Tristram," & a translation of a French book called
"Ariane," & three little boxes of Elizabeth Arden guest soap, tiny cakes,
adorable, & a silk handkerchief she bought in England.[43] She always brings
me things, & I can't stop her, so now I've stopped trying.

May 29 Sunday

Breakfast in the summer-house. Saw a scarlet tanager, & an indigo bunting,
& a yellow warbler, & saw two orioles having a fight, & heard a cuckoo,
all in one morning.

The most beautiful day that ever was in the world.

Let Tom & Molly out in the small pasture.

A man came by with two beautiful pale horses; one was especially
beautiful. So we accosted him, & began to bargain, & almost bought him
for two hundred dollars. But he wouldn't throw in the saddle, & we were
stubborn, so we didn't buy it. Margaret says she can get a beautiful horse
for us for nothing, maybe two, from some Long Island friends who have
too many & don't want to sell them to just anybody.

Betteridge sent back the Conning Tower watch, in spite of what I said, day before yesterday, & it still goes beautifully. Ugin is wearing it. I believe they put another watch in the same case.

May 30 Monday

Harrison climbed to the top of High Hill & saw the sunrise, & saw a scarlet tanager singing against the sunrise. Memorial Day. Beautiful & mild. Drove Margaret to Chatham & left the Mercer with Boright. He is going to bring over a Hudson for us to try.

Gene shingled part of the summer-house, & had his knife cutting the shingle bundle, & a mouse sprang out near his hand, & he struck it with his knife & killed it, & felt awful.

Harrison found two lady's slippers & three painted trilliums.

May 31 Tuesday

Uge went to fetch the Maxwell, but it wasn't ready, so he drove home in Bander's scream of a Lizzie—about as big as a bird-house.[44]

Saw a new nest, under an old clapboard on the side of Tamarack—two tiny faintly blueish eggs in it.

Saw a female bluebird fly out of the hollow tree where last year's nest was.

One of the new rock plants is in blossom—bright pink & tiny.

Steepletop
(June to November 1927)

L ife on the farm at Steepletop—the beauties of nature, birds, flowers, and weather Millay records in such loving and poetic detail—seems nearly idyllic for the first half of 1927. The poet had plenty of peace and quiet time to herself to write new works, and the couple had more than enough good company when they desired it. Indeed if it had not been for needing servants so that the rich couple might live as they wished, the farm would have been a paradise. But the Boissevains' difficulty in dealing with cooks, farmhands, and gardeners was aggravated by Millay's curious disdain for them. And it is in this, her attitude toward "the help," that we begin to see the hairline cracks in the woman's character widen into dangerous fissures.

Her attitude is apparent in the way she called her hired man a "graceless drunken bum"; her housemaid "The Countess Gruffanuff"; and the overweight stenographer Grace "The Three Graces." At one point she even makes the outrageous argument that one must never pay servants what they are worth, because they will take you for a fool, and because they are bound to cheat and steal from you no matter how much you pay them. All of this vituperation culminates in her frightening diary entry on October 3, 1927: "The only people I really hate are servants. They are not really human beings at all. They have no conscience, no heart . . ."

Because nothing like this attitude appears in the earlier diaries, it is clear that Millay is undergoing a change in personality that will affect her life and her work. The change coincides with a decline in her health, which had never been robust, and her increasing dependence on alcohol and drugs.

The problem was made worse by her accident in March when, returning from a performance of her opera in New York, their sleigh was caught in a snowstorm and veered into a thicket, and a tree branch scratched her cornea. The painful injury took months to heal, and required opiates for relief. She had already been in discomfort from symptoms that led, in June, to her having a uterine procedure at Mount Sinai Hospital. "They are lovely here and give me all the morphine I want—ply me with morphine," she wrote. It was not widely known at the time just how addictive morphine is. Her addiction to opiates probably began then, and much of her ill humor and misanthropy may be related to continual withdrawal from drugs.

The following diary entries were sometimes dictated to Eugen. As Millay was devoted to maintaining the diary, she did not mind this, and he was only too glad to serve his wife as amanuensis when she was too ill or too tired to make the entries herself. We may assume, when Eugen is making the diary entry in her stead, that on that day his wife was unwell.

In August of 1927, Eugen and Edna went up to Boston to plead for the lives of the anarchists Sacco and Vanzetti. Toward the end of this chapter, a few poignant diary entries record that sad experience.

June 1 Wednesday 1927

Harry & I worked all day on the garden-house garden, spading & pulling out quack-grass. —Mrs. Tanner didn't come.

We put the pigs in the big pasture, & Stanley made a cute little thatched house for them right by the entrance to the driveway, & put their troughs there, & it stinks like the devil, & the whole driveway stinks, & the whole place stinks. Ugin says they are cute, & they don't stink. But they do stink.

June 2 Thursday

Harrison planted the whole garden-[house garden] to perennials from our last year's seed. It will be too sweet for words,—striped grass in it, too, & bergamot, & iris & Canterbury bells & larkspur & hardy pinks & Sweet William—& lots of other things. —I worked all day mowing the lawn with the dullest lawn-mower on earth. Boright was here to explain that the new cars were not unpacked yet, & he took the mower back with him to sharpen it. Ugin finished shingling the garden-house roof.

The pigs got out & were standing with their fore-feet in the rock-garden when I got to them, yelling & cursing and waving my coat. And they've rooted up & messed up the whole corner of the pasture near the driveway. I hate them.

The road is all fixed up & is splendid.

June 3 Friday [Eugen's entry]

Funny weather.

Transplanted 3 azaleas from road side to shrubbery.

Swarm of bees passed right over our head going somewhere in a straight line in a great hurry.

Boright came with Hudson, & Nash.[1] Tried them both. Didn't like Nash. Loved the Hudson. Drove to Chatham and bought the Hudson.[2] —Met Tess [Adams] at station [Chatham] & got her off instead of going to State Line. —Turned in the Mercer & Maxwell & were allowed $360 for the two![3] Sic transit Gloria mundi.

Boright brought back the grass mower all sharpened.

Edna, Harry & I went for motor drive at night to try out motor.

June 4 Saturday [Eugen's entry]

Wonderful weather. —Tess's birthday. Showed her the place.

Motored to Chatham & went to rotten movie to see Lindbergh, but didn't see him. Bought birthday cake & candles.

Had cocktails & festive dinner for Tess.

Heavy showers at night. Drove Mrs. Tanner home. Had trouble coming back.

June 7 Tuesday [Eugen's entry]

Weather beautiful.

Made up big basket for Tess, rhubarb, flowers, applejack, jelly & plants.

Drove her to State Line. —On return Altair had big fight with a collie when we stopped on the road, talk with Kohler [?] Kohler [unintelligible] Hurt his leg.

Stanley drunk. Discharged him. He asked me to take him back. He may come tomorrow, but swore off for two months, with bet of $5. On returning from State Line, met him in a buggy, white & stupid with liquor.

McCagg got mad when asked about him yesterday. Work. Father & son left.

House finally painted except for one day's work for touching up. — Had supper outside summerhouse.

Edna heard whippoorwill.

June 8 Monday [Eugen's entry]

Beautiful weather. Strong wind.

Motored to Pittsfield—Tess, Edna, Harry & I.

Bought garden furniture, and lumber.

Had luncheon in Pittsfield, music by mechanical violin, first we ever heard.

Stenog. Came—daughter of pig-man—she looks smart and ladylike. American marvel. But poor stenog.[4]

Had gay cocktail party in rose garden, with Edam cheese & crackers.

In the evening Harry played old fashioned popular songs till passed [*sic*] midnight. "The girl on the magazine cover." "And when I told them how beautiful you are." Etc.

Patchwork quilt arrived from Edna's mother.

June 9 Thursday [Eugen's entry]

Wonderful weather.

Hay taken in from lot between drive & road.

Fetched with Brownie & surrey, harry & Edna, 4 azaleas, which we planted along each side of ruins.

Had dinner outside summerhouse.

One gladiola up.

June 10 Friday [Eugen's entry]

Marvelous weather. Got up at 5 a.m. Coffee outside summer house. Went for thrilling drive toward Hillsdale.

Edna & I worked on summer house & Edna finished north side.

Went to Chatham. Bought nails & fixtures for shutters, also tomato & cabbage plants.

Saw John.[5] He's coming back in two weeks.

Stanley drunk. —Promised me to be sober & come to work Monday.

Thunder showers at night. Planted seed garden north of ruins. Cock-eyed [unintelligible] annual garden.

Black team shod. Bailey took them to W. Stockbridge.

June 12 Sunday

Lovely day. Showery. Bright moonlight tonight.

These are the flowers which are in blossom now: buttercups & hawk-weed, for wild flowers & wild geraniums, & the pink azaleas. In the garden, lilacs, forgetmenot, weigelias, & snow-ball bushes almost out; Iceland poppies, hardy pinks; in the rock garden, violas & the little pink rock-cress (or whatever it is) —Also horse-radish is in flower, & the false mitrewort— and the lilies-of-the-valley, the most lovely of all, which I nearly forgot. I have a glass of them beside my bed.

Mrs. Tanner came & paid for the white horse, & she & Stanley took him away. Brownie whinnied quite a lot.[6]

Ugin & I saw, from the upstairs window of Tamarack, a male robin feeding his young ones. He also took the excrement from them, but instead of dropping it on the ground, as the blue birds & phoebes, etc., do, he seemed to eat it. —Four blue eggs in the blue bird's nest. I am keeping Velvet in all the time now. —Ugin set out tomatoes.

June 13 Monday

Beautiful day. —Today by the roadside I saw a piece of roofing paper about a foot square, & thinking it looked untidy, picked it up. Under it lay coiled, apparently asleep, a green snake. He didn't move; I put the paper back, & left him. It is tar-paper, the kind that gets very hot in the sun; I suppose he loves it. Harrison & I cleaned up a lot around the dragon-willow, & pruned it.

Did an enormous washing with the washing-machine, including thirteen rugs; Ugin helped me. A boy came & wanted work, & Gene set him to digging the hole for the gas [gasoline] tank. Kinsey [?] came & looked at our heifers, & insisted on buying them; he almost threatened us. This is not the first time he has been after them! Maybe, like the goose, Dolly will lay a golden calf, & maybe Kinsey workshops golden calves.

June 14 Tuesday

Grey day, sometimes raining. Ugin & I dressed up in our plus-fours & motored to Hudson to inquire about Ugin's naturalization papers, get his driving license, & get the Underwood repaired that was smashed in transit between Sante Fe & Steepletop.[7] Had to take the typewriter on to Albany—thirty dollars worth of damages. —Mrs. Tanner came in the evening & told us that John & Bailey had been drinking our liquor in the cellar daily, sometimes when we were away—crawling in through the cellar window. —And we heard the other day that our lovely faithful old-fashioned cook wasn't sick at all, but just left us to take a job in an orphan asylum in Albany for higher pay. So to hell, to merry hell with the whole bloody canaille.[8]

Stayed up & saw the total eclipse of the moon, at quarter to three in the morning—saw it from Ugin's bed.

June 15 Wednesday

Weather most everything. [*sic*] Marvelous bright rainy sunset with rainbow. Did a big ironing on the machine, eight sheets for one thing. [*sic*] . . .

June 16 Friday

Beautiful sunny day. This morning at eight under the willows in the pasture Dolly gave birth to a beautiful calf, a heifer, white with brown spots. We were having breakfast before the summer-house when we noticed she was behaving peculiarly. —We got Stanley & went down, just in time, & saw the whole thing. First came the fore legs with the hoofs folded; then the head, resting on the folded hoofs, with wide-open eyes that blinked— yes, adorably blinked & blinked, before it was even born. Then Stanley took hold of the legs & pulled hard & Dolly groaned, & it was all over. The little spotted calf lay on the ground, alive, & all wet. And Stanley picked it up & laid it in the sun, & rubbed salt on it, & Dolly licked it & licked it till it was all fluffy & dry. By nine o'clock it was on its legs & sucking. A beautiful calf, they all say. . . .

June 17 Friday

Lovely day. Splitting headache this morning. Took the Hudson in to have the oil changed, having finished 500 miles. They cleaned her up beautifully.

Harrison planted the rest of the roses into the rose garden. I brought some petunias & a rose-geranium & a heliotrope & some aster plants. Saw some old-fashioned garden-heliotrope in Fisher's nursery & insisted on having it, so he's going to let me have two plants the first of September, although he hadn't intended to sell any.

Now that we have done over 500 miles [in the Hudson] we can let her out a little,—today for the first time in our lives we came up East Hill on high. Went for a drive after supper. Ugin wants to be driving all the time now.

June 18 Saturday

Beautiful day.

Stayed in bed most all day. Lovely auction; wanted to go & buy quilts & couldn't budge. The school-teacher, who is also the pigman's daughter, is going to work for us as a house-maid until September. Began today. Hasn't the faintest idea how to make a bed, but is pleasant & willing. Mrs. Belterman here, & brought me the handsomest old iron kettle I've yet seen.

Heard tonight after I got into bed the most frightful shrieks & howls from across the road, as of a cat in mortal agony. I looked from the window, & saw two fearful bright eyes in the field half-way up the hill. Ugin says it was only the barn-cat wailing for her demon lover; but it didn't sound like any feline courtship I ever heard. I can't help thinking she has been carried off by a fox.

June 19 Sunday

Nice cozy rainy day. Ugin & I sat by the open fire & Ugin read me from Upton Sinclair's Oil! I have never liked him much, but his book begins extremely interesting.

No sign of the cat.

June 20 Monday

Fine day, rather cool, but sun very hot. Two splendid red roses in full bloom, an *American Beauty*, & a *Magna Carta*. Stunning—they dress up the whole place, & their odor is incredible.

Stanley did come. Joe didn't come. Gene sat in the big grass chair for a long time this evening before the summer-house, looking down the valley, & just enjoying the loveliness. Harry & I made cocktails, & put fresh mint in the glasses, & got supper, & Ugin just sat & sat & looked down the valley. Usually I am the one who has the privilege. It is the most refreshing thing to do—re-creating. . . .

June 25 Thursday [Eugen's entry]

Got up at 6 a.m. Packed & finally got started at 8:30. Car went wonderfully.

Visited Max. Had lunch with him & Eliena.

Visited Sally.

Visited Floyd Dell, but only heard, & heard, & heard B-Marie.

Arrived at 8 at Margaret's [Cuthbert]. Had a nice dinner with her & Miss [Alice] Blinn.

They left after dinner & stopped for the night outside. —We had a wonderful night all alone in flat.

Saw fireman's parade in Poughkeepsie.

June 24 Friday

Went to see *Chang,* all three of us, the best movie I ever saw.[9] Left car in garage during movie.

June 25 Saturday

Margaret & Alice went out to the country. Gene & I took Charlie [Ellis, Norma's husband] to the theatre where he is playing on the east side & went to see the show—Seventh Heaven.[10] Charlie very good in the lead. Left car in garage during theatre. Went after-wards with Charlie to Jewish restaurant. Came home to 11th Street at about one o'clock—pouring rain, torrents of rain, street deserted. Gene came into the hall with me to let me in & stepped inside to fetch his overcoat, then went out to take car to garage. Returned in a moment to say that the car was gone, stolen. I called up the police at once. A detective came over presently & sent the description of the car to all the police of Manhattan. I'm confident that it will be found.

June 26 Sunday

Telephone call in morning—car found & three prisoners at 68th Precinct Police Station, New [Dorp?], Staten Island—had been found at five o'clock this morning. Gene & I took reporters from the *World* & went to Staten Island. Car badly damaged. Must be repaired. Be a while without a car—unpleasant.

Interviewed by Harry Salpeter for the *World*.

Ugin took me in a taxi to the Mount Sinai Hospital.

June 27 Monday

Operated on—an operation they call a "D. and C."—not a very big one. Very sick in stomach. Can't keep even water down.

They are lovely here & give me all the morphine I want—ply me with morphine.

July 3 Sunday

Gene & I came to Steepletop.

Bought some fire works for Harry in Chatham drug-store. Set some off tonight. Not very good. No Roman candles, or rockets.

July 4 Monday

Set off the rest of the fire-works. Pretty poor. One faint little explosive thing I christened "Debutante's Fart." I was a little tight, I think. We were all very gay.

July 5 Tuesday

Ugin went to New York to appear in court against the man who stole our car.

July 6 Wednesday

Helen & George applied for job.

July 8 Friday

Helen & George came in the evening.

Three months since I smoked a cigarette.

July 10 Sunday

George took Buttercup to the bull. Blossom is giving 12 quarts of milk per day.

July 18 Monday

Wedding anniversary of me & Ugin.

July 23 Saturday

Margaret & Alice Blinn came up to look over a property we thought they might buy. —Witter Bynner came to spend a few days.

Vacuum cleaner man came. Bought cleaner.

July 24 Sunday

Rosie, the white sow, gave birth to nine little pigs, of which six lived.

Wolfe took us all to look at the property, Ugin & Margaret trailing along in the funny 1916 Hudson, a second loan from Boright.

Wolfe took Margaret & Alice to train for New York.

July 25 Monday

Ugin brought home a tiny police-dog bitch, 6 weeks old, terrible cute. We have named her for the present "Double-Toes," her paws are so enormous—"Duboy" for short.

July 26 Tuesday

Gasoline man came & filled our tank, 405 gallons.

Ugin, Hal [Witter Bynner] & I went over to Arthur's property & took a lot of pictures.

July 27 Wednesday

Hal's mother came to fetch him & he left with her, whirled away in her Lincoln Limosine for Windsor, Vermont. Left for me to read a poem he wrote last night about Lindbergh, the worst poem I have read in months, shockingly banal & bad.

Fische, the Chatham florist & his wife & kids came to see our gardens.

Heard from Alice Blinn that the Delineator [magazine] will pay me $200 for my poem about Arthur. . . .

July 29 Friday

Crosby finished the chimney on the cottage, also the foundations.

Put Dulcie & her pigs in with Rosie & hers. All of Dulcie's children nursed Rosie. Dulcie is more interested in her husband than in her children, & they only two days old,—the strumpet.

Ugin gave the little puppy to me, & I named her Lupa. I love her.

July 30 Saturday

Margaret & Alice Blinn couldn't come. But Margaretta Schuyer came with Eleanor DeLamata, to spend the week-end.

Also, just blowing in Mr. & Mrs. Mahon & Janet Kingsley.

Ugin & Harry & the two girls made hay all afternoon, while I watched. I caught a butterfly under my beret, thinking it was a swallow-tail. I chased it a long way & finally caught it. When I looked under my tam it was two butterflies. They had been clasped together in flight, & flew as one. It was two Leto fritillaries, I think. (Don't know how to spell it.)

August 5 Friday

Velvet gave birth to four little kittens, one of them died. I buried the strange little thing.

August 8 Monday

Four months since I smoked a cigarette. Broke my fast today, my abstinence having done nothing at all to improve my condition.

August 9 Tuesday

Major Straight's horse, "Skidoo" which Mrs. Straight's secretary is giving to me & Gene, came from Long Island by motor van today, & Gene met them at Great Barrington & rode him home. He is beautiful. We re-named him Roderick Dhu—& call him "Doo" for short. Fortunately, the saddle & bridle came with him.

I shingled on the back of the cottage while Gene was gone, way up on the scaffolding. A "claim adjuster" from the Home Insurance Company came about our stolen car. They are willing to pay $125, whereas the Hudson people say that the damage is $280 even without the tires, tubes, & rims. I talked down to him from top of my scaffolding, & gave him an earful.

August 10 Wednesday

. . . .

Ugin rode Roderick Dhu all over Arthur's land on this side of the road, & came back thrilled with the beauty of the views from both Arthur's land & ours.

I gave Dhu some lumps of sugar & some apples in my hand. He is so gentle, & so beautiful.

There is something that squeaks, up in the roof of the summer-house. We don't know whether it is baby mice, or faeries.

August 11 Thursday

George took Peggy May Brown to the station at Hillsdale. He left at five in the morning, & was back at 10:30 to help with Haying. He is wonderful. Helen, his wife, is, as she often reminds us, a nervous woman, besides being a pretty bad cook. Except for him, we would never keep her, but George is so wonderful we must keep him at any cost.

I am waiting with anxiety to learn the fate of Sacco & Vanzetti, if they were executed at midnight last night, or have been respited by Governor Fuller.[11]

Gene rode over some of our land & Arthur's on the other side of the road, & came out on top of High Hill. He shouted down & I saw him there, looking splendid on his horse, way, way up in the air, silhouetted against the sky.

August 13 Saturday

Ugin went to Chatham & interviewed our faithless cook, Mrs. Schaefer—I should say—faithless servant, excellent cook. She wants to come back. I feel that we shall take her back. Helen is pretty awful—except for two or three things.

August 14 Sunday

Max Eastman came, with Eliena, & his son Dan. He brought the mss. of his new book. They were drenched with rain when they got here. House full of beautiful flowers marvelously arranged by Harry.

August 15 Monday

Harrison's birthday. Gave him a not-for-sale advance copy of the score of the *Henchman*. He was terribly pleased.

Helen made him a birthday cake which came out wonderful. Usually her cakes are embarrassing.

I showed Max, under protest, the poem I wrote about Sacco & Vanzetti, about my feeling, rather. He was very moved by it, & so I typed it & sent it to the Defense Committee. I felt much happier than I have felt for days.

Max & Gene motored to W. Stockbridge [to telephone] & spoke with Ruth Hale in Stamford, asking if we could help.

August 16 Tuesday (written up October 3)

Max went across to the cottage to work on his book. Eliena cleaned up one of the chambers for him, with a lot of mopping & slopping & splashing of water into the floor below. Then Max decided he didn't like the room anyway, so she swabbed down another. We supplied a table & chair, & he settled down, & worked very hard. He never suggested that I might let him use my shanty, although I'm not working there just now. I was grateful for this. I hate to refuse, but I loathe to have anybody work there but myself.

August 17 Wednesday

Gene began reading aloud to us from Max's book. Found the first half delightful. Max calls the book "breaking Through." I kicked & screamed so at this title that he changed it

[The rest of the page is illegible.]

August 18 Thursday

Gene continued with Max's book. Very interesting stuff about strikes.

Max has used as the crux of his novel the whole unfortunate business of Gene & his coffee adventure with Borden's & the chain stores.[12]

During this time we are trying to get rid of Helen & keep George, at least until the cottage is finished & we can park her over there. Suggest that she go & visit her mother for awhile. All this delivered to George to break to Helen. It is impossible to talk with her. She is the foulest & most verminous slut I have yet had in the house, which is going some. We came upon her one day about to make soup of the bones which Gainer's gives us for nothing but the dogs, swept up from the butcher-shop floor. God knows what we eat.

August 19 Friday

Finished Max's book. I don't like the end so much. Again we have a novel in which the good girl is the dull one. Jo's chapters with the girl we are supposed to accept as his real love fall very flat after the thrilling chapters with the other two.

August 20 Saturday

Called up Ruth Hale again about my going to Boston. —Have decided just to go, & see if there is anything there for me to do. —The whole thing terribly on my mind & on my heart.

August 21 Sunday

Gene & I go to Boston.

We went at once to the Defense Committee, & from there to the Copley-Plaza, where we registered & left our luggage.

Went to the Scenic Auditorium, where Miss Vanzetti was speaking, but arrived just as the meeting was breaking up. Saw Lucy Brannan & took her back with us to the hotel. Elizabeth Merrell was with her, the funny intense little sister of a class-mate of mine. We talked until very late, getting up a sort of program for me tomorrow. Gave out my poem "Justice Denied in Massachusetts" to all the Boston papers.

(Found out later that though all the New York papers used this, none of the Boston papers did.)

August 22 Monday

Began this terrible day in an absurd fashion, shut in the hotel while a tailor across the road struggled with the only dress I had brought, & which I suddenly found, having recently put on at doctor's orders seventeen pounds, I could not nearly get into.

Went down to the Joy Street Police Station & bailed out picketers up to about $800. Shocked to find how few people whose names I knew were here in Boston to protest. Went with Dos Passos, Lola Ridge & about four others to picket the State House, carrying a placard saying, "Free Them & Save Massachusetts![13] American Honor dies with Sacco & Vanzetti!" Walked up & down for about ten minutes, an enormous crowd watching us, were arrested & taken to the Joy Street Station. Bailed out by Gene & Art Hays [Arthur Garfield Hays, lawyer]. Went to see Governor Fuller; talked to his secretary; finally admitted. Very courteous, but gave me no hope. Motored with Gene & Ernestine Evans to Clinton, to see Senator Walsh, a fool's errand, taking precious hours. Senator Walsh not there. Late when we came back. Sat in Art Hays' room with a dozen people & wrote a letter to the Governor. Art & I took it over. Nearly midnight then.

August 23 Tuesday   12 to 1 a.m.

Sat in Art Hays' room, with many others, & waited for news from the Prison. No hope at all now, after twelve o'clock. Everybody quiet. Suddenly I whispered to Art, "Why do you suppose we don't get any word?" Art looked up from a telegram he was writing. "Sacco's gone," he said, & went on writing. So I knew that even at that moment Vanzetti was being strapped into the chair. Agony, agony in my heart to think how late I had come there, thinking there must be thousands here already & I would be just an intruder if noticed at all. So few people to try to help them, only a handful. Poor fellows,—seven years of anguish, & then this barbarous revenge, not for anything they had done, but for what they had said & what they had thought. Barbarous, loathsome capital punishment, never in any circumstances justified, but in this case more hideous than ever, the act of a frightened state against two radicals, who may or may not have committed murder. I believe them to have been innocent. But this was never the point, their innocence or guilt of anything save anarchy.

9:30 a.m.

Appeared in court, with about 150 others, on a charge of "sauntering & loitering." Art Hays made a test case of six of us, including Ellen Hayes, Catherine Huntington & myself.[14] —Art argued marvelously. The judge paid no attention. Art read from books of the Statutes of Massachusetts.

The judge paid no attention whatsoever. In the midst of Art's speech, the judge interrupted with words to this effect: "Mr. Hays, I'm afraid this is just a waste of time. My mind is pretty well made up. I shall find these defendants guilty." Judge Sullivan, his name was. He looked like a very refined & clean little pig in his black robe, pulling his tiny grey beard & chuckling to himself.

Went with Art Hays in the afternoon to see Powess Hapgood, whom the police had chucked into the psychopathic hospital to keep him from picketing & making speeches.

August 25

Went to see Dr. Myerson, whom I met yesterday at the psychopathic hospital, & had him examine me for a possible nervous disorder which might account for my head and eyes. No trouble at all, excepting that my reflex actions are much quicker than in the normal person; even the pupils of my eyes snap shut when subjected to light, instead of closing gradually as usual. He says I must try not to react so thoroughly to the least little thing about me—not to throw myself into things the way I do. —Well—I'll try—God help me.

September 28

Belterman came & made beer, oodles of it, from creamy-malt-& hops.[15] Three twenty-gallon vats & some little ones—also some elderberry wine. —Ugin & I picked the berries.

September 29

Belterman came. Shaefer can't stand her, but after all, Shaefer hasn't used us so well in the past that we should ditch old Belterman for her, after having engaged her aeons ago to make us some beer.

Belterman is to come again Saturday to bottle the beer.

Came home from fetching the mail & found Shaefer just getting into her hat & coat—her daughter's husband had had an accident—several ribs broken—Shaefer sent for—taxi waiting outside. Gene helped her down the steep slope to the car, suspecting nothing.

Word from Belterman that she can't come Saturday.

September 30

Went to call Shaefer at her daughter's—inquired for injured son-in-law. All a put-up job, apparently. Shaefer had left, snuk out with a lie in her throat, just as she did before, the flighty old devil, & taken her satchels with her. And I had really liked her, the elderly Protestant slut.

October 1

Hot—about 80.

Bottled beer, cursing old Belterman's hide for leaving us in the lurch.

Grant says Shaefer left because we were making home-brew. Says she told him so, or something. Heavens, what a good riddance, in that case!

October 2

Hot—over 80.

Bottled some more of the beer. But it's hopeless. There's too much. And we don't know how to do it.

A medieval curse upon that Belterman. Just slipping out & leaving us high & dry. And I've really been good to her, because she was hard-up. Well, I wish her no bad luck—only the hives all summer, & chilblains all winter.

October 3

Beautiful weather—very warm.

I have made no entry in this book since August 15. Many things have happened since then, which I will go back & write up as best I can from memory.

Tanner here.

Sick of bottling beer.

The only people I really hate are servants. They are not really human beings at all. They have no conscience, no heart, no sense of responsibility, no memory of kind treatment or past favours. Even their sins are not human sins but the sins of spiders & magpies, of monkeys serpents & pigs. I do not love them. The only one I love is Hattie, of the old days; she was a darling, even though she treated us badly, too.

October 4

Heavy rain for a short time. Then terrific wind. Hollyhocks blown down for the first time. —Finished my letter to the World in answer to Edmond Pearson & the other Philistines.[16] Gene motored me to Pittsfield, to try to get hold of Mitchell's "Memories of an Editor," from which I wished to quote. We had to go by the long road, through Stockbridge—other road still torn up. Pittsfield Pub. Lib. owned book—book out. Could have wept. Went to three book-shops—only three there were. Didn't have it. Ready to "commit su," as Ugin says. Went back to Pub. Lib. Tried to bribe them to give us the name of the person holding book. They were sympathetic, but firm. Advised us to try Lenox Pub. Lib. which we did—found it! Hooray! —And I was right, & didn't have to change a word. Posted letter to World with loud sigh.

Had Grant pour the rest of the beer into the brook. —All the pears from the Clapp's favorite tree are rotten now, that Shaefer was going to can.

November 4

First snow-fall.

This book never gets written in, except when there's nothing to write. Today in Washington [D.C.] is the opening of the *King's Henchman* on the road with an independent opera company. They are to produce it in about forty cities of the U.S. this winter. —The first snow-fall of the year comes sneaking in on the heels of a two-days' rain. Not more than half the roses are earthed up. The bulbs are not even ordered from Dreer! I am nothing like ready for my reading tour which begins on the 11th. —Dress not back from Jessie Turner, where they're trying to stretch it (I still weight 110)—stocking not yet dyed to match dress—don't know what I'm going to read, with the exception of "Justice Denied in Massachusetts." That should go well, I think, in Worcester.

Steepletop
(1928–1930)
And Texas Lecture Tour

O nce again, in March of 1928, the writer chides herself for not
keeping up her diary, for a quarter of a year this time. She has a
good excuse. At the end of the summer she wrote to her mother,
apologizing for not staying in touch, explaining that she was working full
time writing poetry, poems that would appear in her forthcoming book
The Buck in the Snow (September 1928.) These diary pages are of considerable interest for their literary content, including reference to the writing of
specific poems such as the sonnet "Life, were thy pains as are the pains of
hell," and the literature she is reading, such as Shakespeare's *The Tempest.*
Millay's last visit with Elinor Wylie is detailed here, and the awkward tri-
angle of Floyd Dell, Elinor, and her husband who was called away suddenly by the illness of his father. Finally, we get a glimpse of life on tour,
as Eugen and Edna travel to Texas to promote her new book.

March 22 Thursday [1928]

It is senseless to repine that nearly a quarter of the year has gone by, and
I have made no entry into this book. It is senseless (what *ails* the word?)
senseless [Millay has repeatedly misspelled this word] to recall that not
more than a third of last year's book was filled. It is

SENSELESS

To suppose I shall do any better this year.

It has been snowing for four days. The deepest snow of the year is on the roads, & the snow is still falling thick & furious. All winter we have been able to get through in the car, but today I am very much afraid that Eugen, who has taken Ana to Chatham to telephone New York concerning her mother, who is ill, will not be able to get up the hill again except on foot. Anna is my maid, a treasure, entirely a treasure. Conrad is my Filipino cook, the husband of Anna, who is German-American. We got them through a New York agency, & they have been with us over three months.

P.S. Ugin *did* get up the hill.

[Eugen's entry] This morning the black birds were singing and Ugin was foolish and thought one of them was a blue-jay.

March 24

Llewelyn Powys came to spend a few days with us.[1] While Gene was gone to the station to fetch him, Conrad announced that he & Anna were leaving. I told him firmly that he would have to work his week out anyway, & suggested that he reconsider. But I felt rather sick in the stomach about it all.

Lulu [Llewelyn] & Gene & I walked to the top of High Hill. Lulu is very much impressed by the beauty & wildness of the country here.

Deep snow, but bare in spots.

Took Lulu in to see the cottage. Frank Hill, the man from Austerlitz who is doing the [wall]papering, looked steadily at Lulu as we entered the room where he was working & said, "This gentleman reminds me of Llewelyn Powys." We could not believe our ears. It seems he reads all the time, everything, has read Lulu's latest book, & seen his photo in a review of it.

March 25 Sunday

Anna brought me my breakfast on my favorite little yellow dishes & upon my saying a kind word to her presented me with a little note from Conrad saying that he was sorry & wanted to stay forever, & threw her arms about my neck & wept, saying that she loved me & could never leave me. I am so happy about this. She is an extremely nice girl & I am very fond of her.

Heard the first bluebird. Ran out doors & saw it. Heard the first song sparrow. Ugin saw the first robin. Such a day. Such a rushing of rivers of melted snow!

Read my new poems to Lulu, & he likes them very much.

Conrad & Anna have purchased, with our permission, a police pup named Nancy.

Weather very soft. Got hot walking.

March 27 Tuesday

8:30 a.m. This moment comes a letter from Mitchell Kennerly, saying that Arthur Hooley is dead.[2]

9:30 p.m. Gene has gone to the city with Lulu, to see Dr. Bache again. He is not getting better, in spite of the emetine hypodermics & all the other fussing. —I am without him in this house for the first time tonight. Of course Conrad & Anna are here. But I remember how my mother kept house for me here once for two months entirely alone, & those awful Polish pirates across the road. She is wonderful. The wind is howling like forty furies, & it has been snowing—very cold—roads impassable with deep sink-holes. —Ugin & Lulu had to go by wagon to State Line.

Autti appeared when I was having dinner.[3] In spite of the storm, I sent her home. Read *The Tempest* again.[4] Can't say I liked it much. I believe people like it mostly for extra-critical reasons—identifying S. with Prospero, etc. Pretty silly, that, I think.

At last we have the valances up over the living-room curtains. Aside from this nothing happened today. I tried to type my poems for the dummy of my new book, but the ribbon is no good at all, & there's no stove in my cabin, so I can't use the other typewriter—even the Corona is busto.[5] Didn't go out all day. But I have carefully *dressed* for dinner both last night & tonight, just as if Ugin was here. As the chap said in "Bleak House"—"Discipline must be maintained"—both among servants—and among myself.[6]

I am reading the old copy of Baxter's *Saint's Rest* that Mother gave me.[7] It is a remarkable book—thrilling, really—and beautiful.

Anna told me today that it takes Mrs. Tanner fifteen minutes by the kitchen clock to iron a pillow-case. Well—that helps explain why my laundry bill is speedily soaring to the realm of Big Business.

March 29 Thursday

Anna, Conrad & I are all busy all the morning trimming up the hall & bedrooms of the North wing. It looks adorable.

Gene came home at about 2 o'clock from New York. —Had gone to a new doctor & got some new medicine. The emetine in his arms apparently had not taken hold, had not been put in deep enough.

We left Altair & Lupa outdoors together, thinking they would not run away & leave Nancy, who was tied outside on a leather leash. Nor did they. Lupa bit through Nancy's leash to free her. But Nancy, freed, ran into the house, while Altair & Lupa made for the hills.

Elinor & Bill came up on the evening train. I went with Gene in the car to meet them. Roads frozen. —Elinor was mad about the hall in the wing, & wants to copy the pink paper.

The little pale shoots of several delphinium plants were visible today. I was astonished, & feverish with excitement.

March 30 Friday

We were at luncheon today when a wire came for Bill sent over by motor from Hudson, saying that his father was critically ill & to come at once to Philadelphia. He went back with the driver to Hudson & took the train there.

Gene did not feel well enough to fetch Floyd Dell at Croton, & the roads were so icy with frozen sleet that Curtis refused to do it.[8] So we had to phone him to come by train. He arrived in the evening. We talked before the living-room fire until Gene & I got sleepy, & said it was bed-time, whereupon a great groan went up from the more urban & nocturnal among us. We left Elinor & Floyd downstairs to make a night of it, but they didn't stay long.

March 31 Saturday

Stayed in bed as usual & worked until noon. Wrote an entire sonnet beginning "Life, were thy pains as are the pains of hell"; and the octave of a sonnet beginning "be sure my coming was a sharp offense And trouble to my mother in her bed"—I have never worked so furiously fast before. I seem to be driven by some force accumulated during those years when I have written no poems at all.

Wire from Bill that his father died.

Elinor & Floyd read my poems all the morning, & when I came down we discussed them. Floyd had some valuable suggestions to make, which I shall act upon, & one or two silly ones which I met with loud & joyous boos. Elinor says she thinks this may be my best book.

I said something tonight that hurt Elinor's feelings, but she forgave me. I didn't mean to hurt her, & I felt dreadful. [The following sentence was written in later by Vincent.] * I never saw her again. [Elinor Wylie died on December 16, 1928.]

April 1 Sunday [Eugen's entry]

April fools day, but we didn't know it until afterward.

Vincent wrote in bed. One poem "Seeing how I love you utterly" and half of another beginning "Oh, let forever the phlox & the rose." —Swell, I think.—

Vince & I breakfast together in her room. Floyd & Elinor in Floyd's room. —We took Fl & El to the train in Hudson.*—Returning we bought a rooster, so we could hear him crow morning's [*sic*]. —Put on chains lying in the wet & sloppy mud. The chains were broken & whacked & boomed something terrible, but we got home all right. —The lilies of the valley are beginning to get up. —Some columbine and great many larkspurs. We gave Anna ten bucks for being so nice to our guests. —They may not accept any tips from our guests. —Fine idea that. —Probably mine!

April 2 Monday [Eugen's entry]

Vincent wrote in bed. We had breakfast together in her room, but she worked & had lunch by herself in her bed. —I (Uge) had it outside in the sun with the dogs.

The men [farm hands] walked up from A. as the roads were too bad for their Hennery [*sic*].

Marvelous dinner corned beef & cabage [*sic*]. —The cabage frozen all winter in the cellar in the cottage.

April 3 Tuesday [Eugen's entry]

Men walked up from A. —All the pigs got out. —The dogs had a fine time chasing them! —   Manure was put on the old buckwheat field.

I still love Vincent. —I love her indecently. —and five years married!
Vincent wrote poem "The Cameo"

I finally tried to answer letters but there are still just as many to be answered as yesterday, and always will; World without end!

The rooster has such a high soprano crow, that we fear he is a eunuch.—

Have sold several poems to the S.E.P. [*Saturday Evening Post*] and *Delineator*.—

April 4 Wednesday

Gene & the men tried to burn off the swamp pasture, & while it was damply & reluctantly burning one of the men thought it was a splendid idea to set a match to the ten years mat of dry grass on top of the windy hill. So we had a terrible fire. Everybody out with brooms & burlap bags, Anna & myself feverishly beating it out on the side towards the sheep barn, while the men tried to keep it from the woods. Mrs. Tanner went for help, & all our neighbors hurried to help us. After about six hours we got it under control. (Somebody has been using my pen, damnation!) —Anna is frightfully blistered, hand & foot, my back is as good as broken. Gene is frightfully tired, & the doctor insisting that he rest. —We watched anxiously this evening lest it break out again, but it did not.

April 6 Friday

Elaine Ralli motored up from N.Y. with Frances & Isobel.[9] Frances brought us fresh caviar & marrons glacees & candied ginger & orange peel, & celery & asparagus & many other marvelous things.[10]

I had just gone to bed, worn out, Gene was just retiring. We were without servants as Conrad & Anna left this morning for their monthly three days off. Nevertheless were delighted to have them come, & I got up & dragged myself downstairs & everybody drank lovely cognac which Elaine brought, & we put them to bed in the wing, with only one sheet a piece, the fleet Atalanta who does my ironing being able to put behind her only about three sheets a day without getting a stitch in the side.

April 7 Saturday

Had a lot of fun, the house full of jolly people. Mrs. T[anner]. stayed & cooked us a very good dinner.

April 8 Easter Sunday

Lovely day. —All my roses, or nearly all, are coming into leaf, although I have not yet taken away the earth from the roots. I think I shall have lost very few, possibly the Fran Karl Duschkis—They look pretty bad, for some reason, also the Pink Killarneys. The delphinium is doing wonderfully.

Birds as follows: rusty blackbirds, robins, bluebirds, song sparrows, phoebes, peewees, chickadees, sapsuckers, flickers.

Elaine & Isobel left for New York this afternoon.

April 9 Monday

John Pinney has come back to work here. He went to State Line with the horses to fetch Anna & Conrad, but they did not come. —They came this evening. Walked up from Austerlitz. They had lost our season [train] ticket which we let them take & had been hunting for it all morning. Anna's eyes are red from weeping, poor child. They didn't find it, & as it was quite new, it is a considerable loss.

We had not had our dinner, so Conrad made it for us.

The men took away the banking from about the house today.

April 12 Thursday

Gene & Frances wrote letters all day. I made out my income tax for which I had got an extension of time as they had not enough blanks at the Chatham bank. I find I made over twenty-two thousand dollars last year in royalties from my books & plays & in readings [$350,000 in current purchasing power].

April 16 Monday

Picked pink mayflowers mostly buds, on the bank by the road near the hollow. These are our earliest always. Sent them to Elinor who sails for England tomorrow, so that she can show them to her English friends who never saw them.

Buttercup had her calf, a beautiful little heifer, coloured yellow & white like herself, born in the night. A chicken died, a white leghorn, nobody knows why.

Found upon lifting the hood that the whole water-jacket of the Hudson had frozen tight & burst, forcing out great jagged pieces of iron six inches by four, just by freezing & expanding, breaking the iron as if it had been glass.

Frances left for New York, & for Egypt. John towed her & Gene down the hill with the team, & Curtis towed them to Chatham in his car.

The station-master in Chatham suddenly presented Gene with the lost ticket-book [railroad pass]. It seems somebody had picked it up in the street in New York & turned it in at the Grand Central [Station] & they had forwarded it to Chatham. Anna was delirious with delight. She embraced me & howled,—we are going to call the new calf "Ticket."

April 17

Cold.

Ugin took Brownie & the small wagon to Austerlitz to fetch the groceries. He was going to let Conrad & Anna take her down but I begged him not to. Brownie is gentle & willing, but once in a while just wants to run, & very fast & it takes a clever & strong hand to stop her. She behaved badly, Ugin says. Ugin lost a broom off the wagon coming home.

Two boys from Austerlitz brought it back. They were out hunting for Willie Grant's little black sheep which had run off into the woods.

April 18

Lovely day, but cold in the wind.

Curtis appeared this morning with the black sheep under his arm, a tiny lamb, three weeks old. I fed it from a bottle. We want to buy it, but hear it is a pet of the children, so are not pressing the matter.

The ice-house is finished, shingles & all. The wing has its second coat of paint. Had my old annual garden spaded up in preparation for becoming a perennial garden. It seems to me that larkspur is about the only thing I can depend on in this climate. I always lose a great many of all other plants. Canterbury bells always die. Hollyhocks rot. Oriental poppies become as if they never have been. But larkspur is really hardy. And about the most beautiful of all, too. —Ticket is doing well & her mother, too. The little thing is adorably cute. She has a little white mark on her forehead like a feather curling down from a hat-brim, very chic.

Heard a bull-frog in swamp. Same day as first heard last year.

April 19 Thursday

Last coat of paint put on the wing. One Rhode Island Red has been put in a box to set on 16 eggs, 13 brown & 3 white.[11] Gene & I are sure that Dolly is going to have a calf, & Peggy May Brown a colt, but the hired men say no. Weeded rock-garden a little. Things look fine. Iris is almost up everywhere. Rhubarb is up on this side. Transplanted one honeysuckle from my shanty to summer-house.

Terribly strong winds, irritatingly strong, could not speak. Suddenly changed to hard north wind. As suddenly fell off entirely was still. Dark clouds, but not rain.

Curtis came up without the little black lamb, apparently the children want to keep it.

April 20

. . . . Got news that Tess has another little boy, born the 18th. A great box of linen came today, that Ugin bought at the Fifth Avenue linen shop. —Discovered that all the phlox is up. Bought 10 gals of apple-jack. . . .

Altair & Lupa ran away again tonight.

April 21

Snowing this evening, very thick. —Let buttercup & Ticket out. They went to call on Dolly & Blossom & the children. Cocoa [one of the "children"] was crazy about Ticket. They all were frightfully excited about the new calf. —Paterson came through with the road-scraper.

Ugin & Vincie got drunk & played, "Wat zeg je van nuhb vriend?"

April 22 Sunday

Awoke to see deep snow over all the ground, which remained on all day. Rained all afternoon. Very disagreeable. —The dogs have not come back. Anna & Conrad walked to Austerlitz, came back soaked to the skin. We made out our list of roses from Bobbink & Atkins, 106 roses.

Discovered that our apple brandy is excellent with soda.

April 23

Deep snow. Cold. Old-fashioned Christmas scenes, trees heavy with snow. Made out seed-list & vegetable list from Dreer.

Went out to look for the dogs, thinking they might be caught in a trap. I went on foot, Gene went in one direction on Dhu, Curtis in another on Brownie. Whistled & called, but no sign of them.

April 24

Cold & grey, ground still covered with snow. Horrible spring.

Curtis has taken Ticket away from her mother, & fed her tonight from a pail with his finger in her mouth. Buttercup is giving about 16 quarts a day, lovely rich milk & yellow cream.

Ugin & I pretended we were strangers, & peered into all the windows of the cottage; it looked adorable.

April 26

Cold & disagreeable morning, warmer & fair in late afternoon.

Curtis reported this morning having seen fresh tracks of dogs & whistled, but they did not come. The tracks were very fresh. —I sent Curtis down to Austerlitz on Dhu to put an ad in the Chatham Courier, offering $25 reward for their return. He came back saying they had been seen, or dogs answering to their description, last evening in Green River, just turning off the road into the hills. —Worked very hard all day on a poem about the faun I found once under a tree.

This afternoon Conrad & Anna suddenly burst in & said Mrs. Tanner was unbearable, & that if she didn't leave they would. I promptly went into the kitchen & told her that she was making trouble with my servants, & requested her to leave at once, which she did. I told her I did not know who was at fault, but that I must have a little peace & quiet. I believe she is indeed the cause of the trouble, for I know she can be very disagreeable.

At about 4:30 this afternoon I took the pruning-shears & went down the road towards A. to gather a few branches of yellow pussy-willow & red maple. I had seen again the same dog tracks & was feeling very unhappy. Suddenly a shadow ran across the orchard & out into the road,—it was Altair! He had seen me & came slinking to me at once. Then I whistled & Lupa came running to me up the road. I did not scold them at all. What's the use. And I was so happy to see them, the wicked creatures. God knows where they have been. Lupa was limping, but her toes did not look as if she had been caught in a trap. I rather thought they had gone off on a honeymoon, but Lupa gives no indications of such an episode. Altair's mouth is rather cut up—woodchuck probably. His belly was very fat. They have both had plenty of food; they have been hunting. Oh, for a picture of them as they slept at night under a fallen tree, or a young pine, or a thorn-bush!

April 27 Friday

Wrote a poem called *The Faun* [published in *Wine from These Grapes*, 1934]. Ugin arrived in the afternoon with Margot Schuyler & Eleanor Delamater.

April 28 Saturday

Deep snow. Everything covered with snow. Cold winter day.

Too disgusting to go out.

Lay in bed all morning working on the poem "I met the moth coming out." —Wrote furiously for hours. Was exhausted. Could hardly move.

All sat around drinking, & drank a good deal of excellent apple-brandy. Everybody got very fluent & gay but nobody admitted having touched a drop.

Young man on his way to Chatham—school teacher in Pittsfield—got stuck in his car on the road. We pulled him out twice, once with the team, once with the tractor. Most extraordinarily nervous young man. Gene said he cried, the second time he got stuck.

April 29 Sunday

Tonight we all dressed up in fancy dress! Eleanor went as the Black Pirate; Margot as a Chinese girl in my green brocade Chinese trousers & coat & arbutus stuck over her ears, looking charming; Gene as the Maharaja of Dyokyakarta, in batik skirt, that is to say, a sarong & a little batik tied about his head & an impeccable dinner shirt & pearl studs & black tie, & white mess jacket; I as a general houri, in Albanian under-dress, a Turkish burnous, a headdress from Benares & a pair of slippers from Agia & a brass girdle from Paris.[12] —We sat around the fire & told stories just like the Decameron, thrilling stories & everybody got very thrillingly intoxicated.[13] We did not go to bed until nearly daybreak.

April 30

Another horrible day. This month of April is the most vicious month of stinking weather I ever lived through with a sleeping-tablet on my tongue & a flask of liquor on my night-stand. —The men moved my work-shanty down into the blueberry pasture. Then I changed my mind & wanted it somewhere else, & they got it stuck where the tractor couldn't budge it. *We all* had to stand inside the shanty while they were moving it, out of the most appalling shower which suddenly came up.

May 1

First warm day under the administration of President Coolidge. Lovely nearly all day. Gene got up at dawn & took the girls to the train in Chatham. —Conrad & Anna left for their three days off; Kenneth took them to State Line. —Gene & I pruned roses all afternoon. —Saw—& heard—a purple finch—lovely song.

Raining tonight—I made butter—in half an hour—counting churning & making up. Anna takes ages to churn—must be something wrong.

The rock-cress—aribis—is in blossom in the rock-garden. There is still snow to be seen on the top of High hill.

May 3

Lovely day, somewhat chilly.

Three men on garage all day—all the framework up—looks wonderful. —Gene planted the roses Margot brought us, while I dug dandelion greens—the first this year. We had them for supper. The tenderest & best either of us ever had. —Saw two swallows—thrilling sight, dipping & darting in the high air. Have been doing considerable work uncovering & pruning the roses these last two days.

Started a poem about the Daughters of the American Revolution, & their fantastic infantile Black List ; beginning "Unfilial Daughters of Revolt."[14]

May 4 Friday [Eugen's entry]

Beautiful weather. 78 in shade.

Went to fetch Conrad & Anna in Chatham also Martin Eisenschmidt & Wife & infant of 10 months. Trying them out for the cottage. Put them up at the Inn. They have 6 children, which is a lot! —Probably will not take them.

Dulcie got 10 little pigs. —Vince & I saw them arrive. When 4 had been borne I called Conrad & Anna.

Beautiful moonlight. V & I heeled the plants in, which arrived from Dreer, with moonlight & flashlight.

[Vincent's entry] Vincie heard a cherwink & saw 6 swallows.

May 7 Monday

John took Artie & Gladdy out & ploughed with them just a few furrows to exercise Artie. They are the most beautiful team one could imagine, perfectly matched, & when they plough they pull precisely together & keep step with their feet. Artie lame.

Had Martin set out a young red oak in place of the little white birch that died. Gene & I walked down to the sawdust pile with the dogs. Found some yellow violets which we took home to transplant.

May 8

Lovely day. Motored to State Line to see if roses had come. Not yet.

Dogs ran away again this morning. Motored to Chatham & fetched Mother from the train. The titman of Dulcie's litter has disappeared. He is not at the stall, dead or alive. Nobody has seen him. Great mystery.

May 9

Mother dug dandelion greens all day just as I knew she would. I transplanted, or rather set out, a dozen narcissus* bulbs she is giving Gene for his birthday, the 20th. Put them where he could not see them, is not likely to see them, at least. We gave him ten questions this evening to find out what his present is, & had a lovely, amusing time. He could not guess in eight, & kept two for tomorrow.

Mother brought in the first adder's tongue of the season—very late. Set out the yellow violets, still perfectly good, as we had taken them up with a lot of turf.

Rosie had eleven little pigs this morning,—ten lived.

Took Martin & Frieda away, Ugin did, as it did not seem they would

be satisfactory. They were very nice about it. We just said we had decided we had not room enough for them. Poor people, with six children.
*[Later entry] (April 12, 1933) They were really tulips.

May 11

Lovely day. Ate outdoors all the time.

This afternoon Gene harrowed the whole Buckwheat Field—8 acres—with the tractor in less than four hours. Curtis & George started the first floor upstairs in the garage—it goes diagonally. This afternoon they put the screens on the house. I worked at cultivating the delphinium.

We should have had lots of little chickens by now except that the horrid hens left the nest about a day before they would have hatched. This instinct is all very well, but I'd rather have a little intelligence.

Mother & I got a big bunch of adder's tongues. She also got a lot more dandelion greens. We have them all the time now—very good.

Put in some pansies & mountain pinks Ugin bought yesterday.

May 12

Showery.

Heard a cat bird this morning, just crazy.

This morning Curtis harrowed the Buckwheat Field again, on the bias, & beat Ugin's time & is terribly cocky. But it's easier the second time; he could go all the time in high, & Ugin had had to go in low. This morning John put fertilizer all over the place where the lawn is to be, & this afternoon Curtis sowed the lawn to grass. George finished the floor in the garage. Frank Hill finished the first coat of paint on the cottage. All the buildings will be white, with green shutters, dark green, & red roofs. Ugin & I worked all day in the drizzle on the new rock-garden, & got a great deal done.

July, 1929, Steepletop

I am tired of my husband. It is time he should be tired of me. But the fact that I tired of him first, a fact which he uneasily perceives, lends me an element of charm beyond those which he at one time had for me, and has no longer. We have lived together for six years, during which time though we have had our separate bedrooms, we have constantly slept together, first because we both wanted to, after that because he wanted to, and after that because he had become accustomed to it. In all this time I have never once suggested to him that he sleep in his own bed, although it is my opinion that no bed is wide enough for two to sleep in, unless it be that sleep which follows the exhaustion of love,—when any bed is wide enough. He is as dependent upon me as an infant that cannot get to sleep without its head upon the mother's breast,—he cannot get to sleep without the weight of my head upon his arm. Night after night I lie awake, waiting for his heavy breathing to begin,—then I withdraw from his arm to the other side of the bed, there to compose myself to impersonal slumber.

Every morning I take breakfast with my husband in the dining room, although in my opinion that all persons possessed of sufficient means should breakfast in bed alone, & remain hidden from human sight until luncheon time.

January 1, 1930

On our way home from New York dropped in to see Deems & Mary [Taylor] just in time to drink the New Year in. Spent the night & most of today, loafing and drinking, & talking about the cat-boat Ugin & I intend to buy next summer. Arrived at Steepletop late this evening to find a letter from Autti [James] containing very distressing news as to certain of her recent activities. Looks like the end of Autti as far as I am concerned.

January 2

This evening went over to see Arthur & Gladys to say goodbye before leaving for the coast. Gladys received us in her best Martin Luther manner, full of recriminations that we had not got back in time to spend New Years Eve with them, as in a weak moment I finally after much urging had promised to do.

—Stayed to dinner, but was so sick & disgusted at the scolding Gladys had given us that I could eat nothing. —Left early, and Arthur, who was very sweet as always, set off some Roman candles in our honor as we set off down the road, but did not succeed in taking the dirty taste of Gladys out of my mouth.

Heard dreadful news that the house of Louise Bogan & Raymond Holden in Hillsdale burned to the ground last week.[15] Poor things—everything they had, & Raymond had built most of it with his own hands.

A. & G. said they would come over tomorrow to say goodbye to us.

January 3 Friday

Said to Ugin right out loud over my morning tea that I don't like Gladys, that she is a cold, severe, unripe and unforgiving person, harsh & vindictive, besides being darned dull, and that if it weren't for Arthur's sake I would never speak to her again, except perhaps to tell her to go and one-syllable herself. —Felt much better having got that off my chest. As Cyranno said—or words to that effect—"Je m'ecris avec joie un ennemi de plus!"[16]

Packed all day. —It is now ten-thirty, and Arthur & Gladys have not turned up. Good joke.

January 4 Saturday [Eugen's entry]

We sent Pierrot over to Arthur & Gladys to find out what was the matter, why they didn't come, as we were worried. Pierrot arrived back just in time to take us to train in Hillsdale, with message from A. to say there [*sic*] Kohler on the bum. —Sent Pierre with team early in morning to take trunk to Hillsdale. Found him later on while flying to catch train, drawn up beside Dodd's store abt. halfway to station, regaling himself with a leisurely lunch. Grabbed trunks off the wagon & chucked them in Todd's truck & just made the train. —Pierre is an idiot & should be discharged at once, but we shall keep him on account of the wine he makes and of Suzanne.

Went to N.Y. & stopped at the Vanderbilt.[17] [Margaret] Cuthbert came to have a cocktail & we went out to dinner with [George] Labranch & his girl.

January 5 Sunday [Eugen's entry]

Ugin spent morning talking in conference with Autti, who is in a bad scrape & is a damn nuisance!

Alice Blinn came bringing whiskey for me & gardenia for Vince. —

She saw us off & we caught the 2:15 for St. Louis with the skin of our teeth.

Had drinks in our drawing room & later dinner.

JANUARY 5TH JOURNEY TO TEXAS

January 6 Monday [Eugen's entry]
Arrived in St. Louis 1:20 pm & changed at St. Louis to 2 pm train for Fort Worth.

January 7 Tuesday [Eugen's entry]
Arrived 8:15 Fort Worth. —Met by Station Master, who was terribly polite & nice & I mistook him for a reporter, went to Hotel Texas. —Rooms stinking with white crystals strewn every where. They say it is to scare away the moths, I think more to scare away the guests. Bed room was worst. —I had to lock Vince in bedroom, while I spoke to reporters, and hostesses etc. in sitting room. —When I came back to bedroom Vince was nowhere to be seen, found her in bathroom, sitting in bathtub on a bathmat, with tears rolling down her cheeks. —She had not slept on train, had a head-ache, & the bed stank so she couldn't lie down, & breakfast waiting & getting cold in sitting room, & then this string of strangers! —Poor girl. —That evening she gave reading. —Very well received, but Vince didn't think she was good. —Got roses from the club.

January 8 Wednesday [Eugen's entry]
Packed roses, which were very beautiful & fresh.

Went by motor to Dallas—weather disagreeable & cold & icy road. —Stopped at Hotel Adolphus. Very good.

A big enormously fat woman, Florence Heiser, called up. She is on tour, as press agent, with The Miracle.[18] She gave us tickets. We dressed and went. —I loved it & hated it. —Finally decided a good thing was spoiled, as so often, by a semi-artistic Jew meddling with it. A lovely theme, mar-velously ruined. The Holy Virgin was wonderful.

We had lovely cold chicken & potatoe salad & W & S for supper.

January 9 Thursday [Eugen's entry]

Beseiged by reporters! At one time had man reporters, three girl reporters, two ladies from the women's club and Knott, a cartoonist, making sketch of Vincent, all in sitting room at the same time. A night mare, but the sitting room was charming & full of roses & lilies of the valley people had sent. —We liked Knott, the artist, and one girl reporter Miss Holmes. —one of the women of the ladies club was an unadulterated bitch, the other Mrs. Boggen [?] was very nice.

That night a reading.

Roads a glare of ice. A disagreeable cold. The women's club feared everybody would be kept away as this weather is very unusual here, but there were at least 1200 people to their great surprise. Audience heavy, but very, very attentive & quiet.

Had supper in our room. Vince exhausted!

(continued) One little girl (high school) told me she would not want Miss Millay to hear it, but wished she was my wife! Didn't do anything about it for lack of time.

Calling up room service at midnight for supper, gave name Millay & night girl cashier cried out: "Oh, please let me come up & shake her hand." —she hadn't been able to go to the reading. Nice girl, Miss Betti Dumler. Vince gave her a copy of the Henchman, which made her very happy.

January 10 Friday [Eugen's entry]

Got up at 6:30 a.m. to pack & catch 9 o'clock to Waco. Damned train held up by ice did not get in until 12! Arrived Waco just one hour before 4 p.m. reading. Dr. Armstrong nice fellow to our surprise. —Vince rushed to hotel & dressed as for evening performance. Reading given in an enormous draughty barn of a place. —In spite of icy streets, really dangerous, & cold weather, abt. 1500 people present. Excellent audience, excellent performance on the part of Vince, even Vince was satisfied. —Enormous bunch of roses passed over floor light from woman in audience. Forgot to say Fort Worth roses are still beautiful here in Waco.

January 11 Saturday [Eugen's entry]

Left Waco at noon for San Antonio, (side trip for fun & to see the mission) arrived 6:30.

Went to Hotel [name missing]. Excellent dinner in room.

We like all the colored waiters & bell boys we have seen in the south. They were by far the kindest, best manners, and handsomest men in the south. The white men look rumpled and as if they rarely take a bath, never brush teeth or have their clothes pressed in a word, they have sweaty hat bands.

January 12 Sunday [Eugen's entry]

Bought tea in Waco. Made tea for breakfast—better but not yet good.

Vincent awoke middle of the night with wind blowing on her, looking out she saw the door in the corridor wide open, probably sucked open by our open windows. —Thought she had caught a cold. Pray she is mistaken.

Steepletop
(1933)

The last diary entry in 1930 is January 12. Millay did not write in her diary again until the end of March 1933. These were eventful years for the poet, highly productive, and disastrous.

The reader will have noticed that there is only one diary entry in 1929, in July, the arch and revealing comment beginning: "I am tired of my husband. It is time he should be tired of me." At the end of 1928 she had fallen in love with George Dillon, a handsome poet of indeterminate sexuality who was fifteen years younger. The relationship was doomed in several ways, yet Millay pursued it, and Dillon, at least for a while, could not resist her. Eugen, the "perfect" husband (and a Dutchman with highly evolved morals), not only tolerated his wife's obsession but encouraged it, probably understanding that this affair would sooner or later run its course. And so it did play out, for the most part during the three years that Millay abstained from writing in her diary. It bears repeating that she was most faithful to her diary during periods of relative stability in her life, as long as she was not in the heat of composing poetry.

Inspired by her passion for George Dillon, Millay wrote the extraordinary sonnet sequence that was published as *Fatal Interview* in April of 1931, as well as the sonnets called "Epitaph for the Race of Man," composed in 1933 but not published until the next year in *Wine from These Grapes*. These works represent the last flowering of the poet's genius. Discouraged by her unrequited love for George Dillon and her fading beauty, devastated by his rejection of her in 1933, Millay fell into a depression from which she never fully recovered.

Nevertheless, the Steepletop diary of 1933 is a worthy addition to the record of her passion for nature, for her faithful husband, the dogs that became like family, and her lifelong friends. A new friend mentioned this year is their neighbor William Brann. Brann was part-owner of a horse farm in Maryland, and the Boissevains became silent partners in his racing and breeding enterprise. Millay's twenty thoroughbreds in the 1930s included the famous stallion Challedon, horse of the year in 1939 and 1940.

March 31 [1933]

Returned from Florida. Deep snow all over gardens. Rainy has twin black lambs.

April 2

Sneevw-klokjes are beginning to blossom, the first flowers of the year.[1]

April 10

Ugin planted some peas.

April 11

John (yes, still John Pinney) and Heline, our Swedish farmer, took the covering of leaves off the gardens & the burlap coverings off the climbing roses. My "Canterbury Foxglove" has lived through the winter well. I left it lightly covered today, however.

Hyacinths & tulips are coming up, a few white crocuses are in blossom.

April 12

Sleet storm this morning. Now, at noon it is snowing heavily, & has been for hours. The ground is deeply covered.

Apparently just such a spring as five years ago.

April 13 (Thursday)

Took pictures of winter landscape, everything under heavy snow, trees, roofs, everything. Two feet of snow on ground. Heline went to Austerlitz in sleigh.

April 14

Thawing. Snow-drops sticking up through the snow. Don't mind it at all. White crocuses, too.

April 19

Ugin has been spending several days transplanting Oriental poppies from the corner of the swimming pool. It rains just about all the time, horrible. Think it was yesterday first heard bull-frog, in swimming-pool.

April 20 Thursday

Wire from Deems & Mary that they are motoring up with Joan [their young daughter] Saturday.

April 21

First sun-bath in sunken garden. Third pair of twin lambs born either today or yesterday.

April 22 Saturday

Deems & Mary & Joan came in the afternoon.

Ugin bought 60 beautiful six foot & over arbor vitas from man in Spencertown for 50 collards, to put around the house & south of the swimming-pool & badminton court.[2]

April 23 Sunday

Rock tulips are in blossom in sunken garden. Also purple crocuses, & squills. The snowdrops are nearly gone & the white crocuses. Only one yellow crocus came up of the hundred or so we had two years ago. Don't know whether they blossomed last year or not. Wonder if drought & great heat of summer could have burned them. —Nearly all the peonies are up, also, phlox, delphinium, holly hocks, Madonna lilies, Oriental poppies.

All the poppies Ugin transplanted took fine, except one tiny one we must have forgotten to water.

Joan insists on living in the kennel with Altair & Ghost, or in one of the box stalls with a ewe & two very new twin lambs.

April 24 Monday

Sweetheart's calf, a heifer, born either today or yesterday.

Thought we'd all have a picnic luncheon, so took everything down into blueberry pasture near my old shack where I wrote The King's Henchman. Built a fire for coffee in a little stone fireplace where we'd often done so before, were very careful everybody right on hand in case a spark should fly into the grass, sudden puff of wind blew fire out into the dead grass, all seized our coats & began beating it out, but in less than a minute it was roaring up the hill towards the pasture barn & almost in the direction of the house. Ran to get help. Austerlitz & Spencertown fire departments called out by ranger who saw fire from tower, came very quickly, also many neighbours. Fought fire all afternoon, came within a few hundred feet of kitchen garden. I was sure that the house & everything in it was bound to go. Under control before dark, however. Lost only my shack, which burned flat, and I'm afraid, some beautiful white birches, lovely thorn-bushes, too. Also my little green leather cigarette case, Arthur Ficke gave me, which was in my coat pocket. Tweed jacket of my suit looks pretty exhausted, too. But I am so grateful that the buildings didn't catch fire that I don't mind anything else very much. There were no papers in my shack, either, which was lucky. —Came home nearly dead. Ugin gave all the men white wine.

Deems, Mary, Ugin & I had a bottle of champagne.

April 25

Everybody exhausted. Deems, Mary & Joan left after luncheon.

April 26

Snow-storm.

April 27

Cold, horrible day. Forgot to write that Ugin & I, weighing ourselves on reliable scales the morning after the fire, found that each had lost exactly three pounds since the morning before.

Heard two white-throat sparrows this morning. Never heard them so early before.

April 28

Nasty cold wind. —Ugin planted sweet peas from Dreer, twelve kinds. Just by accident read over & worked a bit on the poem . . . "I met the moth coming out"*. Bad pain in stomach, very queer.

*[Reference to the same poem mentioned in her diary entry on the same date in 1928.]

April 29

Dandelion greens for dinner.

George & Emla [LaBranche] came over.[3]

Saw four swallows. They are early. Dr. Beebe came & says I have *not* an ulcer of the stomach, but must go on a strict diet—no orange juice, & no whiskey. I shall starve. —Harrison Dowd came to stay a week.[4]

April 30 Sunday

No cigarettes! No wine nor spirits!

Did a lot of weeding near house, small hyacinth & tulip beds. Put lots of peat moss around. Look beautiful. Harry & I picked mayflowers, pink ones, from secret place down near where my shack was. Ugin & H. took them over to Emla LaBranche. Blanche Block & her children came over. Ate dandelion greens cold for luncheon & hot for dinner.

May 13 Saturday

Mr. and Mrs. Saxton came, bringing Aldous Huxley & his wife.[5] They are very likely charming, the Huxleys, but everything went wrong, & it was a damned dull party. For one thing, we weren't expecting them until to-morrow & we both looked a sight. For another thing, no sooner had they been introduced to us by the Saxtons than up drove Mr. & Mrs. Renwick, who have *never* been here before, bringing two elegant old people from Englewood, & for another, I can't *stand* people without either a drink or a cigarette & I really need both. Oh, God, it was awful.

May 14

Saw six scarlet tanagers in the dragon-willow, magnificent sight. So brilliant in the sun they were almost too dazzling to look at; they seemed incandescent, six small Holy Grails. —Saw, having first heard him, Baltimore oriole. Saw ruby throated humming-bird. Also, I think it was, a rose-breasted grosbeak.

Ugin swims in the pool every day now, but it is still frightfully cold, & though I love it when it's cold I don't feel quite well enough to go in.

Sweet-peas are up! Miss California is the furthest up,—almost the whole line.[6]

May 15

Fair & cloudy missed.

Worked in rose-garden with Ugin. Heline & John planted arbor vitas south of the badminton court.

Bill & Billie Brann drove up with Mr. & Mrs. Nisbet.[7] I looked a sight. Hurried in to take a shower & change—Had a glass of wine with about a pint of water with my dinner tonight. Same thing last night. Otherwise not a drop of alcohol for over a fortnight, nor a puff of a cigarette. Weight 109¾. have lost about eight pounds, I think. Marvelous. I love being thin. Don't care what the doctors say. They're all cock-eyed. I feel just as rotten no matter what I do, so I might at least look well in my clothes.

Autti & Marie came tonight, from Detroit. Autti is breeding cats, chinchilla & Persian crossed, or some such thing. Brought along five but had the sense to park them at the veterinarians.

Saw scarlet tanagers again today.

May 16

Lovely day but morning very cold in wind.

Heard, then saw, first bobolink. Staked up hyacinths. Autti worked cleaning around the dragon-willow, getting the lilies-of-the-valley out of *la misere.* Ugin finished planting hybrid teas into rose-garden, which looks magnificent with a new path of big flat stones.

Harry Dowd came back. Has fallen off the wagon with a thud, apparently—his eyes had that soft-boiled look.

May 19

Autti & Marie motored all around to find silly toys for Ugin's birthday tomorrow.

While Harry & I were working in the sunken garden, suddenly Floyd Dell drove up, bringing two beef-steaks & the mss. of his autobiography which he wanted me to read.

Planted double Russian violets under maple in hardy garden.

May 20 Saturday

First radishes.

Ugin's birthday. Beautiful day. Floyd spent the night & left after luncheon to go to Arthur's.

At five o'clock we hung all Ugin's presents in the branches of the wild-cherry tree at the corner of the swimming-pool—it is in full blossom—it looked so charming with all the coloured toys among the blossoms. Then we all five took off the few clothes we had on* plopped into the pool like frogs,—Ugin wearing the gold-paper crown be-jeweled with jelly-beans that the girls had made him, & looking exactly like Neptune.

Later in the early evening, we had a terrific hail-storm accompanied by thunder & lightening & followed by a downpour of rain. We had been told there would be a night-frost today (because of the fog on the 20th of February) but the hail-storm apparently took the place of it.

May 21

Grey morning but lovely afternoon.

The tulips are in blossom, & look splendid. The narcissus poeticus are coming out all over everywhere, among the trees.[8] In the rock-garden the red wild columbine is in blossom & the blue phlox & the dark blue large dwarf iris. The moss pink also, but going by, and the rock cress nearly gone. Plant[ed] 31 Platycondons in hardy garden, three white Oriental poppies & three Bleeding Hearts. Planted 3 Pond Lilies in Spring House pool. Planted

pachysandra. Having planted Edelweiss in rock-garden, also everbloom-
ing pinks—yesterday he planted platycondon mariesi.

Ugin's bush lima beans are up.

May 22 Monday

Motored over to see Arthur & Gladys in the evening & invite them to
dinner Thursday.

May 23rd Tuesday

Ugin & I motored to Spencertown in the evening after dinner & crawled
past the first engine & voted for the repeal of the 18th amendment.[9] I wore
my scarlet velvet dress & very handsome black & silver slippers from San-
dari. The people just stared at us silently. —Afterwards we motored over to
Bill Brann's for a moment to see if he had a copy of the American Field.[10]
Ghost is in heat & we want to breed her—the best sire in the country, if
we can find him—but nobody has the American Field & nobody has any
bright ideas & meanwhile the days are passing.

Everybody had whiskey & sodas but me, and I nearly died of weariness & boredom before I got Ugin home.

May 24 Wednesday

Ugin & I motored to Albany & got a couple of hair-cuts—we both feel
pounds lighter. Also went to Cottrel & Leonard & got measured for my
doctor's gown, which I should have got years ago. On June 5th at Russell
Sage College and on June 19th at the University of Wisconsin I collect
two more Litt. Drs. —I confess that I love them.[11] I love the gown, & the
mortar-board with the gold tassel, & the pretty coloured hoods.

May 26 Friday

Heard a cuckoo this morning. Ghost is in her second week now & Altair
is beginning to howl.

May 27 Saturday

Last night awakened by a dog running & barking in the wood, & feared
for the sheep. Turned on light beside my bed & felt same sharp pain in my
right eye I had nearly four weeks ago when Dr. Beebe had just scraped the

cinder out of it. Can hardly see out of the damned eye anyway now, everything is so blurred. Can't read, can't read music. Suppose I'll have to go see some thrice-cursed specialist*

The dog in the wood was Stanley's dog. Ugin went out with a gun & found Heline already out with his gun. Heline gave it a couple of kicks & it went home.

May 29 Monday

. . . . Autti, Harry & I did a lot of cleaning around the driveway near the back of the house, planted geraniums & lilac-bush outside wood shed.

Just one month today since I had a whiff of a cigarette, or a drop of alcohol. Still feel like the devil, but Ugin says I'm getting better, says he can tell by the way I act.

May 30

Nasty cold morning. But had a beautiful fire in my bedroom.

May 31 Wednesday

This evening, just before dinner Eugen's nephew, Dr. Charles Boissevain, drop[ped] up, on his way to Holland. A charming, amusing darned nice fellow, with a fear & dread of "sentimentality" that amounts to a religion.

June 1

Didn't get a wink of sleep until 5 o'clock this morning. Ugin & Charlie sat up & talked until 4:30. It was hideous. Couldn't have a smoke. Couldn't read, my right eye is so blurry. A night of torture. —Charlie left this morning at about 11. I felt too ill to get up to say goodbye to him.

This afternoon Harry found a beautiful shed snake-skin in my rock-garden, doubtless one of pet pair that live there. It is intact, even to one of the eyes. I am delighted with it.

June 2

Today I found the other snake's skin in the rock-garden, very near where the other had been. This one is longer & darker than the first & perfect, absolutely perfect, even to *both the eyes!* I am so thrilled. To have a pair of snakes that you're acquainted with! —Today the snake that always lies on the rock while I'm weeding has not appeared. Probably keeping his tender skin in out of the sun. . . .

The little log-cabin came. It's going to be so cute.

June 3 Saturday

Had my pianos tuned. —Heard cuckoo this morning. Ugin said "Rain before night." Had terrific wind & rain storm just as Ugin & Tess were driving back. Had been very hot day—hottest so far.

Five weeks today since I had a cigarette. I'm going to start smoking again. Whatever is the matter with me, cigarettes aren't it. —But I'll continue to stay off the liquor for a while. Even though today I feel horrible, and I don't get a bit better at all.[12]

Ugin & Harry set up the log-cabin among the arbor vitas in the corner of the badminton court. The whole effect is superb. From a little distance it is as if the tiny cabin were a big cabin, the arbor vitas enormous Douglas firs, and the cabin built on the edge of a precipice, & one were looking at it from a mile away. —My cap & gown have come, velvet stripes, gold tassel & all. —Ugin fetched Tess from train at Stockbridge. —Old-fashioned red peony Mrs. Tanner gave me is in blossom, the first. Tess said the temperature was 90 in the train.

June 4 Sunday

(Got the curse today, of course, so I'll be feeling just fine to sit through the commencement ceremony tomorrow.)[13]

Tess' Birthday. Arthur & Gladys to dinner at night. Never saw Tess look so beautiful, sort of old-rose chiffon with a white fur-piece about her shoulders. She has had her hair cut at last. Never thought she would. Looks marvelous.

Gladys more than normally offensive tonight. I'm afraid I can't put up with her much longer, even for Arthur's sake. Arthur was drunk tonight. Kept repeating himself. What a pity. But you can't blame him. Harry was filthy drunk, perfectly slimy. I of course being perfectly sober had an interesting time observing them all. Ugin was tight, but witty & charming. I couldn't have told that Tess had been drinking at all—she was lovely. Grand dinner. Two bottles of Lanson '21. But I could have only a sip of it. Am smoking again though, thank God. Washed out a white dress to wear under my gown tomorrow. Tess ironed it for me tonight after the party, still in her evening dress.

June 5 Monday

Oppressively hot.

Got up early & Ugin motored me to Troy, where I received the degree of Doctor of Letters at the Russell Sage commencement,—my second Litt.D.

Luncheon with my only* friend Florence Jenney, who taught me Baby German at Vassar. Felt ghastly all day. Horrid pain, & sweating for hours in my cap & gown. Can't have any gin now, of course; can't even have aspirin, it's so bad for my stomach.

Had a very interesting talk with Tess this evening, about how to keep one's privacy & not have people running in and camping on one all the time. A difficult matter, but she's right that one must be firm & even rude & not afraid of making people angry.

---

*I meant to write "old friend!" This could bear looking into—am I getting sorry for myself, or something?

June 6 Tuesday

Hot!

Thunder shower in the night last night.

Played the Grieg Concerto with Tess tonight—the orchestra part—never played so badly.

Ugin took us all motoring in the evening—went to see Autti's house & all around—lovely moonlight!

Was shocked to see on the dinner table a great bowl of peony blossoms, knowing they were the blossoms of my first red peony that is always the first spot of colour in my garden, & such a delight. Tess had cut them, about half the blossoms on the plant, Ugin having said she might! —I felt all mixed up, hurt, astonished, & sad, & so damned furious I cried all the way home in the car, but nobody knew it. —Why can't people let things be in blossom—just simply *be in blossom* for a minute, before they go at them with the shears?—At least, in other people's gardens!

June 7 Wednesday

Hot—everything steamy like a greenhouse.

As if to make up for my ruined peony when I came out this morning the first thing I saw was two Oriental poppies in blossom, about a half dozen blossoms out—gorgeous. —And then—standing by the hardy border looking at the Iris, I heard again the bluebirds in the orchard that I have been hearing so often lately, & followed them quietly just for the fun of seeing the colour of their wings, & saw, to my enormous excitement & happiness, that a pair of them have moved into the bird house which I had John put on an apple-tree only about two days ago! They were going in & out all day, putting down the carpets & hanging up the curtains, as busy as anything—at least, *she* did most of the work, but he did a vast amount of singing, from the ridge-pole of the house.

Gladys motored over to take Tess over to her place to spend the night.

June 11 Sunday

Arthur & Gladys came over. Afraid I was pretty mean to them. But it puts me into a *frenzy* to know that somebody, no matter who it is, is going to come driving up every week on the same day at the same hour as regular as a factory whistle. God, how dull of them to do that! And they *know* we hate that sort of thing.

June 14 Wednesday

Took Tess to train in Stockbridge.

June 16 Friday

Ugin & I took train to Chicago.

June 17 Saturday

Arrived Chicago. Went to Minna Weisenbach's.

Minna went out with us this afternoon while I bought a new hat to go with my brown ensemble, & some white & silver slippers to wear with my white organza dress with the red sash from Louise Boulanger.[14] The hat is right, but I'm not quite sure of the slippers; they look a bit heavy.

June 18 Sunday

Terribly hot.

Minna's Carl motored us up to Madison [Wisconsin]. Stayed at the President's house [at the University of Wisconsin]. Big dinner there this evening. Met Frances Perkins, the Secretary of Labor whom I liked enormously.[15] Zona Gale was there, looking very fragile, like a person who has been very ill.[16]

Wore my white dress & I believe looked very well, but felt awkward, standing up for hours talking to all those people. This dress makes me look such an ingénue that I don't know what to do with my hands. Ugin kept sneaking upstairs after dinner to get himself a drink out of his suitcase. Shocking to see the butler going around the sumptuous dinner-table, reaching between the lilies & roses & over the caviar & squabs to fill up the glasses with ice-water!

Glenn Frank sprang it on me that I was expected to make a little speech over the radio at commencement tomorrow.[17] Froze up at once & told him flatly that I would not do it. But all the time I knew I probably would, I'm such a softie. Evening entirely wrecked for me, hours of anxiety & distress.

June 19 Monday

Frightfully hot.

Commencement exercises at 8:30 in the morning or some such obscene hour. Sat on the platform for hours while thousands of boys & girls filed past me, trying to round off a neat little speech to say over the radio, it seemed so stuck-up & mean not to do it. Finally the awful moment came, & I got up & received my diploma from Dr. Frank & had a very handsome doctor's hood with a lot of red in it put over my shoulders, made my little speech very clippily but without disgracing myself—as, for instance, by saying University of Michigan instead of University of Wisconsin, as I might as well have done in the state I was in, & finally got back to my seat, after bolting off in the wrong direction & nearly stepping on the feet of their funny little Governor.

Went to the State House to hear Frances Perkins address the Senate, which she did very eloquently & without slopping over. Back to Chicago on the train, greatest discomfort from heat I ever experienced, my white dress sticky & filthy with cinders. Even in these circumstances enjoyed talking with Miss Perkins.

June 23 Friday

Midnight train back to Steepletop, & darned near missed it.

June 24 Saturday

Steepletop. —Very tired & glad to be alone, although we had a lovely time in Chicago except for the heat.

Sometime after midnight tonight a car stopped outside. Ugin went down to the door & there was Harry Dowd whom we had told not to come back until we telegraphed him, filthy drunk, driven by somebody of the Jitney Players. They had stopped in at Bill Brann's to borrow some money for gasoline. Ugin & I perfectly furious. Wouldn't let him in. He went on to Auttie's, very sore. Poor Autti! But perhaps she'll learn now that we weren't such meanies after all, trying to keep liquor away from him.

June 25 Sunday

Arthur & Gladys came over.

July 1 Saturday

Motored up to Bailey's Island [Maine] to see Tess.[18]

July 3 Monday

Ragged Island.[19]

July 4 Wednesday

Tess' father & her brother Franklin & his wife came. —Talked with Tess' father about the possible price of Ragged Island. He astonished us by saying that with things as they are now, & the Island being owned by a bank which is in the hands of a receiver, we might get it for as little as ten dollars an acre. —Motored back to Steepletop. On the way stopped in Portland, went to a lawyer named Berman, told him we wanted Ragged Island, & authorized him to offer on our behalf seven hundred & fifty dollars! Felt pretty childish naming such a low price, but it can do no harm.

July 21 Friday

Big thunder storm this evening.

Ugin has just come back from Maine, with the news that Ragged Island is ours! —bought & paid for. So we've done it. We've done what we always wanted to do & meant to do. And I think it is the most beautiful island I ever saw. —I can't believe it. —He says the house is in good condition, too, only a week's work to be done on it by a carpenter & a mason. And then we can go there & stay. I can't believe it.

July 22 Saturday

Efrem Zimbalist & his daughter Maria motored up, & we went back with them to New Hartford.[20] Their house is the old house of Edith Wynne Matt[h]ison, where I visited her & Rann Kennedy when I just was out of college, & where I rewrote a great deal of *The Princess marries the Page.*[21]

Had dinner tonight with Alma's friends the Barneses, a big family of the kind people that Ugin calls "boy-scouty" & I call "browsy."[22]

July 23 Sunday

Frightfully hot.

Went swimming tonight in a lake near Alma's house. Everybody swam out to the float & climbed up on it & swam from the float, but I thought it would be fun to stay in the water & swim about & not climb up on the float at all. So I did, & swam about until it was quite late & everybody was ready to go home—about an hour & a half must have been swimming & I was not a bit tired. I was glad to know that.

Alma's daughter Marie came in & talked to us after we went to bed. We were all quite tight.

This afternoon Efrem played us the piano sketch of his American Rhapsody.

July 24 Monday

Frightfully hot again.

Got the curse. Felt horrible.

Chotzinoff & his wife, Heifetz's sister, & Sascha Jacobsen & his wife, were here to lunch.[23] I liked Chotzinoff, which I hadn't expected to do.

Ugin & Maria & the children went swimming. I went to bed.

In the evening Efrem played some charming Creole songs on the piano for Alma & me, and some Cyril Scott.[24] I don't like Cyril Scott.

July 26 Wednesday

Fine day.

Slept late, & were pleased, pleased but astonished to see Owen Johnson motoring up with his son right after breakfast.[25] Had some wine, & the boy & I went looking for bird's-nests in the orchard. He had glasses with him for studying the birds. I showed him all the nests I know, quite a number. The baby pheasants on the north of the lawn are hatched & gone. We saw the empty shells. The song-sparrows that lived in the Oriental poppy are also gone, and the cedar wax wings. But we saw the open beaks of the baby king birds in their nest in the orchard, & a chipping-sparrow sitting on her nest in another apple tree. —Felt we should invite the Johnsons to luncheon, but they went, & then we discovered that it was five o'clock.

July 27 Thursday

Hattie & Ell, or Perk & Tom, as Ugin calls them, are going to a ball to-night, with Hattie's boy-friend, who is a butler somewhere in North Hillsdale, & another man. We let them have the whole day off, so they could go to Albany to get their hair straightened & have plenty of time to get ready. Heline drove them to the station at about nine this morning. They went off in great excitement, each carrying a big bunch of sweet-peas, which are to be kept in water all day at Hattie's boy-friend's place.

Bill [Brann] came up, saying that H. T. Webster & his wife, whom we met in Florida & who are charming, are visiting them & want to see us.[26]

July 28 Friday

Dinner at Bill's. Mrs. Webster & Ugin did some marvelous stunts from the diving board. She dives beautifully.

I sang a lot of old English songs at the table after dinner "Green Broom," & "The Raggle-Taggle Gypsies" & "Lord Randal," & many others. Felt just like it, & never did them better. —

After dinner got my shoulders all bruised & the skin taken off the back of my neck trying to turn a back somersault on the floor in the hall. Young Bill can do it, & Mrs. Webster can do it, too. I'm going to do it myself as soon as my neck gets healed & I can practice.

July 29 Saturday

Worked all day very hard on "Epitaph for the Race of Man."[27] —Late in the afternoon Ugin & I motored over to say hello to George & Emla [LaBranche] & take them some sweet-peas. Came home by way of Bill's & told them we couldn't stay for the beefsteak supper on the hill, as I had to get back to work.

July 31 Monday

At two o'clock this morning on the big bed in the north guest-room, Ghost's puppies were born, the first of five of them. Ugin & I were with her. The first two & the fifth were alive, but the third and fourth were born dead. She helped get them out of her by licking them & pushing them with her tongue. She bit & tore away the cowls in which they were enveloped & then she bit the umbilical cords in two, & licked the little blind things clean & dry. She was wonderful. Finally, we took the whole family into my bedroom & installed them in the big chair by my bed where Ghost always slept. Ugin went to his room & went to sleep. I kept awake, I was so afraid she'd lie on one of the puppies, & at the slightest whimper put the light on & got up. At five o'clock I hear her licking herself again & I got up & held the three little dry puppies in my lap close beside her, while two more wet ones were born. When Ugin came in in the morning, he stared & rubbed his eyes, to see five of them instead of three. At twenty minutes to eight the last one was born, but did not live at all.

We had Dr. Smith come over to see that everything was all right. Ghost has no fever, & all is well. Sent word to Bill Brann, who gave Ghost to me, & he came to see her, bringing her a great bouquet of asters. She actually leaned over & smelled them. Billie came later. Put Ghost & family into kennel.

August 1 Tuesday

All five still alive & all right this morning. So afraid she'd lie on one. We've named them temporarily, in order of birth, Satu, Dua, Tiga, Ampat &

Lima. Satu is all pure white except for dark ears; will probably be very handsome. Lima is adorably marked, too. They're all cute as hell. —Forgot to say yesterday that Lima, who made much the most noise, didn't know how to suck, so I had to feed him cow's milk all day with a medicine dropper, Dr. Smith's directions. Lima is all right now, though. The last time I tried to lift him out to feed him, he was hanging on so tight I knew I'd never have to feed him again.

Ugin motored down to New Hartford this afternoon & brought back Marie Zimbalist, who wants to make a sketch of me. We all went swimming by moonlight, a rather [illegible] moon, but delightful, & we had a fire by the pool & sat about it & got warm & then went swimming again.

August 2 Wednesday

Ghost & puppies doing splendidly.

Awfully cute note from Bill brought up by his butler this morning, saying he had champagne on ice & what should he do with it, et. cet., so we sent word we'd be right down, & went down & sat around Bill's big pool & drank champagne & swam & had luncheon at the pool in our bathing suits,—heaps of fun. Decided we were having such a good time we would stay to dinner, so told Bill we were going to stay to dinner, & stayed, & had the greatest fun. Bill was all alone, except for his mother-in-law, who ate in the dining-room. We ate on the terrace. Swam some more & drank some more champagne. In the evening were having a grand party in the drawing-room, dancing & being ridiculous, when who should walk in but Alma! —bringing Mrs. Smith. The man at the garage had told her where we were. We were all a bit taken aback; Marie was furious, & promptly got drunk. Ugin called me out to attend her in the bathroom, she was sick as anything. Bundles her into our Cadillac without letting Alma, & Miss S. following. Got Marie into my bed before Alma got here. Good work. Alma & Miss S. slept in wing. —Going to the races with Bill tomorrow. Opening day at Saratoga.

August 3 Thursday

Ghost & puppies all fine. Ghost is beginning to behave more like her old self again. Alma came into my room this morning while I was drying my hair, & insisted on having a talk with Ugin & me about Marie, what a difficult child she has been to bring up, with poor Marie sitting right there. I'm so fond of Alma, & I felt so sorry for her; but it seems to me that for a mother who is anxious to draw her child close to her, she has a perfectly fiendish gift of doing exactly what will push the child away. —Alma & Miss Smith left for N.H. & Marie, Ugin & I drove to Saratoga with Bill in his Rolls, which is very elegant, but to my mind a pretty inferior car. Partly the chauffeur's fault, a regular old auntie,—but whatever the reason was, there we were, very much afraid we were going to miss the first race, in which Bill had a horse running, tearing up the concrete at the dizzying speed of fully 35 miles per hour. We were all sweating with annoyance, except Bill, who didn't seem to mind. We bet on all the races, picking our horses for the silliest reasons, "Beret" because Tess Root [Adams] had just given Ugin a basque beret; "Shot & Shell" because we'd been telling so many lately,—about Marie getting sick & everything. And all our horses came in on top, & we made loads of money. Except "Swatter," but we betted on him because he was Bill's horse. Also I picked "Tambour" for his looks, & he came in second to "Equipoise."

August 4 Friday

Marie made a sketch of me this morning, which I like. Ugin & I drove Marie home to New Hartford. I took down some books of mine for Efrem which he hadn't got, & some photographs which he wanted. But he wasn't there. I was very disappointed. Played "bagatelle," & stayed to dinner, motored home in the evening.[28]

August 5 Saturday

Getting back to work again. Working quite a bit on the "Epitaph." Also some other things.

Ugin motored over to see Arthur, to ask him if it was all right for Mrs. Tanner to cut his hay, but Arthur & Gladys are visiting the Dwight Wymans & Theodore Dreiser, or so their very unpleasant servant told Uge.[29] Ugin then went to call on John Cowper Powys, whom we hadn't seen for ages, & had the most marvelous time with him.[30] Says he is the most beautiful & thrilling-looking creature he ever saw in his life, & wants me to hurry up & get a look at him before he gets a hair-cut. He has his hair cut about twice year, I think, & then has it absolutely shaven.

August 6 Sunday

Finished reading "La Main Tendue" of Phillippe Heriat.[31] Awfully good things in this book, but somehow it is tedious & annoying, badly put together. At any rate, I've been a long time finishing it, which I feel is a bad sign, I so seldom really leave a book till I've finished it, & I read so rapidly.

Ugin is reading "The Fortunes of Richard Mahoney," at my recommendation, which I read at Efrem's recommendation; & he gets so furious at the pompous stick of a humourless Irishman who is its hero, that every once in a while he yells out "CHRIST Almighty!" & leaps up & tears his hair & stamps & pours himself a stiff drink & then goes right back to reading it.[32]

August 7 Monday

Ghost's babies were a week old this morning. In a couple of days now they should be getting their eyes open. Ghost has her appetite back now & eats enormously, raw meat twice a day, & quarts of milk & cream. The puppies are getting so fat. Ghost is quite her old self, cries to come out at suppertime, & goes leaping & running about.

Worked hard most all day, changing, correcting, typing. Motored to Hillsdale in afternoon to send off Harry's suitcase, & Ugin called up Norma. Charlie is showing his paintings for the first time, in New York City somewhere, for a fortnight. I *MUST* see them, I'm so excited about it, but God, how I dread to get into a bunch of those venomous copperheads that are Norma's neighbours in New York City.

Am practicing the Chopin G minor prelude, which I once heard Myra Hess play so marvelously.[33] It's not hard, not hard to play badly, that is. Tess told me recently that Myra Hess is a Jewess. I felt greatly relieved, for it had been bothering me considerably how an Englishwoman could play like that.

Europe and England
(1934)

With few exceptions Millay's diary is seasonal, beginning in the late winter or spring and ending in the late summer. And so the Steepletop diary of 1933 concludes with a full entry on August 7. In July she and Eugen purchased Ragged Island, one of the outermost islands in Casco Bay, near Brunswick, Maine, eighty acres of rocky soil with a small house on it. They spent much of the summer and autumn settling in to the house on Ragged Island. In letters she speaks of regaining her spirits and health by swimming and sunbathing there, in preparation for a journey to Europe for the winter.

So it is unusual to have a continuous winter diary, chronicling a journey to southern France, Paris, and England from January to April. These are extraordinarily rich entries that describe the beauties of France as well as encounters with famous writers such as Somerset Maugham and Llewelyn (Lulu) Powys, the painters Pavel Tchelitchew and Romaine Brooks, and the actor Laurence Olivier and his wife. During the mornings Millay worked on her manuscript reports and recommendations for the Guggenheim Foundation; hours each day are devoted to tennis; and the evenings are given over to casino gambling at Cannes where Eugen devised some remarkable system for beating the house.

March 10 she traveled alone to Paris for several days to visit George Dillon. The longed-for rendezvous proved disappointing. If she had hoped to breathe a flame from the embers of their passion she was unable, at this late date, to manage it.

During these months she was fighting a losing battle with her alcoholism, continually swearing off the bottle and days later complaining of night-long bacchanals, and crushing hangovers. A reference to morphine on the ship home (on April 22) suggests that she has either been prescribed the drug by the ship's doctor, or is craving it. Meanwhile it is an astonishing witness of character and evidence of stamina to see this forty-two-year-old writer functioning at such a high intellectual level (as the Guggenheim reports prove), and playing a decent game of tennis daily, while poisoning her system nightly with liquor and opiates.

This pattern will continue upon her return to Steepletop at the end of April, and it would appear that the habit is related to her depression over the loss of George Dillon's affection.

🖏

January 1 [1934]

S. S. Excalibur—6 days out from New York, bound for Marseilles. We passed the Azores today, the first time I had seen them, as the *Cabo Tortosa* two years ago did not pass in sight of them.[1] Saw what looked like an extinct volcano. —Without exception there is the mangiest, lousiest bunch of passengers on this boat that I ever saw anywhere. Among them is a certain Don Luis who says he is the brother of the king of Spain. He looks Bourbon enough. But otherwise he looks just like everybody else, i.e., lousy.

January 2

On deck at five bells to see the sun rise—gorgeous. It is getting so lovely & warm now. A very good crossing, except for the passengers, & the food.

January 3

Saw the light of Cape St. Vincent tonight at about 10.[2] —There is a really attractive little girl aboard, a Jewess named Ruth Starrel, brainy, too. Talks about being Jewish just as a Frenchman might talk about being French. If they would only all be like that! —so unselfconscious, and uninferior. Tells interesting things about Jewish customs. The manager of the line is aboard, too, a jolly nice fellow. But the average is very low.

January 4

On deck at five bells again. Land sighted about eight bells. Stood way out on the bow & saw about a hundred big porpoises swimming & leaping & plunging in front of the boat right under. Beautiful flashes of blue & green colour they make under the water. Stopped briefly in Gibraltar.

January 5

This morning the manager & the chief engineer took us all over the boat,— kitchen (I mean galley) refrigerator, crew's quarters & engine room. Really splendid. Learn to my astonishment that our cargo is FISH. We are exporting fish to Marseilles and Naples. Also to England! Tons of frozen fish!

January 6

"Houzee," Cap d'Antibes.[3]

Furious yesterday because they wouldn't let us off at Mallorca. Wanted to find the Spanish riding-master we were such friends with two years ago and get the address of the poor bootmaker who is still wondering why Ugin doesn't come back for his boots, or at least pay for the ruined leather. We were simply furious, and sat at the bar all afternoon, scolding & getting tighter & tighter. Last night & this morning terrible wind blew up suddenly, and the ship pitched & shuddered like anything. Such a surprise after the calm days we've been having. Nearly always like that in the gulf of Lyons, according to the night-watchman who came balancing in with tea at about six-thirty. Had the most awful hangover this morning, and all our packing to do, & in that sea! I must have been darned drunk last night. I don't remember leaving the bar and going to my cabin at all. But apparently I came down just before dinner and got into bed and fell asleep like a shot. I awoke about midnight when Ugin came in. I remembered nothing, but my clothes were all over the room, and I never do that. Disgraceful. Got to cut it out. Not only that the doctor says so, but that I'm getting a tummy. —Sea perfectly calm when Ugin went to bed. Storm came up in about five minutes. —This morning packed somehow with the help of seven gin-rickeys. Left the boat at Marseilles about 3 p.m. — Declared all our cigarettes down to the half-smoked butt and got through customs nicely without having to open every box of Kotex. Train to Antibes at 6 o'clock. Dinner on train. Best braised endive I ever tasted. But of course *anything* after the food aboard the *Excalibur.* Taxied to Jan's [Eugen's brother's] cottage on the rocks, & found the man, a Russian, waiting for us.

January 7

Didn't drink a drop or smoke a cigarette all day. Didn't want them. Up at sunrise. Breakfast on the porch. —Sun-bath—partial one—on the rocks. Lovely in the sun, but the wind chilly, & in the shade cold. To bed very early.

January 8

Wired Jan to come and visit us in his own house. Took sun-bath—altogether one—on rocks. Eugene-the-Russian drove us to Antibes where we ordered a Badminton set. The court here is in good condition, but all the things are rotted. Uge & I took lovely walk along the road. Lots of pines here. Australian pines, I think. Heaps of fun picking up cones & small branches for our open fires. Drank nothing. To bed at nine. Up at sunrise.

January 9

Day overcast. Played two sets of badminton. Not in such bad condition as we feared. But went to bed pretty tired. Wire from Jan, coming Thursday. Drank two very small *fines-a-l'eau* & a half glass of *pinard.* Smoked two cigarettes. To bed at nine. (We were up at seven.) Ugin beat me: 15–7; 15–13.

January 10

Up at sunrise. One set of badminton before breakfast. Ugin beat me one set 15–13. Read Conrad Aikens' Selected Poems.[4] Like the second half of book (the later poems) very much. Little claret for dinner. 3 cigarettes.

January 11

Up at sunrise. Terribly stiff from the badminton. Could hardly walk. But played two sets before breakfast. Ugin beat me the first one 15–3. I beat him the second 15–12. Hooray! —Nan came along while we were at breakfast out on the grass. We pretended we couldn't speak French so we wouldn't have to talk with her. Ugin gave her 8 francs. She went away mumbling, but whether cursing him or saying a prayer for his soul, we could not make out. Picked flowers for the house today. [unreadable] (like daisies), purple stock, pink geraniums, hundreds & hundreds of them—they climb the walls like ivy here—and two rose-buds, all from the garden. Also some yellow blossoms—some kind of vetch, I think,—from high bushes.

January 12

Jan came last evening from Amsterdam, bringing presents of *roggebrood* and a yellow cheese with aromatic seeds in it from Hilda de Booy.[5] Today it was rainy, it drizzled & rained. Ugin & I took an early morning walk, lovely but I'm still quite stiff in my legs & every step hurts. Learned from our lugubrious Russian servants that our expenses, chiefly for food, have been about 1200 francs in these five days—over seventy dollars! If we can't stop that, we'll have to leave the place. Decided to take our dinners out, cheaper to eat in restaurants than at home. Besides, Helene's cooking is very bad.

January 13 Saturday

This morning very strong wind blowing. The harbor of Cannes very blue, the snow-topped Alps very handsome and clear. Ugin & I walked to Juan-les-Pins, beautiful walk. Bought a beret each and a walking stick each in the village. Had a café-au-lait at a little bistrot near the sea. In this lane just before reaching there discovered along the roadside many flowers like or-chids, sort of brown & green,—what they were *really* like, both flowers and leaves, was tiny Jack-in-the Pulpits. Picked a large bouquet for the dining table, very effective.

This afternoon Jan & I left Ugin at the Casino in Cannes to try out the System, while we went hunting for a cheap place to dine. Found a little place called "Le Pingouin" which looks nice. Ugin says System works, but very slowly.

January 14

Had the curse & felt awful—a week overdue—Couldn't have played bad-minton anyway, the mistral is blowing so hard.[6]

In the afternoon pulled myself together & we all went to the casino.

System worked like a charm. It is frightfully exciting. Dinner at La Pingouin. Perfectly all right, & only 10 fr. Vin compris.[7]

January 15

Terrific wind blowing. Ugin made 820 francs today at the Casino.

January 16

Mistral still blowing.

We *are* drinking again, of course. But my God, you have to do something to fight off the mistral.

Tonight Ugin won for a while, & then things went against him to a point where he had no money to stay in with, taking a loss of something over a hundred dollars.

January 17

Saw Corsica today quite plainly, although it was a misty day here. Jan says it is the second time he has seen it in eight years. —The wind has died, but the weather is grey & misty.

The three of us went out tonight with the express purpose of getting lit,—went to several bars & had heaps of fun, but didn't really get lit. Had dinner at a nasty little place stinking of gas—prix fixe 12 f. & no wines! & the proprietor made us pay a cover charge! —for a paper table cloth! We smiled at him strangely & bade him a sweet goodbye.

January 18

Tonight the opening of the Casino at Juan-les-Pins—or at least so we supposed. We went there tonight & saw the play, "Jean-de-la-Lune." First two acts amusing & charming, last act all wrong, peachy & sentimental. Learned to our disgust that the gambling rooms are not to be opened until June! —nothing but *boule* to play there! —They are going to have roulette tables this year & apparently it will take till June to train the croupiers. But why can't they train them somewhere else & in the meantime let us have the *baccara?*[8] It's just a stall. They've driven all the Americans home by making the prices so high, that's what's the trouble, and they can't afford to open. —The mangiest bunch of people there tonight, all spread out in their chairs drinking *limonade,* or all spread out on their feet doing nothing. Where *did* French women get their reputation for being smart? From the high-class cocottes, I thought, but Ugin says those are mostly Russian & Viennese. —Sat at the bar drinking champagne cocktails a while. Came home early.

January 19

Rained a little last night. Court wet this morning, but dried up later. Played fifteen sets, very strenuous ones, five singles, & the rest Uge & I against Jan, or Jan & I against Ugin. We are all playing darned well. I never sweated so; it was marvelous; I felt grand. —Grey day all day, not cold, no wind. Two battleships in the harbor tonight signaling frantically, waving searchlights, sending out *verrie* lights (if that's the right name) very lovely, like flying golden balls, & then shooting off a cannon. Target practice right in the harbor in pitch darkness, & nothing to warn people off but a modest notice in this morning's *"Eclaireur."*[9] Glad I was not a little sloop just tacking in from Corsica. The silly idiots! The bastards!—

Dinner in tonight. But Helene still insists on feeding us cotellettes d'agneau [lamb cutlets] at vingt francs la bouche, and as I persist in my refusal to be consulted about the *menus,* we'll just have to eat out again.

January 20

Rained again last night. Court wet this morning. A young Italian girl who is staying at the practically empty Hotel du Cap scrambles up the wall every morning & sits there, watching us play badminton. I am sorry for her—it must be very dull at the hotel—but I am sick of her. This morning after the court had dried I was just starting out to play when I saw her— there she was again, sitting on the wall. I suggested that we go to the tennis club & play tennis instead. Which we did. Twenty francs for the three of us for the day. I've always played tennis wrong—wrong stroke—& now Jan is trying to teach me the right. The upshot is that I get a black & blue lower forearm & that I can't play at all. —In the late afternoon played badminton & was pretty good. —

The woman at the bar at the tennis club gave me a bunch of beautiful large white violets which she had picked. She says they are rare. I had never seen them before. They smell sweet.

January 21

10 a.m. The weather is perfectly filthy. Haven't seen the sun for over a week, except for about an hour on Thursday. This morning icy wind blowing from the east, grey sky. Sea pale greenish blue & very handsome, surf on our rocks. But I have a headache & feel nervous & irritable. Think I'll get drunk.

Have been busy ever since we got here reading all the poets for the Guggenheim Foundation. So far the only ones I'm excited about are Conrad Aiken & Walter Lowenfels.

February 1

Went to Cannes this evening to hear Lucie Delarue-Mardrus speak & to hear the music.[10]

February 2

Bought myself some adorable white linen shorts at Spaldings in Cannes. Also a white tennis skirt. Also a beautiful white pull-over sweater. Also a white belt. —Bought a new girdle, too, at another place. Left it to have the garters altered, & Ugin went to collect it. The woman, seeing that I was not with him, made him pay 170 francs for it, instead of 136, the price she had told me. He suspected her, & when he came back to the car asked me about it. Then he went back & made her fork over 34 francs. These French shop-keepers certainly are a thievish bunch, particularly the women.

On the way home stopped at the Miramar Bar for a champagne cocktail. Delightful there, looking right out upon the sea. —Couldn't play tennis because I turned my ankle last night stumbling over the stage to try & find Mme. Mardrus,—& it still hurts.

February 4

Played six or seven sets of tennis. Very strong wind, though, pushed back our rackets & blew sand in our eyes. —In the late afternoon Ugin & I went for a lovely walk, all up & down strange little lanes, & finally out upon the Antibes road about 2 miles from home. Probably walked about 4 miles. Not bad, after all that tennis. On the way home stopped at a little shop & bought a bottle of too expensive Scotch—seventy francs—& even at that we had to beat him down from eighty.

February 5

Three years ago today my mother died. I kept it out of my mind all day long, on account of Jan, because it is his birthday, & gave him a lovely birthday. We sent Eugen out early this morning to get a bottle of champagne & some sweet biscuits, & at eleven o'clock we sang Happy Birthday to Jan & the champagne was brought in. He was astonished that we knew about it, & so pleased. We played about seven sets of tennis, & I played ever so much better than before. Had one set of singles with Jan & won two games out of the set. Of course he was giving me easy balls,—but one of the games was a love game, & I was serving! I was terribly proud.

Ugin made a delicious New England fish-chowder dinner—we were all dressed up & very handsome—and afterwards we went out & drank champagne cocktails, first at the Carleton Bar & then at the Casino in Cannes. Saw Dickie Gordon in the Carleton Bar. She is sailing for New York tomorrow, from Ville Frenche.

February 6

We arrived here a month ago this evening. Most beautiful sunny day. Some wind, but not too strong. Played three sets of tennis this morning. I felt that I played very badly in comparison to yesterday. But Jan & Eugen said that I was not so very bad. I had a slight hang-over from last night, however, & was quickly tired. I *must* cure myself of saying "Damn!" every time I miss a ball. Eugen says my language is quite improper for an elegant & refined game like tennis. —

Luncheon outside, & sunbath on Jan's terrace. The sun is getting to feel very hot. —Have got my weight down to 107.

February 10

Jan took to Cannes today & exchanged for a much more expensive Underwood, the awful little Remington with half its vital parts missing that I bought without having looked at it in New York the day I sailed. The Underwood has to have its keyboard changed from French to English. I wish I had my big Underwood here, though. I hate all these new portables. —And I wish to God I had my Oxford Dictionary here. It seemed such a chore to be carting the ponderous thing all over Europe, that at the last moment I left it behind. I wish now that I had left all my clothes behind instead.

Played about ten sets of tennis, & was never so near being a tennis player. Beat Jan 6–4 set, singles. Of course he was letting me use the double court, & he was giving me easier serves than he would to a real player—still—I do feel encouraged. Sat outside on the clubhouse terrace & drank Vermouth & Casis with seltzer.

February 11

Got the curse, but don't feel very bad yet, so played tennis this afternoon. Wasn't very good, though Jan says, however, that the game is getting much faster, that they are giving me more difficult balls, & that's why I feel myself not improving. Ugin & I played against Jan, four sets, & Jan beat us every one. —This evening we played three-handed bridge before the fire. God I'm slow! I don't see how anybody can have the patience to play with me. Drank a lot of pretty awful champagne in the course of the evening, and smashed a champagne glass. But came out ahead in the game.

February 12

(About 10 a.m., I think. All the clocks seem to have stopped.) I am sitting on the porch of the "Grand Villa Houzee"—the house we live in is the "Petite Villa Houzee"—this villa has not been rented & Jan sleeps over here. This is where we always take our sun-baths when it's too windy on the rocks, or when we are feeling lazy. Both Ugin & I have the most horrid hangover from last night—the champagne was really not fit to drink. I have my back to the sun as I write & am getting a swell tan. We are having simply glorious weather now. Glad I'm not in New York, where the temperature is over fourteen below zero (I mean *under* fourteen) or in Steeple-top, where it must be 25 below. Worried about swimming pool. Heline will have to cut the ice every fifteen minutes to keep it from cracking in this weather.

February 15

The Russians left this morning, thank God, & Ugin, Jan & I are alone. They left in a great huff, having failed to cheat Uge out of four extra days' pay. It is unpleasant to have servants go away hating & insulting you, but the following reflection, which I passed on to Ugin, comforted us both considerably, if your servants *don't* leave in a huff, it just means you've been a sucker.

February 16

Tennis. Went to the Casino at Juan-les-pins. Practically empty. While we were there, the King of Denmark came in with another man & two ladies. —ladies-in-waiting to the queen, the barman told us.

February 17

Tennis this afternoon. Uge & I beat Jan one set & he beat us three. The sets stand now 7–3 in Jan's favour. The match is as follows: Jan must win 25 sets before we win 10, other wise he is defeated & must give us a beautiful silver cup. —I was awfully sick in the night last night, threw up most of my furniture, except such things as were hooked on the decks. Result of the foul choucroute garnie we had for dinner at the *Viking* last night, worst I ever tasted.[11]

February 18

Beautiful day. Motored over to Cap Ferrat, just beyond Nice, & had luncheon with Somerset Maugham, just the three of us, Dr. Fairchild—who is a sister of Rebecca West—Mr. Maugham & the man who lives within, his secretary, et cet., Gerald Hexton, I believe his name is.[12] Beautiful place, up on the hillside overlooking the water, delightful gardens with the most succulent-looking green grass here & there in tiny lawns & lanes. They get the grass-seed from England, & they have to dig up the lawns & re-seed them every year. I must say it is worth it.

I liked S.M., but somehow it was not very much fun, something wrong somewhere. So few people know how to give a good party. —Motored back early, stopped in at the Casino at J[uan]. les P[ins]. for champagne-cocktails. The barman told us that the King of Belgium had just been killed in a motor accident. He was driving his own car, alone, as I understand it.

Poor fellow. —Still, it was quickly over. —In the evening turned on the radio; most lovely music from everywhere: a Beethoven violin & piano sonata, a Hayden sonata (adorable) a Mozart symphony, a Mozart quartet for flute & strings (lovely), some of the Gotterdammerung, & all of the Rimsky-Korsakov Scheherazade. Of course some of it was gramaphone records, but it was awfully good.

February 19

Those odious battleships are still here, ruining the beautiful calm days with their hateful cannon-firing, & machine-gunning. And last night, right in the midst of the gay, innocent music (the Haydn, it was) their dirty wireless cut in & kept tac-tac-tackey-tac-tacing for a long time. It was dramatic & poignant to hear the gentle gracious music so horribly invaded, yet going serenely on. I came damn near crying. —Unreasonable enough, perhaps, since without the radio I should not have been hearing the Haydn at all. Still, it was not the radio I was objecting to. —There they go now—crash, boom—crash, boom—crash, boom.

February 20

It seems that the King of Belgium was killed by a fall while climbing a mountain. I feel sad about him. He seemed an awfully nice fellow. Even my Dutch husband & brother-in-law say he was a nice fellow. And for a Dutchman to have a decent word to say for a Belgian, is news.

February 22

My birthday. —Didn't think anybody would know about it. But this morning before I was up Ugin & Jan stood outside my door & sang "Happy Birthday." And then, they came in. Ugin with a beautiful bouquet of mauve stock & pink geraniums from the garden, & Jan with a great spray of almond blossoms from his little *propriete* on the hill—too lovely for words. What beautiful blossoms they are, almond blossoms!

In the afternoon played tennis, or rather both morning & afternoon, lunching on the terrace at the clubhouse. Played nine sets & by winning two of them (10–8; 10–8) Ugin & I won the match from Jan, he ending with 22 sets in his favour, & we with ten. Great excitement.

Forgot to say had champagne for breakfast.

February 23

Vacation's over. I'm working like fury now on my Guggenheim Fellowship applicants. I've read them all by now, & thought about them a lot, but now I want to re-read them, & collect my notes on them, & then I must write my report. —It's a terrible job, all right. But I knew it would be.

March 4

Slaved all day in my room on my reports for the Guggenheim Foundation. Twenty-one poets I have read & re-read & thought about & finally written about. —Practically finished tonight. All typed, just a few corrections to make in the morning. —I've given hardly a moment to my own work for these two months—tennis, & reading & pondering on these twenty-one writers, that's all I've done—I'm recommending Kay Boyle, Conrad Aiken, Isador Schneider, Walter Lowenfels &—for rather special reasons—John W. Andrews.[13] —Their own pet, for some reason, seems to be Horace Gregory, who means to me, if I except certain of the bawdier among the Catullus translations, precisely not a damn thing. —I wonder who will get the fellowship.

Weight down to 105, I've lost more weight sitting up in bed writing this report than I've lost playing tennis—from seven to ten sets a day!

March 4

At last my report is off to the Guggenheim. Finished correcting & typing it this morning, & Jan & Eugen motored off to get it aboard the train so that it will catch the "Paris" at Havre. —God, what a terrible job. I'm exhausted. Have hardly left my bedroom for three days. Haven't stuck my nose out doors. —Wonder if they have any idea how much thought & care & downright drudgery go into these reports I do for them.

Washed my hair & got into my shorts & leaped out into the sunshine. Felt as if I were out of jail. —Played tennis this afternoon. Played better than I ever did—took plenty of time, got into position, waited for the ball— nothing made me nervous. —Afterwards went to the Casino at Juan-les-Pins & drank buckets of champagne-cocktails. Danced with the professional; first time I ever danced with him when I felt like it; he complimented me, but in a patronizing way. Thick-headed little Frenchman. I dance so much better than he does. He just knows a few little steps I'm not familiar with, that's all—and even at that I follow him like his shadow. Stupid little beast.

March 6

Went to the tennis [illegible] early this morning & played six sets before luncheon. Beautiful day, just a bit chilly. Had luncheon at the club, outside on the terrace, omelettes fine herbes & lovely tender lettuce, fresh from a little garden right beside the courts—not much like the burdock leaves they sell you in the shops here. —Had three more sets after luncheon. Then home & hurriedly bathed & dressed to go to Nice & hear Raquel Meller, whom neither Ugin nor I had ever heard.[14] She was marvelous. I sat between Jan and Ugin & they were both crying & openly wiping their eyes about half the time. I didn't cry, but I came near it. — Ugin & Jan are both in love with her, terribly hard hit—they told me so. When she threw the violets they were both frantic for fear they shouldn't get any. But she threw them each a bunch. And I got one, too.—

Dinner at *Pergola* in Nice. Excellent. But I wish the proprietor would stay away for a moment to let one eat, instead of sticking around asking how every mouthful tastes.

March 7

Cable from Mr. Moe [Henry Allen Moe, secretary of the Guggenheim Foundation], anxious to know if my report is on the way. Thank God it is.

10:30 a.m. The mistral is blowing like hell. It looks as if we were in for three solid days of howling & hooing & booming & swishing & rattling, and little Golfe Juan looking like a particularly dirty piece of mid-Atlantic, and the curtains standing out in the room as if the house had a heavy list to port.[15]

It is impossible to work; you simply can't think. They only thing to do is to get drunk & stay drunk until it blows itself out, & read detective stories. —I've just had my first gin-fizz. And it's not going to be my last.

March 8

Must go to Paris tomorrow for a few days.

March 9

On the P.L.M.

Very luxurious compartment, all to myself, very de luxe. I wanted to travel cheaply, we're so poor this year, but of course I had to go & get the curse this morning, so Ugin insisted I should be as comfortable as possible. —Which is not too darned comfortable, even at that. I feel like the devil. And the sheets are of cotton, & I hate cotton sheets. These are particularly cheap & offensive. They feel like very old paper-covered books with dust on them. —Thank heaven I have a flask of gin along.

March 10

Arrived in Paris at 11:30 this morning. Raining, of course, —While I was getting dressed—or rather before I had a stitch on, & was sitting on the edge of my bed wiping off the cleansing-cream & applying a pat of skin-tonic—the door, which I thought locked, suddenly opened, & there stood the frousy, rumpled porter saying "Quinze minutes." I yelled "Get out of here!" which he promptly did. Unspeakable fellow. Liar, too. There was fully three-quarters of an hour before we were due to arrive.

Went to a little hotel called the *Magellan,* in the Avenue Marceau, very reasonable rates,—fifty francs a day for bedroom, sitting-room & bath, & the petit dejeuner included— Had luncheon with George [Dillon] at his hotel, a charming place in the rue Galilee. —Came back to the hotel & washed my hair—in water that was absolutely cold!—but absolutely—no difference whatever in the temperature from the two faucets. Took a bath in ice-cold water, too. My grandmother would be sure that I shall get my death of this, what with the curse & all. I shan't, though. —Had dinner with George—didn't notice where—and went to the theatre, "Au Grand Large," which is a translation of the American play "Outward Bound."[16] Some of the acting very good, & some things in the play,—but awfully sentimental for the most part, frightfully obvious & boring toward the end. —Went somewhere afterwards & had some drinks.

March 11

Had luncheon with George at his hotel, & much to my horror found we were hopelessly entangled with a friend of his who is also staying here, but who, he had sworn to me, never comes down to luncheon. She is an old lady from—of all places on God's green earth where she *might* have come from—the Cap d'Antibes! She is the widow of a famous Greek poet, whose name I have heard, but forget. It seems she had found out in some way that George was having a guest to luncheon—so in she butted. I liked her, rather, but thought her an old nuisance. How *can* people do things like that? Got away finally & went & had some drinks. Then came back to my hotel & showed George a lot of my new poems. So happy that he likes them. He made one or two extremely intelligent & valuable suggestions, which I shall at once try to carry out. —Had some whiskey & sodas sent up. —Went out to dinner rather late. Had some excellent *chocroute garnie;* & some beer which G. liked because it reminded him of Munchner, but I found it too sweet, preferring the bitter blonde beer of France. Came back to my hotel & talked some more & read some more poems.

March 12

George left this morning at 10:30 to catch the boat-train for Le Havre. He sailed on the *City of Havre* for Baltimore.

Went to the National City Bank building in the Champs-Elysees to look up Dick Labouchere. He had already gone out to lunch, but his son got him on the phone for me. Arranged to have tea with him. —Went forth then to try to find news of my dear old Pauline.[17] Had not heard from her for nearly a year, & was so afraid I should learn she had jumped into the Seine again—and no Ugin around to fish her out.

—Went to her old address in the rue des Dames, cluttered narrow street, strange forbidding quarter. A young man, husband of the concierge, finally answered my knock, in his shirt-sleeves, looking very cold & suspicious. I put my question. "Can you give me information about Pauline Venys, who lived here about ten months ago?" He looked at me with an expressionless face & called over his shoulder "Somebody here asking if you know anything about a Mme. Pauline Venys." Instantly a young &

very handsome woman entered & the man went out. She looked at me very proudly & coldly. "What do you want?" she said. I repeated my question. I could tell by her answer—a simple repetition of the name of Pauline that she did not remember her at all. My heart sank. I felt frightfully sad, "Oh, please," I said, "if you remember her at all, if you have any idea what has become of her, please tell me!" The woman looked at me for a moment in silence. Finally she said, simply, "elle habite toujours ici." —"Oh," I cried, "I'm so very glad, so relieved! —is she in the hotel now? Could I see her?" —Suddenly the woman's face changed entirely, & she smiled at me with the most beautiful smile. "She'll be in in a minute," she said, "She's working. She always comes in about one. Come in, & sit down & wait for her." She smiled at me again, so sweetly & kindly, & went out, leaving me in the little front room.

I waited for nearly an hour, & finally Pauline came in, looking very well & strong, her cheeks very red, & laid down an armful of newspapers on the table. —She is selling papers for a living. —We were so happy to see each other. —Before I went I gave her two hundred francs that I had in my purse, & she insisted on my having a glass of chartreuse with her. —I shall see her again soon.

Had tea with Dick at his house. His daughter Alix, a lovely girl, was there & two pretty young friends of hers. They played on the gramaphone a record of the Gershwin *Rhapsody in Blue* arranged for eight pianos, & then played it as arranged for harmonicas. I thought it much better on the harmonicas. —Went with Dick to have cocktails with his brother Jacques & his wife. —Afterwards Jacques played me on his radio-victrola the most beautiful Bach records I ever heard. —Jacques took me out to dinner. I didn't notice where we were going. Sitting at the table I thought the place looked familiar, & picked up the menu, "La Biche du Bois," I said, "why, there's a place by that name on the avenue Victor Hugo!" "This is the avenue Victor Hugo," Jack said. —I was just around the corner from my old apartment in the rue Benjamin Godard. It gave me a very queer feeling. —Meant to leave Paris tonight, but Dick had persuaded me to stay & have luncheon with him tomorrow.

March 13

Had luncheon with Dick & a friend of his, a terribly nice man, at the *Ane Rouge* at the top of the rue des martyrs. (Another old haunt of mine—the *Auberge du Clou* is just next door. Paris is really getting to be too full of ghosts. —(Paris is really just a great big beautiful old haunted house.) — Had cocktails first at the Crillon bar. Had champagne with caviar at the *Ane Rouge,* followed by a most lovely Bordeaux (some kind of Haut-Brion, I think) & ended up with the most perfect & most powerful liqueur I ever tasted,—a *framboise.* Dick's friend called up his doctor & cancelled an appointment to be examined for his life-insurance, & then we all went somewhere else. Finally we found ourselves at Bisdom's place *"Neliare."* "Where do you get your hats, Edna?" Dick said. "Suzanne Talbot," I replied. "I'll show you some hats," dick said, & took me to "Neliare," & insisted on buying me two!—perfectly adorable, one big one in a yellow Milan straw, the other smaller & black. —I don't know where we went after that. I think we were all pretty tight.

—Finally got back to my hotel, packed hastily, & left for the Gare de Lyons. I was anxious to know, just out of curiosity, in what way *this* French hotel would cheat me; it turned out to be *petits-déjeunes;* they denied they were included in the price of a room, & charged me five francs a day for a cup of café-au-lait & one roll. I had no time to argue; besides I am getting to hate the French so for their lying & cheating & rude manners that I can hardly look them in the face; they give me the creeps. So I paid up & leapt forth. —My money which I was expecting from Harper's not having yet arrived, I had to travel second-class & sit up all night (of course I knew I shouldn't have given Pauline that two hundred francs, but I couldn't help it, especially as she was so courageous, not asking for help at all. She probably went out & got drunk on it,—but lord! Who doesn't?)—

March 14

Spent about the most uncomfortable night I ever spent in my life. Got onto the train last night at eight o'clock with a few francs in my pocket & no dinner under my belt, waited until 9:20 for the train to start, was dying of thirst by that time, having got so tight in the afternoon, & nothing to drink on the train but *eau non potable,* until we should get to *Lyons* at about four in the morning.[18] I was desperate. —There were two obviously "first-class" American girls on the seat opposite, & one only too obviously "third-class" passenger, a young Frenchman, on the seat beside me. He was very nice, asked me my nationality, saying that although I sounded like a French girl I didn't look like a French girl, & finally saved my life by giving me a cupful of red wine mixed with water from a bottle he carried in his suit-case.

—I was very grateful to him; but after the lights were all out, with the exception of the dim little blue *veilleuse,* & it became a question of sitting bolt upright for sixteen hours or succumbing to the situation & discreetly stretching out on the seat with my feet in the young man's stomach, he began to present certain difficulties, & became increasingly difficult throughout the night. By daybreak, I was thoroughly worn out, what with gently & repeatedly pushing him off, & having him as gently & doggedly return. Of course I could have complained to a guard or somebody, but I wasn't quite sure which I should find more objectionable—the rude coldness of the official, or the polite though much too persistent warmth of the strange young man. —Anyway, I managed to get through the night without serious mishap, & my three fellow passengers descended at Marseille, leaving me alone in the carriage until I got off at Antibes. Reached Antibes at 1:47, Ugin & Jan were waiting. They had the house simply full of flowers; two big potted cinerias, one white with blue edge & one pale magenta; a big bowl of white iris, several bouquets of stock, hyacinths, & anthemis, & in my room sweet-peas, and little daisies and a camellia.

March 15

Rainy & stormy. Stayed in bed all day & worked on my poems. Made some excellent changes, I think. And Ugin gave me a marvelous suggestion about *The Hedge of Hemlocks.* On the whole, however, I distrust the mood I am in, & dare do nothing definite. These poems look too darned good. A dangerous state of mind.

March 16

Drank too much last night, we all did; or the champagne was bad, which I suspect, for I awoke with one of my old-time headaches which I so seldom have now, at least, seldom so cracking. And everybody felt awful.

Managed to play five sets of tennis. Jan beat Ugin & me the first three sets: 6–0; 6–1; 6–1. —Later we pulled ourselves together & beat him 6–4; 11–9. But we all played as if we were in diving-suits. —This morning a cablegram from Mr. Moe saying that my report on the Guggenheim poetry applicants reached him safely—the day before the committee meeting! "Today thank God it arrived Magnificent" he cabled. I was pleased. I had worked very hard on it. (It really arrived yesterday.)

Received also a notice that I have been elected to membership in the Cosmopolitan Club of New York—and this although I dynamically do not want to be a member of their club, & never did want to & said clearly to several of their members who approached me on the subject in December, the day before I sailed, that I would rather be found shot in a nightclub *cabinet* than be caught dozing over a copy of *Town & Country* in the Cosmopolitan Club. Not that I have anything in particular against this particular club,—but I don't like clubs & I'm darned if I'll join them.

March 17

This is St. Patrick's Day. And it is the anniversary of my mother's wedding. —Once when I was on a reading-tour, & Ugin was with me & Mother was in Newburyport, we sent her two dozen American Beauties on this day. And she was so happy with them.

March 22

Have been working very hard these last few days on my *Epitaph for the Race of Man*. Have finished several of the sonnets which I began years ago [as early as 1920]. Am having a bad time with the one beginning "When Death was young & bleaching bones were few." The trouble is I need to have my dinosaur both a brontosaurus and an allosaurus—herbivorous in the third line & carnivorous in the seventh line! —And I'm afraid I just can't work it. —Played tennis this afternoon, & never played so well. Jan said it was for the first time really tennis. Very tired afterwards, however. Went to the Casino & drank martinis.

March 23

Worked on the epitaph all day. Finished "See where Capella with her golden kids." Ugin read the whole series aloud to me, seventeen of them.

I keep getting shivers up my spine & at the end found myself very shaky. A strange experience.

March 24

Charlotte [Jan's wife] arrived in Cannes today on the Conte di Savois from New York. At least, she docked in Cannes. She is here.

Couldn't sleep last night so worked all night—from 3 o'clock on—on the Epitaph. Wrote a whole sonnet "What rider spurs him from the darkening east."

March 25

Well, our peaceful bachelor establishment is invaded by the lewd presence of woman. Awoke this morning to hear Charlotte scolding Jan because he didn't have a lady's maid waiting to unpack for her. They had a terrible row. And she's been home just one day.

March 26

This morning while I was packing Charlotte came into my room all primed for a fight, started right in without a word of preamble to say that she'd have me know she wasn't a bitch, et cetera. I was never so astonished. I simply stood there. Finally I said that I didn't know what she was talking about but if I'd said anything to hurt her feelings I was sorry. After a while she went away. I was horribly upset, all cold & shaky. I can't stand such things. I can't *stand* people who like to row & make scenes. Eugen & I have been married nearly eleven years, & we have never had a quarrel, but *not one.* Two or three times one of us has been irritable or spoken sharply to the other, but the other has never taken it up, so it has always stopped right there. —Uge & I left tonight on the train for Paris, & I must say we were both relieved to get away without further trouble. Women are awful, really. I have very little respect for them, with a few exceptions. They are so uncontrolled & self-indulgent, & *so noisy!* I'm a stout feminist, and all that, but I do think that for the most part women are pretty awful.

March 27

Paris, Hotel Galilee. Very nice. Dick came to have cocktails with Ugin, but I was exhausted & stayed in bed.

March 28

Cocktails, or gin-fizzes rather, at Dick's house. Later cocktails with Jack at his house. Ugin got very tight, I fairly so.

March 29

Went to see "Tovaritch," at Dick's suggestion. Didn't like it much. Amusing, but pretty thin.

March 30

Went to see the Fratellini at the Cirque d'Hiver.[19] The funny little old circus stank so I was afraid I shouldn't be able to stand it until they came on. Did, however, & loved them. So silly, & part of it very tedious, but so sweet.

April 1

Easter Sunday. Also, pathetically enough, April Fool's Day.

April 2

Saw "La Croisiere Jaune," a movie.[20] Turned out to be just a great big advertisement for Citroen [automobiles] & we paid very high prices for the seats. Hated it.

April 3

Saw Mae West in "I'm No Angel" at the Cameo. Also a hot tip of Dick. Thought her awful. She exercised no come-hither at all upon Ugin,—nor upon me, either, & I am far from unsusceptible to women's charms.

April 4

Happened in just by accident upon a film called "Vol de Nuit," & thought it excellent.[21]

April 5

Saw Cecile Sorel at the Casino de Paris.[22] Left at the first intermission. Incredible! I can't see why they don't tear her down. Really, she's a public menace.

April 6

Went to see Henri de Regnier & found him most charming.[23] Lucie [Mardrus] had said he was very cold, & so had Natalie [Barney], & I was scared to death. But he was perfectly lovely to me, & I had a delightful talk with him.

April 7

Taken by Natalie Barney & Romain[e] Brooks to the studio of a young man named something like Chillichef [Pavel Tchelitchew], to see his paintings.[24] Liked some of his paintings quite a lot, but thought quite a number of them pretty silly. Also liked the young man, though this, I am sure, was purely physical. He was insufferably conceited, talked all the time about nothing but himself, can't stand any paintings but his own, Rembrandt is awful, Vermeer is awful, everybody is awful, except Chillichef, who is wonderful. Somebody told me that he is Edith Sitwell's *grand amour.* Well, I can understand it in a way. But God! What a selfish man. Still, things like that never seem to stop us.

Took Lucie Mardrus & Germaine de Castro & a young French Communist friend of theirs to Maxims' for supper. Had a wild gay time. I got lovely tight. Instructed the taxi-driver to take us to a perfectly dreadful place, all naked girls walking about or sitting on your lap, or spiriting twenty-franc pieces off the table either with the *derriere* or the *devant.* Lord, I must have been plastered to take the party there! Still everybody had a fine time & L was very much interested, never having seen anything like it before. These Parisians don't know anything about Paris.

ENGLAND

April 9

London. Came over on the Boulogne-Folkestone boat. Came to *Berner's Hotel,* it being the only address we could think of that didn't sound too expensive. Hate it here. Rooms icy cold. No way of heating them except by a little electric gadget which you feed with six pences not supplied by the hotel. Saw the forty-eight dowdiest women on earth all at the same time right here in the lounge, & the ninety-six largest feet. Must be a convention.

April 10

Dinner with Neville MacDonnell, Ugin's cousin at his club. Saw Elisabeth Bergner in "Catherine the Great" this afternoon.[25] Good. Saw Sybil Thorndike in "Double Door" this evening. Lousy. (Yet I used to think her marvelous. Perhaps she was.) Have decided that Berner's Hotel should change its name to "Pension for Poor Relatives." Snobbish, nasty, dreary place.

April 11

Neville showed us church were Queen Elizabeth gave thanks after Mary Stuart was beheaded, & the tavern in which she lunched on "pork & peas," the dishes are still there. We saw the church where Pepys used to go & where he is buried, and a section of the Roman Wall built around ancient London to keep out Queen Boadicea.[26] It is in a warehouse in Cooper's Row. Saw Noel Coward's "Conversation Piece."[27] Charming, but not filling. Took Jill Desmond & Laurence Olivier to supper at Savoy Grill.[28] Champagne, lots of fun. Went home with them afterwards to their house in Chelsea. Late back to the hotel,—and the later the better, to this damned hole.

April 12

Called Jill & told her I could not come to luncheon but would come for a cocktail. Did so. Larry came in from a rehearsal of "Biography," astonished to see me there, was very distraught, did some steps of a tap-dance, put a ship on the mantle & loved it there & hated it there, went out to get some green paint to paint the trellis, returned without it et cet. All very droll. I felt uncomfortable & beat it as soon as I could. —Met Uge at bar of Hotel Cumberland, crowded, thousands of most awful people. Went to see Ann Sten as Nana, & liked her. Supper at the Hungaria, goulash & tokay. Talked with the waiter about Budapesth.

—I loved London. And I loved the people. Everybody is so gentle, the taxi-drivers, the shop-keepers, the bobbies, all so polite & kind. Coming here direct from Paris, where you have the rudest taxi-drivers, et cetera, on earth, the shock is almost too great. It's hard to keep the tears back. (It's the English would-be-upper-class&-can't who's so mean.)

April 13

Went to Anderson & Sheppard, where Ugin was measured for a suit of evening clothes, & about time, too, his old ones being rather worse for wear & for Seine water. Went to see an exhibition of paintings by Cedric Morris, whom I used to know about twelve years ago in Pourville near Dieppe.[29] Felt sad to feel myself disappointed by them. Lovely flowers, well done, but that was *all;* no eloquence of any kind. —By train to Wareham & by motor to Ludworth Cove to see Lulu [Llewelyn Powys].

April 14

Cover Hotel, Lulworth.

Awakened very early, about 3 or so, by the sea-gulls, screaming as if they were being murdered, a horrible strangling sound. Worked on the preface of H. van Stockum's "A Day on Skates." —Bleak day. Walked to Chydock [*sic*] over the sea-downs to see Lulu & Alyse [his wife], about three miles. Lulu looking beautiful with his curly white hair, & a beard, & looked better than I had dared hope. Left my notebook of typewritten poems for my new book [*Wine from These Grapes*] for them to read.

Lulu gave me a pomander. I did not know what a pomander was. It is an orange so covered with cloves stuck in it that you wouldn't know it had ever been an orange, a round brown ball smelling very sweet. You make them at Christmas & give them to friends. —Met Lulu's sister Gertrude, very handsome, as all the Powys are. Lulu says that Keats wrote "Bright star, would I were steadfast as thou art" here in Lulworth.

April 15

Lovely day, (Heard & saw many skylarks walking over the downs.)

Spent morning working on a poem "Pinch now the down, etc," a sonnet. Not very good. But it is fun to be working again. Lulu's brother Willy, who is here on a brief holiday from South Africa, came to ask us to luncheon. Walked over to his cottage, near Lulu's. On the way saw a snake lying across the path ahead of me. Was not startled at all. First time I ever saw a snake without that "Zero at the bone" that Emily Dickinson writes about. Yet it was an adder, the first poisonous snake I ever came upon. I felt sure it was an adder & later when I described it both Willy and Lulu said it was. It lay still a minute, then went off into the grass. Waded through some horrid brambles & climbed an ancient thorn-bush to see some magpie's eggs in an enormous nest at the top. Saw the magpie fly off as I climbed, all black & white. At first could not get high enough to see the eggs, so reached in my hand & lifted one up to look at it,—pale blueish-green speckled with brown like a song-sparrow's egg. Later managed to get a few inches higher & could see six of the eight eggs which Willy said were there. Got scratched a bit but managed not to tear my pale-green tweed. Tea with Lulu & Alyse. They liked my new poems. I'm awfully pleased.

April 16

This is Shakespeare's birthday. —Oh, no it's not! —What am I thinking of—1616, most likely.

Awakened at about four o'clock by the screaming of the seagulls. Very foggy. A fog horn (I wonder if it is Shambles light-ship) blowing continuously. Ugin up at seven & left for London to have his evening clothes fitted. While it was still dark & I could not sleep, wrote a poem about the gulls & the fog-horn. Have a coal-fire in my tiny grate which measures no more than three inches across the back & seven across the front. Kipper for breakfast, as usual. (I must find out if the magpie went back to her nest. I feel dreadfully guilty.) Walked over alone to see Lulu.

Ugin returned this evening.

April 17

Wrote a poem for Lulu, a sort of ballad, using many lovely names of this district. Walked over with Ugin & read the poem to Lulu & Alyse, who were happy with it, although Alyse cried.

April 18

Returned to London. Went to the Gro[s]venor House, a darling hotel.

April 19

S.S. President Roosevelt. Sailed from Southampton tonight. Dog-tired. Feel a perfect wreck.

April 20

Ugin & I stayed in bed all day & read detective stories.

April 21

Stayed in bed all day. Got up for dinner.

April 22

Stayed in bed. I'm so dying to get home that I can hardly bear it. I wish I could be kept under morphine that whole way until we dock. Don't want to go on deck, can't *stand* it to have to talk to people. Just want to keep on drinking & reading detective stories until we hit New York.

April 23

Invited by the captain to tea, so *had* to get up. And who should be there but Mrs. Theodore Roosevelt, the widow of the president, a charming person, & her daughter Ethel, Mrs. Derby, & ex-Governor Whitman of New York & his wife, all delightful people.

April 24

Ugin has deserted me. & plays chess in the smoking-room with Mr. Whitman.

Steepletop
(1934–1935)
Also Cuba and Florida

M illay's delight in returning to the farm on the hilltop pours
forth in her exquisite observations of the birds, the rose garden, and even the frogs and the snakes in the swimming pool
during the month of April. By May she is working on poetry again, poems
that will appear in the book *Make Bright the Arrows.*

The spring section of the 1934 diary is one of Edna's best contributions
to this book and requires little editorial comment. There is rich narrative
about the couple's social life: her ongoing drama with Arthur Ficke and his
wife, Gladys; the affectionate relationship with the Branns, and also with
the Powys family of writers.

The diary breaks off, predictably, on the last day of May and resumes
briefly at Ragged Island on September 1. "I shall love to see Steepletop
again," she writes on September 6, "but I hate to leave the island." She
dreads the poetry reading tour that will take up much of the autumn. In
the winter of 1934–1935, the Boissevains would become snowbirds. The
diary resumes on New Year's Day, on a ship bound for the Virgin Islands,
and a few entries in February record visits to St. Thomas, Haiti, and Cuba.
From Havana in March they traveled to Delray Beach, Florida, where they
rented, for the first of several seasons, a house near their friend William
Brann, who had another horse farm nearby.

In the spring of 1935 Millay's diary resumes at Steepletop once more,
briefly, with some mundane observations about property maintenance,
complaints about her health, and an amusing story about the dogs, Ghost
and Altair, who had wandered off for several nights. By May of the year it

is clear that Millay is losing interest in writing in the diary, or lacks the energy for it. And with the exception of a generous entry made in February of 1938, there will be almost nothing henceforth in the Millay diaries and journals apart from reflections and notes on her illness.

🦋

April 28 [1934]

Docked at 8:30 this morning. Norma was there to meet us. Went to see Saxton about my new book.[1] And FOUND MY NOTEBOOK! It had accidently got deposited with a bunch of things at the Guaranty Trust.[2] Ran into George & Emla on the platform at the Grand Central, just back from Florida. We all traveled up together on the 1:40. —Never was so glad to get home. Caught a nasty cold on the boat last night, damn it.

April 29

Walked all about the place today, looking at the trees & plants. All the climbing roses, even the Dorothy Perkins, have been killed back almost to the roots by the terrible cold last winter. But the wisteria look all right. And Ugin's little peach trees are all alive, much to my astonishment. Most things look wonderful. Poor Ugin found his beautiful wine, six or seven years old now, all frozen in the cellar, a bad blow for him.

April 30

Saw two swallows. Heard a gay & familiar song, & realized with happiness that "Wohin" [spelling uncertain] had returned from the south again,— one of my favorite song-sparrows.

May 1

Find that the wine, though impaired, is still pretty good. So relieved. —Find that in my rose garden practically all the hybrid-perpetuals are alive, and also, to my complete astonishment, many of the hybrid-teas!—including a Radiance, a Red Radiance, a Francis Scott Key, a Joanne Hill, a Rowena Thom, a Mrs. Jules Bouch, a Madame Butterfly. Yet they were unprotected—

not even earthen up! & in the same garden that Dorothy Perkins died back to the ground!

May 5

Saw two frogs in the shallow water of the swimming pool this morning in what any of the Powys brothers would term "a fond embrace." They would swim out together for a bit & then sit on the bottom. Ugin prodded them gently with a stick & even pushed them a little way along the bottom, but they were quite oblivious. The female is much the larger.

May 6

My two frogs still embraced in the pool. Five young snakes swimming around near the edge. Don't know whether they belong there or just fell in. Reached down a stick to one of them but he wouldn't climb aboard.

May 7

Heline cleaned out the swimming pool, putting the frogs & things outside to find another home. Started the water. But it came rather cloudy, so shut it off for the night.

Ugin's left leg feels very heavy again & aches from the phlebitis he got in India. He has been spading trenches for the sweet-peas, & that's what did it, I think. It's so strange, he can play ten sets of tennis & not suffer from it; two years ago in Mallorca we walked from Pollensa to Sollas [spelling?] over the mountains, over the Ping Major, more than twenty miles of the most frightful trail, & Ugin stood it perfectly well, though Jan & I were exhausted.[3]

May 8

Swimming pool over half full. Ugin & Heline went up High Hill & cleaned the spring this morning. Now the water is beautifully clear. Sitting by the pool looking at the water this afternoon, heard a sudden sound in the leaves & grass behind me & looked around to see a big stripped [striped?] snake dragging off a tiny frog to swallow it alive, as I knew. I grabbed a rock & threw it at him. He dropped the frog which hopped away quite unhurt. I threw some more rocks on the snake & killed it. Horrid business. I was shaking all over when it was done. But I'm going to stop trying to like snakes. I just can't. Their table manners are too revolting.

May 9

Heline has finished planting out the 200 Narcissus Poeticus bulbs which came last autumn just as we were starting off on my lecture tour. Don't know how they will act, but they are all sprouted. Put most of them in the new pine wood. "The New Forest," I think I'll call it.

Cold wind. Worked in rock garden all day. Nice & sheltered there. Heard the first bobolink. Saw rose-breasted grosbeaks, very handsome. A chewink sat in the snowball bush for a long time & called & sang. I never heard his song before. It is rather soft, & like the wood-peewee's. Saw what I think was a red-start, in the crab-apple. I can already smell the crab-apple way across the lawn, though it's not in bloom yet. Swimming pool full.

May 10

Thunder storm & hail this morning. This afternoon stifling hot. Ugin went to see Nisbet about our dogs, which he had had for the winter to train. Satu is the best, it seems very good.

May 11

Sweet-peas are beginning to come up. Forget what day Ugin planted them. Worked all day in the rock-garden, did a great deal. John [Pinnie] is working for us for a while. He took away wagon-loads of dead brown honeysuckle; very sad. Ugin weeded the peonies on the lawn. Yesterday afternoon John went all around the place & along the road, burning the nests of the tent caterpillars. Never saw so many as this year. —The beautiful tall mountain ash we brought down from the Hamlin place when it was a baby, is covered with umbels of buds this spring.[4] I'm so excited. That means red berries in the fall, too.

May 12

Stayed in bed all day with a nasty cold. Wrote Mr. Saxton & sent him sixteen poems for the dummy of my book. It will really be two books. I think, published together—some of the poems need a definite separation from the others.

Dave Love, Bill Brann's superintendant, brought us up a big salmon, one of two which "Webby" sent Bill from new Brunswick. Bill & Billy [his son] are coming home tomorrow. Had a letter from Bill asking us to come over Monday.

Ugin brought up a bottle of Marsala, & we drank it. It made me feel nice & warm. —It was his mother's favorite wine.

May 13

This morning ice again in the dog's drinking dish, & the tomato plants frozen. —A pair of wrens are building a new bird-house Heline just put up in the orchard. And the three last year's houses are still empty. Last year, too, I remember that day after John put up two new houses, or a few days after, one was taken by a pair of wrens, & the other by a pair of bluebirds. Yet all the bird books say they won't go near new houses.

Weather still cold, & mostly overcast.

May 14

Bill & Billy just motored up from Frederick today, & this evening motored up to see us. They've had better luck with their horses this year & made a lot of money at the races.

Saw a bobolink sitting & singing on one of the young maples north of the kitchen garden which we put in last year; he has a particularly charming song, very long & varied. —The smaller mountain ash has one blossom. A song-sparrow is nesting in the juniper bush. I saw the nest a fortnight ago, but it looked deserted. Yesterday I saw four pale blue speck-led eggs in it, & this morning saw the bird sitting on them. I am glad. But I miss Nip & Tuck, the chipping sparrows who nested in that bush for three or four years now. I wonder where they are.

—Worked in my rock-garden. It's beginning to look beautiful—Saw ruby-throated humming-bird. Same day as last year. Sweetest letter from Bill Bullitt today, from Moscow.[5] Wants us to come there. Wish we could go over for a week this summer.

May 15

Went down to ask Bill's advice about doing a broadcast of my poems for the Kraft Cheese Hour—it really sounds too awful). He advises against it unless they want me for a whole series. Stayed to luncheon. —John & Heline spent all day burning caterpillar nests along the roadside. I transplanted wild anemones.

May 16

Beautiful sunrise. Ampit wakes me up every morning at six o'clock. He sleeps in Ugin's room, but always comes in to wake me up first. By putting his nose on the bed & then, when I open my eyes, putting his paws on the bed. Then he goes back & wakes Ugin. He doesn't want to go out, particularly. He just thinks it's time to get up.

Read in the paper yesterday evening that Mary [Taylor] has got a divorce from Deems in Reno.

Went to dinner at Bill's. Ugin wore his beautiful new smoking [jacket].

Yesterday ordered two birthday presents for Ugin, James Warburg's "Money Muddle," which he is dying to read, and a shooting-stick from Abercrombie's.[6] He has been using my shooting-stick a bit lately when walking about the place looking at things, & it's ever so restful for his leg. Got Bill to post my two letters without Ugin knowing.

May 17

We are having the most marvelous soups & salads now, using all kinds of herbs from Ugin's herb-garden. Ugin makes a beef bouillon & skims the fat off twice, then lets it come to a boil for just a few minutes. It is delicious, either served hot, or in jelly. Then we make a salad with herbs in it, tarragon, & chives, & sage, and a few leaves of spearmint. The thyme was winter-killed. The hyssop smells rather good, but doesn't seem to have much taste, so we're waiting to find out how to use it. And the sweet-mary, of which I gave Ugin two plants from my hardy garden, tastes just like grass, though it has such a pungent & delightful smell; so we're going to use it just to put in finger-bowls. (The sweet-mary is from mother's garden in Camden. She gave them to me to take home & set out at Steepletop, when we were driving back after having brought her the little mountain laurels & set them out. She gave me some little fir trees, too, tiny ones, which she dug up with her hands on Sherman's Point the day before, when we drove her out there. She stood by the car as Ugin packed the plants in the back;

there was some penny-royal too. And she stood in the yard as we drove away. It was the last time I saw her alive.)

May 18

Beautiful day, though wind very strong. Ugin & I weeded rose-garden without any clothes on & got a wonderful tan. Ugin went for a swim, first time this year. I didn't go in. because there were no towels there, & I was too lazy to fetch one, & didn't want Uge to fetch it for me because his leg isn't quite right yet, though much better.

—Letter from Abercrombie's saying the shooting-stick is on its way, but I'm so afraid it won't get here for Ugin's birthday Sunday. Only one more post.

Heline mowed the big lawn today with the motor-mower & mowed right past the juniper bush before I had time to tell him to use the hand-mower there. The poor little song-sparrow must have been terribly frightened. But she went back to the nest afterwards. I expected to see her feathers gone snow-white from terror, but she looks just the same.

The tulips are in blossom in the sunken garden & look gorgeous. Ugin transplanted some rock-cress into the border of the hardy garden in front of the peonies. They look sweet. —I still can't tell whether the big red one is alive that John & Heline set out on the lawn last year. I'm so afraid it's gone. Yet the white oak they transplanted at the same time looks marvelous. And another Hybrid Tea rose has come to life, a Margaret McGredy. Yet some of the apple-trees are half winter-killed. This is a cock-eyed year.

May 19

The crab-apple tree by the front door is in full blossom & was never so beautiful as this spring. I think it is the prettiest thing in the world.

May 20

Came into the kitchen this morning from going over the place as usual & found on the table a birthday cake with candles & a bottle of gin,—a present to Ugin from Heline & his wife. Ugin's shooting stick came last night & he was so curious about the parcel that I had to let him open it. He was delighted with it. He calls it his "walking-sitting stick." Today I gave him his book, and a little rose tree about three inches high, potted in a big pot. It is a seedling from one of the beautiful small-blossomed white rugosas by the summer-house.[7] Also, I brought him the first three narcissus poeticus to blossom, down by the dragon-willow. Also, for another present, showed him a green bud high up on the wisteria by the front door. —Ugin made a bread-pudding under my direction, but insisted on putting in too much molasses & it was awful.

May 22

Motored over to say goodbye to Jack Powys & Phyllis, who are leaving for England tomorrow to live in the barn-cottage on Chaldon Down where Ugin & I had luncheon with his brother Willy. They will be close to Lulu, & Lulu adores John so & is longing to see him. But I believe poor Phyllis is wretched at leaving her little house & her garden that she loved so & worked so hard in.

—A car stopped outside & there was Arthur, just back from Florida a few days ago (as we learned later from Gladys. Poor Artie had told us he just got back yesterday, so we wouldn't be hurt that he didn't come to see us sooner.) Went to Arthur's from Jack's, where Gladys told me that she had been sick & in pain constantly for years, & had been relieved by a slight operation in Florida, & now feels perfectly well & no longer nervous & irritated. I felt she was trying to tell me that this was why she had often been so nasty about little things. Perhaps it was. I hope so. Anyway, I'm glad she feels well.

—Arthur is very embarrassed now when he is with me. We both think of the evening shortly before I sailed last winter when he told me he doesn't like my poetry any more, & held up to scorn specifically the phrase "cool and aimless beauty," finding it execrable. "That's not 'Beauty's massive sandal,'" he said. "But," I started to say, "it's a different kind of thing entirely,"—then I shut up. "See here, Arthur," I said presently, "you don't like the poems I've been writing lately, & you don't like the poetry of Leonie Adams, or of George Dillon, or of several others that I admire. You & I just don't agree about poetry any more, that's all, & that's all right. Let's forget it, & talk about other things. Only you mustn't keep asking me how my new book is getting along & things like that, now that you are convinced it will be an awful book, and think I am wasting my time on it."

—Poor Arthur, he just can't look me in the eyes now; he doesn't dare ask how my book is getting along, and he can't think of another darned thing to say.

May 23

Dinner at Bill's. Marvelous dinner, all kinds of sea-food, including soft-shell crabs & lobster. But I *don't* like this fat, Crisco or whatever it is, people fry things in, everything tastes much much more of Crisco than of itself. Had sherry instead of cocktails before dinner. Such a relief. —It was fun, just the three of us, Bill & Ugin both so handsome in their evening-clothes & the most beautiful dinner service I ever saw—a joy just to look at the plates, white with a broad embossed dull gold trim. —Later in the evening, Bill brought out a sheaf of clippings from newspapers & confronted me with them, all the dull & insipid reports of interviews with me on *President Roosevelt,* et cetera sickening. "Don't do it!" said Bill. "Don't talk to the reporters!" "But Ugin *made* me talk to reporters!" I retorted, angry & miserable. "Write out a statement to hand them!" said Bill. "She *won't* write out a statement!" roared Ugin. So there we were, & the evening was spoiled; we began to pour out our drinks & tramp about. I wished I were all alone in the hermit's hut on top of the Merbaboe.

May 24

Felt awful all day. Most horrible hang-over. Yet I wasn't tight last night at least not very. Don't understand it. Worked in rock-garden transplanting.

May 25

Letter from Mr. Moe, saying they very much wanted me to be a member of the Advisory Board of the Guggenheim Foundation. —Gave a thorough cleaning to my room & Ugin's room & our bathroom. Devilish old weather.

May 26

Hellish cold. Rained nearly all day. Spent the day house-cleaning the hall. Chucked nearly everything out of the closets, & rearranged the furniture somewhat. Then Ugin & I decorated the place with Havanese brass and red grays from Burma, & I put a big bowl of tulips on the table, & it looked so beautiful we could hardly believe it. It's been such a terrible mess lately, full of trowels and seeds and garden-gloves and old coats & muddy galoshes and unanswered letters. I bought some wax to use on the slate floor, it brings out the colours beautifully, but I was too tired at the end, so just wiped up the dust with a wet rag. Picked the last of the hyacinths today, put them also in the hall, on the gun-rack. Picked pansies for Ugin's bedroom. I have three narcissus poeticus, very tall & white & perfect, in a silver vase on my dressing-table. Of all the flowers I love I believe this is the one I love best. When I first fell in love with it I was ten years old. It was growing in the grass of a house called the old Coffin house on Rings Island [Massachusetts], which we had rented. The house & grounds of this place seemed to me much grander than anything we had ever had, & very romantic. The yard was infinite; in the back it ran right down to the marshes; but in the front, it was infinite with something else, I never knew quite what; & the pheasant's eye narcissus, which I had never seen, & which I suddenly came upon in the grass there, was as much like a voice as like a flower. —It had always been like that to me. Years later I learned it was called *narcissus poeticus,* so now of course I never dare admit to anybody but Ugin that it is my favorite flower.

May 27

Isobel came motoring up just at luncheon time, terribly drunk & bringing an unpleasant woman with her. Ugin made her some black coffee & I made her take a swim in the pool to sober her up, but it didn't do much. If she'd been alone & sober I should have invited her to stay a week; as it was, we didn't even ask them to luncheon. In sudden panic lest, this being Sunday, other people should come to call, we lept into the Cadillac and hurtled off after snatching a bite of food. That is to say, we both felt that if we stayed at home & Arthur & Gladys came driving up, methodically beginning one more summer of Sunday afternoon calls, we should shriek, & bite all the buds off the peonies, & then go jump into the pool with a couple of volumes of the Oxford Dictionary in our arms. —Motored around the country-side for awhile, looking at caterpillar nests along other people's roadsides & feeling very superior, but very furious at having been driven out of our beautiful place like that. Sunday, of all days, when it might be so peaceful; no servants, & no men working around, & we might have been naked in the sun, or working naked in the garden around the pool, & not a sound except from birds.

Finally, went to see Owen & Peggy Johnson at Stockbridge, to let them know we were back from Europe & explain why we couldn't have Christmas dinner with them last winter. Their lawn is the most peaceful & lovely thing I've seen for a long time, so broad & so long & so almost flat & so well-kept, & lovely trees. Stayed & had supper with them. Owen made an excellent Welsh rabbit, & Peggy a fine salad with herbs in it.

May 28

Arthur & Gladys *did* come yesterday! Can you bear it!

Bill came up & had a drink with us & invited us down to have a drink with him & to a cold supper.

May 29

Arthur & Gladys came, bringing a good-looking but dull girl, who went for a swim in the pool. —They invited us to dinner Saturday, to meet some nice people (the young couple who bought Jack Powy's house); but we didn't want to meet any nice people. So we're going to have dinner with them alone a week from Saturday. —Arthur inquired after my forthcoming book of poems,—I knew he would. And I knew he was going to for minutes beforehand, he was so obviously in dry labour. I answered politely, yes, it was true I had a book coming out in the fall. He couldn't let it go at that. "Going to be good?" he asked. Poor Arthur. Why must he be so false and so indiscreet? He knows he's read most of the book, & doesn't like it. The moment was ridiculous, & painful.

May 30

Beautiful day. The last few days have been lovely. —The men were not working because it was a holiday, Memorial Day, & we had the place to ourselves. I worked weeding in the forget-me-nots and maiden-hair ferns that are in the shade of the big cherry-tree at the corner of the pool, & also the narcissus poeticus beside the white bench there. That side of the pool looks so lovely; in the back the long hedge of arbor vitas, tall & unclipped; just in the middle, close up against them, the long slender white bench with its beautiful pure lines (the bench alone with the tall evergreens behind it is a perfect setting for a Greek play); at either end of the bench a small clump of tall white narcissus—one has four blossoms, the other two; further along, between the arbor vitas & just in front of them, two clumps of green & white striped grass. The whole thing looks formal & restrained. The effect of all that green & white is exquisite. I must *never* let the clumps of striped grass get bigger than they are now.

Did all of my weeding without a stitch on, and got a marvelous tan. This morning motored down for the mail and to Dodds' for some bread and dog-meat. —on the way home, as we approached the hollow, I heard several thrushes all singing at once and Ugin stopped the car and we listened for a long time. There were several Wilson thrushes making their thrilling descending arpeggios all at once, and one wood thrush with a song so marvelous that only the nightingale's can be compared with it.

Ugin's pole beans are up.

May 31 Thursday

Took some asparagus & rhubarb down to Billy, who is alone this week, Bill being in New York until Saturday, & who loves asparagus, which Bill detests. Took a beautiful drive along the back-roads. On our way home stopped the car in the hollow again, & heard the same beautiful concert as last night. We felt so happy.

The tiny seedlings of parsley which I found self-sown & put into pots are growing very fast now. And the wisteria keeps putting out her buds higher up the stalk. And one of the grape-vines that I thought was dead isn't dead at all. But the big red oak on the lawn that John & Heline set out last year hasn't shown a sign of life yet. Such a pity. —Hardly any blossoms on the lilies-of-the-valley. Few blossoms on the iris. But peonies splendid.

—Had squab tonight for dinner, first two this year. Didn't much want them, but Heline had killed them & put them in the ice-box, & that *supposed* to be what we keep pigeons for. —It's not, however. We keep pigeons, & let them eat up all the first sowing of sweet corn & half our sowing of peas (which is precisely what they have done this summer) because they look so pretty flying, against the green hill, & pecking at the gravel in the driveway.

September 5. Wednesday

Ragged Island—We have been here just four weeks today, and I haven't had a moment in which to write about how wonderful it has been. Entirely alone. I have stepped foot on shore just once all this time, and that was on Orr's Island, where I went into the store to try on some oilskins.[8] I haven't seen a soul that I had to speak to in all this time, except that once the store-keeper. Once in a while John Johnson, who is going to be our care-taker here, comes over in his lobster boat with a telegram or something, and then we all have a little drink together, and once in a while there's a lobsterman hauling his traps just outside our harbour, & we shout good-morning to him. Twice we've crossed to Orr's Island in our dory, once sailing & once rowing; and I've sat in the board tied up at the wharf & read while Ugin did something. —Nothing was ever so quiet & so beautiful. I don't know when I've been so at peace.

We fish for cunners off the rocks, & have our own lobster-trap— which never comes up empty!—and dig clams, and fetch water from the well among the spruces, or gather driftwood, & swim, and read, and sit on the ledges looking out to sea. We have almost no furniture, beyond two luxurious new beds which did not get here until four days ago, four weeks after we ordered them! —We've been sleeping on army-cots with no mattresses. We have no chairs except two unpainted kitchen chairs we brought along with us, and a funny little falling-to-pieces old Windsor which was in the kitchen when we came, and no tables except some that Ugin has put together out of old lumber,—things like that. I have a fine big heavy ugly office desk for my typewriter and other writing supplies, which we bought fifth-hand in Brunswick for five dollars.

Tomorrow we expect to leave for Steepletop. I shall love to see Steepletop again, but I hate to leave the island. —Ugin hopes to get back here in ten days or so, but I don't think we can. My reading-tour begins about the 8th of next month, God help me, & I have to get some new clothes for the attraction to appear in. Also I must work out a new program. Haven't got my page-proofs corrected for Harper's yet, either, & I expect they're frantic. One line in one of the sonnets of the Epitaph is causing all the trouble. I simply cannot get it to suit me. I work at it off & on all through the day, in my head. I never slave so over anything.

1935

January 1st [1935]

On board S.S. Scanperus, out of New York, bound for Virgin islands.

January 2

Landed in St. Thomas.

Feb. 12

Benefit reading for the poor of St. Thomas (almost!).

Feb. 23

Farewell dinner with darling Robert Herrick.

Feb. 24—Sunday

Paquebot St. Dominque. Due to leave St. Thomas at 4 this afternoon. Did not leave until 10 tonight.

Got the curse this morning & felt perfectly horrible. Lila brewed me some tea out of the dane piece senna David Bar gave me, sticking a dash of gin in it. Spent almost all night last night packing. —Felt sad saying goodbye to Lila; "I'll see you again," I said standing by the taxi and pressing her hand, but her eyes filled with tears, & she turned away abruptly & went into the house. Sweet thing, with her black face & her enormous pink hat.

Rufus came on board with us. He was dying to come along to New York. He confided in me that he was going to stow himself away in one of the life-boats, and I really believe he seriously considered it. However, we saw him off finally in one of the (?)-boats. Met the captain, & Ugin and * promptly fell in love with him,—a charming young Frenchman named Pierre Lescarret. Had dinner with him tonight. Such fun to be talking French again.

Feb. 25—Monday

In bed all day. Most frightful headache, in addition to the rest of it. Sent Ugin finally to ask the doctor for an ice-bag. So in comes the doctor in person, young Frenchman, pretty bored, I imagined, & dying to be doing something. Put hot compresses on my head, gave me all sorts of pills & potions, and made off with my bottle of gin. Bad for my head, he said. Of course. But swell for some other things.

Feb. 26—Tuesday

Got up for dinner tonight, at the special request of the captain, who was so sweet I simply couldn't refuse, though I felt precisely like hell. I am so grateful to him for taking away all the sore places and dirty tastes that some of his countrymen have left with me. It was a gay and delicate subtle dinner, excellent conversation, & good wine.

Feb 27—Wednesday

Jac-mel, Haiti. Went ashore here for the day. Abducted the captain, & took him along with us. Got a car with two native chauffeurs and started through the mountains to Port-au-Prince, on the other side of the island, taking along some beer and a picnic lunch. Found ourselves suddenly up to the running-boards in a river, and were informed we had thirty-two of these to ford, some not so deep, some deeper & swifter. The driver, having waited to shift gears until we were well awash, stalled us in mid-stream, where, seeing nothing better to do, we got out our beer & sandwiches & had luncheon. Finally we succeeded in persuading our young man, who had settled down to a peaceful day of meditative pushing at a starter which had been dead for years, to look for a crank. He made many objections, but did at length produce one from under the seat, and was reluctantly preparing to make use of it when, catching sight of a group of native women wading across down-stream with skirts held high above their knees & baskets of oranges on their heads, he called to them to come & shove us out. Which, much to my astonishment, they did.

Feb, 27—Thursday

Les Cayes (Haiti).

March 1—Friday

Santiago-de-Cuba. On the bridge at dawn to see our entrance into the harbour—marvelous harbour—entrance entirely hidden until very close— long, winding entrance more like a river. Had coffee on the bridge.

—Went to Hotel Casa Grande. Captain Lescarret came ashore to have dinner with us, his sailing being postponed until one o'clock tonight. Horrible dinner. Indeterminate sort of wine, whose label informed us that it was a Chambertin, and also that it was made in Bordeaux. Later went back on board the sweet little St. Dominque, and stayed with the captain until it was time to sail.

March 2—Saturday

Flew to Havana. Flight of about six hours from Santiago,—coming down for a few minutes in five other air-ports. Ugin scared white, though he has flown so many times before; I feeling sort of numb, but my hair gently stirring at the roots as if something were moving around in it, and saying to myself, "Well, here you are, you consummate ass, you air-minded earth-worm, and you got into this seat of your own free will, and payed money for it besides, and if you're going to crash you're going to crash and there's not a darned thing you can do about it, so you might as well look out over those thousand square miles of cotton-wool clouds, and observe that curious rainbow round as a doughnut, a rather fuzzy doughnut that has "soaked fat"; and relax and ride the bumps like a lady and a scholar and a sailor, and think about poetry, or think about your lovers, or fall asleep.["]

March 3—Sunday

Hotel Nacional, Havana. Beautiful hotel, looking right out upon the Caribbean—or has it stopped being the Caribbean & become some other name?

Went to the races & lost a horrible lot of money.

March 4—Monday
[Havana]

Very windy. Played some tennis, but too windy.

Luncheon, all Cuban dishes, some very good, on the sidewalk before a café in the Prado.[9] They've gone & changed the name of the Prado, the tiresome louts, to the Paseo del marti (as very likely they have changed the Caribbean to something else). But anyway, everybody still calls it the Prado. How I hate these square white beans that never quite get done. —The Prado is one of the loveliest boulevards imaginable—a park all down the middle of it. And Havana is one of the most beautiful cities I ever saw.

Had dinner at a place Robert Herrick told us about, El Patio. Attractive enough. But awfully dowdy tourists there.

In the midst of dinner there came a loud crash from some street nearby. A waiter hurrying past saw our thoughtful expressions & said, "No es bomba."

March 5
[Havana]

Hardest time finding a decent place to have a drink. Everything looks so untidy & dirty. Went to La Florida, which a girl on the air-plane, the only other passenger, had said was the best place in Havana. Liquor good, but place so dirty & dull it was no fun. Went to the Plaza Bar. All smudgy.

Tonight went to the casino. Charming place. Made a little money at vingt-et-un.[10]

March 6
[Florida]

By train to George La Branche's place in Islamorada [Florida]. They met us at the station. Discovered that it was their wedding anniversary. Gave them the presents we brought them from St. Thomas. For George mahogany swizzle-sticks & some little straw cups to set highball glasses in, & for Emla a tea-cloth & napkins with the most lovely drawn-work & her initials in—dozens of initials—she has as many as I have.

March 7

George & Ugin went bone-fishing. Ugin had a big one on but it got away from him by winding itself all up in a mangrove. He is wild. And George is wild. —I worked all day on the Guggenheim poets. Must get my report off right away. It has been nothing less than slavery this winter; new stuff from a dozen of them pouring in all the time right up to the end of February, up to the 23rd, to be exact. Would have my mind all made up about somebody and his report half done & then along would come some new stuff to consider & maybe I have to change my mind. Inexcusable, really, I think, to do this to me.

March 8

Uge caught a big bone fish. And Alonzo speared a turtle.

April 2

Night train to Charleston.

April 19

[Steepletop]

It has snowed every day since we got home, until today. One day there was a real blizzard, and all the other days for a fortnight it snowed steadily, but steadily, all day long. Incredible. —Oh, have I just forgotten? Bill [Brann] didn't want us to come north. He wanted us to go back to Boynton Beach after Charleston. He says that in New England and part adjacent April is winter, it is a winter month, and that it is the English poets who have made April so attractive to us, and that we've never had the sense to notice it. —However, today is the first day of spring. It is beautiful. And the truth is, we like it to snow and be winter for a fortnight after we come north, so that we can really see the spring come.

April 20

At last we're having the badminton court made into a badminton court. We're getting putting-green grass seed, and having lots of top-soil put on, and having it raked and rolled, and it's going to be beautiful.

Almost two hundred dollars worth of plants & roses this year again from Dreer. —We're having the house painted white with black shutters, and all the other buildings, too, black & white.

April 21

John saw the first swallow in the barn today, a single one, very early. Ugin & I are very anxious about the swallows this year. We had to tear down the old barn where so many of them always nested; it was dangerous, and the most shocking sight. But we think that perhaps we shall have to build them an old barn somewhere where it's not so conspicuous. Not to see them wheeling & dipping over the pool, eight or ten at a time, and skimming the surface with their throats wide open, not to have them about here any more, would be too awful.

April 22

We have a beautiful new Ford station-wagon called a "Suburban." It is very swagger. Troy gave us $75 for the old Ford. I don't see why. —Got the curse. But worked all day scratching around the roses. Most of the hybrid teas lived through this winter again, with no protection. And almost all of the Dorothy Perkins died. What's the use of believing anything? —The rabbits were very destructive last winter. They're hateful, the way they gnaw all the way around, instead of just a little bit here and a little bit there.

April 23

Today Charlie & Norma are giving a party at the Montrose Gallery [in New York City], where Charlie's first show is being exhibited. I feel too awful to go.

April 24
[New York]

Went to New York & to the St. Regis. My hair was dirty and I was too ill to wash it and I felt awful, but Ugin felt just like having a party, and he was so cute I couldn't scold him—though we really came down here seriously, I to see Charlie's show, and he to engage three servants. Supper of fresh caviar and sour cream, I in my flannel bath-robe and dirty hair, and later Tess and Frank & later Deems over, and I think Ugin ordered up nine bottles of champagne, I think it was nine, and he was so gay and so terribly cute, that I really couldn't mention it at all, even though we'd meant to eat at Childs and save money.

April 25
[New York]

Awful hangover. Couldn't crawl out to see Charlie's show, four blocks away.

April 26

Saw Charlie's show. Beautiful. Very impressive. Everybody is impressed by it—critics—even friends!—even friends who also paint!!! —Came home to Steepletop by late afternoon train. Met George & Emla at train gate. Had dinner with them at High-Holt, but I was tight from too much Irish whiskey on the train, and went to sleep in the red room instead of eating it.

April 27

First swim in a swimming-pool. Achy. (Achey?—Ache-y?) Anyway we ached terribly in the legs for a minute after getting out. But we felt grand. Went in four times. But didn't stay in a second. Plopped in and scrammed out.

May 1—Wednesday

Painters didn't show up this morning. Ugin thought it was because he scolded them yesterday for having done only one door and two shutters among the three of them. But it appears they thought it too cold to work. I should have thought it too cold to do anything else. Heline went down & rounded them up and they painted in the garage all afternoon, and did thousands of shutters—

Wrote a letter to President Roosevelt tonight, protesting against filibustering and boosting the Costigan-Wagner anti-lynching bill.[11] Also wrote a letter resigning from the National Committee for the Defence of Political Prisoners, but have to look up a quotation before I send it, so probably shall never send it . . . quotation from a letter by Jack Lawson, and have lost the letter.[12] —The carpenters have finished cutting off the edge of the roof on one side of the house and have started on the other side. It's going to be an enormous improvement.

Our new station wagon is all smashed up in the back where somebody crashed into Heline. We just want to howl. We haven't even got drunk.

May 1, Wednesday

Going to bed very tight—on nothing but claret, so far as I remember—It was very cold today—snowed a bit last night or in the early morning. Ugin & I spent the day cleaning out our desks—how funny my handwriting looks—how funny to get tight on just claret.

May 2

Wrote seven letters today. Don't know what's got into me. Wrote to Hal Bynner, and to V. Sackville-West, and to Dr. Lipscomb of Lynchburg, and to Eugene Goosens, and to Pierre Lescarret of the St. Dominque, and to old Mrs. Morrill of Rockport, Maine, whom I have not seen since I was nine, and to my darling Pauline.[13]

The painters are making the kitchen green-and-white, instead of blue-and-white, for a change. I never want to see a blue-and-white kitchen again—John and Heline made a sort of rustic pergola for the grape-vines at the top of the kitchen garden. It looks sweet. Dozens of the *narcissus poeticus* that Heline set out in the grass among the pines last spring are up and thriving. It was in May we set them out after they had set all winter forgotten in a kitchen chair while Uge & I were in Europe! Yet there they are.

The plasterers charged us only $24.30 to put an entirely new ceiling in the kitchen and do quite some patching in the drawing room.

The peas are up, that Ugin planted on the 21st and the all-foliage turnips, and the lettuce & radishes and onions from onion sets have been up for days. The dill has seeded itself all over the herb garden. Some of the lavender actually looks as if it had lived through the winter, under a litter of leaves. But moles got under it and killed a lot of it. —No sign of asparagus yet.

Ghost and Altair [the dogs] have been gone two nights now, and no sign of them. This will be the third night. I'm really sick and tired of them. I really don't know whether I ever want to see them again or not. And of course I keep imagining that Ghost is caught in a fox-trap and Altair is just watching beside her and that they are both starving; or that Victor Brooks has shot them.[14] Things like that. And I wish to Christ they'd come home.

May 3

Bitter cold. Suddenly found out, much to our delight, that we are insured! Took out all kinds of motorcar insurance years ago, but had a feeling we had dropped it, along with all the other insurance. But we hadn't! So now we get the back of the Ford all good as new for nothing. —

Wrote letters all day. Never had such an experience. Don't know myself. —Ugin has smoked only three cigarettes today, and only had a half-glass of claret. I've had two gin-fizzes, besides two gin & bitters. I'm bad. —Three new servants arriving tomorrow. Am in a perfect sweat about it.

The dogs have not come back. It's awful.

May 4—Saturday
[Steepletop]

The dogs have just come back. It is about nine o'clock in the evening. We were sitting here in the drawing-room before a bright wood fire, and the door was open onto the lawn, because after three days of distressing cold it had suddenly grown warm & felt like spring. —Altair just walked in through the open door. He didn't shiver, or cringe, or bark, he just walked in. —I said, "Puppy!" and put my arms around his head. I've called him Puppy for ten years. Then we were anxious, because Ghost was not with him, so we said, "Where is Ghost?" And then she came in, on her belly, because her memory is better than his and she knew that five days ago she ran away. She looks like a whippet, she is so thin. We didn't scold them. We just gave them a big bowl of milk here on the rug, and some hunks of raw meat. She is so tired she can't stir. She is curled in her chair, and Ugin says she looks no bigger than a kitten—I wonder where they have been. John said today they had been seen in Harlemville—20 miles from here— with a big German police-dog and a little English setter. What a marvelous time they have had.

May 5, 1935

This morning it snowed, a proper snow-storm. Very cold all day, until late afternoon. Now the wind has changed from east to west, & we hope for better weather.

The house is in the most awful state. The kitchen has been painted, but is not yet dry enough to set things on or chuck things in. So everything is stacked in the dining room. The carpenters are making cupboards to hold the things that can't be put into the kitchen—but they are not yet finished!—and this afternoon we sent Heline to Pittsfield to buy sheets & blankets & dressing tables for our imminent servants, & at 5:30 he got back & at six he went to fetch them, & at six-thirty they arrived. We've not seen them yet—since that brief interview in the St. Regis. —How difficult for them, dumped into a strange place like this—and how difficult for us.

Well, it may really be spring tomorrow. And, anyway, the dogs came back.

The Final Diaries
(1938–1949)

Just as Millay's early diaries illuminate the mystery of her precocious genius, so the final diaries and journals reveal, in harrowing detail, the nature of her decline and demise.

What follows here are some of the most curious, sad, and shocking documents ever to see the light of publication. It is a wonder that they survived those years of turmoil after Eugen's death in the summer of 1949. The notebooks that contain the records of Millay's drug use in the 1940s were hidden by her sister, Norma, in the poet's grand piano in the parlor of Steepletop for decades after her death of heart failure on October 18, 1950.

From spring of 1935 until February of 1938 the diary is suspended. Those years included the writing and publication of two important works: Millay's collaboration with George Dillon on an English translation of Baudelaire's *Flowers of Evil,* published in the spring of 1936, and *Conversation at Midnight,* an intellectual verse drama published in the autumn of the same year. In 1937 she found time to accept half a dozen honorary degrees at such institutions as New York University, Tufts, and Colby College.

She continued to complain of health problems. In the summer of 1936 she was thrown from her car while Eugen was driving, injuring her shoulder. In the summer of 1938 she wrote to her sister Kathleen, "I have been seriously ill, had collapse from overwork." In a letter to George Dillon dated September 14, 1940, she described her medical condition thus: "I have been very sick . . . in constant pain, due to an injury to certain nerves in my back, referred to by the ten or twelve different doctors and surgeons who have tried to cure the trouble, as nerves 4, 5, & 6 of the dorsal spine . . ." She explained that the nerve injury was the result of having been thrown from the moving car. "I have had three operations on these nerves and should be quite well now, I think, if I were not still, naturally rather weak." In an earlier letter to Ferdinand Earle, Boissevain stated that his wife was "in such constant pain that she is obliged to be given hypodermic injections of morphine several times day."

At the same time, Eugen's homeland was overrun by the Germans. Rotterdam was destroyed in May of 1940; the couple was exasperated by America's isolationism. Millay, with what little energy and concentration she had in reserve, had begun to write propaganda poems such as those that were included in *Make Bright the Arrows* (1940). The book was received politely at best by the critics, respected for its sentiments, and roundly dismissed as poetry.

The diary entry I have dated March 28, 1942, is a riveting and incisive self-portrait of Millay as she was struggling with her drug addiction during World War II. It is one of a few diary entries in this book that were not dated by Millay herself. The heading "Riggs Clinic," in parentheses, was written on the loose pages in pencil by her sister Norma, and refers to the Austen Riggs residential psychiatric treatment center in Stockbridge, Massachusetts. Millay was a patient for several weeks there in the spring of 1942, and I have estimated the date from circumstantial events such as "the fall of Java and Sumatra" to the Japanese troops in March of that year. Millay's reflection is in the form of a furious address or apostrophe to one of her physicians, a kind of rant that might possibly have been the draft of an unmailed letter. Yet it is directed more to the writer than to any putative reader, and since it has no address or heading or salutation it belongs more to the category of diary writing and reflection than correspondence.

After this, the diary entries consist mostly of meticulous records of Millay's drug consumption. The circumstances of her recovery from drug addiction are not well known, but sometime during the year 1946 she underwent a successful cure at Doctors Hospital in Manhattan.

Eugen died of cancer on August 29, 1949. Millay died at Steepletop from heart failure when she fell down the stairs on October 18, 1950.

February 19, 1938

Steepletop. Saw first female downy woodpecker I've seen this winter. There have been several males around all winter, eating the suet in the pine just outside my window.

—Dozens of chickadees on my bed eating (or rather picking up to carry off with them sunflower seeds), while I write this. I put my bed close to the open window, & spread the seeds out on a towel. Of course I have been preparing them for this by putting seeds on the window-sill, etc. If I take the seeds away from the sill & hold them in my hand, they hop or fly to my hand, & perch on my thumb, or sit on my wrist, or walk around in my hand, picking up the seeds and throwing them away till they are satisfied. There is one that insists on taking two at a time. It is funny to watch him. Saw a weasel in his ermine coat down by the brook this morning, very conspicuous, because it has been thawing and raining, and there is no snow on the ground there. How beautiful he looked moving over the brown leaves! —Once he half stood up on his hind legs and his beautiful sinuous body and [illegible] head were plainly visible. He finally went under the bridge out of sight. Strange, thrilling apparition.

December 31, 1940
Chart / Miss Millay

Awoke 7:30, after untroubled night. Pain less than previous day.

7:35. — urinated. No difficulty or distress.

7:40 – 3/8 gr. M.S. [Morphine solution] hypodermically self-administered in left upper arm. Profuse bleeding, almost instantly quenched.

7:45 to 8 — smoked cigarette (Egyptian) (Mouth burns from excessive smoking.)

8:15 — Thirsty, went to ice-box for glass of water, but no water there. Take glass of beer instead, which I do not want. Headache, lassitude and feeling of discomfort and stuffiness from constipation.

8:20 — cigarette (Egyptian) 9:00— " "

9:30—Gin Rickey (Cigarette) 11:15—Gin Rickey

12:15 Santine [*sic?*] four cigarettes 12:45–1/4 grain M.S. and cigarette
1:00 pain back and also in lumbar again
No relief from M.S.

March 11, 1942

Steepletop. 5:30 A.M. —Made tea & then slices of buttered bread &
brought up to Ugin. —Put on a tray a few buds of sneeuwelokjes from
under the tamarack on the round lawn. They will soon be in blossom in
big circles under the tamaracks!

[Undated entry, 1942?]

Advice to Little Nancy [Millay's alter ego]

Exercise Will Power in *all things,* big or little, Don't become self-indulgent, don't become sloppy in *anything,* in your thinking, in your dress, in
anything.

Don't fool yourself. If you feel nervous, don't *purposely* (half-subcon-
sciously) make yourself *more* nervous. Instead, turn your attention at once
upon something which interests you, or do at once something which you
enjoy very much doing.

Have a drink instead, sometimes.

Never let the other person see you using the hypodermic, or know that
you are about to do so, or have just done so. *Never* leave the syringe about
where you see it.

Things I must do for Eugen if I truly love him—and I *do,* more than anybody ever loved anybody.

1. Even if I am suffering TORMENT, speak in a voice with *no hint* of pain,
speak in the strong, gay rich voice he loves, the voice of a person vitally
interested in things, deeply amused by and full of laughter at other things,
even when I don't care *anything* about *anything;* let my *Diaphragm* do the
work, even when every deep, proper breath is like the thrusting in and wrig-
glingly drawing out of a Javanese kris under my shoulder-blade. DON'T
WHINE! Never, even when you are dying, if you are still conscious, permit
yourself to speak in a SICK VOICE. CRY AS LITTLE AS POSSIBLE!!
But NEVER whine.

2. KEEP THE CORNERS OF YOUR MOUTH UP! DISGUISE YOUR FEELINGS!

3. When Ugin is in the room, smoke very little, drink very little! (When he is *out* of the room, try to cut down too—do the best you can, but don't let yourself get to the point where you begin biting your Finger-Nails!

4. Go outdoors *often*. Let Ugin *find* you outdoors, instead of *Still in Bed,* or in your *SPECIAL CHAIR* (Pah!—Old Woman!) in the drawing room.

5. Wash your hair the way you used to, twice a week at least, *even if it hurts* TERRIBLY. Keep young, keep pretty FOR UGIN. Don't *ever* let him see you with STRINGY HAIR!

6. Stop airing the same Grievance *over and over*. Stop having Hobby Complaints. Don't EVER spoil a moment when Ugin is feeling a little bit gay, by bringing up *something unpleasant*—even if it is *something important*. Wait just a *little while!*

*

1. Care for *Nothing* so much (after your poetry) as to make YouKnowWho happy. Put everything from your mind but this, and your work. (and what's more, *keep* everything else but these two things out of your mind!)

2. *Never* mention yourself, if possible to avoid it, *especially* before YOU-KNOW WHO(M)

Never bring the conversation round to yourself *even for a minute, even to illustrate a point,* or in a brief parenthesis, to show that you understand what YOU KNOW WHO is saying. *Never* mention anything from your past, any incident of your childhood. Forget that *you* exist.

[March 28?, 1942]
(Riggs clinic)

Me with my Savile Row riding breeches just longing for the ice to get off the country roads so that they can go out and have the doeskin rubbed up a bit on the insides of the knees! *Me* with my two Top Flight tennis racquets just singing for the court to be raked and rolled and the lines put down so they can start whacking about the balls that as early as last autumn I teased a pro friend to sneak to me a few at a time! *Me,* whose weight without troubling to diet, eating all that I like of whatever I like, is 109 lbs. stripped, and who looks my best when wearing neither brassiere nor girdle!

Me, who never show my face (or perhaps it's my figure) in New York without having four attractive men of my acquaintance dialing their phones, to take me out to the Stork Club, or 21, or a Noel Coward opening! *Me*, to be stuck in a looney bin with a contingent of bulging old biddies too arthritic to divide their own Iris, holding a distaff in one hand and a spindle in the other, and wondering when the hell the nurse is coming to take me for my invigorating quarter-furlong breeze around the circle of the driveway!

Me, who stand every afternoon beside the frozen swimming pool, trying to measure with my eye how many inches the round black eye of open water in the middle has broadened since the day before!

Me, with my old clothes by *Worth* and my new clothes by Bergdorf Goodman, me, with my Tweeds by Henri of Bond Street and my hostess gowns by Jessie Turner, waddling and hissing out of the dining room midtaste in order to get my 4 ½ AA's by I. Miller onto the fender before some other old lady does! *Me*, going in for *Swaraj* and uplift and getting "teamy"! *Me*, turning on the radio to hear, what, War News?—No! —Recipes and sermons and knitting stitches!

Me, getting devilish and arguing with the minister with many girlish titters as to whether or not the arches in the croquet set are wickets or hoops. Whoops!

Me, a busy woman like me, with a score of interests and a dozen occupations, me, speaking over short wave to England for the British American Ambulance Corps, me, speaking at dinners in the Waldorf ballroom for China Relief; me, up to the neck in work for the Office of Facts and Figures, the Red Cross, and a half dozen other organizations—instead of writing my article for the Author's Guild Bulletin, instead of finishing my poem for the Red Cross, instead of writing Miss Monroe explaining to her my difficulty *re:* "Make Bright the Arrows"; instead of answering Mrs. Roosevelt's letter, telling her I'm sorry but I'm afraid I *can't* do a five-minute broadcast for the Youth Groups—instead of doing any one of the things I should have been doing and wanted to do, sitting for two solid hours in your damned office telling you a bunch of things that were none of your business, and all because a little squirt of an M.D. in Great Barrington who wouldn't know whether a baby were coming head-first or feet first has apparently got it into what he doesn't use in place of a head, that I am a congenital defective with criminal tendencies, an alcoholic, a drug-addict and a generally undesirable member of our civic group! What he told *me* was: that at your place I would be able to find out what drugs to take to help me get to sleep (after listening to the 10 o'clock newscast of the fall of Java and Sumatra, where two of my Dutch husband's beautiful nieces are now, in the paws of the Japanese, a fact which their mothers, his sisters, who are like my own sisters to me, and who are starving, actually starving to death in Holland, as we know quite well and can do nothing about it—a fact as I was saying, which their mothers in the Netherlands will have heard by now) You, daring to say to *me* that if I have trouble sleeping at night it is because I need to be Adjusted to Life, and that *You,* The Riggs Foundation, can bring about this adjustment! You, pouncing on *me,* after two idiotic and inexcusable hours in your office with your Elementary Psychology. "Why can't you remember where you left your coat and hat?"

If I weren't mad enough to spit, I might be amused enough to laugh, and I dare say by this afternoon I shall be getting a good laugh out of it. But this morning the whole absurd encounter makes me sick enough to chuck up, the pontifical solemnity of it, varied at just the most offending intervals by the "Ha-ha! I'm a good fellow!";ship!—the cockeyed reasoning that if I am *aware* of Life, touched by it, moved by it, troubled by it, hurt by it, in other words *sensitive* to it, (and life on this harassed planet what it is today!) I must be ill-adjusted to it! And the further insolence of all such institutions,—the unmitigated gall to assert that . . . [the manuscript ends here]

*

[September–October 1943, daily drug summary]

3 tablets to 2%[1]   VINCE

Sept.	28	12	=	3 grain[2]	←
"	29	13 ½	=	3 ⅜ "	←
"	30	10 ½	=	2 ⅝ "	←
Oct.	1st	8 ¼	=	2 1/16 "	←

Oct	2	8 ⅝	=	2 5/16 "	
Oct	3	7 ⅞	=	1 31/32	←
Oct	4	6 ¾	=	1 11/16	←
Oct	5	7 ⅛	=	1 25/32	
Oct	6	7 ⅞	=	1 31/32	
Oct	7	6 ¾	=	1 11/16 [9]	
Oct	8	6 ⅜	=	1 19/32	←
Oct	9	6 ⅜	=	1 19/32 [9]	←
"	10	6	=	1 ½	←
"	11	8 ⅝	=	2 5/32 RED DAY. M.D.'s order	
"	12	5 ¼	=	1 5/16	←
"	13	9	=	2 ¼	
"	14	8 ¼	=	2 1/16	
"	15	11 ⅝	=	2 29/32	
"	16	9 ⅜	=	2 11/32	
"	17	8 ¼	=	2 1/16	
"	18	2 1/[7]	=	1 5/16 [drawing]	
"	19	6	=	1 ½	
"	20	7 ⅛	=	1 25/32	

[Note, referencing Oct. 13–20: "Bad intestinal and gastric. Very uncomfortable."]

Friday   8th Oct [hourly drug-use summary]   Vince

9.15	2	
10.30	2	1 gr. Codeine. 1 P.G.[3]
11.00		1 vit.—2 Tabs—Diastase[4]
12.20	1	
2.00		2 Taba [*sic*]—Diastase
2.45	2	
2.55		1 gr. Codeine	½ Tab. Benz.[5]
3.15		1 G. + G.[6]
3.30		½ Tablet Benzedrine
5.50	1	
6.30	2	

8.00	1	
9.10	1	$1\ \frac{1}{2} = 4\ \frac{1}{2} = 1\ \frac{1}{8}$
11.05	2	
11.50	2	
1.45	1	
	17	

$2\ \frac{1}{8}$	=	$6\ \frac{3}{8}$	=	$1\ 19/32$
	[crossed out: 8.20		1/4]	
				1 19

Monday   10/18   Vince

5.30	2	12 hrs. 30 m—9/8	
9.40	2	17 hrs.—12/8	
10.45	1		Betaxin (10?)[7]
2.50	2		nembutal (3.00)[8]
6.00	2		½ Benzedrine (10?)
8.45	1		
10.00	2		
1.00	2		
14		= 3 + 9/16 = 3 7/16 tablets	

9/4	$1\ \frac{3}{4}$
$5\ \frac{1}{4}$	
1 5/16	

$3\ \frac{1}{2}$ + 1/16 tablets

14/8 = $1\ \frac{3}{4}$ hypo =

3 + 9/16 tablets = $3\ \frac{1}{2}$ + 1/16 tablets

¾ [¼?] of 14/8 = 42/32

[crossed out]   5/16

[Vertically written note:]

never since I first began taking it have I felt so free of it, both mentally + physically, today.

[Horizontally written note:]

during day 4 nembutal

lots of codeine

Tuesday   10/19   Vince

10.45	3	V. slept from ± 1 [unintelligible] 10.45
11.15	1	feeling pretty good
1.40	1	this A. M.
2.30	1	
3.40	1	codeine
4.14	2	
5.20	2	1 nembutal
9.15	1	16/8 = two hypos
9.30	4 2	
3.30	2	

$16/8 = 2 = 6 = 1 ½$

Friday 10/22 '43   Vince

6.30	2 (full strength)		⅛ 2.05
10.00	2 " "		1 grain C
1.25	1 " "		1 grain Codeine
1.30			
5.50	1 " "		
6.35	1		
7.15	2 (at ¾ strength)		¾ of ⅝ = 15/32
8.20	1 "		
8.55	1 "		¾ of 8/8 = ¾ of 1 = ¾ gr.
9.10	1 "		
9.50	3 " → →		½ grain Codeine
9.50			
11.00	1 ½ tablets Codeine		
12.05	1		
1.25	2		

2.15   1
                 1 29/32

⅞ 28/8 3 ½

11/8 1 ⅜ 4 ⅛

7 25/8   1 29/32

[Note next to 1.25:] what happened to that other ⅛ grain? Did it leak out?—they some-times leak.[9] I feel sure I didn't take it. (Later) Evidence—it leaked. The codeine hypo did the same thing.[10] They had both been left slanting downwards

[Note next to "1 ½ tablets Codeine":] Either 1 grain + ¾ gr. Or ⅞ gr. + ⅛ gr. = 14/8 gr. = 7/4 = 1 ¾ g = or 13/8 = 1 ⅝ gr. = (at a quarter to eleven this evening) 1 ½ grains (plus ⅛ gr.) which is too much, but not discouraging, considering in how many different kinds of pain I was.)

Vince   Tuesday, 10 26 "   October, 1943

Dr. Cassel

3 o'clock
Orange Juice!

3.30
Jelly!

4.30
Insulin!?!?!

Wednesday   Thursday   10/28   Vince

4 AM	2	
4.30	1	
8.00	2	
11.30	1	
12.15	1	½ Codeine
1.25		¼ c.c. Insulin ↓5 units
1.30		1 nembutal
2.-	1	

2.30		1 winterwheat[11]
5.20	2	Hyoseine[12]
5.40	1	
8.-	1	
8.30	1	¼ c.c. Insulin
10.30	2	5 units
11	1	13/8 = 1 ⅝ hypos
		= 3 15/32 pellets[13]
	13/8	= 1 7/32 grain
3 15/8		
	1 ⅝	
	4 ⅞	
	1 7/32	

Friday   10/29   Vince

	⅓ ¾	5 ¼ = 1 5/16
9.30	2	
10.-		1 gr. Codeine
11.15		1 tps. Nervosine (anti-jitter)[14]
12.15		2 tbsp. appetizer
		1 pint Ginger ale[15]
12.40	2	
12.45		2 Taba [*sic*] Diastase
1.25		5 units Insulin
2.02		½ Tablet Hyoseine
5.20	2	3/2 grains Codeine
8.20	2	2 nembutals
9.05	1	
9.10		5 units Insulin
10.10	1	
11.30		
12.20	2	1 grain codine
2.30		1 pellet codeine (½)
4.40		1 pellet codeine
4.45	2	

4.50	14/8	1 nembutal

1 ¾ hypo

[Next to 12.20 2:] But 4 ½ grains Codeine!

3 nembutals!—½ Tablet Hyoseine!!

[1943]

[awake all night with sore throat —   Vince

No fair! —Last week it was a burned finger; the week before a sprained knee! —How am I to give up taking morphine when I need it all the time for one darned thing or another? It must be hard enough when it's just a habit!—everybody says it is = everybody says its impossible, when you go to the hospital and have nurses injecting insulin + hyoscine into you all day long!

Friday   11/2

1.- (A.M.)	2
4.-	1
5.30	1
6.15	1
6.20	2
9.00	2
11.-	1
12.30	2-
1.45	2
2.50	1
5.00	1+
6.20	1
6.30	1
8.20	1
8.50	2
10.00	2
10.45	2
12.15	1
12.45	1

Friday   11/5   Vince

9.	2	15/8 = 1 ⅞ hypo.
12.40	1	¾ of which =
2.20	2	3 pellets + 21/32 grain
4.30	1	= 5 pellets 3/32 gr.
5.40	2	= 1 ¼ + 3/32 gr.
7.40	2	= 1 11/32 grains
9.00	1	
10.10	2	15/8
11.40	1	
1.15	1	
8.40	2	
9.30	1	
11.40	1	
12.15	2	1 gr. Codeine
3.30	1	
5.40	1	
6.50	2	
8.30	2	1 ½ gr. Codeine
10.45	2	
11.45	1	5 nembutal
2.20	1	

Thursday   11/11   Vince

9	2	
10.15	2	
12.-	2	
2.45	2	
4.-	1	1 ½ pellets Codeine
6.45	1	
7.40	1	1 ½ pellets Codeine
9.10	2	

9.50   2

11.10   1

16/8

(=2 hypos, ax ¾

Grains the hypo,

= ¾ of 8/4 = 6/4 =

1 ½ grains

[Note, written vertically under 1 ½ codeine:] "Happy I am, to see so many friends about me! for them I know, I prosper."

Sal—Hepatica[16]

Vince   been sick   Vince
Tuesday 11/16

10.30   1

11   2

11.45   2

1.-   1   15/8 + 4/8 = 19/8

2.40   1

3.50   2   ¾ of 19/8 = 57/32 = 1 25/32

5.30   1

7.45   2

8.30   1

12 midnight   1

1.35   1

////////////////////////////

3.35   4

6.50   2

7.30   3

10.-   1

12.-   1

1.-   2

2.-   2

6.-   2

Wednesday, 11/17

[begins at "6.50   2" See above.]

20/8 = [crossed out]

¾ of 10/4 = 30/16 = [crossed out] 1 ⅞ grains

7.15 - 1

7.50 - 1

9.05 - 2

10.30 - 2

12. - - 1

1 ⅞ grains

11-30-1943

Establishment is shocked,

—stir / seek no adventure

Above this splitter granite

[1943–1944 (no date)]

1./ Daily medicines

Calcium Gluconate (6)[17] | 3 Tuesday 2

Taba [*sic*]—Diastase—6 (^2 directly after each meal)

Vitamin special →

(2 ^**per day** Ruby grapes of Proserpine[18]

Anti-gas Tablets—(2 several times a day)

Anti-Jitter—1 tsp. 3 times per diem

Iron (liquid, as directed)

Appetizer (1, 3 times per diem, before meals)

Insulin (10 to 15 to 20 units twice a day)
↑to be followed immediately by lumps of sugar, and/or candy, and meals of potatoes, bread (rice)

2./
Dilaudid, if necessary, (as per necessity) to be given subcutaneously[19]
Codeine (1 grain 3 times daily hypodermically ^if must)
Nembutal (several times daily and 2 just before retiring)
new Drug (2 pellets twice daily ← to be given hypodermically)
1 coffee—spoon Bicarb. Soda (dissolved in 1 cup hot water—first thing upon washing)
Sal-Hepatica (morning)?
Scraps [*sic*] (night)?
Betoxin (vitamin B,) hypodermically

3.15 - 2

8-9-11 - 1.00 - 3.15

(2 each) = 10/4 = 2 ½ hypos
= 6 + 1 ½ = 7 ½ pillules[20]
= 15/8 = 17/8 grains

Tuesday [1944?]

Between 8.20 + 3.20 - 11

Wednesday

Between 8.30 + 2 35 - 6

In approximately 6 hours
a cut of ⅝ hypo

a hypo is ¾ of 8/8 = 6/8

⅝ of 6/8 = ⅝ of 24/32 = ¾ x 5 = 25/4

= almost ¼ grain

AM   Monday   March 13 [1944]

6.30	-	3	
8.00	-	3	
9.00	-	4	
10.30	-	2	
" "	-	-	- 1 gr. Codeine
11.00	-	-	- 2 tps. hervosine
12.00	-	-	- 2 gram pills (Iron)[21]
1.00	-	2	
2.30	-	2	
2.30	-	2	1 ½ gr codeine
3	-	2	
.6	-	2	1 ½ gr codeine
9	-	2	
9.45		2	(1 sleepy injection)[22]
10		3	
AM			

12.15	-	-	1

30/8 = 15/4 = 3 ¾ hypos = 9 9/16 pellets

= 9 ½ + 1/16 pellets = 2 ¾ app. grains

Thursday, 3/16

6.30	2	
7	4	1 gynegen[23]
9	2	1 sleepy powder[24]
12.30	4	
2.30	2	
3.30	2	

6.00   2

6.45   2

A.M.   Friday, March 17   1944

4.45   2

6.30   2

8.30   2

9.15   2

10.00   3

11.00   2

PM 1.00 1

1.20   2   (1-2-3-4)

2.40   3   (1-2-3-4)   [1 pellet Dilaudid, 2 Codeine]

3.05   3   (1-2-3-4)   Sleepy Powder

3.30   2   (3-0-0-4)   Headache Tablet[25]

4.20   2   (3-0-0-4)   2 aspirins

4.35   3   (3——4)

6.35   2   (3——4)

7.30   2   (3——4)   Headache Tablet

8.15   2   (3——4)

10.15   2   "   "

12.30   2

2.10   2   nembutals (since afternoon -4)

             35/8 = 17/4 + ⅛ (at 3 to 4 cc, sterile water)

41/8   [calling it 18/4 = hypos = 13 pellets

       + 1 pellet = 14 pellets = 3 ½ grains Delaudid

5 ⅛   1 Sleepy Powder - 1 p.m.

15 ⅜

Vince   Wednesday, Apr. 5, 1944   Ugin

AM

2.45	2	(3.30 - 2 cc Demoral)[26]	8.30	2
8.30	2		4.40	1
10.30	1		8	2
11.40	1	(11.40 - 1 c/c Dem)	10.30	2
12.50	1	(1 cc. Dem. - 12.50)	12	I
2.35	1	(1 Luminol amytal-circa 1)[27]		
4.45	2		8/8	
5.30	2	(1 cc De. 7.30)		
7.35	1	(1 cc Dem. - 9.00)		
9.00	1	"		
10.55	1	"		

15/8   = 3/16 grain m of pillule
(1 cc Dem. -)

Thursday, Apr. 27

Vince			Ugin	
2.30		2 A.M.		
3	3	(1 " " 10)	9	2
	2	given by Ugin—when?)	1	2
		" " " when I	7	2
		Was dictating over phone	10	2
1.30	1		12	1
7.10	2	[6/8 of a hypo spilled		
10.30	2	by me! —When Hilda		9/8
12.00	2	said she was getting		
		discouraged.][28]		
16/8				

(Demerol several times)

Vince   Wednesday 3 May   Ugin

3 AM	1	(2 c/c 5.45)	9	2
9.30	2			
12	2	(1 cc Dem - 1 o'clock)		
2.00	2 (?)			

PARATHYROID [?][29]

poisoned by Dil[audid]   poisoned by Dil[audid]

May 10, 1949

The rabbit that just loped up to my cabin to get away from Sabat, who is howling and yelping giving chase in exactly the wrong direction, was grey, not brown at all, and looked sort of mortified and moth-eaten, and yesterday when I was breaking the last year's stalks from the lemon scents of balm, John [Pinnie] called me to look at three deer grazing in the pasture, and they were grey too.[30] I mentioned them to John, and he said at this time of the year they are always that color, because they haven't yet lost their winter hair (at least that's what I think he said. I'll ask him again, and about the rabbits, too.)

NOTES

Finding Her Voice (1907–1910)

1. *Triss: Or Beyond the Rockies* was a play written in the late nineteenth century by David Hill.

2. Consumption is a wasting disease, such as pulmonary tuberculosis, common before effective antibiotics were developed.

3. Booth Tarkington (1869–1946) was an American novelist and dramatist, known for the novels *The Magnificent Ambersons* and *Alice Adams* (for which he won the Pulitzer Prize for fiction in 1919 and 1922, respectively.) His first book, *The Gentleman From Indiana,* was published in 1899.

4. Washington Irving (1783–1859), the American short story writer and biographer, first published his book of short stories, *Tales of a Traveller,* in 1824 under the pen name Geoffrey Crayon.

5. Ethel and Martha Knight were sisters and close friends of Millay's during high school. Together, they belonged to a reading group called the "Huckleberry Finners."

6. Millay attended Camden High School, where she graduated with honors in 1909.

7. On November 16, 1909, a short dramatic film called "The Gypsy's Secret" was released. This entry is dated before that film was released.

8. Megunticook Lake, at the foot of Mount Megunticook, is about three miles north of Camden.

9. *Dombey and Son,* a novel by Charles Dickens from 1848, was first published in monthly installments, with illustrations by Hablot Knight Browne, better known as "Phiz." Its plot explores many of Dickens's themes of arranged marriages, class distinctions, and exploitation of children.

10. Abbie Evans was the minister L. D. Evans's daughter, with whom Millay was very close—she was Millay's "best friend." Evans was a few years older than Millay, and led several girls in Sunday school. In 1910, Evans enrolled in Radcliffe College with scholarship aid.

11. From "Comin' Thro' the Rye," a poem written by the Scottish poet and lyricist Robert Burns in 1782. The words were written to the melody of the Scottish Minstrel *Common' Frae The Town,* a variant on *Auld Lang Syne.* Burns is considered the national poet of Scotland.

12. The political scientist Melissa Harris-Perry describes the "Mammy" as a figment of the American imagination in her book *Sister Citizen: Shame, Stereotypes, and Black Women in America,* published in 2011.

13. *St. Nicholas* was a popular monthly children's magazine from 1873 to 1943. The *St. Nicholas League* was started in 1899, and sponsored contests for younger readers. Millay's poem "Forest Trees" was published in the magazine in October 1906, when she was fourteen. Her poem "The Land of Romance" was published in March 1907.

14. Silas Heale was a dance instructor who organized events at Cleveland Hall in Camden.

15. Felix Mendelssohn (1809–1847), German composer, pianist, and conductor in the early Romantic period. His birthday was actually February 3, not January 3.

16. I.O.O.F.: Independent Order of Odd Fellows, a secular non-political fraternal order founded in 1819, a branch of the eighteenth-century brotherhood known as The Odd Fellows.

17. Leila Bucklin French, Millay's piano teacher. Before taking lessons with Mrs. French, Millay was "discovered" by her mother Cora's patient, a former member of the New England Conservatory and composer, who after hearing Millay play an original composition offered to give her piano lessons for free.

18. Beethoven's "Moonlight Sonata" (Piano Sonata no. 14 in C-sharp minor), *Quasi una Fantasia,* one of the composer's most popular pieces.

19. Millay had a strong social commitment to teaching Sunday school that eventually came into conflict with her iconoclastic religious beliefs.

20. Probably "La Lisonjera [The Flatterer]," a piano piece by Cécile Chaminade, Op. 50 (1897).

21. Fred was Stella Derry's boyfriend.

22. Refers to *The Rubáiyát of Omar Khayyám,* a series of poems traditionally thought to have been written by the twelfth-century Persian astronomer Omar Khayyam, and first translated into English by Edward Fitzgerald in 1858.

23. In German, *Lieder ohne Worte,* "Songs Without Words," short musical compositions by Felix Mendelssohn.

24. A hair coronet is a braided hairstyle that wraps all around the head.

25. Bert Millay was Edna's paternal uncle.

26. A corset cover was worn over a corset, to protect a woman's modesty and soften the angles of a bone corset.

27. Frieda Langendorff (1868–1947) was a German contralto. She made her Metropolitan Opera debut in 1907.

28. Frederic Chopin (1810–1849), Prelude, Op. 28, No. 15, often called the "Raindrop Prelude," because it invokes the sound of raindrops.

29. "The Cry of Rachel" is a song written in 1905 by the American soprano Mary Elizabeth Turner Salter (1856–1938) and L. W. Reise.

30. "Spanish Dance" probably refers to *Danzas Españoles* ("Spanish Dances"), a nationalistic composition by Enrique Granados (1867–1916), not to be confused with Manuel de Falla's (1876–1946) "Spanish Dance No. 1," from his opera *La Vida Breve* ("The Brief Life"), which was first performed in 1913.

31. *Carmen,* an opera by Georges Bizet, first opened in Paris in 1875. It tells the story of a Spanish soldier seduced by Carmen, a Romani woman.

32. "The Alley Cat's Kitten": A children's book by Caroline Fuller (b. 1873), published in 1907.

33. Castine is a coastal town across Penobscot Bay from Camden.

34. Crème de menthe is a sweet, minty alcoholic drink.

35. The voyage of Abbie Evans's parents to Egypt and then across the Mediterranean to Greece was unusual then.

36. Alfred, Lord Tennyson (1809–1892), poet laureate of Britain for forty-two years.

37. *The New Sophomore* is a novel by James Shelley Hamilton published in 1909.

38. *Sonnets from the Portuguese* is a collection of love sonnets, published in 1850, by the English poet Elizabeth Barrett Browning (1806–1861).

39. The Grand Army of the Republic was a fraternal group for veterans of the Civil War. As the members of the G.A.R. grew frail and died, women's groups formed to take care of their families.

40. A serge is a heavy, durable woolen fabric.

41. "Sprigged" refers to a fabric imprinted with a floral pattern. Organdie is a sheer cotton cloth.

42. *Bella Donna* is a 1909 novel by Robert Smythe Hichens (1864–1950), and *Stradella* is a novel from the same year by F. Marion Crawford (1854–1909).

43. "Aladdin's wonderful magic lamp" is a folk tale from *Arabian Nights.*

44. *The Mill on the Floss* is a novel from 1860 by George Eliot (the pseudonym of Mary Ann Evans; 1819–1880).

45. "High yellow" or "yaller" was a term used to describe light-skinned biracial people, of mixed black and white ancestry. It is understood as an offensive anachronism today.

46. "Maying" refers to springtime merrymaking, outdoors.

47. "Humoresque" is a piano cycle written by the Czech composer Antonin Dvořák (1841–1904) in 1894.

48. A portiere is a curtain hung over a doorway.

49. The Three-Part Inventions is a series of short pieces Johann Sebastian Bach made for piano students.

50. *Lorna Doone: A Romance of Exmoor* is a historical novel by Richard Doddridge Blackmore from 1869. "John Kidd" refers to "John Ridd," the farmer's son whose murder is the inciting incident for the whole book.

51. Millay refers to a volume of poetry by Robert Browning throughout her diaries as "Browning."

52. Henry David Thoreau (1817–1862), American poet, philosopher, transcendentalist, and essayist best known for his book *Walden,* his reflection on life in the woods.

53. The *Bangor News* is a newspaper devoted to rural Maine, published six times a week in Bangor, Maine. It was founded in 1889. A puff is a complimentary newspaper article.

54. Clara Schumann (1819–1896), German composer and pianist; her *4 Polonaises pour le pianoforte* was published in 1831.

55. The girls in the reading club were reading *The Adventures of Huckleberry Finn* by Mark Twain.

56. Wolfgang Amadeus Mozart (1756–1791) composed his Requiem in D Minor in 1791 in Vienna, but it was unfinished when he died.

57. Arthur Foote (1853–1937) was an American composer; his "Pierrot & Pierrette" was published in 1893.

58. "In Old Madrid" is a song by Henry Tortere and Clifton Bingha written in 1890. Bolero is a Spanish dance with foot-stomping and sharp turns.

59. Don Quixote, the eccentric antihero of the Miguel de Cervantes novel from 1620, had a chaotic study.

60. *The Innocents Abroad,* by Mark Twain, was published in 1869.

61. Two silent films called "Saint Elmo" were released in 1910, one on April 23, by Vitagraph Studios, and another on March 22, by the Thannerhouse Company. Both are melodramas based on a domestic novel by Augusta Jane Evans.

62. Beauchamp Point is a scenic peninsula near Rockport, Maine, just south of Camden.

63. "B & I." may be a personal notation referring to Millay's menstrual cycle.

64. Auntie Bines is most likely a made-up character.

65. From Shakespeare, *Julius Caesar,* Act III, Scene 2.

66. Ethelbert Nevin was a pianist who wrote a setting in 1902 for this air from Shakespeare's *As You Like It.*

67. *The Man on the Box* was a play written in 1907. It was turned into a film in 1914, directed by Oscar Apfel.

68. *Anne of Green Gables* is a novel by the Canadian author Lucy Maud Montgomery, published in 1908 and a children's classic.

69. She means Chopin's Scherzo no. 2 in B-flat minor, published in 1837.

Vigils with Imaginary Lover (1911)

1. "Intellect is but half of the man: the will is the driving wheel" is a paraphrase of the German philosopher Arthur Schopenhauer.

2. Rarebits, or Welsh rabbit, is a dish with a sauce made from melted cheese poured hot over toasted bread.

3. Bon-ami was a brand of household cleaning products.

4. "Flow Gently, Sweet Afton" is an 1837 song by American Jonathan E. Spilman based on a 1791 poem by Robert Burns.

5. *The Golden Heart* is a novel by Ralph Henry Barbour published in 1910.

6. Robin Goodfellow, or Puck, is a mischievous fairy in English folklore. The word "Puck" meant "demon" in Old English. In Shakespeare's comedy *A Midsummer Night's Dream,* Puck is a shapeshifter and a comic figure who deceives other characters in the play.

7. "Robin Adair" became a popular ballad in the mid-eighteenth century, written by Lady Caroline Keppel with composer Charles Coffey about Keppel's husband. "Auld Robin Gray" is a ballad written in 1772 by the Scottish poet Lady Anne Lindsay, and tells the story of Robin Gray, who marries a younger woman in love with another man.

8. "Amaturus" is one of a cycle of poems in a collection published in 1858 by William Johnson Cory, a nineteenth-century English poet and teacher.

Sweet and Twenty (1912)

1. *Robert Kimberly* is a novel from 1911 by Frank H. Spearman (1859–1937), who wrote about the American railroads.

2. Molokai is a Hawaiian island in the Central Pacific that maintained a leper colony from 1866 to 1969. The island is featured in the novel *Robert Kimberly.*

3. *The Garden of Allah* (1904), by Robert Hichens (1864–1950), is a romance about a young English woman journeying through the Algerian desert.

4. Elbert Hubbard (1856–1915) was a homespun writer, artist, and philosopher known for his heroic essay "A Message to Garcia."

5. Yankee is the speech dialect of eastern New England.

6. Mitchell Kennerley (1878–1950) was an influential modern publisher, art dealer, editor, and collector of books. After moving to New York from England, he published the literary magazine *The Forum,* and began a book publishing firm that produced important works by Walt Whitman, Oscar Wilde, and D. H. Lawrence. He was arrested and prosecuted for "obscenity" under the Comstock Act in 1913.

7. William Stanley Braithwaite (1878–1962) was an American poet, and anthologist. The son of a British Guiana immigrant and the grandson of an enslaved North Carolina woman on his mother's side, Braithwaite had only a seventh-grade education before discovering his love of poetry at a typesetting job. Edward J. Wheeler (1859–1922) was an American poet. He was president of the Poetry Society of America; also the editor of *Current Opinion* and *Current Literature,* magazines published between 1888 and 1925. Millay's poem "Land of Romance" was published by *St. Nicholas* magazine in 1907.

8. Humoresque is a cheerful, upbeat, and humorous type of musical piece.

9. Whitehall is an inn in Camden where Millay's sister Norma was waiting on tables. The sisters often performed music during the summer tourist season for the well-off guests from New York, Ohio, and elsewhere. On this occasion Millay played piano and sang a number of her original songs. Enchanted, her audience then prompted her to recite her poem "Renascence" for the first time in public. Pierrette is the feminine counterpart of Pierrot, a stock mime character of seventeenth-century *commedia dell'arte*, popularly known as "the sad clown."

10. These were all songs Millay had composed, and she accompanied herself on piano.

11. Caroline B. Dow, the dean of the YWCA Training School in New York, soon took charge of a group seeking to become Millay's benefactors.

12. Some of the wealthy visitors at Whitehall were so impressed by Millay's literary talent that they began talking about paying her tuition to attend Vassar College, in Poughkeepsie, New York.

13. Postal: postcard.

14. Aemora: The spelling is unclear; may refer to an oboe d'amore.

15. Others among her would-be patrons, especially Mrs. Julius Esselbourne, were proposing plans for Millay to attend Smith, the small liberal arts women's college in Northampton, Massachusetts.

16. Witter Bynner (1881–1968) was an eminent poet and cultural figure who served as president of the Poetry Society of America from 1921 to 1923. He and Millay maintained a close friendship until her death. Arthur Davison Ficke (1883–1945) was an American poet and playwright influenced by Japanese artwork. Ficke was well known for his sonnets, and his traditional approach to poetry. He and Millay were longtime friends and lovers.

17. Louis Untermeyer (1885–1977) was one of the best known American poets of this time, as well as the editor of numerous poetry anthologies and the literary editor of *The Masses*. He and his wife Jean went on to became friends of Millay's. He was awarded the Gold Medal by the Poetry Society of America in 1956.

18. Floyd Dell (1887–1969) was an American poet, critic, newspaperman, novelist, playwright, and magazine editor. His groundbreaking writings on feminism, politics, and psychoanalysis shocked his middle-class readers, and were highly influential. Untermeyer did write a glowing review of the poem for the *Chicago Evening Post* daily newspaper.

19. William Marion Reedy (1862–1920) was the editor and owner of the *Saint Louis Mirror*, or *Reedy's Mirror*, in 1912. He was an advocate of several up-and-coming writers, including Sara Teasdale.

20. By "over-virilized Masefield," Reedy is referring to John Masefield (1878–1967), an English poet and children's novelist. Masefield served as poet laureate from 1930 to 1967.

21. "The Earth Passion," one of Ficke's poems, was published in volume form in 1908 along with several other of Ficke's poems.

22. "The Happy Princess" is one of Arthur Davison Ficke's poems. It was published in volume form, along with other poems, in 1907.
23. Nicholas Vachel Lindsay (1879–1931) was an American poet known for bombastic singing and chanting of his poetry.
24. Crane's Linen Lawn was a luxury brand of "superfine" paper.
25. *The Breaking of Bonds: A Drama of Social Unrest* is a play by Arthur Davison Ficke, originally published in 1910.

"Lest We Forget": College in New York (1913)

1. Following the euphoric reception of her poem "Renascence" when it appeared in *The Lyric Year* anthology published by Kennerley, he continued to launch her career by publishing many of her other poems in *The Forum,* as well as her first book of poetry, *Renascence, and Other Poems,* in 1917.
2. This may refer to *The Moth,* a book by William Dana Orcutt published by Harper & Brothers in 1912. Orcutt (1870–1953) was an American publisher, typeface designer, historian, and author.
3. Charles Vale (1874–1928) was the pseudonym for Arthur Hooley, Millay's elusive lover from 1913 to 1917. Hooley was an Englishman, novelist, and editor. January 6, 1913, is probably the first time Millay ever saw Vale's name. After reading his rhapsodic review of her poem, Millay wrote to him and enclosed a photograph of herself. This led to their romance, sparked at a dinner party at Mr. and Mrs. Kennerley's mansion.
4. "B.&M." may be a personal notation referring to Millay's menstrual cycle. Ditto for "T.T.M.M.," three entries later, under January 10.
5. Mr. Seymour was an autograph collector and an early fan of Millay's.
6. A monkey-cap is a knitted hat with an opening for the face or eyes. It is often used as cold-weather gear by mountain climbers and skiers.
7. "Freckles" may refer to Neil Twomey's stage adaptation of a novel by Gene Stratton-Porter published in 1904. The play was staged at the Grand Opera House in New York in 1912. The story concerns an Irish-American orphan traveling between Indiana and Chicago. It was made into a film starring Jack Pickford in 1917.
8. "The Dead Path" may be a poem that Millay was beginning to write.
9. *Poetry: A Magazine of Verse* is a literary magazine that began publishing in Chicago in 1912.
10. Mrs. Tufts may be the wife of John Tufts, Cora's former patient who volunteered to give Millay piano lessons for free.
11. Gladys Niles, Mr. Dunton's granddaughter who attended law school.
12. Founded in 1910 in New York, the Poetry Society of America (P. S. of A.) is the oldest American poetry association. Past members besides Millay included Langston Hughes, Wallace Stevens, and Robert Frost.
13. Millay was redecorating her home office in a sporty aesthetic.

14. Most likely Waterville, Maine, a city about forty-five miles from Camden.

15. *A Pair of Burglars: A Farcical Sketch in One Scene* was written in 1908 by Byron P. Glenn.

16. Milbank Hall is the oldest building on Barnard College's campus. Designed by the architects Lamb & Rich, it was built in 1896–1897.

17. The New York Philharmonic, founded in 1842, is the oldest of the "Big Five" symphonies, regarded as the finest in America.

18. The Young Women's Christian Association (YWCA) in midtown Manhattan was the oldest YWCA in the United States. Caroline Dow had arranged for Millay to room there while she studied at Barnard College in Morningside Heights.

19. Mr. and Miss Babbott.

20. Grand Central Terminal in New York had only recently opened in February 1913 when Millay first passed through it. Henry Churchill King (1858–1934) was president of Oberlin College in Ohio from 1902 to 1927, where he taught mathematics, theology, and philosophy.

21. Sara Teasdale (1884–1933) was an American lyric poet. She won the Pulitzer Prize in 1918 for her collection of poems *Love Songs*.

22. Madison Avenue Presbyterian Church was founded in 1834; the church moved from the Lower East Side to the Upper East Side in 1858. Dr. Henry Sloane Coffin (1877–1954) was the church's minister, and later the president of Union Theological Seminary in New York from 1926 to 1945. As the author of many books on religion and an influential advocate for addressing social problems through Christianity, he became nationally famous, appearing on the cover of *Time* magazine in 1926.

23. Talcott Williams was the director of Columbia University's school of journalism. Annie Russell (1864–1936) was a British-American stage actress. *She Stoops to Conquer* is a play by the Irish playwright Oliver Goldsmith. It debuted in London in 1773.

24. Oswald Yorke (1866–1943) was a British character actor.

25. The MacDowell Club of New York existed from 1905 until 1942, and was one of many MacDowell Clubs around the country that were dedicated to music appreciation and the arts. Parker H. Fillmore (1878–1944) was an American writer and folklorist, known for his publication of Czech folk tales. *The Bookman* (1895–1933) was a New York literary journal, edited by Arthur Bartlett Maurice (1873–1946).

26. S. S. McClure (1857–1949) was an Irish-American publisher who became very involved in investigative, or muckraking, journalism.

27. Established in 1826, Lord & Taylor is a luxury department store on the Upper East Side. It is the oldest department store in the United States.

28. This may be Sarah Adelaide Trowbridge, widow of the novelist John Townsend Trowbridge.

29. On a bustop: The top seats of the bus were uncovered.

30. *Helen of Troy & Other Poems* is Sara Teasdale's second collection of poetry, published in 1911.

31. Riverside Drive, near Barnard College, occupies the most western part of Upper Manhattan.

32. Aeolian Hall, built in 1912, is a concert hall in midtown Manhattan.

33. Norman Wilks (1885–1944) was a Canadian pianist and music teacher.

34. The Vanity Fair Tea Room was at Fortieth Street, across the street from the New York Public Library.

35. Geraldine Farrar (1882–1967) was an American soprano and movie star, whose young female followers were known as "Gerry-flappers."

36. Jessie Belle Rittenhouse Scollard (1869–1948) was an American poet, anthologist, and secretary of the Poetry Society of America. Edwin Markham (1852–1940) was an American poet. Between 1923 and 1931, he was the Poet Laureate of Oregon.

37. Horace (65–8 B.C.) was the greatest lyric poet of the Augustan Age of Rome.

38. "Honey Bee" was a poem that Millay submitted to the youth magazine *St. Nicholas*.

39. Miss Goodale was Millay's classics professor at Barnard.

40. Miss Jacobs was a neighbor, perhaps Millay's landlady.

41. Educators was a brand of cracker.

42. Gertrude Elliott (1874–1950), or Lady Forbes-Robertson, was an American stage actress married to Johnston Forbes-Robertson (1853–1937), an English actor and theater manager.

43. *Die Walküre* is a musical drama by Richard Wagner.

44. Johanna Gadski (1872–1932) was a German soprano opera singer. Louise Homer (1871–1947) was an American operatic contralto. They appeared in *Die Walküre*.

45. Alfred Noyes (1880–1958) was an English poet, playwright, and short story writer known for his narrative poems "The Highwayman" and "The Barrel-Organ."

46. Charles Hanson Towne (1877–1949) was a well-known author and editor. During the mid-1920s he edited several magazines, including *Harper's Bazaar*. Rose Cecil O'Neill (1874–1944) was an American cartoonist, perhaps best known for creating Kewpie, the most famous cartoon character before 1940. Hildegarde Hawthorne (1871–1952) was an American writer who specialized in stories with supernatural themes. Florence Van Leer Earle Coates (1850–1927) was an American poet.

47. *Mademoiselle de la Seiglière* is a novel from 1848 by Léonard Sylvain Julien Sandeau (1811–1883).

48. Anna Hempstead Branch (1875–1937) was an American poet, celebrated during her lifetime.

49. This may refer to Dugald Stewart Walker (1883–1937), an American illustrator.

50. *Drake* was an epic poem about Sir Frances Drake, the Elizabethan naval commander, published in two volumes, in 1906 and 1908. Anna Hempstead Branch's *The Heart of the Road and Other Poems* was published in 1901.

51. Refers to the Armory Show, an international art exhibition in midtown Manhattan held from February 17 to March 15, 1913.
52. Anna Gertrude Hall (1882–1967) was an American children's and young adult book author of great renown. She won a Newberry medal in 1941 for her novel *Nanson*.
53. Brooks Hall was Barnard College's first residential hall, built in 1907.
54. Meaning she was delighted.
55. A pianola, or player piano, is a piano with a built-in mechanical device that permits it to self-play.
56. Bloomingdales, now a luxury department store chain, was once a small retailer of hoop skirts on the Lower East Side. Eventually, the store moved up to Midtown and became a mecca for shoppers.
57. A stereopticon was an early slide projector, patented by a Massachusetts chemist, John Fallon, in 1860. "Livingstone" probably refers to David Livingstone (1813–1870), a Scottish physician and missionary, who was a celebrated explorer during the Victorian era.
58. Br'er Rabbit is a character from folk tales that may have partly inspired our modern concept of the "Easter Bunny" figure.
59. Trinity Chapel may refer to New York's Third Trinity Church, a historic Episcopal church on Wall Street in Manhattan. It was founded in 1839.
60. May refer to Madison Square Presbyterian Church, which was founded in New York City in 1854.
61. Calvary Church is an Episcopal church, founded in 1848 on the east side of lower Midtown in Manhattan.
62. John Milton (1608–1676), the English poet, best known for *Paradise Lost.*
63. Henry Harland (1861–1905) was an American novelist and editor. *The Cardinal's Snuff Box,* a novel he wrote in 1900, was his first widely-read book.
64. Lewis Carroll (1832–1898), the English children's book writer celebrated for his absurdity, wordplay, and fantasy, epitomized in his novels *Alice's Adventures in Wonderland* (1865) and *Through the Looking Glass.*
65. Gilbert Patten (1866–1945) was an American novelist perhaps best known for his dime-store Frank Meriwell novels and short stories.
66. Andrew Marvell (1621–1678) was an English poet, satirist, and politician.
67. The Balkan Wars began in 1912 and continued until July 1913, months after this journal entry.
68. John William Mackail (1859–1945) was a Scottish academic at Oxford who wrote a classic book on Latin literature.
69. This most likely refers to a hat fashion show.
70. Wilhelm Bachenheimer (1892–1942) was a German Jewish baritone singer. He managed the Czech soprano Maria Jeritza (1912–1935).
71. *Songs of Sappho* is an English translation of the classical Greek poet Sappho (630–570 B.C.).

72. Jerry McAuley (1839–1884) was an Irish-American missionary who spent time in Sing Sing Prison before founding the Water Street Mission with his wife, in 1872, the first of hundreds of missions set up to help the homeless, poor, sick, and "fallen" during a period of heavy immigration from Europe.

73. *Cyrano,* a four-act opera based on the French play by Edmond Rostand (1866–1918), premiered at the Metropolitan Opera in New York City in February 1913. It was composed by Walter Damrosche (1862–1950).

74. *Twelve Japanese Painters* was one of Arthur Brown Ficke's two works of nonfiction, published in 1913.

75. A public park on the Bronx River, home to the Bronx Zoo, founded in 1899, and the New York Botanical Garden, founded in 1891.

76. This rhyme is also quoted in *The Deke Quarterly,* vol. 33 (1915), on p. 253.

77. Arthur Guiterman (1871–1943) was a writer of humorous verse. Berton Braley (1882–1966) was an American poet.

78. The John Wanamaker department store, which started in Philadelphia in 1876, also had a store in New York at Broadway and Ninth Street.

79. Meaning the Statue of Liberty in New York Harbor.

80. Sailors Snug Harbor was a home for retired sailors in Staten Island, New York. Today, it is a botanical garden.

81. Millay is probably referring to Kennerley's *Forum* "anthology." Two of her poems had been accepted for publication in the magazine.

82. In the late nineteenth and early twentieth centuries, "tea rooms" and luncheon restaurants were places where ladies socialized and exchanged handcrafts.

83. Beginning in 1892, Ellis Island was the port of entry in New York Harbor for immigrants arriving in America on steamships. The immigration procedure included a medical examination, and those deemed sick or otherwise unfit to enter the United States might be detained there. The facility later was an immigration prison and hospital, until it closed in 1954, after which it became a museum.

84. The Hungarian Rhapsodie no. 6 in D-flat Major is the sixth of nineteen "Hungarian Rhapsodies" by the pianist and composer Franz Liszt (1811–1886).

85. Sarah Bernhardt (1844–1923) was a French stage actress who rose to fame in the late nineteenth and early twentieth centuries. *Camille* was the Anglicized title of *La Dame aux Camélias,* which the author Alexandre Dumas simplified, and sanitized, in order to appeal to American audiences. This was Bernhardt's most performed role, which she played more than a thousand times from 1880 until her death.

86. The "Bohemian church" is St. John the Martyr Church, founded by John T. Prout in 1903 to serve the Bohemian Catholics of the Upper East Side.

87. The Horatian epode is a lyric poem in which lines of iambic trimeter (three beats) alternate with lines of dimeter (two beats).

88. Bliss Carman (1861–1929) was a Canadian poet who served as Canada's poet laureate for a number of years.

89. Mamaroneck is a town in Westchester County, about twenty miles north of Manhattan.
90. Manursing is an island in Long Island Sound, close to the Connecticut border.
91. The Coney Island neighborhood in Brooklyn is famous for its amusement parks, especially Luna Park, which opened in 1903.
92. "He" may be Arthur Hooley.
93. "Briarcliffe" probably refers to Briarcliff Manor, a town near the Hudson River about thirty miles north of Manhattan. Sleepy Hollow is a village on the Hudson River in Westchester County, New York.
94. Herbert Kaufman (1878–1947) was an American newspaperman.
95. Charles Buzzell was Cora Millay's brother. Bristol is a city in central Connecticut.
96. Lake Compounce, in Bristol, Connecticut, has an amusement park that has been in operation since 1846.
97. Henry was an old friend of Millay's, with whom she has an on-again off-again flirtation.
98. "Iced and soda'd" meant they drank several sodas and were accordingly energized.
99. Collinsville is a town in Connecticut north of Bristol.
100. *Brewster's Millions* is a 1914 film adaptation of a play from 1902 by George Barr McCutchen (1866–1928).
101. Fannie Stearns Davis (b. 1884) was an American poet.
102. Dark Harbor is a village on the island of Islesboro, across Penobscot Bay from Camden.
103. A "bacon bat" is a picnic or binge with sports.
104. A small island just off the coast of Camden; it was renamed Curtis Island in 1934.
105. Spruce Head is a town about fifteen miles south of Camden.
106. Gwendolyn was Ellen Young's baby. "Wump" is Millay's sister Kathleen.
107. *The Pink Lady* was a 1913 film.
108. "Samps" may be short for "samples," or "examples," possibly photographic proofs.

Vassar (1913)

1. Probably refers to *Oliver Twist*, by Charles Dickens, his novel from 1838 that features a scene of the hungry orphan begging for more food.
2. "Called up on campus" was a term for being reprimanded.
3. The *Miscellany News*, established in 1866, was (and still is) Vassar College's student newspaper.
4. "For a bushel" alludes to the expression "Don't hide your light under a bushel (basket)."
5. "Hygiene lectures" is a euphemism, perhaps for sex ed.
6. Anthony Comstock led efforts in the United States during the late nineteenth and early twentieth centuries to censor materials that he considered obscene, including

even information about birth control. People jokingly called him "Miss Comstock" in a pejorative way.

7. Ernestine Schumann-Heink (1861–1936) was a great German-American contralto.

8. Katharine Tilt was a classmate of Millay's, with whom Millay had a close relationship and most likely a romantic and sexual entanglement.

9. Translates as, "Do you know too much to be in this class?" Perhaps Millay was being condescending.

10. Her "feet are mates" means both are the same size.

11. "Hall play" might refer to regular student theatrical productions.

12. "Head Proctor" refers to an upperclassman who acts in an advisory role in the dormitory.

13. Catherine Filene Shouse (1896–1994) was a fellow Vassar student with whom Millay most likely had a romantic and sexual relationship. She later became a philanthropist for the arts.

14. Josephine Preston Peabody (1874–1922) was an American poet and dramatist.

15. *The Singing Leaves* is a collection of Josephine Preston Peabody's poetry published in 1902.

16. *Mr. Faust* is a play, published in 1913, by Arthur Davison Ficke. It is based on the Elizabethan play *Doctor Faustus,* by Christopher Marlowe.

17. The YWCA Training School where Millay stayed while attending Barnard College during the spring semester of 1913.

18. The Knights of Pythias is a brotherhood organization established by the government treasury clerk and composer Justus H. Rathbone in 1864. The order promotes good works and community through acts of charity.

19. The verb "rag" refers to a fast and high-stepping dance to ragtime music.

Europe (1920–1921)

1. Meaning the city in Tennessee.

2. The hotel is on the Left Bank in the 7th arrondissement in a former home built in the seventeenth century.

3. The Latin Quarter, on the lower Left Bank of Paris, then a working-class neighborhood where artists and writers lived and gathered.

4. Montmartre is a neighborhood similar to the Latin Quarter on the Right Bank, on the hill beneath Sacre Coeur Church.

5. In eighteenth-century typography, the letter "s" looks similar to a modern "f." "Aussi" is the French word for also.

6. Allan Ross Macdougall (1893–1956), was an American writer and a biographer of Isadora Duncan. Henri Barbusse (1873–1935) and Anatole France (1844–1924) were French novelists.

7. Brindisi is a port city on the eastern coast of Italy, on the Adriatic Sea.

8. Durazzo, now Durres, is the second largest city in Albania.

Steepletop (March to May 1927)

1. Stanley was a regular farmhand hired at Steepletop.
2. West Stockbridge is a small town just across the state line in the Berkshires of rural western Massachusetts, the next town over from Austerlitz.
3. Dr. Bache was probably an internist.
4. *The King's Henchman* had opened two weeks earlier at the Metropolitan Opera in New York with Millay in attendance, and went on to great critical and popular success. The *New Yorker* called it "the greatest American opera so far"; her libretto sold more than ten thousand copies soon after its publication in book form.
5. Austerlitz is a town in upstate New York, on the Massachusetts border about a hundred miles north of New York City. Today, the Edna St. Vincent Millay Society is based there. Frank Wolfe was probably a real estate agent.
6. Pittsfield, Massachusetts, is twenty miles from Millay's home in New York, and about ten miles north of West Stockbridge.
7. State Line was a nearby village.
8. The *New York World* was a local New York newspaper that ran from 1860 until 1931.
9. "Bunny" was the nickname of Edmund Wilson (1895–1972), the prolific writer of fiction and essays and one of the most important literary critics of the twentieth century. He had also been one of Millay's lovers earlier in the decade.
10. Belladonna is a poisonous plant that is used in many medications, including eye drops.
11. John Pinnie was a faithful worker for the Boissevains until Millay's death. McCagg was an occasional helper. Madeleine was a surly and uncooperative housemaid.
12. Mrs. Tanner was a sometime housekeeper of Millay's.
13. Maison de Blanc was a luxury Belgian textile company, founded in the 1800s.
14. *'Tis Pity She's a Whore* is a dramatic tragedy written by the English playwright and poet John Ford (1586–c. 1639) involving themes of incest.
15. William Rose Benét (1886–1950) was an American poet and editor. In 1942, Benét was awarded the Pulitzer Prize for his memoir from 1941, *The Dust Which Is God*. Wylie was his second wife.
16. Millay is referring to an argument over the poet Percy Bysshe Shelley (1792–1822).
17. *Epipsychidion: Verses addressed to the noble and unfortunate Lady Emilia V—, now imprisoned in the convent of—* is a poetical work by Percy Bysshe Shelley written in 1821. *The Eve of St. Agnes* is a romantic narrative poem written by John Keats in 1819.
18. "Ode to the West Wind," an ode by Shelley written in Florence, Italy, in 1819.
19. "Ode on a Grecian Urn," a poem by Keats from 1819.
20. *Mortal Image* was a novel by Elinor Wylie published in 1927.
21. *Wayfarer* is a novel written by Millay's sister Kathleen in 1926.
22. Cora disapproved of Elinor's notorious adultery.

23. Great Barrington is a town in the Berkshires, approximately ten miles south of West Stockbridge. A shingled haircut is a very short bob, tapered in the back, with a curl against each cheek, that was popular in the 1920s.

24. Francesco Caruso was a Sicilian immigrant convicted of murdering Dr. Casper Pendola, a twenty-seven-year-old physician who Caruso was sure had murdered his six-year-old son, Joey. Joey had in fact died of diphtheria, and Pendola had attended to him on his deathbed.

25. Betteridge is an American jewelry business, established in 1897.

26. Thomas Hardy (1840–1928), the English Victorian realist novelist and poet.

27. Max Eastman (1883–1969) was an American critic, essayist, and aesthetician. He was a leading socialist who founded and edited notable magazines, such as *The Masses* and *The Liberator,* devoted to the promotion of liberal and radical causes. Eastman was close friends with Eugen before and during his marriage with Millay. Eastman's wife, Elena Krylenko, was a lawyer who pursued painting, poetry, and dance; she was the sister of Nikolai Krylenko, Joseph Stalin's prosecutor general.

28. The National League of American Penwomen, an organization dedicated to fostering the work of American women writers, had invited Elinor Wylie to be the guest of honor at a dinner. Because of gossip about her love life, the group canceled the invitation.

29. Dreer is a nursery near Austerlitz.

30. Millay sometimes could not accustom herself to the use of motorized farm machinery, seeing it as a heartless and mindless juggernaut that demanded the sacrifice of everything in its path.

31. There is a patrician Dutch family with the surname van Eeghen. She may be referring to a cousin of Ugin's.

32. Achillea are yarrow flowers.

33. The Copake Inn was in Copake, New York, the Taconic Mountains.

34. Fred Millay, the brother of Millay's father.

35. Molly and Tom were draft horses. Old Hamlin place was an abandoned mansion.

36. Velvet was the house cat.

37. Weigelias are a pink flowering shrub.

38. The shadbush or serviceberry, a low tree with white blossoms that blooms in early spring.

39. Charles Lindbergh (1902–1974), the first aviator to fly solo across the Atlantic, departed on his historic flight that day.

40. A whiffle-tree is the wooden cross-tie that yokes two horses to a plow or vehicle.

41. Buttercup was a heifer on Millay's farm, as were Blossom and Dolly.

42. Margaret Cuthbert (1887–1968) was a Canadian pioneer in radio broadcasting, and a publicist for NBC Radio. She persuaded her friend Millay to broadcast her poetry on the airwaves, helping to promote her work to the public.

43. "Tristram" is a book-length narrative poem written in 1927 by the American poet Edwin Arlington Robinson (1869–1935).

44. Bander was the local auto mechanic. The Lizzie is an old Model-T Ford.

Steepletop (June to November 1927)

1. Hudson and Nash were automobiles produced during the first half of the twentieth century. In 1954, the two companies merged to form the American Motors Corporation.

2. Chatham is a small town in eastern New York.

3. Mercer and Maxwell were American automobiles manufactured before 1925.

4. Short for stenographer, one who writes in shorthand or takes dictation.

5. John Pinnie was a longtime handyman for Millay. He was the one who discovered Millay dead on October 19, 1950.

6. Brownie and Gynie were Millay's horses.

7. The Underwood company manufactured what was generally considered the first successful modern typewriter. By 1939 the company, headquartered in New York City, had produced five million machines.

8. Derived from *canis,* the Latin word for dog, "canaille" is a derogatory term for the "common people" or "the masses."

9. *Chang: A Drama of the Wilderness* (1927) is a silent film about a farmer's struggle to survive in the jungle of Nan Province, Thailand. The film was nominated for the Unique and Artistic Production award at the inaugural Academy Awards in 1929.

10. *Seventh Heaven* was a popular Broadway musical in the 1920s, a love story set in France during World War I.

11. Alvan T. Fuller (1878–1958) was governor of Massachusetts from 1925 to 1929. He was widely criticized for his handling of the trial of Nicola Sacco and Bartolomeo Vanzetti, ending his political career.

12. Eugen had formerly been in the import business and probably ran afoul of wholesale dealers.

13. John Dos Passos (1896–1970), an American novelist, and Lola Ridge (1873–1941), an Irish-American poet, were part of a group of well-known writers who traveled to Boston in a last-ditch effort to save the anarchists Sacco and Vanzetti from the electric chair.

14. Ellen Hayes (1851–1930) was an American mathematician and astronomer. Catherine Huntington was an American actress. They joined the group of high-profile writers and activists who protested the trial and execution of Sacco and Vanzetti.

15. Belterman was probably a neighbor who did odd jobs for the Boissevains.

16. Edmund Pearson (1880–1937) was an American librarian and "true crime" writer, best known for his account of the Lizzie Borden murder case.

Steepletop (1928–1930): And Texas Lecture Tour

1. Llewelyn Powys (1884–1939) was a British essayist, novelist, memoirist, friend and lover of Millay. Millay sometimes referred to him as "Lulu," and she and Eugen maintained a correspondence with Powys until his death.

2. Arthur Hooley, a mysterious figure, was the main romantic interest in Millay's life from 1913 until she graduated from Vassar in 1917. Born in England, Hooley arrived in America in 1908, and his cousin Mitchell Kennerley hired him as an editor of the magazine *The Forum.* Millay wrote several important sonnets about this elusive lover.

3. Autti James was an eccentric friend of Millay's to whom the poet wrote in a letter, "If I wasn't so busy finding out what horses won the races in Maryland today, I might have time to write."

4. Shakespeare's *The Tempest,* believed to have been performed around 1610, was one of the Bard's final plays.

5. Smith Corona typewriter.

6. *Bleak House,* a novel by Charles Dickens, was published serially in 1852–1853.

7. "The saint's everlasting rest, or, A treatise on the blessed state of the saints in their enjoyment of God in Heaven" is a Christian devotional text by English Puritan poet and Church leader Richard Baxter published in 1650.

8. Croton-on-Hudson is a village in Westchester County, in the northern suburbs of New York City.

9. Elaine Ralli and Isobel Simpson were fellow students with Millay at Vassar, and were among her lovers while they were in college. In spite of jealousies and rivalries during those years, they went on to maintain lifelong friendships with her.

10. Marrons glacés are glazed chestnut sweets that originated in Italy and France.

11. The Rhode Island Red is a breed of chicken. In addition to chickens, they were also raising pigs, cows, and horses.

12. In Muslim theology, houri are beautiful maidens who accompany faithful Muslims into Paradise. A "burnous" is a hooded garment created in the Middle East in the sixth century. Benares is a city in northern India on the banks of the Ganges, regarded as the holiest of the seven sacred cities in Hinduism and Jainism. It also became an industrial center famous for its production of muslin and silk fabrics.

13. *The Decameron* is a book of novellas by the fourteenth-century Italian author Giovanni Boccaccio. A cast of seven women and three men seclude themselves in a villa outside Florence to escape the bubonic plague. To pass the time, they tell stories.

14. Founded in 1890, Daughters of the American Revolution is a service organization open to those who are related to a person involved in the fight for U.S. independence. In 1928, D.A.R. allegedly had a blacklist of individuals believed

to have communist allegiances; these were not permitted to speak at D.A.R. functions.

15. Louise Bogan (1897–1970) was an American appointed in 1945 as the fourth U.S. poetry consultant to the Library of Congress, the first woman to hold the position. Raymond Holden (1894–1972) was an American novelist, poet, and publisher. Bogan and Holden married in 1925, and divorced in 1937.

16. "With pleasure I write off one more enemy."

17. The Vanderbilt is a 54-room mansion in Hyde Park, New York, overlooking the Hudson River. It was once owned by the industrialist Frederick William Vanderbilt.

18. *The Miracle* is a play written in 1911 by the German philologist Karl Vollmöller. The play is wordless, and tells the story of a nun who deserts her convent with a knight; in her place, a statue of the Virgin Mary comes to life and takes the nun's place in the convent until at last she returns.

Steepletop (1933)

1. *Sneevw-klokjes* are known as snowdrops or the common snowdrop.

2. Arbor vitas (or arborvitae) are members of the *Thuja* genus of coniferous trees, or cedars, native to North America and eastern Asia.

3. The LaBranches were neighbors of Millay at Steepletop. George LaBranche wrote books about angling.

4. Harrison Dowd (1897–1964) was an American poet, pianist, and actor. Along with Arthur Ficke and Arthur Hooley, Dowd was one of Millay's romantic interests when she was a student at Vassar and frequently visited New York City. Dowd portrayed the character Pierrot in Millay's antiwar play from 1919, *Aria da Capo.* The two stayed in touch throughout their lives.

5. Aldous Huxley (1894–1963), the British writer and philosopher, was best known for his visionary dystopian novel *Brave New World* (1932).

6. "Miss California" is a fuchsia plant with a large pink flower.

7. William L. Brann (1877–1951), an advertising executive turned horse owner and breeder, owned a farm near Steepletop and was one of Eugen's best friends. In the mid to late 1930s Millay developed an obsessive interest in horse racing, and she sent letters with instructions to Brann about training the horses she owned that he oversaw. Millay's most successful horse, Challedon, was the runner-up in the 1939 Kentucky Derby, went on to win the Preakness Stakes the same year, and was inducted into the Thoroughbred Racing Hall of Fame in 1977. Fearing that associating her name with gambling would sully her reputation, Millay used the pseudonym Nancy Boyd (the name she used in writing stories) for her horse dealings.

8. *Narcissus poeticus* is a daffodil named for the beautiful youth in Greek mythology who fell in love with his own image reflected in a pool of water.

9. On June 27, 1933, New York became the ninth state to ratify the Twenty-first Amend-

ment to the U.S. Constitution, repealing the Eighteenth Amendment's prohibition of alcohol.

10. The *Field Dog Stud Book* is the oldest purebred dog registry in the U.S. Its records date back to 1874.

11. Russell Sage College is a women's college in Troy, New York. Along with Russell Sage and the University of Wisconsin, Millay received honorary degrees from New York University, Tufts University, and Colby College.

12. Here she's premenstrual, but in general she's got eye pain, gut pain, and bad nerves. Plus, she's a hypochondriac.

13. "The curse": a woman's menstrual period.

14. Louise Boulanger (1878–1950) was a French fashion designer prominent in the 1920s and 1930s.

15. Frances Perkins (1882–1965) was the first female member of the U.S. cabinet, serving as secretary of labor from 1933 to 1945 under Franklin D. Roosevelt.

16. Zona Gale (1874–1938) was an American fiction writer and playwright, best known for her 1920 novel, *Miss Lulu Bett,* adapted for a Broadway production and a silent film. She won the Pulitzer Prize for drama in 1921.

17. Glenn Frank (1887–1940) was the president of the University of Wisconsin–Madison from 1925 to 1937, and formerly the editor of *The Century Magazine.*

18. Bailey Island is in Casco Bay on the coast of Maine, northeast of Portland.

19. Ragged Island is a small island in Casco Bay near Bailey Island.

20. Efrem Zimbalist (1889–1985) was a Russian-Jewish concert violinist, composer, and teacher. New Hartford is a town in Oneida County, New York, near the Adirondack Mountains.

21. Edith Wynne Matthison (1875–1955) was an English-born actress and renowned acting coach who instructed Millay following her graduation from Vassar when the poet pursued an acting career. Matthison's instruction influenced Millay's theatrical style in her poetry readings. Charles Rann Kennedy (1871–1950) was an English-born playwright married to Edith Matthison. The couple was among a group of patrons vying for Millay's attention after her graduation from Vassar, hoping that she might choose a career in acting. *The Princess Marries the Page* is a one-act play Millay wrote and starred in at Vassar, debuting on May 12, 1917; it is the story of a princess who falls in love with an enemy prince. In 1919, the play opened the third season of the Provincetown Players in New York.

22. Djuna Barnes (1892–1982) was a novelist, poet, and visual artist, part of the early-twentieth-century modernist movement; she was among the group of American artists Millay interacted with in Europe. "Browsy": suitable for light reading or browsing, rather than serious sustained interest.

23. Samuel Chotzinoff (1889–1964) was a Russian-American pianist; his wife, Pauline, was the sister of the Russian-American violinist Jascha Heifetz; Sascha Jacobsen (1895–1972) was a Russian-American violinist and teacher.

24. Cyril Scott (1879–1970) was an English composer and writer.

25. Owen Johnson (1878–1952) was an American writer best known for his stories about the character Dink Stover.

26. Harold Tucker Webster (1885–1952) was a cartoonist whose syndicated strips *The Timid Soul, Bridge,* and *Life's Darkest Moments* were popular from the 1920s to the 1950s. Fans compared him to Mark Twain.

27. "Epitaph for the Race of Man," Millay's eighteen-sonnet sequence, was published in 1934.

28. Bagatelle is a billiards-derived table game of French origin; the object is to navigate balls past wooden pins into holes.

29. Dwight Wiman (1895–1951) was an American silent movie actor and director; Theodore Dreiser (1871–1945) was an American novelist who espoused the literary movement of Naturalism.

30. John Cowper Powys (1872–1963) was a British philosopher, novelist, and poet.

31. Philippe Hériat (1898–1971), a French novelist, playwright, and actor, published his novel *La Main Tendue* [The Outstretched Hand] in 1933.

32. *The Fortunes of Richard Mahoney* is a three-part novel by the Australian writer Ethel Florence Lindesay Richardson published between 1917 and 1929.

33. Dame Myra Hess, DBE (1890–1965), was an English pianist.

Europe and England (1934)

1. *Cabo Tortosa* was a Spanish cargo ship.

2. Cape St. Vincent is the southwestern-most point of Portugal.

3. "Houzee" is an interjection meaning Hurrah! Cap d'Antibes is a peninsula on the French Riviera.

4. Conrad Aiken (1889–1973) was an American poet and fiction writer.

5. *Roggebrood* is a Dutch sour-sweet rye bread.

6. "The mistral" refers to a cold dry wind from the north.

7. "Vin compris" means wine included.

8. Baccarat: a gambling game with cards.

9. *Eclaireur,* which is French for scout or spy, was the name of a newspaper.

10. Lucie Delarue-Mardrus (1874–1945) was a prolific French journalist, poet, and novelist who translated sonnets in *Fatal Interview.*

11. *Choucroute garnie* refers to sauerkraut with sausage.

12. Somerset Maugham (1874–1965) was an English playwright and fiction writer. Rebecca West (1892–1983) was a British journalist and author.

13. These were all poets who had applied for Guggenheim Fellowships, and Millay had spent weeks evaluating their poems.

14. Raquel Meller was a Spanish vaudeville performer, famous for singing "La Violetero," the violet girl.

15. Golfe Juan is the gulf where the resort town of Juan-les-Pins is located on the French Riviera, between Antibes and Cannes.

16. *Outward Bound* is a play by English writer Sutton Vane (1888–1963).

17. Pauline Venys, a working-class girl, tried to drown herself in the Seine in 1932. Ugin leaped into the treacherous river in evening clothes and managed to save this desperate stranger. The incident made international headlines.

18. *Eau non potable* means undrinkable water from the faucet.

19. The Fratellini were three brothers famous as circus clowns in the 1920s, known for their wit.

20. *La Croisiere Jaune* [The Yellow Journey], a film about a road trip.

21. *Night Flight,* a movie based on the novel by aviator Antoine de Saint-Exupéry.

22. Cécile Sorel (1873–1966) was a French comedienne.

23. Henri de Regnier (1864–1936) was a famous French symbolist poet.

24. Natalie Barney (1876–1972) was an American playwright who kept a salon in Paris. Romaine Brooks (1874–1970) was an American portrait painter. Pavel Tchelitchew (1898–1957) was a Russian painter and designer.

25. Elisabeth Bergner (1897–1986) and Sybil Thorndike (1882–1976) were British actresses.

26. Queen Boadicea was a Celtic ruler who led an uprising against the Romans in A.D. 61.

27. Noël Coward (1899–1973) was an English playwright. His musical comedy *Conversation Piece* premiered in London in 1934.

28. Laurence Olivier (1907–1989), probably the most celebrated English actor of the twentieth century, and his wife, Jill Desmond, a minor actress.

29. Cedric Morris (1889–1982) was a British artist.

Steepletop (1934–1935): Also Cuba and Florida

1. Eugene Saxton was editor-in-chief of Harper & Brothers and handled all of Millay's relations with the publisher until his death in 1943. The "new book" was likely *Wine from These Grapes,* her collection of poems published in 1934.

2. Guaranty Trust is the former name of her bank, J. P. Morgan & Co.

3. Mallorca is the largest of the Balearic Islands, which belong to Spain.

4. In botany, an umbel refers to a cluster of flowers in which stalks emanate from a common center.

5. William C. Bullitt (1891–1967) served as the first U.S. ambassador to the Soviet Union. In June of 1940, soon after Bullitt was reported to be in German "protective custody," Millay published "Lines Written in Passion and in Deep Concern for England, France and My Own Country," in *The New York Times,* attacking America's isolationism.

6. James P. Warburg (1896–1969) was a German-born American banker, and financial adviser to President Franklin D. Roosevelt.

7. The rugosa is a species of rose native to eastern Asia, also found in northeastern China, Japan, Korea, and southeastern Siberia.

8. Orr's Island is in Casco Bay, in the Gulf of Maine.

9. Prado is a promenade in Havana, Cuba, near the old city wall.

10. Vingt-et-un is French for twenty-one, a family of casino card games including blackjack.

11. The Costigan-Wagner bill sought federal prosecution of law enforcement officers who failed to respond to lynching incidents. Millay and others attempted to persuade President Roosevelt to support the bill, but he did not, fearing he would lose the next election if he lost Southern white votes. Congressional Southern opposition managed to prevent the bill's passage.

12. The National Committee for the Defense of Political Prisoners was founded in 1931 by the Communist Party of the United States of America in order to "aid workers to organize and to defend themselves against terror and suppression." Jack Lawson (1881–1965) was a British trade unionist and a Labour politician.

13. Hal is a nickname for Witter Bynner; Vita Sackville-West (1892–1962) was an English author and garden designer; Eugene Aynsley Goossens (1893–1962) was an English conductor and composer.

14. Victor Brooks (1918–2000) was an English film and television actor, best known for his roles as a police inspector.

The Final Diaries (1938–1949)

1. "3 tablets to 2%" described a dilution of morphine comparable to three oral tablets.

2. Millay was keeping a record of how much morphine (and other drugs) she was consuming to manage her pain. In the column at left, following the date, she listed the number of doses of morphine she took that day, either as pills or by injection. The pills were a quarter grain each; higher doses were delivered by injection. The right-hand column gave the total amount for the day, in grains. (In apothecary systems, one grain is equal to approximately 64 milligrams.) A standard dose of morphine for acute pain is 10 milligrams. By the time of the record shown here, Millay had developed a three-grain per day morphine habit. She was also supplementing that with four grains of codeine on some days, as well as Nembutal tablets.

3. "P.G." may stand for "per grain."

4. Diastase is a digestive aide. "Vit." stands for vitamin.

5. "Benz." is an abbreviation for Benzedrine, the first amphetamine marketed in the United States to treat mood disorders, like depression. Because its addictive nature was not well understood, the drug was often abused.

6. "G." might stand for grain.

7. Betaxin is a nutritional supplement.

8. Nembutal, the brand name for Pentobarbital, is an anticonvulsant and sedative medication. The drug often leads to paranoia or suicidal ideation, and it can impair

memory, judgment, and coordination. It is particularly dangerous when paired with alcohol.

9. When Millay mentions "leaking," she is referring to a mechanical issue in injecting her drugs.

10. She was also self-administering codeine hypodermically.

11. Refers to an organic supplement.

12. Hyoscine is a medicine that has been used as an anesthetic for surgery, childbirth, and pain since the 1890s. It results in the foggy state known as "twilight sleep."

13. "Pellets" refers to pills.

14. Nervosine is an anti-hysteria medicine composed of reduced iron and naturally occurring ingredients like licorice. As Millay writes, it may have been prescribed as an anticonvulsant.

15. Perhaps taken for stomach ailments.

16. Sal Hepatica was a salt mineral laxative, distributed by the Bristol Myers company from 1887 to 1958. The tablet was dissolved in water, and recommended for conditions ranging from kidney problems to liver disorders to gout.

17. Calcium gluconate is an intravenous calcium supplement.

18. Ruby grapes of Proserpine may refer to nightshade. The English romantic poet John Keats (1795–1821) referred to poisonous nightshade in this way in "Ode on Melancholy" in 1820.

19. Dilaudid, the brand name of hydromorphone, is a narcotic drug used to treat moderate to severe pain. It is highly addictive.

20. Pillules are small pills.

21. Two grams is a huge amount of supplemental iron to take at once. A normal supplement is 15–27 milligrams daily.

22. Either Nembutal or morphine.

23. Perhaps a hormonal supplement.

24. Probably the drug Veronal, which was invented in 1902 and used widely in the 1920s and 1930s.

25. Probably aspirin.

26. Demerol is a narcotic pain medicine that is extremely addictive and potent.

27. Luminal is an anti-seizure medication.

28. Perhaps referring to Hilda de Booy.

29. The parathyroid is a structure in the body that regulates calcium levels.

30. Sabat was Millay and Ugin's dog.

ACKNOWLEDGMENTS

This book has been the work of many hands, beginning with Edna St. Vincent Millay's handwriting and ending finally, if imperfectly, in this published book.

I would like to acknowledge the contribution of previous, unpublished transcribers of various sections of Millay's diaries, most notably the poet's sister Norma Millay, who transcribed the Steepletop diaries of the 1920s and 1930s with fair accuracy fifty years ago. The late Elizabeth Barnett, literary executor to the Millay estate and founding member of the Millay Society, transcribed some of the early diary entries. Barnett's daughter, Vincent Elizabeth Barnett, was kind enough to send me a copy of her mother's efforts. Thanks to Millay biographer Nancy Milford for her groundbreaking use of the diaries and her kindness in answering my questions. Millay's handwriting is sometimes difficult to read, and my keen-eyed partner Sarah Longaker helped decipher some perplexing sentences.

All of Millay's extant diaries and journals are collected at the Library of Congress. I am grateful to Elizabeth Barnett, who granted me access to the unprocessed papers of Millay in the 1990s in connection with the biography I was then writing about the poet's life and work. Dr. Alice Birney, literary manuscript historian at the Library in 1999, helped me to locate most of Millay's diaries in the unprocessed collection, which was then chaotic. Twenty years later, when I was granted permission to edit and publish the diaries for this book, Barbara Bair, manuscript historian and curator for Literature, Culture, and the Arts—and longtime advocate of Millay scholarship—was accommodating in helping me locate all of

Millay's diary and journal entries. This task would have been impossible before the painstaking work of Nan Thompson Ernst with the assistance of Michael W. Giese, Jewel R. Parker, and Chante Wilson in organizing and categorizing the Millay papers. Having seen the papers before and after "processing" I can testify that theirs is a work of outstanding scholarship.

Jeffrey M. Flannery, the chief of the manuscript reading room at the Library of Congress, has been for more than twenty years a friend and an extraordinary support to all researchers, and I am fortunate that we were able to work on one more book together. Bruce Kirby, at the main desk there too, was ever helpful. My friend and neighbor Chris Whittaker provided technical support in copying manuscripts and transferring electronic files.

I want to thank Sarah Miller, who first acquired this book for Yale University Press with the advice of Jennifer Banks, Senior Executive Editor for Religion and the Humanities; and Miller's successor Heather Gold, who has seen it through production and publication with the assistance of the very able and patient Eva Skewes. I am grateful for the graceful and meticulous work of the copyeditor Phillip King in polishing a book that presents unusual textual challenges.

I am indebted to my assistant India Kotis, for her great patience and good humor in preparing this complex manuscript for publication, long distance, in 2020. Her understanding of Millay's life, and her contribution to the footnotes and index, were crucial. I also want to thank Nate Gordon, who assisted us in researching and writing the footnotes.

Finally I want to express my gratitude to my friend of many years Holly Peppe, the literary executor to the Millay estate. We share a lifelong passion for Millay's work. It was Holly who finally gave me the green light to edit this book, knowing just how long I had wished to do it. She has been involved in every aspect of the publication including assembling the photographs and writing the kind Foreword.

INDEX